4. IT HAS ONLY ↑HROW ↑NO ↑ S
TIME IS SCARP ↑ P — IT R
IS EX ↑INST ↑ OST £1
TODAY — + LL B↑C
WITH MUCH MORE BY SITE↑
AUDACITY — BY FLINSIN'S ↑
WERE I THE EQUIVLANT OF
ON TH↑ ↑CT ↑ ↑CKIER↑
↑I AVE FOR T↑
PLAYIN CE O
EN PL I TIM
BIRTHP NOT
MUST YOU
TS TI ? PN
MARVE ? BO
LAST RIEN↑
PER ↑A C AS↑
DAL ↑. TIFUL
BUT NOT ↑S ↑E↑
YOU HIS TEETH SEEMED
W↑↑NS + YOURS DINO

FRIEND — A L
DEC↑ ↑E + WROT
TH↑

THE
VISITORS'
BOOK

THE VISITORS' BOOK

In Francis Bacon's Shadow:
The Lives of Richard Chopping
and Denis Wirth-Miller

JON LYS TURNER

Constable • London

CONSTABLE

First published in Great Britain in 2016 by Constable

1 3 5 7 9 10 8 6 4 2

Copyright © Jon Lys Turner, 2016

The moral right of the author has been asserted.

A CIP catalogue record for this book
is available from the British Library.

ISBN: 978-1-47212-166-0 (hardback)

Typeset in Bembo by SX Composing DTP, Rayleigh, Essex
Printed and bound in Great Britain by CPI Group (UK) Ltd, Croydon CR0 4YY

Papers used by Constable are from well-managed forests and
other responsible sources.

MIX
Paper from
responsible sources
FSC
www.fsc.org FSC® C104740

Constable
An imprint of
Little, Brown Book Group
Carmelite House
50 Victoria Embankment
London EC4Y 0DZ

An Hachette UK Company
www.hachette.co.uk

www.littlebrown.co.uk

Every effort has been made to obtain the necessary permissions with reference to copyright
material, both illustrative and quoted. We apologise for any omissions in this respect and will
be pleased to make the appropriate acknowledgements in any future edition.

For Dicky and Denis

Contents

The Fall, April 2008   *1*

1   The Search for Bohemia   5

2   The New World   28

3   Little Yellow Papers   45

4   Benton End   55

5   Butterflies and Grandeur   72

6   Prison and Wivenhoe   94

7   The Storehouse   104

8   Bacon Arrives   122

9   Colony of Artists   139

10   The Party Line   161

11   Escapades   188

12   From Dicky and Denis with Love   202

13   Golden Roses   219

14   Chippy Chopping   231

15   The Fire   251

16   Lust, Aberration and Death   264

17   Bad Behaviour   277

18   The Death of Dyer   294

19   In a Muddle   321

20   A Monstrous Companion   336

21   Absence   359

Retrospective   *371*

Endnotes   375

Acknowledgements   380

Bibliography   381

Index   387

The Fall, April 2008

Early postcard showing the Wivenhoe waterfront. *(Author's personal collection)*

*F*irst light. The bell of St Mary's in Wivenhoe has just called the hour but the town is otherwise silent.

Behind the Georgian facade of the Storehouse, a 90-year-old man has woken at the sound of the chimes. He is in the kitchen, the same kitchen where over the decades Francis Bacon pissed in the butler sink; the same kitchen that Terence Conran designed after someone, probably George Dyer, set the room alight courtesy of a cigarette end. The kitchen cabinets now have a film of grease. The house is falling into decay.

The old man is lying prone, his cheek hard against the floor, in the same position he has been throughout the freezing night. The sound of the bell prompts him to call out again.

'Denis!'

His voice is too weak. He tries again.

'Denis! Help me, Denis!'

Dicky Chopping is calling the man with whom he has shared his life for the last seventy years. Together they achieved artistic success and defied convention. They witnessed the faltering of society's approbation until, with both men aged around ninety, they became one of the first legal civil partnerships in the country.

He has been calling Denis on and off since the day before, with no response from upstairs. Dicky's care worker had not appeared. Infirmed and with his eyesight failing, he had been left lying in the hospital bed set up in the sitting room. As the afternoon wore on, he had become so thirsty that he decided to attempt the journey to the kitchen tap by himself.

He had made his way towards the kitchen, one hand gripping a crutch, the other clutching a large cordless phone. The phone was to be by his side at all times, ready for any emergency.

He had reached the kitchen doorway and rested, preparing himself for the careful coordination that would be required at the sink. He would need to keep his gravity centred while putting down the phone, turning on the tap, filling a glass and turning off the tap, all while still gripping the crutch.

He had set off again and was nearly there – a metre from the sink – when the crutch slipped on the floor and he fell. His head smacked onto the ground.

He was still conscious, but he had lost grip of both the crutch and the phone during the fall. His first instinct had been to try to rouse Denis, but he knew the chances of being heard were slim. In any case, he feared that the man he had loved for so long would not help him. While Dicky had become weak of body, Denis had become weak of mind. His senility and confusion had filleted away his charm, leaving him cold, aggressive and hostile.

Dicky could dimly see the handset. He put his hand out towards the phone but it was beyond his reach. In desperation he started calling weakly for Denis. No response. Time passed. He called again. The cold crept up from the kitchen floor and his thirst worsened. He started to lose the sense of where he was. The church bell sounded again as he slipped into delirium.

The bell has woken him and he detects the early morning light. He is freezing but his mind is clearer now. He starts calling again. There is still no response. He has a memory from last night, but he is not sure if it was a dream: Denis in the kitchen while he was on the floor, making his dinner as if he wasn't there. He banishes the image as just a product of his delirious state.

The bell sounds the hour several more times before he hears dull thuds progressing down the staircase. He hopes that there is enough left of the real Denis to help him.

His partner walks into the kitchen and steps over his body. He begins preparing his breakfast. Denis's eyesight is poor, too, but he is not deaf. Yet he does not seem to hear Dicky's pleas. He mushes a blackened banana into a bowl of bran and then finally looks down at Dicky, assessing his plight. He then smashes his foot down on the telephone.

Denis eats standing up by the cluttered sink. Banana-slime drips from the corners of his mouth. A drop makes a tiny splatter on the floor not far from Dicky's face. Another tiny splatter follows. Denis puts his bowl into the sink, turns on his heel and heads back upstairs.

Dicky starts to cry. He admits to himself that the man he loves is no longer in possession of his senses. He no longer calls out.

The church bell rings again and again, and Dicky weaves in and out of consciousness before he hears the familiar thud of Denis descending to the kitchen once more.

Once again, Denis steps over him as if he is not there and sets about preparing his meal. Once again, when he finishes he clatters his dirty *plate into the sink. And once again, he turns around, steps over Dicky's head and disappears upstairs.*

Alone, Dicky fears that the end is coming now. He has spent years in this room, entertaining, cooking, writing, drawing and obsessively archiving. He wanted to record everything, to put together a full account of the extraordinary life he and Denis had led together. It is the story of the madness of the twentieth-century art world, the tale of a bohemia now evaporated. The story lies in box after box of archives, diaries, letters, programmes, notes and the discarded drafts of an autobiography. It lies in the simple list of names and dates in the Storehouse's visitors' book. As an artist he had been the most famous book-jacket designer in the world; as a writer his first novel had been a scandalous bestseller. But he has failed to tell his own story. He closes his eyes and waits.

I was a close friend of Dicky Chopping and Denis Wirth-Miller for the final thirty years of their lives. After their deaths, their archive was entrusted to my care. As I opened the boxes, I was soon immersed in a story that melded tales of the last of the Bloomsbury Group and the artistic bohemia of the 1950s with details of their bizarre and long-enduring three-way relationship with Francis Bacon. I sat among the boxes and decided to fulfil Dicky's wish to tell their story.

Chapter 1
The Search for Bohemia

At the age of twenty, Richard 'Dicky' Chopping was in search of a London he had heard about but barely seen. His teenage years had been charged with stories of a bohemia that had emerged in a few square miles between the Euston Road and Holborn. The Bloomsbury Group were transgressors. Writers and artists such as Lynton Strachey, E. M. Forster, Virginia Woolf, her sister Vanessa Bell and Duncan Grant combined innovation with boundary-breaking relationships. He had heard stories of love triangles, bisexuality and homosexuality.

By 1937 their light had faded and several members of the set were already dead, but in the streets of neighbouring Fitzrovia a new artistic bohemia was arising – classless, anti-establishment, sexually liberated and even wilder. At the same time, the West End theatre scene was dominated by Noël Coward, who combined arched campness with a talent and confidence that allowed him to subvert the resistance of the establishment.

Chopping was painting in his spare time and had already flirted at the edge of the worlds of journalism, theatre and art, but to no great effect. He was yet to find his feet. He was also trying to come to terms with his emerging sexuality. There had been a physical adventure with a half-Russian, half-Irish au pair called Olga, but he remembered more keenly his chaste crushes on fellow schoolboys.

In June 1937, he used what little money he had to buy a ticket for Noël Coward's 'Theatrical Garden Party' in Regent's Park. It was an open-air charity event in which theatregoers would be allowed to mix with the stars. There was a chance that it would open the door to a world of possibilities.

He had a specific intention in mind. He knew that Peter Blackmore, a 29-year-old playwright whose *Lot's Wife* was playing at the Aldwych, would be there. They had met at a party in St James's Park, and Blackmore had taken Chopping back to his flat. Chopping had believed he was about to sleep with a man for the very first time when the playwright had excused himself and left the room. He returned ten minutes later and said, 'I think you had better go now', without further explanation. The episode had frustrated Chopping and he was determined to make something happen at the garden party.

Chopping was young, tall, handsome and charming, and he dressed carefully for the occasion – a grey flannel Hector Powe suit and brown suede brogues. Nonetheless, once inside the party, he felt out of place and his lack of confidence took over. He felt that everybody else knew each other. Except for the pockets of young bohemians whose loucheness made them appear indifferent to proceedings, the guests were several tiers above his station. He could not find anyone with whom to talk. Even if he had been able to find Blackmore, he realized that he would have been too embarrassed to approach him if he was among friends.

In the gents, he ran into Rodney, a young man he had met at Sadler's Wells theatre. They had arranged to meet again, but Rodney had not turned up. Despite this, Chopping was relieved to find him and his German friend. Similarly out of place, they claimed they were already bored by the garden party and were heading to a 'Hungarian goulash party' in South Kensington. Chopping agreed to abandon Regent's Park and join them.

He regretted his decision. He became frustrated by their continual show of world-weariness and admonished himself for his lack of confidence at the garden party. After the meal, and fortified by wine, he headed back to Regent's Park and tried again to find Peter Blackmore, without any luck. He resorted to standing aloof once more, trying to get a glimpse of Noël Coward. He was embarrassed by his social ineptitude and increasingly envious of the noisy bohemians who seemed effortlessly to dominate the space around them.

When someone finally spoke to him, it was not one of those young men but a middle-aged woman who was helping to run the charity event. He soon found himself roped into selling tickets to a promotion for Optrex eye fluid. He was told to ask the glamorous guests: 'Want to buy the eyes of the stars?' Further indignity was hoisted on his shoulders in the form of a large, Optrex-liveried sandwich board.

He could have no idea that in the years to come Coward would claim that Chopping had saved his life and would become a friend. That associates of the proto bohemia of Bloomsbury – Frances Partridge, Nina Hamnett, Noel Carrington, Kathleen Hale and Julia Strachey among many others – would become close friends and associates. That the new bohemians such as Francis Bacon, Lucian Freud, Johnny Minton and Colquhoun and MacBryde would do likewise, as would many of the century's other great artists. Almost all of them would travel to his home at Wivenhoe and have nights that rivalled the decadence of Fitzrovia and Soho. At that moment he was just a 20-year-old man who had been forced into wearing a sandwich board.

He successfully sold some sixpence tickets to the Optrex promotion and, having ran out of his own money, conjured the sort of plan he thought a bohemian would admire. He took off the sandwich board and used some of the proceeds to buy himself a drink. When that was finished, he donned the board again to raise funds for his next gin and lime.

On one round in his sandwich board, he noticed a young man by the dance floor, eyeing the spectacle on stage with a drink in his hand. He was good-looking and of medium height, and his swept-back hair had fallen forward over his right eyebrow, adding a louche touch. He wore a bow tie and an unpadded, single-breasted suit, and projected exactly the kind of nonchalance to which Chopping aspired. The man seemed mysterious and had the air of an artist: he was undoubtedly one of the new bohemians that Chopping envied. Emboldened by several gins and with the excuse of his sales pitch, he approached the man.

'Want to buy the eyes of the stars?'

The man kept looking at the stage, ignoring him.

'Want to buy the eyes of the stars?' Chopping said again.

The man finally looked at him and spoke.

'Why don't you fuck off?'

Richard Wasey Chopping was born to Ezekiel and Amy on 14 April 1917. He was an identical twin but his brother died when an epidemic of Spanish flu swept through Essex just a year later. The family, which included an older brother, Ralph, lived on the outskirts of Colchester towards the Suffolk border. Ezekiel Copping, a respectable Conservative who served as mayor of Colchester in 1921–2, owned shops and mills, and claimed to produce the whitest flour in Essex.

The 1926 General Strike had a long-term effect on the family, with Ezekiel Chopping's mills brought to a standstill alongside factories, buses and trains. During the chaos, blacklegs who attempted to work were attacked, as was Ezekiel, who had volunteered as a Special Constable in order to help quell disturbances in Colchester. Nine-year-old Dicky, a sensitive lover of Victorian illustrated fairy-tales, watched as a mob dragged his father from his home and severely beat him. Ezekiel would be in extreme pain for the remainder of his life and died when Dicky was still a schoolboy.

At the age of ten, Chopping was sent to Gresham's, a boarding school in Holt, Norfolk. His schooling seems to have been of little note. He contributed an ode to a dragonfly to the school's *Grasshopper* magazine in 1931 and began an interest in art. Towards the end of his schooldays, with the rising threat of another war in Europe, Chopping declared himself a conscientious objector, a stance that had the bonus of getting him discharged from the school's Officer Corps. He was influenced by Philip Smithells, the gym teacher at Gresham's, who was an advocate of pacifism and appeasement. He had recently written a children's book titled *World Without War* (1934), and forged links with the Anglo-German Fellowship, an organization – later accused of being pro-Nazi – that fostered cultural ties between British and German youth.

In 1935, Smithells arranged for Chopping and fourteen other Gresham's pupils to tour a play around Germany. Chopping, who had never been abroad, was excited by the European adventure and determined to use the opportunity to smoke as many cigarettes as he could to effect an air of sophistication.

The propaganda element of the tour later became obvious as they were taken to see Adolf Hitler and other major Nazi figures make public appearances four times in just three days as they made their way through western Germany. Chopping was innocently impressed by the pomp and ceremony of the events and rallies, as well as by the members of Hitler Youth tasked with chaperoning the English boys in their free time. He thought the

German boys were well turned-out, handsome and disciplined. He admired their devotion to the Führer and Fatherland.

The Gresham's pupils were advised not to take photographs, but Chopping managed to capture a series of blurred shots of Hermann Göring inspecting troops at a parade. 'He looked very nice . . . young and handsome', he recorded in his diary.

The political agenda continued with a visit to the scene of the Beer Hall Putsch, during which Hitler had attempted to seize power in Munich in 1923. Then, in Frankfurt, the boys visited a labour camp. The prisoners looked clean and well-fed as they worked in organized teams. The boys' Hitler Youth guides explained that the camp had been set up to 'rehabilitate' criminals and Bolsheviks.

It was only on the final day of the tour that Chopping saw anything to sway him against national socialism. For the first time, the boys were without adult supervision and they drank beer with their dinner in Frankfurt. Some of their Hitler Youth counterparts began a series of anti-Semitic rants. A few others hesitantly admitted that they held reservations about Nazism. They even intimated that the labour camp had been a sham: the real camps were squalid, violent places, and the prisoners were treated as slaves. One boy stated that he had not given up thinking for himself as others had, but he knew that having an independent mind in Nazi Germany was futile. In years to come, Chopping would wonder how long the boy had lasted before he had been executed or imprisoned.

The next morning, the Gresham's boys boarded the boat-train back to London. Chopping wrote thirty-five years later:

We left Germany, some of us never to come back, some to return as conquering heroes; others as dead meat plummeting out of a sky full of flack onto a land of sadistic

cruelty, starvation and disillusionment, soaked from innocent blood. Those who had eyes to see during the last
sixteen days of April 1935 had seen it all along.

He then chided himself: 'I was almost totally blinkered.'

Chopping left Gresham's a few months later. He was captivated
by London and managed to find work experience at the Regent
Street office of the magazine *Decorations of the Modern Home*. Aged
just eighteen, he was soon given the title of sub-editor, which
compensated for the fact that the position remained unpaid.

He moved into a dilapidated room in a flat off Fetter Lane,
which he shared with the twin children of the Chopping family
doctor, along with an older woman who worked as a probation
officer. To get into the building, Chopping had to slip through
a narrow gap in a twenty-foot advertising hoarding and into a
little back-alley. Inside his room, the lathe and plaster walls were
full of holes he needed to stuff with newspapers to block both
the draught and the noise of the sexual antics of the neighbours.

As sub-editor, Chopping accompanied Gerald, a small man
with a bushy moustache, on photographic assignments. One of
these was to the country house of Norman Hartnell, who would
become the Queen's dressmaker. Chopping was impressed by
the gardens, in which the designer had a collection of all-white
animals, including pigeons and a peacock strutting around the
grand lawns.

Another home that Dicky and Gerald photographed was the
St John's Wood flat of the Freud family, who had left Nazi
Germany in 1933. There, Chopping first met Lucian Freud, the
grandson of Sigmund, but he later had little recollection of the
event. Meeting a gangly teenager, five years younger than him,
was not of much interest at the time but their lives would soon
become entwined.

As well as Gerald, the magazine's staff included Margery, who looked after the lonely-hearts column. 'What do you think of this one?' she would ask Chopping among chuckles. Chopping learned that she was something of a lonely-heart herself, perpetually engaged to the large, always perspiring accountant who resisted the altar. The characters at the magazine would form the template for the office-workers Chopping would depict thirty years later in his first novel, *The Fly*.

During this time in London, he resolved to lead a 'normal' sex life, which led to him losing his virginity to the Irish-Russian au pair, but he suspected that his taste lay elsewhere. When he was sixteen, he had seen John Gielgud in a matinée performance of *Richard of Bordeaux*. Not yet thirty, Gielgud was on his way to becoming a household name having established his reputation in Shakespeare productions at the Old Vic. Chopping had been transfixed by him – his voice and 'noble' profile – and sought out his entry in *Who's Who* when he next visited Colchester Library. To his surprise, he shared his birthday with the actor. He started sending him a birthday telegram each year, and went to see him as Mercutio in *Romeo and Juliet* with Laurence Olivier as Romeo.

Chopping was still stuck fast in a sexual identity crisis. Homosexual activity was illegal (and would remain so for the next thirty years) and he was afraid of what his sexuality might mean for him. Nevertheless, as an experiment, he allowed himself to be picked up by a slightly older man he had met on the number 15 bus when heading home from Regent Street. The two travelled back to the man's flat in Victoria, and Chopping climbed the stairs full of trepidation. When the man went into his kitchen to prepare them both a drink, Chopping lost his nerve and rushed out the door.

He left *Decorations of the Modern Home* after ten months. The magazine's finances were in a poor state and he finally accepted that he would never be paid. It went bankrupt shortly after he left.

His mother Amy had been indulgent towards him, especially since the death of his father. She had financed his time in London while he was at the magazine, but following his resignation he had needed to return home. Before long, in 1936, she attempted to help him get a foothold on an artistic career by paying for an apprenticeship with the sculptor, Barry Hart. While teaching at the Royal College of Art, Hart had taught Barbara Hepworth and Henry Moore, and became such a friend to Moore that he was his best man in 1929. He was already a sculptor of some repute who, in the future, would design memorials at Broadcasting House, the Savoy and Brasenose College, Oxford.

During his time as Hart's apprentice, Chopping would be given artistic exercises, which he would undertake in the cellar of his mother's house, but he was rarely impressed by his own efforts. They included a still life of food – a raw chicken next to a plum pie with a slice cut out to reveal the blood-red filling – which he later recalled as 'a dreary affair'. The bird's carcass began to stink out the cellar in the summer heat. He convinced his mother that he needed to practise landscape painting instead. She agreed to finance a trip he wanted to make to Finchingfield in north-west Essex, but Chopping had an ulterior motive: he had found out where Gielgud lived.

Chopping travelled by bus to Finchingfield, which was only a short walk to Gielgud's country house, Foulslough Farm. He stayed in a local pub and the next morning set out with a sketchbook and watercolour paints towards Gielgud's home. He made sure he was clearly visible from the house and wore a wide white sun hat to emphasize to any onlookers that he was an artist at work. He proceeded to paint a sketch using only yellow ochre, cobalt blue and crimson-lake red – a rule that had

Richard Chopping painting near Finchingfield, Essex, *c*.1936.
(Author's personal collection)

been set by Hart in order to restrict his wild palette. The result, he reported, was 'mediocrity'.

He fantasized that he would hear Gielgud's mellifluous voice shouting an invitation for a gin and tonic from the drawing-room window or that the actor would send out a maid to fetch him. His hopes waned over the course of the day. He realized that he was unlikely ever to lie on a bed and hear Gielgud deliver the same words he had whispered to Gwen Ffrangcon-Davies in *Richard of Bordeaux*. He went home.

Overall, Chopping was not impressed by Hart. The feeling was mutual. The relationship faltered further when Hart falsely accused Chopping of reading his letters and telling his wife, Editha, about his secret girlfriend.

The one benefit of Chopping's first introduction to the art world was the leasing of Daffodil Cottage. Hart had a country retreat called Wiston Cottage, in the Stour Valley, where Chopping would visit him to show him progress on his artistic exercises. To reach Hart's cottage, Chopping would take the bus to Wormingford and walk the remaining eight miles. He may not have liked the end destination but, as he was interested in the natural world, he enjoyed the walk along the Stour, past the home of the artist John Nash.

Near Wiston, he would pass an uninhabited and dilapidated worker's cottage with a drooping, thatched roof. On one occasion he investigated its interior and found that it had no running water or electricity, and the outside lavatory consisted of a bucket – but it appealed to Chopping. Enquiries led him to a neighbour, a 'wild-toothed, crazy-haired, phlebitis-legged Irishwoman', who gave him the address of the Humes, the owners of the cottage.

He entered their more modern house and was greeted by a squawked 'Hullo!' from Buster, the Humes's parrot. Chopping described Mrs Hume as 'almost completely spherical, coarse skinned and slippered'. Mr Hume, meanwhile, was 'mild, quiet, spare'. He barely spoke from under his bristly white moustache, but he made his presence felt. Every few minutes, he would hawk phlegm into the fire. Chopping secured Daffodil Cottage for 2/6d per week.

When Chopping accompanied Hart to Manchester to paint flying sausages and kitchen utensils onto the ceiling of a gas showroom extension, he decided that his artistic education was not going as he had hoped. He resigned shortly thereafter, but he kept Daffodil Cottage on. Chopping's fantasy was that, away from his mother's prying eyes, the cottage would become his illicit love nest where he could take London conquests.

Dicky Chopping's obsession with Gielgud, rather than his commitment to fine art, determined his next move. In 1937, he enrolled in a course at the London Theatre Studio – he had found out that Gielgud was on its board of directors.

He studied stage design under Michel Saint-Denis, who directed Laurence Olivier in *Macbeth* in 1937 and would later set up the Drama Division at Juilliard in New York. The French director's theories would go on to have a major impact on drama tuition, helping to initiate professional training for actors, but they had little effect on Chopping. He was put in charge of the stage lighting for the school's public shows, alongside a woman called Jennifer, but neither of them had any aptitude. During a production of the students' yearly show, they accidentally implemented the lighting sequence for the second act throughout the first. The result was chaos.

Gielgud was not much in evidence at the school. Chopping only saw him in the flesh once, disappearing into a board meeting. He was continually disappointed but would soon have a strange liaison with the actor away from the school.

As he described it, Chopping was walking along Shaftesbury Avenue when he bumped into someone. He looked up to apologize and was shocked to see that it was John Gielgud. He kept his composure and strolled on, but he could not resist looking over his shoulder. He saw that Gielgud had stopped walking and was pretending to look in a shop window while glancing at Chopping. The young man turned back, passed behind his idol and walked the whole length of Shaftesbury Avenue, making sure that Gielgud was following. He then entered a newsreel cinema in St Martin's Lane and went into the dark auditorium.

He scanned the rows of seats behind him and eventually saw that the actor was sitting on an aisle seat six rows away. As Gielgud was so far back, Chopping convinced himself that the actor was not interested in him at all; he made no move so perhaps had genuinely just wanted to see the news all along. Chopping stood up and walked up the aisle, hesitating slightly by Gielgud's seat. He then pushed through the exit, past a lavatory door and out into the afternoon sunshine.

He waited outside the cinema to see if he would be followed, but Gielgud never appeared. He felt like a fool for thinking that Gielgud could have been interested in him.

The Café Royal near Piccadilly was first opened in 1865 by the French wine merchant Daniel Nicholas Thévenon and by the 1890s it was London's unofficial arts club. Composers, writers and artists including James Abbott McNeill Whistler and Walter Sickert would meet among its gilt mouldings, mirrors and pilasters. They were attracted to its famous wine cellar and the decadence suggested by its exotic 'Frenchness'. Aubrey Beardsley and Oscar Wilde would often hold court there. In 1895 Frank Harris, Wilde's friend and biographer who had some legal knowledge, went to the Café Royal to attempt to persuade the playwright to drop his libel case against the Marquess of Queensberry, father to his lover Lord Alfred Douglas. Wilde ignored him and was subsequently imprisoned for gross indecency.

The Café Royal continued to attract notable figures, from the Bloomsbury set to Noël Coward, as well as the wilder elements of high society. Its importance as an intellectual and hedonistic gathering place for artists was underlined when Charles Ginner, Harold Gilman, William Orpen and Nina Hamnett all painted scenes there within just a couple of years during the second decade of the twentieth century.

In 1937, not long after the Theatrical Garden Party, Dicky Chopping followed the long line of would-be bohemians and young artists – as well as pimps and criminals – who trooped to the Café Royal. He was drawn by its reputation for glamour and iniquity. For company he had a pale-haired friend called John. He could only afford a coffee.

As soon they reached the counter area, a young man in a bow tie walked towards them. Chopping was disconcerted. The man's hair was flopped decadently over one eyebrow. It was the same young bohemian who had been rude to him at the Theatrical Garden Party. When the man asked if they had met before, Chopping warily admitted that they had.

'Good,' the man said. 'I can't join you now because I am with some friends, but when the café closes at midnight why don't you come back to my studio for a drink?'

Chopping was intrigued by the mention of a studio and by what he later described as the prospect of a 'never-before experienced type of hospitality'. He forgave the young man's previous rudeness and agreed.

After the man had left them, John confessed that he did not want to go to a stranger's house. 'I don't think Uncle would like it if I am so late home,' he said.

'All right, don't then if you feel like that, but I shall go.'

The man who had approached them was Denis Wirth-Miller, an aspiring artist. Although only two years older than Chopping, he was already becoming a fixture at the Café Royal. His circle of acquaintances included Prince Yusupov, the White Russian who had murdered Grigori Rasputin in 1916 before being exiled as a result of the communist revolutions. Although he had recognized Chopping, Wirth-Miller would later claim that he had no recollection of snubbing him at the Theatrical Garden Party. The inspiration for approaching him was merely the sight of him – 'beautiful' and tall – walking through the Café Royal.

While Wirth-Miller returned to his own party of friends and associates, Chopping eked out his coffee in the company of John. His friend left him just before midnight and Chopping waited alone. He suspected this would be yet another of his failed adventures.

He was surprised when Denis Wirth-Miller appeared as promised, by now unsteady on his feet. He ushered Chopping through the Café Royal's swing door and into a taxi.

'Curiously, I can no longer recall what happened in the taxi', Chopping later wrote. As the taxi followed the arc of Regent Street, veered right at Oxford Circus and then turned north, he would have realized that he was in the company of one of the Fitzrovians – the bohemian set who inhabited an artists' quarter north of Oxford Street, the other side of Tottenham Court Road from the more refined Bloomsbury.

Fitzrovia had a poor reputation and places were cheap to rent. It had become the unofficial home of innovative contemporary art, with Fitzroy Street as its epicentre. As Jane Rye wrote of the abstract artist Adrian Heath's move to 22 Fitzroy Street in 1949, the street 'had a suitable avant-garde pedigree for a young artist with aspirations to be at the forefront of things'.[1] Paul Nash had lived on the street, while Augustus John was currently living at number 18, the former studio of the Vorticist Wyndham Lewis.

In October 1937, not long after Dicky Chopping and Denis Wirth-Miller's taxi drove up the street, the Euston Road School was founded at no. 12 by Victor Pasmore, William Coldstream and Claude Rogers. In 1939, Pasmore, one of the pioneers of British abstraction, took a studio for himself at no. 8, which had previously been used by James Abbott McNeill Whistler and was rented from the Bloomsbury Group's Duncan Grant. The writer Stephen Spender and the critic Lawrence Gowing would attend classes at the Euston Road School, which moved to nearby Euston Road in 1938, and Vanessa Bell and Grant would teach there. Rodrigo Moynihan and Graham Bell, who had been leaders of the Objective Abstraction art movement in the mid-1930s, were also associated with the school.

The taxi pulled up at no. 19, the studio and home of the confident young artist in the bow tie. The building had previously been rented by Walter Sickert and had become the headquarters of the avant-garde Fitzroy Street Group in 1907. Along with the Camden Town Group and their joint successor the London Group, the Fitzroy Street Group pushed at the boundaries of mainstream art. Part of Sickert's power lay in his depiction of the figure, particularly in the *Camden Town Murder* series, which, in its transgressive content (a clothed man with a naked woman on a bed) if not its style, would prove to be a forerunner to the work of Wirth-Miller's friends, Francis Bacon and Lucian Freud.

'I knew that according to the law we were about to commit a crime,' Chopping wrote about the unfolding scenario. 'Why had I ever been so weak as to start on this primrose path?'

After Wirth-Miller had unlocked the large front door and led the way down a sloping passage past a shared lavatory stinking of urine, Chopping finally stepped into the world of artistic and sexual liberation that had so far eluded him.

The studio room was large, illuminated by a light above a long window covered by pink-and-white striped mattress ticking Wirth-Miller had deployed as a curtain. Underneath two skylights were an elliptical Victorian drinks table and an olive-green, S-shaped sofa. There were matching glass-fronted cupboards at either end of the love seat, and a green baize table supporting a white plaster bust of Mercury.

In a corner, on a pink baize table, there was a life-like wax bust of a woman's head with glass eyes, along with eyelashes and a wig made from human hair. Wirth-Miller explained that Sickert had seen the bust in an old-fashioned barber's shop window and had bought it for the artist Nina Hamnett, his then mistress. Hamnett, known as the 'Queen of Bohemia', had burst

Denis Wirth–Miller, 19 Fitzroy Street, London, 1938. *(Author's personal collection)*

into Wirth–Miller's studio one day and made him a present of the bust as she regarded it as a legacy of the studio's past. Wirth–Miller and Hamnett had soon become friends.

Chopping also saw one of Wirth–Miller's artworks for the first time: a large, boldly rendered painting in gouache on paper of Elijah being fed by ravens. It confirmed to Chopping that he was in the company of a talented artist.

'I began to learn what homosexual men really did together,' he reported, 'having previously only kissed with firmly closed lips and only suspected what other orifices could be employed.'

Chopping remembered thinking the next morning as he left Wirth–Miller's studio: 'My body had cried out for deliverance from this pressing sexual need. Sin conquered finally. I must never do such a thing again.'

Dicky Chopping remained wary of Denis Wirth–Miller. The artist was charming and humorous, but he was unorthodox and had a dangerous edge to him. Chopping also had a lingering attraction to Peter Blackmore, the writer he had searched for at the Theatrical Garden Party.

Nonetheless, when Blackmore declined his invitation to join him in the Upper Circle at Drury Lane to see a ballet, saying he was going to the countryside, Chopping telephoned Wirth-Miller, who agreed to his offer immediately. Chopping pushed all thoughts of Blackmore aside when he saw that, far from being in the countryside, the playwright was laughing with wealthy friends in the foyer at Drury Lane. He imagined they were laughing at the boy who had invited Blackmore to join him in the cheap seats.

After the performance, Wirth-Miller treated Chopping to supper at the Café Royal, but Chopping held back from accepting his invitation to stay at the studio again. As well as intimidating in his knowledge of the art world and literature, the slightly older man was evasive when asked about his background. Chopping thought that his upper-class drawl and mannerisms seemed slightly affected. It was clear, though, that the two men were deeply attracted to each other, and Chopping was intrigued by the artist.

After he walked back to the shared house on John Street where he had been living while attending the theatre school, he was given a frosty reception. He felt as if his suspicious housemates knew that he was now a practising homosexual, and were judging him for it. He realized that he no longer wanted to live a life of restraint and to subvert his inclinations. He resolved to see the mysterious Denis Wirth-Miller again as soon as possible.

Denis Wirth-Miller's unwillingness to talk about his background was born of a traumatic childhood. He was born Dennis (with a double 'n') Wirthmiller in Folkestone on 27 November 1915.

His mother, Eleanor, was from Northumbria and had gone into service as a between maid at Castle Howard at the age of thirteen. His father, Johann Warthmiller, was Bavarian, and together they ran a downmarket hotel. Dennis was the third child, following a daughter, also called Eleanor, in 1910, and a son, William John, born in 1913. All three children were registered with the slightly anglicized name Wirthmiller.

Many years later, Wirth-Miller would claim to his friend David Douglas, the Marquess of Queensbury (David Queensbury), that, during the First World War, his father avoided internment as a German national by living in the hotel basement and was later shot as a spy in the Tower of London. While the claim that he was executed was untrue, it is possible that Johann Warthmiller may have been interned, perhaps before Dennis's birth. In any case, he played little part in the childhood of Dennis and his two older siblings.

The father's absence left the family destitute and they were continual victims of anti-German sentiment in Folkestone. When his mother wheeled his pram through the streets, mother and child were sometimes spat at for their association with the enemy.

Local animosity became so intense that before Dennis was a year old, his mother moved him, his brother and his sister to the coastal town of Bamburgh in Northumberland. They were again ostracized by the community and remained in poverty. The situation did not improve after the war, with Wirthmiller frequently humiliated and degraded at school for being half-German. He learned to hide his emotions and understood the importance of looking tough and emotionally impregnable — facets that never left his personality. He and his elder brother are also believed to have taken up petty thievery when young, spurred on by their poverty.

The young Wirthmiller developed a passion for drawing and, without any tutoring or encouragement, taught himself the rudiments of line, perspective and shading. From there he progressed to handling paint. Although he may have taken trips down to Newcastle to see John Martin's paintings in the Laing Art Gallery, his self-education mainly consisted of copying illustrations from periodicals and newspapers.

When he finished school at the age of fifteen, he had no formal qualifications, but resisted the temptation to follow in his brother William John's footsteps and become a career criminal. Through persistence, Wirthmiller was given a job in the design department at Tootal Broadhurst Lee, a textile manufacturer in Manchester.

By this point, both Wirthmiller boys had further freed themselves from their German ancestry by calling themselves Miller. In later life, Wirth-Miller kept few photographs, letters or paperwork that related to his family, although he maintained contact with his sister and corresponded with Sister Agatha, a niece who had joined a nunnery. Eventually, in 1983, he was to fall out with Sister Agatha over a gift of some wigs that Dicky Chopping presented to the nuns for their Christmas production of *The Sound of Music*. The nuns were horrified to discover that the wigs had previously been used for a drag act. As a gesture of goodwill Wirth-Miller sent a cheque to the nunnery to assist a charitable project but thereafter all communications ceased.

Wirth-Miller's mother and sister returned to live in Kent. His sister Eleanor married in Folkestone in 1935 and it was around this time that Wirth-Miller lost his virginity to an Indian cricketer while people passed by on the port's Leas Promenade, just a few feet away.

Occasionally, he was sent down from Manchester to London to help out at Tootal Broadhurst Lee's outpost in Cavendish

Place and, like Dicky Chopping after him, became increasingly aware that the capital offered both artistic and sexual adventures that were difficult to find elsewhere. After a year at the Manchester office, he asked if he could be transferred to Cavendish Place. His request was accepted. He soon proved adept at designing textile patterns and putting together window displays for the London office.

Once in the capital, Wirthmiller used the anonymity of the big city to reinvent himself further. He styled himself as a bohemian artist and was gregarious, witty and an enthusiastic drinker. He Gallicized his forename to 'Denis', adopted the double-barrelled surname Wirth-Miller, and cultivated his accent. He started concentrating on his art in his spare time and soon moved to Sickert's former studio in Fitzroy Street.

It was not only its recent art pedigree that attracted Wirth-Miller and other young artists and writers to Fitzrovia in the 1930s. Its narrow streets and small squares between the thoroughfares of Warren Street to the north and Goodge Street to the south were dangerous, but the area was cosmopolitan as well as cheap. Before post-war Soho started to flourish as the down-at-heel but exotic quarter of London, Fitzrovia attracted French, Greek and Italian immigrants who set up shop and offered an antidote to typically reserved English taste and culture.

In contrast to the almost exclusively Oxford-educated Bloomsbury set, class was irrelevant to the Fitzrovians. Even the richest of Wirth-Miller's contemporaries affected not to care about social hierarchies or the mores of the day. Debauchery and drunkenness crossed all social and sexual distinctions. The new bohemians shared with the Bloomsburians a rejection of bourgeois ethics and constraints, a love of art purely for its aesthetic value, and an emphasis on personal relationships and individual pleasure. They could never be called an artistic or literary movement: there was no united style or intellectual synchronicity to their creativity beyond the desire to push boundaries. While Vanessa Bell and Duncan Grant and other Bloomsbury artists collectively broke the distinction between framed art, design and decoration, the young Fitzrovians for the most part pursued more individualistic artistic transgressions while in their studios or at their desks. Their collective action was merely to drink excessively together and enjoy the ensuing chaos. The most important characteristic was to be interesting.

Fitzrovia's pubs and foreign restaurants became a destination for artists, writers and cultural tourists. The Fitzroy Tavern, with sawdust on the floor and a mechanical piano, and the mock-Tudor Wheatsheaf provided the social axis, with Augustus John, George Orwell, Dylan Thomas and Nina Hamnett all regulars.

Thomas was still in his early twenties but had already published his second acclaimed volume of poetry, having been discovered by T. S. Eliot and Stephen Spender. In 1936, Thomas lured his future wife Caitlin away from the artist Augustus John in the Wheatsheaf. Caitlin had run away from home to be a dancer – a typical story among the mix of people in Fitzrovia's pubs and restaurants. The privileged rubbed shoulders with struggling artists and performers, as well as a low-life element, and Wirth-Miller quickly became friendly with the Fitzrovia regulars.

Fitzrovia's hostelries also included the rough and violent Marquess of Granby, Madame Buhler's Café, the Bricklayer's and the Black Horse. European restaurants included L'Étoile, Schmidt's, Bertorelli's, the Tour Eiffel (which became the then exotic Greek restaurant the White Tower a few years later) and Poggioli's, which were glamorous and theatrical in their foreignness while serving cheap food. Like Wirth-Miller, many

Fitzrovians, if they had enough money, would complete the evening by heading down towards Piccadilly to take advantage of the late licence at the Café Royal.

Wirth-Miller soon introduced Chopping to his world, starting with dinner at Poggioli's, the cheapest restaurant in Charlotte Street. Wirth-Miller arrived late with an unexplained black eye not entirely covered by an eye-patch, and apologized to Chopping for having to request cash to pay the taxi driver. As Wirth-Miller ordered the wine, Chopping realized that he would have to foot the bill. Once again, he wondered whether Wirth-Miller was too unconventional, too wild for his palate. But, as the meal progressed, he acknowledged that he was also too charismatic and interesting for him to give up on. And in turn the outlandish, self-assured artist seemed to find him equally interesting.

That night, Chopping stayed at Wirth-Miller's studio. He spent the next night there, too. Then, on the following day, he agreed to move in.

Chapter 2

The New World

Within a few months, Chopping's life had changed completely. Wirth-Miller convinced him to drop his half-hearted theatrical ambitions and pursue his art. He believed that his new lover already showed great promise as an artist and helped him to improve his skills. He kept his own job at Tootal Broadhurst Lee to help fund their joint life together and also accompanied him to evening classes at Goldsmith's College in south-east London twice a week. Chopping's time at the London Theatre Studio had not been entirely worthless, however, as a very young Jocelyn Herbert, who would go on to design many productions at the Royal Court and National Theatre, asked him to produce costume designs for a production of *Hamlet*. Jocelyn Herbert would remain a friend, and would become the artist John Minton's close confidante.

Wirth-Miller also helped Chopping to free himself of his teenage obsession with John Gielgud, which had led him towards a career in the theatre in the first place. When Chopping described the incident in the news cinema, Wirth-Miller gave him a primer in the rituals of sexual assignations. He explained that, with the threat that being caught in a homosexual act could lead to a custodial sentence, only an idiot could expect an encounter with a well-known public figure in the stalls of a cinema. That was what the lavatory was for. Chopping realized

A 1937 Wirth–Miller window design for Tootal Broadhurst Lee,
Regent Street, London. *(Author's personal collection)*

that while he had been waiting back out on the street, Gielgud
had probably gone to find him in the gents.

Knowing that the actor used public lavatories in search of
sexual gratification (a fact confirmed in 1953 when Gielgud was
arrested in a public lavatory in Westminster) was a blow to his
idolatry. Wirth-Miller then dealt the killer punch. He admitted
that, a few years earlier, he too had been picked up by Gielgud
and taken to his flat. There, on the actor's bed beneath a portrait
of Peggy Ashcroft and Edith Evans as *Juliet and the Nurse* painted
by Walter Sickert, he had been fellated by the actor 'to the
sounds of muffled choking'. Gielgud had placed his false teeth
in a glass of water at the side of the bed before commencing.
The birthday telegrams stopped from that point on.

The radical and unconventional nature of the bohemian scene in
Fitzrovia benefited both men. Chopping was able to come out of
his shell in terms of his personality, sexuality and artistic ambition.
Meanwhile, Wirth-Miller started to receive commissions from

fellow Fitzrovians even though he was untrained and still working in textiles and window-dressing. He had become friendly with Richard Buckle, a flamboyant young ballet critic and later biographer of Nijinsky and Diaghilev, who lived nearby on Fitzroy Street. It was probably he who helped Wirth-Miller secure commissions for illustrations in Royal Opera House programmes. The illustrations he produced were modernist line drawings that owed a slight debt to Vorticism. In 1939 Buckle also commissioned Wirth-Miller to illustrate the first edition of *Ballet* magazine.

Chopping and Wirth-Miller became friends with Robert Buhler, who was their age, when they ate at Madame Buhler's Café. It was run by his Swiss mother, who also sold foreign-language newspapers and books to the cosmopolitan clientele. Buhler had already trained at St Martin's School of Art and the Royal College of Art (RCA) by the time Chopping and Wirth-Miller became friends with him. The two men, as artist-outsiders, related to Buhler's artistic rebelliousness: he rejected both the RCA's formal teaching methods (he had left after six weeks) and the role of the aristocratic Bloomsbury set as the sole progenitors of progress in British art.[2] That he would go on to teach at the RCA after the Second World War was a sign of how quickly the orthodoxy and deference imbued in British art was turned on its head within a couple of decades.

Chopping and Wirth-Miller also became close to Sonia Brownell and William Coldstream, who were seeing each other despite the latter's continuing marriage to the artist Nancy Sharp. Coldstream, who had worked with W. H. Auden and Benjamin Britten as part of the GPO Film Unit, had just returned to painting full-time, thanks to a stipend from Kenneth Clark, the young director of the National Gallery. Like Buhler, Coldstream was politically concerned about the place of the working rather than the aristocratic artist in society. He too would play a major role in post-war art education, becoming principal of the Slade School of Fine Art. Through him, both men came to know Victor Pasmore, who would become the leader of a new generation of British abstract artists following in the wake of Ben Nicholson. In the future, Pasmore would collaborate with another of Wirth-Miller and Chopping's friends, the architect Ernö Goldfinger, on a constructivist sculpture for *This Is Tomorrow* (1956). The exhibition was a watershed in British art, announcing the arrival of British Pop Art.

It was Sonia Brownell, a young editor, who would become a long-term friend of Chopping and Wirth-Miller. She lived on Charlotte Street above the Tour Eiffel restaurant, where Chopping and Wirth-Miller and their young artist friends would often eat, and she was a regular at all their haunts. In time she would have an affair with Lucian Freud, marry George Orwell on his deathbed in 1949 and become a close confidante of Francis Bacon.

Older, established artists also played a role in the young men's initial life together. They would regularly see Augustus John on Fitzroy Street, while Lucien Pissarro, the oldest son of the Impressionist Camille Pissarro, came to their studio for tea. Pissarro, who had been living in England since 1890, already knew the interior of their studio well as he was a close friend of Walter Sickert. As the most high-profile landscape painter that Wirth-Miller knew prior to the Second World War, it is possible that Pissarro imparted some wisdom but there is little evidence of this in his early works. Wirth-Miller was far from concentrating on landscape at this time.

Nina Hamnett was the member of the older generation who had the greatest role in Wirth-Miller's life. The former mistress of Sickert lived opposite the studio in Fitzroy Street in a tiny attic flat.

Born in 1890, she had lived in Paris and been a model for
Pablo Picasso as well as the Vorticist Henri Gaudier-Brzeska and
the Bloomburians Roger Fry and Duncan Grant. She had mixed
with the avant-garde crowd of Jean Cocteau and Serge Diaghilev,
and was fond of declaring that Modigliani had told her she had
the best breasts in Europe.

In 1932, she had published a memoir-cum-history entitled
Laughing Torso about her bohemian life. It had sold well and she
was still living off the proceeds, having fended off the occultist
Aleister Crowley's attempts to sue her for libel over allegations
of black magic. She was fearless, unconventional, bisexual and
promiscuous. Having previously been known to dance naked
on the tables of Montparnasse, she haunted the pubs of Fitzrovia
and the Café Royal from the 1920s onwards and was often
referred to as the Queen of Bohemia.

Among a catalogue of drunken incidents, she had once
objected to a young woman sitting with her friend, the poet
Roy Campbell, at one of Augustus John's parties. She had
walked behind the sofa they were sharing, grabbed the woman's
hair and yanked her backwards so hard that she fell over the back
of the couch. Blood poured from her scalp, and Campbell had
to call a doctor. Another anecdote tells of Hamnett carefully
throwing up in her handbag before clipping it shut, delicately
wiping her lips and resuming drinking.

Such stories and the success of *Laughing Torso* overshadowed
her early reputation as an artist, which had been bolstered by
showings at the Royal Academy and the Salon d'Automne, and
by her work with the Bloomsbury set's Omega Workshop. By
the time Wirth-Miller became friendly with her in 1937, her
life had already descended into alcoholic squalor, and she could
often be found in the Fitzroy Tavern singing sea-shanties in
exchange for drinks.

According to her biographer Denise Hooker, Hamnett's first words to Wirth-Miller were, 'My deah, what's your name? You look evil!' – perhaps in response to his dark, parted hair slightly reminiscent of Adolf Hitler. From that point on, she would always introduce him with, 'Here's Denis Wirth-Miller – he's evil my deah, evil!'[3] They were a strange yet compatible match despite the twenty-five-year age gap: they were both direct, opinionated and drank to the extreme, but they were also sociable, witty and good company. The letters from Hamnett to Wirth-Miller dating from 1938 to 1952 show that the bond between them was strong and enduring.

After moving into the studio, Chopping was wary of the imminent introduction to Hamnett as she and Wirth-Miller had become so close. He had an uncomfortable feeling that he was about to be subjected to a test of approval. He worried that if Hamnett did not like him, Wirth-Miller would be disappointed in him.

As it turned out, their first meeting was brief. Hamnett was drunk by the time she met them but showed no outward hostility: she was more concerned about asking for money. When Chopping complied, she immediately left them and went in search of gin.

Soon, they went out drinking with Hamnett regularly in sessions that teetered on chaos. Chopping was daring, but a streak of conservativism initiated by his family life remained constant within his character. While Wirth-Miller, Hamnett and the likes of Francis Bacon would push excess to its furthest limits and, in doing so, offend without compunction, Chopping never wanted to be the cause of distress. The difference would play a key role in Chopping and Wirth-Miller's relationship – and in their joint relationship with Bacon – and was evident in their art. While he enjoyed Hamnett's company when they were out on Charlotte Street, Chopping wondered whether he was accepted by her.

Another friend to whom Wirth-Miller introduced Chopping was the modernist poet Anna Wickham, who drank in the Wheatsheaf. Born in 1883, she had married a solicitor and had four sons before falling in love with the American playwright, Natalie Barney, and going to live in Paris in the early 1920s. Shortly before she met Wirth-Miller, she had helped to support fellow poet Dylan Thomas financially following his marriage to Caitlin. She accompanied Chopping and Wirth-Miller to the Café de Paris on a regular basis where, if provoked, she would bite people on the head or pull their breasts.

Robert Colquhoun and Robert MacBryde were Chopping and Wirth-Miller's frequent companions as they drank their way around Fitzrovia and Soho in the 1940s and 1950s, and there is evidence that they were already friends in the late 1930s. Like Wirth-Miller and Chopping, Colquhoun and MacBryde, known as 'the Roberts', were provincial outsiders but they had received an art education at the Glasgow School of Art. Colquhoun, born in Kilmarnock in 1914, and MacBryde, born a year earlier in Maybole, met while young and became an inseparable couple. Although often described as a single entity and their work is frequently shown together, they each had a distinct style, with their different use of line and colour making their work distinguishable; Colquhoun later became a more figurative painter while MacBryde veered towards still life and landscape. Colquhoun was the more sensitive looking of the two men and the more cerebral; MacBryde was shorter, dark and sensual.

Even at this stage, both showed artistic promise and, like Wirth-Miller, they had a determination to succeed as artists. In September 1936, Colquhoun won a grant that allowed him and

MacBryde to travel to London for the first time to visit the Tate
and the National Gallery. As Wirth-Miller knew the Roberts
before starting his relationship with Chopping in 1937, he may
have met them while they were on this trip – they would become
co-conspirators in excess. According to Chopping's recollections,
the Roberts must have visited London again temporarily either
before or during their extended travels, courtesy of another
travel grant, in France and Italy in 1938–9. Chopping always
regretted not accepting their invitation to join them in Italy in
early 1939. A decade later, when the Roberts were returning
from another trip to Italy, the four men met up in Paris.

The Roberts were a formidable duo, prone to excessive
drinking, promiscuity and fighting, including each other. In
contrast to Chopping, who stood at the edge of the London
artistic scene waiting to be introduced, the two Roberts arrived
in loud voice, crashing into the centre of the party wearing
kilts and revelling in their outsider status. They made a
performance of their 'otherness' and were rarely forgotten. Yet
it was the quality of their work, initially influenced by the
work of John Piper and Graham Sutherland, that would lead
to their exhibitions at major commercial galleries while still
young men.

The Roberts would become leaders of the younger artists
involved in the neo-Romantic movement. The neo-Romantics
found inspiration in the work of the eighteenth-century
British artists William Blake and Samuel Palmer, but
simultaneously combined it with the more contemporary
cubist influence of Pablo Picasso and André Masson. The
work of the Roberts, Johnny Minton and Keith Vaughan
quickly heralded a new era for British art. All of them were
young homosexual men exploring their art in a similar neo-
Romantic direction.

Unlike the working-class Roberts and Wirth-Miller, and the provincially middle-class Chopping, John Minton came from a cossetted background and was an artist of independent means. He was flamboyant and gregarious, and was regarded as handsome in an otherworldly, exotic sense, with tanned skin and olive-green eyes.

Born on Christmas Day, 1917, Minton was still only twenty at this time and studying at St John's Wood Art School (also known as 'The Wood'), and before long would leave for Paris. He had recently been introduced to the neo-Romanticism of Graham Sutherland, John Piper and Paul Nash by his friend and fellow student Michael Ayrton. Minton was yet to tell even Ayrton that he was homosexual and he led a partially clandestine life before he left for France. This is likely to have involved trips a few stops down the Northern line to Fitzrovia, an area of London where a homosexual artist was sure to find similar pleasure seekers, and his path may well have crossed that of Wirth-Miller and Chopping. They formally met when Minton visited the Benton End art school in about 1941.

While Chopping and Wirth-Miller attempted to establish their careers and ignore the prospect of war, they careered from the Wheatsheaf to the Fitzroy to the cheap restaurants in Fitzrovia, but they also often headed towards Soho.

The Gargoyle, housed in two upper storeys on the corner of Meard Street and Dean Street, opened in the late 1920s. It laid the foundations for the Colony Room – which opened across the street in 1948 – to shift the focal point of bohemia from Fitzrovia to Soho in the 1950s. Before the war, the Gargoyle was effectively an offshoot of Fitzrovia, with Augustus John and Dylan Thomas as well as Wirth-Miller, Chopping and friends making the trip across Oxford Street. The spies Burgess, Maclean and Kim Philby would also visit the club, as would the writer

Joan Wyndham, who would become famous for her diaries that traced her days in bohemia. On her first visit to the Gargoyle, she witnessed a drunken Philip Toynbee throwing up all over the sofa he was sitting on without an eyebrow being raised. Toynbee, an anti-fascist activist and novelist, was at the time going out with Lytton Strachey's niece, who would become a friend of Chopping.

The Gargoyle had been founded by the socialite David Tennant, and designed by a combination of the architect Sir Edwin Lutyens and the artist Henri Matisse. His *L'Atelier Rouge* (painted in 1911 and now in the Museum of Modern Art in New York) was displayed on the wall until 1941. Matisse cut up antique mirrors to create 20,000 wall tiles for its Moorish interior, and the club had a gold and silver staircase connecting its bar, coffee room and ballroom. Noël Coward, Tallulah Bankhead and Fred Astaire all became members, and the club gained a reputation as a den for both artists and aristocrats seeking excess.

Minton would later become notorious at the Gargoyle for his unique and enthusiastic dancing style, and also for drinking too much when he lacked the robust constitution of the two Roberts, Chopping and Wirth-Miller. Possibly bipolar, at a certain point of the evening his gregariousness would metamorphose into depression and whining self-pity. Wirth-Miller would always tolerate him but others were less fond. With its heightened atmosphere and lack of inhibition, the Gargoyle was, in Francis Bacon's phrase, 'a place for rows', which he enjoyed.

Francis Bacon, who would become such a pivotal figure in Wirth-Miller and Chopping's life, lived in Chelsea and was not a regular in Fitzrovia but he was already a strange and notable presence in the wider bohemian scene. The Gargoyle would remain one of his favoured destinations for years to come.

His early life had been unusual. He was born in Dublin on 28 October 1909, the second of five children in an upper-middle-class English family. They moved to England during the First World War so that his father Edward could take up a military post and, when they returned to Ireland, they faced the increasing threat of violence from Irish nationalists.

Bacon's father, a racehorse trainer, seemingly had little time for his asthmatic son. His idea of punishment for the wayward boy was to hand him over to the male grooms, who took it upon themselves to whip and bugger him, setting in train a masochistic streak that would never leave him. At fancy-dress parties he would dress as a flapper in a backless dress, but when his father caught him wearing his mother's underwear at the age of sixteen, he was apparently told to leave home (although Bacon was an unreliable and mythologizing source when it came to the biographical details of his own life).[4] Bacon's biographer Michael Peppiatt wrote, 'Before his life had really begun, he had been rejected by his own kin and branded as an outsider . . . from the moment of his rejection, Francis Bacon set out to take rebellion to its furthest extreme.'[5]

Bacon went to London, where he lived by the grace of older male associates, became a thief embroiled in the homosexual underworld, and worked as a manservant.[6] One employer was outraged to find Bacon, who already had a taste for switching between high-life and low-life, dining at the Ritz at the same time as him. He was consequently dismissed. Edward Bacon then made the decision to send his son to Berlin in 1927 with an older relative, Harcourt-Smith (his Christian name is likely to have been Cecil), in order to straighten him out. It was a decision that he may have regretted as Berlin was the hedonistic capital of Europe and Harcourt-Smith was a sexual sadist. Bacon said of him: 'Very tough – a real brute. I really don't think it made the slightest bit of difference to him whether he went with a man or a woman. He fucked everything that moved.'[7] And that included Bacon.

He also furthered Bacon's taste for luxury as they stayed at the Hotel Adlon. Harcourt-Smith soon tired of him, however, and abandoned him after a couple of months. The 17-year-old Bacon then relocated to Paris, learned French and, having seen Picasso's work at the Galerie Paul Rosenberg, began to draw and paint: 'They made a great impression on me, and I thought afterwards, well, perhaps I could draw as well.'[8]

Bacon returned to London in late 1928. Recent evidence has emerged that he lived with a former attaché to the British Embassy in China, Eric Allden, who was twenty-three years his senior. Allden had met Bacon on a cross-Channel ferry in July 1929, when the artist was making a brief return trip to Paris. He noted in his diary shortly after meeting Bacon: 'I like this boy, who is extremely intelligent, but he has the complexion of a girl, with big blue eyes and long lashes. He is really too pretty for a boy, and his ways are rather effeminate.'[9] In September 1929 Bacon and Allden went to Co. Galway in Ireland and stayed in a bungalow near a holiday cottage rented by the artist's family. On their return to London, the two men lived together, along with Bacon's former nanny, Jessie Lightfoot, in a maisonette in Vincent Square, Westminster, followed by 17 Queensberry Mews West in South Kensington. James Norton, who discovered the older man's diaries, writes that 'Allden often describes separate sleeping arrangements, scrupulously giving reasons when occasionally they had to share a room . . . Although the relationship may not have been sexual, there were evidently strong bonds of feeling on both sides.'[10]

The return trip to Paris was to buy items for a prospective furniture shop, but by 1930 Bacon emerged refashioned as a furniture designer, rather than retailer, in the Kensington Directory: 'Francis Bacon – Modern decoration, furniture in metal, glass and wood; rugs and lights'. His success was immediate. In August of that year, his work was highlighted in 'The 1930 Look in British Decoration', an article in *The Studio*, alongside that of Vanessa Bell and Duncan Grant.[11] His tubular steel and glass furniture and abstract patterned rugs, made by Royal Wilton, may have been influenced by both the Bauhaus designs he would have seen in Germany and by the work of the Irish-born designer Eileen Gray, who had made her name in France.

By 1930, Bacon was also concentrating on art, aided by his mentoring the Australian painter Roy de Maistre. He soon also gained the financial support of a businessman named Eric Hall, who superseded Allden as Bacon's quasi father-figure. In the early 1930s, Bacon painted a series of X-ray-like crucifixions, marking his interest in the distortion and metamorphosis of the human figure. He came to immediate attention when the influential critic Herbert Read placed an image of one of the works alongside Picasso's *Female Bather with Raised Arms* (1929) in his book *Art Now: An Introduction to the Theory of Modern Painting and Sculpture*, and showed it in a group exhibition at the Mayor Gallery in London in 1933. The work was purchased by the collector and art educationalist Michael Sadler, who commissioned a further painting.

This was to prove the highpoint of Bacon's pre-war career as an artist. In 1934, when he mounted a solo show at the Transition Gallery (actually the basement of his friend Arundell Clarke's Mayfair mansion, converted specially for the purpose), he was disappointed. Apart from qualified praise for Bacon as an 'interesting colourist', *The Times* review of 16 February 1934 was damning: 'Mr Bacon does not get beyond the creation of uncouth shapes which are the common form of dreams.' Only three works were bought – two by his cousin Diana Watson and one by Allden, even though he reported in his diary, 'I can't say that I care about the rather gruesome distortions of heads, bodies etc. in which he seems to find his only self-expression at the present moment.'[12] Bacon subsequently destroyed all of the remaining works. During his career, he would criticize his own work more harshly than reviewers, and destroyed several hundred canvases. Denis Wirth-Miller would adopt similar traits.

Herbert Read then rejected Bacon's work for inclusion in the *International Surrealist Exhibition* in 1936. In January of the following year, his work was included in *Young British Painters* at Agnew's alongside paintings by Graham Sutherland, John Piper and Victor Pasmore. Eric Hall was responsible for mounting the exhibition and including Bacon's work; although married with children, he would become obsessed by the artist, paying his rent and supporting him for several years before moving in with him. The exhibition earned the approbation of the *Daily Mail*, which called the paintings 'the nonsense art or pseudo-art of today' and Bacon's work was not exempted from criticism by the *Sunday Times*. One of Bacon's 1937 works was *Abstraction*, which featured an extended, distorted form with bared teeth, which would return in *Three Studies for Figures at the Base of a Crucifixion* (1944). With that Bacon disappeared, at least as an exhibiting artist, for the next eight years.

It was following those disappointments that Denis Wirth-Miller and Richard Chopping first saw Francis Bacon in the Gargoyle Club. He had already taken to wearing foundation and rouge and using boot polish on his hair, and would fix fellow drinkers with his intense stare. Initiating a conversation was ill-advised as he was given to tirades against both abstract art and the neo-Romanticism that was being adopted by Minton and the Roberts. Bacon and Wirth-Miller were yet to begin the friendship that would last for fifty years until Bacon's death in 1992, but the older artist made an impression on the Fitzrovians.

Having quelled his conservatism and embraced a life without inhibition, Dicky Chopping soon began to make a name for himself. In July 1939 he exhibited two paintings in the annual *Goupil Gallery Salon* at the New Burlington Galleries. The Goupil had hosted the first shows of the London Group from 1914 onwards, showing the work of Sickert and Wyndham Lewis. The exhibiting of Chopping's works in the salon was the first assertion of his legitimacy as an artist: his paintings *The Ash-grounds*, an oil, and *Flowers with Hands*, a watercolour, were shown alongside works by Lucien Pissarro, his future friend John Nash, Jacob Epstein and Duncan Grant. The prices of his paintings were a mere 6 guineas and 3 guineas respectively, compared to 150 guineas for a Pissarro oil, but it was a beginning. Inspired by the characters who populated Fitzrovia, his works at this time were humorous and sometimes cruel caricatures, which revealed his observational skills and curiosity. The titles of the unknown works at the salon, though, suggest that he was already drawn towards nature. In the future, his precision, eye for detail and analytical skills would come to the fore in botanical works.

By this time, Chopping and Wirth-Miller's relationship had become solid, but their life was not without ructions. A year into their relationship, Wirth-Miller's brother William John, who had also moved to London, was arrested for his involvement in the burglary of a country house in Derbyshire. He and three other young men were summed up by the King's Counsel at Derby Assizes as 'idle young men' who had taken to 'drinking and fooling their way round Mayfair and the West End'.[13] They had been caught stealing jewellery among other items. During the court proceedings, William John Miller asked for several other offences to be taken into account.

A further blow to the family followed on the day after he was sentenced to eighteen months in prison. On 19 November 1938, the *Daily Mail* ran the headline: 'Father of Gaoled Playboy is Gassed'. Johann Warthmiller, by now calling himself John Wirth Miller, had committed suicide in Folkestone immediately after news broke of the imprisonment of his estranged son:

> While a relative was convinced last night that his son's imprisonment had not led to Mr. Miller's death, a friend said that he was worried by it.
>
> 'William's extravagant living and escapades were always a source of anxiety to his father. He used to go to expensive places in London and hand out the most ridiculously large tips to waiters. He was a spoiled young man.'[14]

Throughout his life, Denis Wirth-Miller hid the truth about this tragedy even from close friends such as David Queensberry, preferring to claim that his father was executed as a spy. Chopping would later say that William John also committed suicide while he was in prison. There was a hereditary strain of darkness within the family, and Wirth-Miller was not without his own troubles and mood swings.

Although affectionate and besotted by Chopping, he was sometimes given over to petty jealousy and rowing. Chopping, meanwhile, was tiring of Nina Hamnett's constant invasion of 19 Fitzroy Street. One afternoon in the spring of 1939 Chopping, as he wrote years later, returned to the studio to find Wirth-Miller in the midst of a hard drinking session with Hamnett. Chopping made the mistake of believing that he was on sure enough ground to object. He laid down the ultimatum: 'Either she goes or I do.' He had underestimated Wirth-Miller's affection for Hamnett. Wirth-Miller simply replied, 'Well, you'd better leave immediately then.'

Chopping did not leave, however. Their affection for each other was already too intense for a small disagreement to cause a permanent rift. Bar the odd excursion Chopping took back to Essex to see his mother Amy, they had by now spent almost every night together for two years.

Soon they would be forced into breaking up their home in Fitzroy Street but that had more to do with the barrage balloons already floating over London.

Chapter 3
Little Yellow Papers

On 4 September 1939, the British Prime Minister Neville Chamberlain declared war on Germany following the invasion of Poland. London prepared for what seemed an inevitable attack. 'Now is the future I never wished to see,' Dicky Chopping wrote in his diary, quoting the writer and artist Ruthven Todd.

Frances Partridge, a member of the Bloomsbury Group who would become a very close friend of Chopping, wrote in her diary in early 1940 that the Air Raid Protection (ARP) authorities were 'expecting 70,000 deaths in the first raid on London, and had enough papier mâché coffins ready'.[15] The anticipated number would have been much higher if, even before Chamberlain's declaration of war, the government had not evacuated almost one and a half million women and children from Britain's cities. A further two million, the majority from London, left the major cities hurriedly of their own accord. Among them were Chopping and Wirth-Miller.

Nina Hamnett was savage in her attacks on anyone 'cowardly' enough to leave Fitzrovia. For all his attachment to Hamnett, Wirth-Miller was by now willing to follow Chopping – even to a run-down workers' cottage in rural Essex – and abandon his job at Tootal's. There seemed little point in staying in Fitzrovia to await the bombs.

Daffodil Cottage, Wormingford, Essex, 1937. *(Author's personal collection)*

Daffodil Cottage, the house near Wormingford that Chopping had rented since his apprenticeship with Barry Hart, would finally prove useful. It had never become the illicit hideaway Chopping had imagined. Since 1937 it had remained empty except for a couple of short visits made by the two men.

In the chaos of the first few days of September 1939, the two artists packed all the belongings they could carry. London's railway stations were overrun in the panic so they attempted to hail a cab. It took them a long time to find a taxi driver willing to make the journey to Essex and, when they finally got going, the cab broke down while still in the capital's suburbs. They carried their bags to a local station, and eventually reached Wormingford by a combination of train and local bus. Still laden, Chopping then led Wirth–Miller down the familiar eight-mile walk along the River Stour.

Little had changed since the day Chopping had first discovered the cottage. Constructed of wattle and daub, it was rudimentary and very small, and the main room was dominated by the kitchen table. There was still no electric light; the only water source was the unreliable pump outside; and the lavatory consisted of a wooden slat over a bucket in a shed. It was not, Chopping noted, very conducive to romance.

The two men would soon find friendship with near neighbour John Nash and his wife Christine, a friend of the artist Dora Carrington with whom Nash had initially been in love. While John's older brother Paul was regarded as one of the great British artists of the era, combining landscape with abstraction and surrealism, John Nash himself was also a high-profile painter. Born in 1893, he was a founding member of the London Group in 1914 and, like Chopping over twenty years later, his early work was shown by the Goupil Gallery. After joining the Artists' Rifles during the First World War, he became an official war artist and painted his most famous work, *Over the Top* (1918). Since then, he had become a teacher (he was teaching at the Royal College of Art in 1939) and a successful landscape artist – he undoubtedly influenced Wirth-Miller in his move towards the genre during the Second World War. One of the earliest known landscapes that Wirth-Miller executed, an untitled work probably begun at Daffodil Cottage in 1939, has a fracturing of planes and bare trees slightly reminiscent of Paul Nash's *The Menin Road* (1919) while other works bear a perspectival relationship to some of John's landscapes.

John Nash described Daffodil Cottage, which, even though small, was two workers' cottages knocked together, as 'two very lichened shells'. The ceilings were so low that, following an initial visit, Nash wrote to the six-foot-one Chopping, 'I did like the cottage awfully but I was a bit worried about you not being able to stand up properly.'

Living in the cottage was a challenge to Chopping and Wirth-Miller's relationship. Although they had been together for more than two years, they had been caught up in the whirlwind of bohemian London, constantly surrounded by friends and never more than a few hundred metres away from a pub. Now, stranded hours from the nearest railway station, they were on their own. They were glad of Christine and John Nash's occasional company, even if the older couple's connection to the Bloomsbury set of old had grown weak with time and settled married life.

The situation was not ideal but tolerable. Both worked long hours, crouched around the kitchen table, filling sketchbooks and experimenting with oils, inks and watercolours. Wirth-Miller's illustration commissions dried up in the first few weeks of the war, but this period laid the path for both of their future careers. With their metropolitan lives put to one side, Wirth-Miller and Chopping found their calling in landscape and nature illustration respectively. They took on odd-jobs to make ends meet, including a stint as gardeners at a convent, where the nuns washed their clothes in return for a few hours' work.

Wirth-Miller and Chopping enjoyed the early autumn weather and the bucolic scenes around the Stour, picking field mushrooms and fruit and picnicking. They bathed in pools and photographed each other posing naked in the water ('Greatly daring at that time,' as Chopping noted). Other photographs show the pair on painting expeditions to the fields, wearing white shirts and straw hats. The photographs show an innocent tenderness between them. Wirth-Miller also soon took up the hobby of bee-keeping, which provided them with honey.

John and Christine Nash ensured that they would not be as cut off from society as much as they had first feared. Nash was sent to work for the Admiralty in 1940 as an official war artist, having initially joined the Royal Observer Corps, but before he left he introduced them to like-minded locals. While Wirth-Miller may have benefited from the guiding hand of Nash, Chopping found a friend and mentor in Robert Gathorne-Hardy. In 1938, his book *Wild Flowers in Britain*, featuring illustrations by Nash, had been published by Batsford. He would go on to write several books on gardens, as well as fiction and biographies. He gave Chopping invaluable help regarding nature writing and illustration – which would become his chief occupation over the next decade.

Gathorne-Hardy, born in 1902, was older but a willing participant in the young men's hedonistic exploits in the country. He in turn introduced them to Fidelity, Countess of Cranbrook, who was married to his brother Jock. The group often took lunches, teas and suppers together at the Nashes' home, and Chopping and Wirth-Miller would sometimes paint there and stay the night.

Perhaps oblivious to the fact that they were a homosexual couple, other locals were also welcoming and helpful. When her nephew was killed in action early on in the war, an old woman named Miss Woodhouse presented Chopping with his barely used three-speed bicycle. Chopping passed on his old £1 Raleigh bike to Wirth-Miller, who admitted he had no idea how to ride it. Chopping resolved to teach him how to cycle and, after many falls, Wirth-Miller eventually began to get the hang of it. They were now free to range the countryside, one riding confidently along the lanes while the other wobbled along behind. Wirth-Miller's cosmopolitan worldliness meant nothing in the country and Chopping, the former ingénue, often had to lead the way in their new lifestyle.

They took long afternoon teas at the house of John Green, the farmer who let out the Nashes' cottage. Green was 'a nice man but a hopeless farmer', who provided small luxuries that would become rarer as wartime shortages were introduced. They enjoyed his cake, 'heavy with dried fruit', and a custard called beastings made with the colostrum produced by cows after giving birth.

'Slaughter seemed like another planet away', Chopping wrote about life in Wormingford during the first few months of the war. No summons to serve arrived for him, while Wirth-Miller was one of only 3,000 British citizens given exemption from war work. His status may have been related to his half-German nationality but he avoided internment. Even the 16-year-old future artist Eduardo Paolozzi, the son of Italian immigrants, was briefly interned in 1940 although he was born and raised in Britain. The matter of Wirth-Miller's exemption remains a mystery as the couple would maintain silence whenever the topic was raised.

Despite the panic in September 1939, no gas attack came and no bombs flattened Fitzrovia in the first eight or nine months of the war. Many people who had evacuated London, including a great number of children, returned to the capital during the Phoney War. Chopping and Wirth-Miller may have been tempted to follow them but they stayed at Daffodil Cottage as they had taken to country life and were able to concentrate on their work. It was lucky that they did not return. In the Blitzkrieg of 1940, their home on Fitzroy Street was obliterated by a bomb.

The mild autumn of 1939 gave way to the coldest winter in forty-five years. In parts of Essex, the sea froze along the coast. Chopping and Wirth-Miller's bohemian peasant clothes were replaced by thick sweaters and tweed, and using the outside privy was put off until essential. In Wiltshire, Frances Partridge wrote of 'trees covered with icicles', every twig 'encased in ice as thick as a man's thumb'. It was, she recorded, 'like being kept in a refrigerator'.

The weather deteriorated further in the New Year but the two artists continued to work – near to the fire so their hands would not become too cold to hold a pencil or brush.

Then, on 10 January 1940, Chopping received an envelope stamped by the army. He knew exactly what it meant before opening it. It was what he called his 'sinister little yellow call-up papers'.

In accordance with the National Service (Armed Forces) act, 1939, you are called for service in the Territorial Army and are required to present yourself on Wednesday 17th Jan 1940 at 10 a.m. or as early as possible on that day.

In less than a week, he was to report to a municipal building in Ipswich. For a young man who had spent the past two years doing as he pleased, it meant giving up all independence, ambition and potentially his life to the anonymity of a serial number.

Chopping later wrote in his memoir that by the time he got up on the morning of 17 January, it had been snowing unremittingly for twelve hours: 'White sky met white ground in a swirling curtain of falling flakes. We rose from our tear-drenched pillows to face a world the beauties of which were invisible to our red-rimmed eyes.' At Colchester station, he waited alone on the platform watching mothers, wives and girlfriends kissing the other young men goodbye. Earlier, he and Wirth-Miller had to say what might be their final goodbye in private.

Chopping, described by Frances Partridge as 'affectionate, gentle, kind and inquisitive', was an obvious outsider as soon as he stepped inside the carriage of noisy conscripts. After the journey, while waiting in the recruitment office, other men parroted his middle-class voice whenever he dared to speak. The humiliation continued until Dicky was processed and issued with a new identity; he was now 601972 Private Chopping of the 2/5th East Essex Regiment.

The new recruits were marched back to Ipswich station and the regiment was transported to Sussex. There, Chopping continued to be the whipping boy for his fellow conscripts, especially after it was revealed that he had been a pacifist while at public school. Chopping believed that, rather than protecting him, the officers encouraged the bullying.

'The brutality, boredom and uselessness of it all makes me despair,' he wrote to Wirth-Miller. 'We are continually being called on parade and each time I dread to find myself in the front rank.'

In May 1940, after Chopping had endured four months of drills and weapons training, the Phoney War ended. Within a month, France had capitulated and the British Expeditionary Force had been pushed back, evacuating mainland Europe via Dunkirk. An invasion of Britain seemed likely and Chopping's hope that he could survive the war without fighting was seemingly gone.

By then Chopping was already despondent, emaciated and acutely lonely. He was also suspicious that somebody was stealing his correspondence with Wirth-Miller. He eventually convinced his platoon's openly hostile sergeant to put his name down for an interview with an army psychiatrist. The meeting went on for two hours while Chopping spoke of his victimization and admitted to his homosexuality, but it appeared that his case merited no further action.

Then, one morning in July, he was summoned to an office beside the barracks. He walked into the room and presented himself to a panel of bored officers, who asked him to strip and stretch out his arms. A young doctor took his measurements as he stood there naked and the panel passed comments back and forth. After disappearing to a side room for several minutes, the medic returned to whisper a brief statement to the officers. They consulted for several minutes as the emaciated Chopping watched, his arms still outstretched.

'You can pull your trousers up now,' the medic finally told him.

Within an hour, 601972 Private Chopping of the 2/5th East Essex Regiment was no more. After seven months, he had been discharged from the army as he was deemed incapable of serving in any capacity, apparently because of the ratio of his limbs.

'I was considered completely unfit for any military duty,' he wrote, 'secretly because of homosexuality and, thank fate, because they didn't know what to do with me.'

Back in London, even the asthmatic Francis Bacon was given war duties while Chopping was erased from the service register. Bacon had avoided active service, supposedly by provoking his asthma by sleeping alongside a dog. Nonetheless, he volunteered for Civil Defence and worked for Air Raid Precautions. An ARP warden's duties included enforcing the blackout, helping to fight fires and pulling bodies from rubble. The cataclysm inherent in Bacon's view of the human condition, already revealed in *Abstraction* at his exhibition of 1937, was made real. Eventually he would have to give up his ARP role due to the effect the dust had upon his lungs.

Fitzrovia was no longer the bohemia Chopping and Wirth-Miller had known in 1939. Some of the artists, writers and eccentrics remained, but rationing and conscription had emptied the pubs and restaurants. Many artists became involved in war work even if they were conscientious objectors. Although he had registered as a conscientious objector in 1939, John Minton joined the Royal Pioneer Corps in 1941 and briefly became a commissioned officer before being discharged on medical grounds in 1943. Robert MacBryde was declared medically unfit while Robert Colquhoun worked for the Royal Army Medical Corps as an ambulance driver before he too was discharged as unfit in 1941.

None of these artists was yet held in high enough esteem to be protected by the British War Advisory Scheme of the War Artists' Advisory Committee. The brainchild of Kenneth Clark, the scheme gave artists the official paid role of depicting war scenes at home and abroad rather than serving in frontline action; Augustus John, John Piper, Graham Sutherland, Paul Nash, John Nash and Henry Moore, some of whom were too old to serve in the military in any case, all served on the scheme. The first artist to die while working as an official war artist was Eric Ravilious, a close friend of John and Christine Nash, who was killed in 1942 when his plane was lost in action.

Chapter 4

Benton End

Dicky Chopping's return from the army brought him relief from bullying and removed any danger of dying in combat, but an attack on the British Isles was still imminent and there was a permanent undercurrent of fear. 'We are told that parachute drops on England "are now extremely likely"', Frances Partridge wrote at her desk in Wiltshire on 14 May 1940. '[My] greatest preoccupation is with the question of how to get a supply of lethal pills. I feel it would be the greatest possible help to know we had death in our power.'

On 7 September, when the German attack finally began in earnest, it came in the form of the Blitzkrieg rather than invasion. The Luftwaffe attacked London with 348 bombers and 617 fighters, and the bombing raids continued for 57 days. London was now a war zone.

Wirth–Miller and Chopping had little work or money, but there was now no point in risking their lives by returning to Fitzrovia. They saw out 1940 holed up at Daffodil Cottage in Essex. They had no idea that an artistic bohemian community was flourishing only six miles away, just across the county border with Suffolk.

Cedric Morris and Arthur Lett-Haines, known as 'Lett', set many precedents for the future lives of Dicky Chopping and Denis

Wirth-Miller. First among these was that they proved that it was possible to have an openly homosexual, long-standing relationship that would provide the bedrock for their careers as artists.

The self-styled 'English Surrealist' Arthur Lett-Haines was born in 1894. He was educated at St Paul's and served with the British Army during the First World War. In 1916, at the age of twenty-two, he married Aimee Lincoln, but just two years later he met and fell in love with Cedric Morris. Five years older than Lett-Haines, Morris was a Welsh artist who was studying in Montparnasse at the outbreak of the First World War. He attempted to join the Artists' Rifles but was declared medically unfit. He spent the war looking after army horses at a stables in Berkshire in the company of fellow artist Alfred Munnings, the future president of the Royal Academy, who would become a bitter rival. Unconventionally, Morris moved in with the Lett-Haines couple. The three of them were due to emigrate to the United States in 1919, but only Aimee went, leaving the two artists to live together for the remaining sixty years of their lives.

They moved to Newlyn, Cornwall, in 1919. Morris's approach at this time has been described 'simple and direct'.[16] His paintings, in which he brought modernist ideas into the realm of landscape painting, stood in contrast to the more old-fashioned and heavily detailed style of Stanhope Forbes, Munnings and other leading Newlyn School artists.

The couple spent the next decade living a bohemian existence in Cornwall, Paris (where they were friends with Duchamp and Man Ray) and among the Bloomsbury set. Their love of excess and eccentric characters, and their sense of artistic freedom, helped pave the way for the younger generation of artists they would teach, as well as the Fitzrovians. In 1929, they moved to a farm in Higham, Suffolk, and formed a loose artistic colony. The sculptor John Skeaping came to stay there after the end of

A picnic at Benton End with Lucian Freud (left) and
Arthur Lett-Haines (right). *(Author's personal collection)*

his marriage to Barbara Hepworth in 1933 and created a
sandstone sculpture of Lett-Haines.

In 1937, Morris and Lett-Haines established the East Anglian
School of Painting and Drawing at Dedham near the Essex–
Suffolk border, with help from the highly successful artists,
designers and illustrators Eric Ravilious, Edward Bawden and
John Aldridge. It was a revolutionary institution. There were
no formal classes and there was a complete absence of gender
bias. Its existence irked the ultra-conservative Munnings, who
lived nearby, but the East Anglian School thrived and had over
sixty students by the close of the year.

In 1939, the 17-year-old Lucian Freud came up from London
to join their number. He had already studied briefly at the
Central School of Art in London and was regarded as an
exceptional talent. According to legend, when the East Anglican
School burned down later that year, Freud was responsible,
having left a cigarette burning in his room. Munnings reportedly

made a point of driving past on the next day, yelling: 'Down with modern art!'

Teaching continued in a local pub but before long Morris used an inheritance to secure the large premises of Benton End, on the outskirts of Hadleigh in Suffolk. The establishment continued to attract aspiring artists who were resistant to the old-fashioned, restrictive teaching methods of the likes of Henry Tonks at the Slade. Rather than a formal school, it was a place for the free exchange of artistic ideas and techniques. The school was anti-hierarchical as well as anti-patriarchal, with little in the way of structure or rules, and provided a setting for sexual as well as artistic liberation. The new premises were large enough to enable the students to live-in as an extended family, and they shared the chores.

The unorthodox art school continued for a further forty years until Lett-Haines died in 1978. Maggi Hambling recalls visiting Benton End as a 15-year-old in 1960 and being invited by Lett-Haines to come and paint. On the first day of her school holidays, too intimidated to walk up to the house, she sat and painted in a ditch near the gates until she was eventually discovered by Lett-Haines and Morris and welcomed into the school. She was to become so close to the pair that Morris bequeathed half of his estate to her. He had often asked her if she would run the art school at Benton End after his death, but Hambling always declined as her priority was her own work.

A local 20-year-old artist, Joan Warburton, who would go on to have her work shown at the Royal Academy and Leicester Galleries, sporadically attended Benton End soon after it opened while also undertaking war work. She knew of Chopping and Wirth-Miller as she lived nearby and, in spring 1941, decided to invite them to a party that evening at Benton End. She cycled over to Daffodil Cottage from the house of her 'awful Scots mother and her down-trodden retired Colonel father', as described by Chopping, to find that Chopping was suffering from mumps. Wirth-Miller, although still wobbly on his bicycle, agreed to join her for the six-mile ride along the Stour Valley.

Wirth-Miller was impressed by the grand house at Benton End. It was a large Tudor building with outbuildings and small, walled enclosures that sheltered vegetable patches and flowerbeds. Many birds freely ranged the grounds including a lemon-crested white cockatoo, a blue and crimson macaw and a squadron of ducks that Chopping would later claim bore a resemblance to Joan Warburton's father.

Inside, artists' paraphernalia covered the floor space and books were stacked high. The people who greeted Wirth-Miller, dressed in eccentric and outlandish clothes, would not have been out of place in Fitzrovia. The guests included poets and writers as well as artists, drink was being consumed recklessly, jazz was playing, and Wirth-Miller was able to dance for the first time in eighteen months. It was, he told Chopping when he returned to the cottage, as if a huge dressing-up box had been thrown open. Even though the show had been recast, London's bohemia had been transferred to the Suffolk countryside.

A second invitation to Benton End followed when Chopping felt strong enough to make the journey. His enthusiasm matched that of Wirth-Miller. The location was, he wrote, 'as ideal a position as could be imagined'. Chopping immediately took to both Morris and Lett-Haines.

Morris and Lett-Haines were daringly unconventional, and the atmosphere at Benton End was markedly hedonistic. While large-scale aerial attacks on London were continuing at the time of Chopping and Wirth-Miller's initial visits, life at Benton End was characterized by parties, and, partly due to their vegetable gardens, Morris and Lett-Haines's cooking was not compromised by wartime austerity. Ronald Blythe, the local Suffolk writer, would later sum up Benton End: 'there was a whiff of garlic and wine in the air . . . The atmosphere was . . . robust and coarse, and exquisite and tentative, all at once. Rough and ready and fine and mannered. Also faintly dangerous.'[17]

By comparison, Daffodil Cottage now seemed damp and depressing, and the Nashes were no longer on hand to provide social variety. When Wirth-Miller suggested they enrolled at the school, Chopping agreed. They may have been progressing with their art but neither was trained to any substantial degree. They knew that, even without formal instruction, they would learn much from Morris, Lett-Haines and their fellow students. They cycled over to the Humes's house to terminate their tenancy of Daffodil Cottage, although they did return there briefly during the holidays while at Benton End.

The final image of the Humes lodged itself in Chopping's memory. He described the landlady as swaddled in a 'slowly revolving ball of clothes', while her silent, moustachioed husband sat hunched in front of a fire, despite the fact that by then it was high summer, and Buster the parrot gabbled in the background.

Their departure from Daffodil Cottage was tinged with more regret than they had anticipated. Their initial semi-isolation in the countryside had brought happiness, invigorated their art and strengthened their relationship even further. Years later, in 1974, Chopping would note in his diary: 'The smell of damp grass and standing water fringed by dragonwort, mint and crowfoot reminded me of Wormingford where cares seemed less pressing and hope for the future more optimistic.'

There was an immediate problem regarding Chopping and Wirth-Miller's transfer to Benton End: they could not afford the fees. Morris and Lett-Haines obliged with a solution. If the young men performed odd jobs around the house and gardens in their spare time, as well as joining in the communal chores, they were welcome to stay and study for as long as they pleased. Chopping and Wirth-Miller adopted the job titles of 'apprentice gardener and head bottle washer', and also filled in as life models.

While the couple would always admire the strength of Morris and Lett-Haines's relationship, it also provided a warning for their future conduct together. Their hosts often bickered, with the tension escalating into rants. 'You filthy, stinking, grey old piece of fish!' Chopping recalled Morris shrieking at Lett-Haines. In 1984, after Chopping and Wirth-Miller's own relationship had become beset by fights, Chopping would write, 'we really should have known better'.

While Chopping described Morris's art as 'rough but distinctive' and 'cheerful', and Lett-Haines's work as 'not great', they took their work seriously. Lett-Haines's style owed a debt to Giorgio de Chirico, particularly his *Dark Horse* watercolour, gouache and chalk of 1934, now in the Tate collection. Morris was a very keen gardener, and developed almost a hundred varieties of iris during his lifetime. As well as portraits, he painted many still-lifes of flowers in his primitive post-Impressionistic style and would be a key influence on Chopping's early career.

Chopping soon took a new approach to his work and put his interest in caricatures behind him. His technique changed when he watched Morris paint for the first time. Without any preliminary marks, the Welshman would start at the top left-hand corner of a canvas, then pull a curtain of paint down over the surface. He would then begin his vivid depictions of both rare and familiar flowers.

Conscription, illness and the prospect of a German invasion had kept Chopping's artistic profile low and there was no momentum following the Goupil salon. Both he and Wirth-Miller had been worried that their artistic dreams might have come to a dead end, but Benton End pushed them in new directions and gave them important contacts. The democratic values of the East Anglian School proved beneficial, and ideas and materials were freely shared. Wirth-Miller and Chopping were encouraged to challenge their established painting and drawing techniques. Gradually their confidence in their ability increased, thanks to the help offered by Morris, Lett-Haines and their fellow pupils. No house-style was imposed on the students and guests but the characteristics of Morris's style, with his straightforward and direct addressing of the subject, set the precedent. This was apparent in the work of the young Lucian Freud, as well as that of the older, eccentric local artist Lucy Harwood.

The more successful artists would pass commissions down the pecking order and were willing to arrange introductions to publishers and gallerists. In July 1941, a work by Chopping was printed alongside Lucian Freud's in *Art & Industry* magazine. Meanwhile, Wirth-Miller was toying with ideas. His 1941 oil on stucco, *Garden Landscape* (which he presented to Morris and Lett-Haines as a gift and is now in the collection of the curator and gallerist James Birch), makes a play of geometric forms in Benton End's gardens and is severely scrapped down; in contrast *The Beekeeper*, also painted in the early 1940s, is a distorted portrait against a landscape more reminiscent of Graham Sutherland's early work.

For the majority of their time at Benton End, Chopping and Wirth-Miller counted Freud as a close friend. When the artist Mollie Russell-Smith knocked on the door at Benton End as a visitor, it was 'flung open by three young men [Chopping, Wirth-Miller and Lucian Freud]. They bundled me in, assuming that I had come to be a student, and Dicky showed me all over the house with great enthusiasm and charm. I was enchanted.'[18]

Lucian Freud being painted by Sir Cedric Morris, Benton End, 1941
(the painting is now in the Tate). *(Author's personal collection)*

One of the chores with which Chopping and Wirth–Miller earned their keep was managing the accounts of the school, detailing expenditure and earnings (Wirth–Miller would later prove adept at financial management). They also assumed a medical role. One account entry shows that when Freud had a bout of constipation, they prescribed him a special diet of fresh fruit and bran. At the age of twenty, Freud was already the star of the group. The social circles of the three men would intersect for the remainder of their lives but their friendship would not last.

Cedric Morris painted portraits of both Chopping and Freud while they were at Benton End together. The 1941 portrait of Chopping – 'his subject dark-haired, sloe-eyed, duffel-coated and alert' – was included in the Tate's 1984 Morris retrospective.[19]

Among the materials found in Chopping and Wirth-Miller's archive of Benton End memorabilia is a rare photograph of Lucian Freud sitting as a model for Morris in one of the school's studios. Morris's sexual preference, according to Chopping, was evident in his flattering portraits of men and unflattering portraits of women.

Lett-Haines was equally happy to express his tastes. One morning, when Chopping was tasked with taking a cup of tea up to Lett-Haines's bedroom, the older man drew back his sheet to reveal his erection. 'Would you like to do something about that?' he asked. Chopping didn't – but others were not so reticent.

The Benton End couple's relationship was completely open, even though this would sometimes lead to bickering and jealousy, especially with regards to Kathleen Hale, one of the notable figures to visit Benton End regularly.

Hale was born in 1898 and brought up in Manchester; bright and rebellious, she went to art school against the odds. She mixed with the Bloomsbury set after she became Augustus John's secretary and was a friend to Vanessa Bell and Duncan Grant. She met Morris, Lett-Haines and their circle in Paris in the 1920s, and recounted, 'I remember Cedric and Lett coming gracefully towards us along the boulevard like gazelles, the two of them extremely handsome and elegant.'[20]

While still in her twenties, she established a reputation as a successful illustrator and book-jacket designer, and in 1938 published *A Camping Holiday*, the first of her highly successful *Orlando the Marmalade Cat* series of children's books. At Benton End, Hale became known as 'Mog' due to the fame of Orlando the cat.

Although she was married to a doctor, the relationship was 'semi-detached' and her behaviour was often out of keeping with her growing reputation as a children's author. She once said,

'I broke all the rules of decent behaviour', and one of those rules was not sleeping with her friend's partner.[21] During drunken evenings at Benton End, she would declare that she had never achieved orgasm until encountering Lett-Haines's 'very substantial' penis.

It was not Lett-Haines unfaithfulness that irked Morris, but the fact that he was bisexual. Chopping wrote of Hale in his diary, 'to Cedric's 100% homosexual Welsh character she was an anathema to be tolerated with snide asides'. Nonetheless Hale and the two men continued to be close friends and Morris was very helpful to her progress as a painter. In 1948, she told Chopping in a letter that she felt that some of the artists at Benton End laughed at her paintings but 'Cedric never does, he really tries to pull me out of my difficulties.' Whatever problems Hale may have brought to the relationship between Morris and Lett-Haines, she would change Dicky Chopping's life.

When Hale met Chopping at the school she had already been told about his drawing skills by a mutual friend. Chopping showed her a story for children he had written and illustrated called 'Gwladys, the All-British Giraffe'. Mog's enthusiasm led to an introduction to Noel Carrington, the brother of the artist Dora Carrington. Noel Carrington had worked for Oxford University Press and was now involved in children's book publishing. He soon took an interest in Chopping's illustrations and introduced him to Country Life as publishers. Although nothing came of 'Gwladys', it was only another two years before Chopping, still aged only twenty-six, would start to see his illustrated books in print.

Hale was to become a lasting friend to Chopping and they would exchange many long letters over the next five decades. She would be one of the many artists and writers who would sign the visitors' book at the Storehouse, Chopping and

Wirth-Miller's future home. While staying there with her young sons, Mog would often work alongside Dicky.

As well as new acquaintances, the Fitzrovians started to stagger back into Chopping and Wirth-Miller's lives courtesy of the parties at Benton End. In the 1920s, Nina Hamnett had known Morris, Lett-Haines and their circle in the bars of Montparnasse in Paris, and came out to Suffolk to reacquaint herself with them and with the younger artistic couple. In the meantime, despite the worsening of her alcoholism, she had become a guest of the literary salons of Nancy Cunard and Lady Colefax in Chelsea.

Robert Colquhoun, Robert MacBryde and John Minton also arrived for these parties or lunches. Another visitor was the young communist writer Stephen Spender, whom Chopping and Wirth-Miller already knew. He had enjoyed an interesting career by this time. By 1941, he had published several volumes of poetry in the 1930s, helped discover Dylan Thomas, covered both the Moscow Trials and the Spanish Civil War for the *Daily Worker*, and married twice. In 1942, he joined a fire brigade as part of the war effort.

In a note dating from 1941, Chopping recorded that Wirth-Miller had started to get on particularly well with Francis Bacon, who made trips to Benton End. They had never spoken more than a greeting at the Gargoyle Club in Soho, but on one of Bacon's visits he and Wirth-Miller started talking and found they enjoyed each other's company. They had much in common. The two had grown up as outsiders – Bacon as an unusual English boy in Ireland and Wirth-Miller as a half-German outcast in England – and had spent much of their childhoods left to their own devices. They had taken to petty crime during their youth, and were not disposed to hide their homosexuality. They treated their painting with equal seriousness. And, as far as the

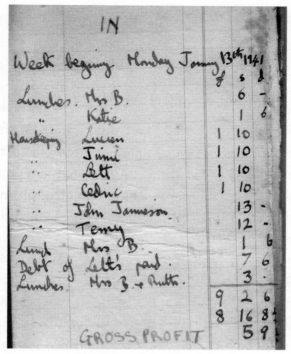

IN

Week beginning Monday January 13th 1941

		£	s	d
Lunches, Mrs B.			6	-
" Katie			1	6
Haustaping Lucian		1	10	
" Jimi		1	10	
" Bett		1	10	
" Cedric		1	10	
" John Jameson			13	-
" Terry			12	-
Lunch Mrs B.			1	6
Debt of Bett's paid.			7	6
Lunches, Mrs B. + Ruth.			3	-
		9	2	6
		8	16	8½
GROSS PROFIT			5	9¾

Benton End account book 1941,
mentioning Lucian Freud and John Jameson.

Benton End gatherings were concerned, they would still be drinking when everybody else had passed out or retired to bed.

As one friendship began to form, another was becoming strained. Wirth-Miller was starting to lose patience with what he perceived as Freud's arrogance – typified by the younger artist taking it upon himself to alter one of Chopping's flower paintings. Freud could do no wrong in Haines and Morris's eyes, a fact that irked Wirth-Miller while he was still trying to prove himself as a painter. By this time Freud's work had already been seen in *Horizon*, the new art and literary magazine edited by Cyril Connolly. A competitive wedge was coming between the two painters.

Chopping was becoming aware of how much Wirth-Miller's past had affected his character: he was still given to impulsive theft. One afternoon, the pair cycled into the Suffolk countryside for a picnic. On the way back, they stopped to have a look around a village church. When they got home to Benton End, Wirth–Miller took off his jacket and Chopping noticed a bulge in the pocket. Curiosity got the better of him and he pulled the object out of the jacket pocket: it was a prayer book from the church. Embarrassed on Wirth–Miller's behalf, Chopping cycled back to the church to return it.

Soon, Wirth–Miller's compulsion to steal and his growing dislike for Freud would be the possible cause of their time at Benton End coming to a sudden halt.

There is some uncertainty as to how a possible portrait by Lucian Freud came into Chopping and Wirth–Miller's possession. The painting of a young man with parted hair, narrow, focused eyes and bowed lips was long believed to be Freud's portrait of John Jameson. He was one of the grander figures who frequented Benton End. In 1780, his family had established the Jamesons distillery, which produced one of the world's most popular whiskies. He was apparently unconcerned about keeping up the family reputation. According to Glyn Morgan, who attended the East Anglian School from 1944, Jameson was reputed to have only two interests: witchcraft and cruising the streets of Norwich for sex. He commissioned young artists whom he met at the school, including Morgan, who went on to have a successful career as a landscape artist, and Freud.

Another possibility is that the painting, executed in Freud's typical palette of the time, is a portrait of Stephen Spender, which is possible due to Spender's association with Benton End in the early 1940s.

Wirth–Miller said that Freud had given the work to him while they were at Benton End so that he could use the reverse

side of the canvas for a painting of his own but in old age, while
suffering what appeared to be signs of the onset of senility, he
once contradicted himself by saying he happened upon it in a
junk shop. A close friend of Chopping and Wirth-Miller, who
wishes to remain anonymous, also reported after their deaths
that there was another version of the story.

This story suggested that the artists at Benton End were
asked to exhibit their best work for a competition in a county-
show tent in the nearby village of Tendring. That morning the
sky was 'as blue and cloudless as the Mediterranean, hot, full
of promise', as described by Chopping. According to the friend,
when the tent was opened Freud's painting, which had been
expected to win the competition, was missing; the artist never
saw the portrait again and the work mysteriously ended up in
Wirth-Miller's possession.

Given Wirth-Miller's tendency to obfuscate and sometimes
sensationalize details from the past, it seems likely that if he
hinted to his friend that he had stolen the painting, he was
merely playing with the truth in order to brag that he had got
one over on Freud. There is no corroborative evidence for
the story, and Chopping never alluded to this version of events
in either his personal diaries or the multiple drafts of his
memoir.

Chopping and Wirth-Miller left Benton End, where they
had lived happily for the previous year and a half, around this
time. The reason is unknown, even if a link could be made to
the 'disappearance' of the Freud painting. Yet they maintained
their friendships with Kathleen Hale, Arthur Lett-Haines and
Cedric Morris, all of whom would be guests at their future
home, the Storehouse, so it is highly unlikely that they left
Benton End under a cloud of suspicion. It was the end of the
school year and they had no funds, so it seems more likely that

they simply chose to conclude their studies and concentrate on earning a living from their art. By this time, Chopping's association with Noel Carrington, courtesy of Kathleen Hale, was starting to bear fruit.

One thing is certain: after they left the school, neither Chopping nor Wirth-Miller would say a complimentary word about Lucian Freud ever again due to his behaviour while at Benton End.

Chopping lists the reasons behind his continuing animosity towards Freud, 2004. *(Author's personal collection)*

Over sixty years later, on 29 March 2004, Chopping scribbled down a list of events that fuelled his personal animosity towards Freud. The entries, detailing episodes that mostly took place during the early years of the Second World War, are somewhat cryptic.

Chapter 5

Butterflies and Grandeur

Dicky Chopping and Denis Wirth-Miller were now homeless. They did not return permanently to Daffodil Cottage as, despite their affection for it, they could not face another cold winter there. Both artists – particularly Chopping as his first illustration commissions involving Noel Carrington were approaching deadline – quickly needed to find a more permanent space where they could live and work. The two men, however, had no money with which to pay rental fees.

In October 1942, after several months as itinerants, Wirth-Miller's new friend Francis Bacon provided a solution.

Bacon's relationship with his mentor, the Australian artist Roy de Maistre who had aided his transition from furniture designer and decorator to painter, had weakened since the early 1930s. By now Bacon was already well on the way to establishing his unique visual identity, far away from de Maistre's figurative cubism, and was working towards *Three Studies for Figures at the Base of a Crucifixion* (1944), the exhibition of which would transform his career. Roy de Maistre also had a new subject for his mentoring skills, the young Australian novelist Patrick White, who would win the Nobel Prize in 1973. Despite the weakening of his relationship with de Maistre, Bacon would remain on familiar terms with the wealthy patrons, connoisseurs and artists in his mentor's circle, including Geoffrey Houghton Brown.

An eccentric amateur artist and connoisseur, Houghton Brown was born in 1903. His paintings were very close in style and religious figurative content to those of de Maistre, but his principal concern was restoring grand properties. In the words of one obituary writer, 'He would take on rather derelict great houses – Clouds, Oving Hall, Felix Hall, Winslow Hall – which, for he was a somewhat ruthless improver, he was wont to leave less great than he found them.'[22] In 1939 he had bought Felix Hall (also known as Fillol's Hall), a crumbling, fifty-six-room manor house in Kelvedon, Essex, in 1939. During the Blitz, he acted as a voluntary fire-watcher in an attempt to protect Westminster Abbey from incendiaries, but he failed to take similar precautionary measures to protect his own property. Felix Hall was torched in 1940.

Houghton Brown had made no attempt to repair the building, so Francis Bacon saw a solution and introduced him to his friends. Houghton Brown immediately asked Chopping and Wirth-Miller if they would move into Felix Hall in order to look after it pending its restoration.

Not long after they moved in, Houghton Brown sent them a letter, concerned about their washing facilities: 'How's that old bath? Still gurgling and cranking?' As far as the couple was concerned, it was an improvement on the unreliable pump and outside privy they had put up with for almost two years at Daffodil Cottage. The Hall was partially in ruins and draughty, and a flock of geese Houghton Brown had bought honked loudly, day and night, but they enjoyed the ruined grandeur of their new address.

For Wirth-Miller, having endured an impoverished childhood, living at Felix Hall expanded his horizons and initiated thoughts of creating his own stylish home. It also allowed him the space and light to paint as he wished, waking at dawn and finishing at lunchtime. He would then spend the afternoon gardening and bee-keeping. His work was becoming more individual and emotive; the bleakness and threat that characterizes his best work was beginning to manifest itself in his new material. He had now been in East Anglia for over three years and he was responding to its landscape.

A bonus of living at Felix Hall was that it allowed Wirth-Miller and Chopping to host their own parties for the first time. Setting in motion a trend that would continue for much of their remaining lives, friends from London would travel to their home to take advantage of their hospitality. In exchange, the guests would help with the house's maintenance. While cigarettes and alcohol were not rationed in the war, they were often in short supply, so the hosts and guests would pool their resources to purchase the best available merchandise on the black market.

Chopping and Wirth-Miller were also able to seek entertainment in London regularly for the first time since 1939, and to see their friends such as the Roberts and Johnny Minton back in the familiar territory of the pubs and clubs of Fitzrovia and Soho. The blackout was still in force and the standard of living much reduced, but by the end of 1942 German bombing raids had become less frequent.

The war had inadvertently created a new kind of nightlife. Soldiers and military personnel from the USA and other allied nations were beginning to flood into the capital and were eager for entertainment. Quentin Crisp described the US servicemen as 'labelled "with love from Uncle Sam" and packaged in uniforms so tight that in them their owners could fight for nothing but their honour'. They were an exotic distraction for both womenfolk and those deemed 'unfit to serve'. As summed up by Crisp, who was rejected from military service with the unusually explicit diagnosis 'suffering from sexual perversion':

'never in the history of sex was so much offered to so many by so few'.[23]

The blackout made dusk an effective curfew for most Londoners. For the adventurous among the city's homesexual underworld and for soldiers away from home, it provided cover for assignations made more urgent by a heightened awareness of mortality.

According to Michael Peppiatt, Bacon 'was attracted to men who were basically heterosexual yet could be momentarily seduced – by money, or by novelty, or by their own defiance. Cities under siege abounded with such encounters.'[24] Chopping and Wirth-Miller both sought out similar clandestine moments.

One of the stranger items in their archive is a large, dented biscuit tin filled with buttons from military uniforms. Each time either of them had a sexual liaison with a serviceman, they would snip a memento from his uniform as a keepsake. The tin contains approximately 200 buttons.

Dicky Chopping was rapidly establishing himself as an illustrator of natural history and children's books as a result of his meeting, arranged by Kathleen Hale, with the publisher Noel Carrington.

Cedric Morris's nature illustrations of insects, plants and animals influenced much of Chopping's output over the next decade. Morris's posters for Shell in the 1930s, including *Summer Shell* depicting an aerial view of two large Red Admiral butterflies circling above a white petrol pump, were a particular inspiration for Chopping's first book for Puffin. *Butterflies in Britain* was 'Written and lithographed by Richard Chopping' and published in 1943.

Chopping's introduction to Noel Carrington could not have been more timely. In 1939, Carrington had persuaded Allen Lane, head of the fledgling Penguin publishing house founded in 1935, to allow him to set up an imprint for children's books. This was to become Puffin Books, and Carrington would remain in charge until his retirement twenty years later.

Chopping often had to work fourteen hours a day to complete his highly detailed and delicate illustrations for the book, which were then overlaid with colour fills. He was given a single large zinc plate by the printers, onto which he drew the illustrations for each of the thirty-six pages with lithographic ink. To his frustration the specialist ink continually clogged his fine-nib pen and slowed down the process. He had to work so close to the plate that, in cold Felix Hall, his breath would condense and the moisture would prevent the ink from properly adhering to the plate. He took to wearing a handkerchief over his mouth while he worked.

In return, the financial reward was low. Carrington offered Chopping a 5 per cent royalty, rather than the more standard 10 per cent, on each £2/6 book. A note Carrington added to the contract shows that he was a shrewd judge of Chopping's priorities: the resultant funds would be 'enough to throw a party or two anyway'. Chopping was not in a position to refuse the offer, and gambled that Carrington would hold true to a promise that there would be international royalties, too.

Initially issued as a paperback, *Butterflies in Britain* was a success, especially when it became an approved school textbook. Chopping was soon commissioned to produce an additional edition, with decorative endpapers, for a hardcover reprint, and the book remained in print for many years. Penguin also issued international editions including a French one, *Jolis Papillons*, in 1947. In years to come, despite the low royalty percentage, Chopping and Wirth-Miller received a regular flow of income from the book.

In 1942 Chopping was also working on illustrations for a King Penguin publication, *A Book of Spiders*. The author was

William Syer Bristowe, an eccentric English naturalist and head of personnel for Imperial Chemical Industries (ICI). Chopping and Bristowe jointly pitched the project to Allen Lane and Nikolaus Pevsner, the editor of the King Penguin list who would later become a household name due to his 'Buildings of England' series.

Chopping was responsible for one of the more minor setbacks in progress when he was starting to put together the book's illustrations. As he confessed to Bristowe, 'I am really sorry to tell you that unfortunately I killed your Segestria while drawing.' Ever inventive, Chopping set out to remedy the situation himself. 'I caught another in Westminster within a hundred yards of Bob Hope and Burgess Meredith being filmed in Dean's Yard.' The death of a spider was unlikely to have upset Bristowe. He enjoyed cooking and eating large spiders, and described their taste to Chopping as 'quite nutty'.

A more substantial problem was the printing of the book. At a meeting between publisher, printer, author and illustrator at Allen Lane's Westminster home, the reproduction of the very detailed illustrations in a nine-colour process was deemed unachievable. Reluctantly the project was dropped at the time. (*A Book of Spiders* was eventually published in 1947, with twenty-four colour plates, but without Chopping's illustrations.)

As Chopping and Lane left the flat together and headed down Birdcage Walk, Lane offered the deflated Chopping some consolation: 'What I really want to publish is a book of British flowers.' Eager to advance Penguin's reputation, he explained that he wanted to 'throw it down on other publishers' tables and say, "there you are, there's the Scarlet Pimpernel, the Blue Pimpernel, every type of bloody Pimpernel!"' Impressed by Chopping's increasingly individual, precise and detailed style, Allen wanted the young artist to be involved.

Allen requested that the book should be as comprehensive as possible. Daunted but unaware exactly how many illustrations that would require, Chopping's first instinct was to contact Noel Carrington, who recommended a potential collaborator to concentrate on the text. Her name was Frances Partridge.

Frances Partridge was born on 15 March 1900. She grew up in Bloomsbury's Bedford Square, the sixth child of the architect William Marshall, who sent her to the progressive Bedales School in Hampshire. While studying there, she met her lifelong friend Julia Strachey, whose Uncle Lytton was the lynchpin of the Bloomsbury Group. In time, Partridge would become famous for her wartime diaries, published as *A Pacifist's War* in 1978, but she would always be associated with the group and was regarded as its last surviving member before she died in 2004.

After finishing her degree in English and Moral Sciences at Cambridge in 1922, Frances took a job at David 'Bunny' Garnett and Francis Birrell's bookshop, near the British Museum. The bookshop was used by many members of the Bloomsbury Group and she became closely acquainted with Vanessa Bell and Duncan Grant. She spent time at Bell and Grant's house, Charleston in Sussex, and often spent weekends with Julia at her uncle's home, Ham Spray House, a Victorian manor house in Wiltshire. Lytton Strachey had become one of the most significant literary figures of the early twentieth century on the publication of his irreverent biographical work, *Eminent Victorians* (1918). He lived at Ham Spray House in an unconventional triangular relationship with Noel Carrington's sister, the artist Dora Carrington, and her husband, a young First World War veteran named Ralph Partridge.

Strachey made little secret of his homosexuality but Dora was besotted with him. Ralph, a friend of Noel's from university, was introduced to them in Hampstead and fell in love with Dora. She agreed to his marriage proposal, but on the condition that she could continue to live with Lytton.

Dora bought Ham Spray House in Ralph's name, and the three set up home together. The ménage à trois suited no one, and became further complicated when Dora also fell in love with Ralph's friend, Gerald Brenan. All this was open: according to the unofficial principles of the Bloomsbury set, there was little wrong with infidelity as long as there were no secrets.

Frances was the catalyst that partially solved the problem. Within months of meeting, she and Ralph had begun an affair. They set up home together in London while Lytton and Dora remained at Ham Spray. There was no bad blood, however, and Frances and Ralph continued to visit Wiltshire on weekends.

Lytton Strachey died of stomach cancer in 1932 and Dora Carrington committed suicide a few months later. Ralph and Frances moved to Ham Spray House, and within a year had a son. They named him Lytton after Strachey but always called him by his second name, Burgo. Ham Spray became a literary salon populated by old Bloomsburians and new friends. As a social and intellectual nexus, it was Bloomsbury's rural twin. Ralph and Frances worked on Lytton's unfinished project to publish the unexpurgated memoirs of Charles Greville, the courtier and diarist who provided insight into the lives of George IV and William IV. They were published in eight volumes in 1938.

When the war began in 1939, Ralph and Frances declared themselves conscientious objectors. Ralph had fought heroically in the First World War, but had been horrified by the carnage. The war inspired Frances to keep a diary of her observations, which would become acknowledged as one of the most incisive records of wartime Britain.

In late 1943, when she received a letter from Noel Carrington outlining Allen Lane's proposal, Partridge was hosting the young family of her protégée Janetta Woolley. Partridge was intrigued.

In December 1943, Dicky Chopping cycled alongside Noel Carrington and his wife Catherine to a pub in Hungerford to have his first meeting with Frances Partridge about the flower-book project. Chopping recorded that he was nervous as Partridge was almost twenty years older than him and a notable figure in literary circles. He was expecting to meet a privileged and austere woman. He was desperate to make a good impression but feared he would be hampered by his head cold as well as his nerves. During the ride he distracted himself, as usual, by looking at the natural world around him. He noted how the trees 'scintillated by the side of the shining road that was sparkling in the winter sunshine with pure white snowdrifts'.

During the meeting, he soon realized that Partridge was a sympathetic, kind and surprisingly 'normal' woman. A week later, Partridge wrote to Chopping for the first time, recording the 'hellish cold' at Ham Spray House. It was the start of sixty years of correspondence and friendship.

Partridge had enjoyed the company of homosexuals ever since she had first become familiar with the 'Bloomsbury Buggers', as she called Lytton Strachey, E. M. Forster and their homosexual associates. She noted that Chopping had 'all the practical companion ability of many buggers' but none of the possible 'silliness'. This was a reference to the high-campness and frivolousness that had more noticeably permeated homosexual culture since the First World War. She would soon learn that Wirth-Miller and Francis Bacon were not fey or pretentious either, even if their speech could be arched and Bacon wore fishnet stockings under his trousers as well as make-up. When they veered towards camp, it was satirical rather than exuberant.

During this period Chopping hoped to rent a room in London so he could be near Kew, making it easier to undertake his botanical illustrations. John Nash, who by now was an acting major in the Royal Marines and still an official war artist, wrote offering help. He asked if Hampstead would be too far from Kew: 'Tirzah Swanzy, Eric Ravilious's widow, is looking to let a large double-bedded, bow windowed room on the ground floor in her home at 169 Adelaide Road, you may know it, it used to belong to Ivon Hitchens. You have to put pennies in the geyser and buy your own coal.' The idea never came to fruition; Chopping lacked the funds to pay anything but a nominal rent.

While Chopping was trying to find a cheap base in the city, the urbane Bacon was surprisingly getting out of it. His relationship with the married businessman Eric Hall, who lived in Steep, near Petersfield in Hampshire, was ongoing. Bacon decided to rent a property there to see whether he could adapt to country life. The experiment was a failure. By late 1943, he had returned to the familiar territory of South Kensington, living and working at 7 Cromwell Place, which had been the home of the Pre-Raphaelite painter John Everett Millais from 1862. Bacon's former nanny Jessie Lightfoot continued to live with him there, sleeping on the table due to lack of space and helping him to run a sporadic illegal casino. She would take the coats and serve the guests drinks.

The following January, 1944, Chopping and Partridge were summoned to a meeting with Allen Lane, whom Chopping called a 'Napoleon character', about the flower-book project. Partridge already knew Lane, remembering him as a forceful spiv who had tried to push her into bulk-buying his titles when she worked at Garnett's bookshop in the 1920s.

The meeting at Penguin was short. The editors and account-ants revealed that, rather than a couple of volumes, the project was to comprise twenty-two separate books for which Chopping would need to draw every genus of flower in the British Isles. The ambition of the project began to dawn on Chopping. Prior to this, he had not fully considered how many genera of flower existed in Britain.

As far as Chopping and Partridge could ascertain, the figure twenty-two for the number of volumes was arbitrary. The Penguin accountants repeated the figure and seemed assured that the project made financial sense. Their confidence was odd: although Penguin was doing well, the publisher had never previously undertaken a commission on this scale.

Richard Chopping searching for flora, 1944. (*Author's personal collection*)

The project may have been immense in scope, but the co-authors were eager and almost immediately set to work. They independently scoured the countryside for samples of the thousands of flowers. Carrington had been wise in suggesting Partridge: it had not been a case of casually picking someone from the extended Bloomsbury family and she was no less enthusiastic than Chopping about the project. She soon wrote to Chopping, having returned from a research trip:

> I have just got in from a long day of bicycling. I am sleepy and sodden with sun, air and exercise. My word! How pretty everything is just now! I feel I never before saw quite such a combination of yellow buttercups, fresh green grass and crumbly white of hawthorn and cow parsley.

Meanwhile, Denis Wirth-Miller was finding some level of success as an artist. Well before the war had ended, the group of young artists who had started to inhabit the pubs and clubs of Fitzrovia and Soho in the late 1930s and early 1940s were starting to forge ahead in their careers. The Kensington home of Robert Colquhoun and Robert MacBryde, 77 Bedford Gardens, became the usual first-port-of-call for Wirth-Miller and Chopping on their trips to London. Wirth-Miller in particular had cause to make the journey from Felix Hall, while his partner was spending so much time in the countryside looking for flora. Aside from the fact that he had known the Roberts since before they lived permanently in London and enjoyed drinking with them, he was confident enough in his recent work to take it around the major galleries. Although none stepped forward to represent him at this stage, there was enough interest to justify his self-belief.

The Roberts had endured a difficult time since they returned from Italy in 1939. While MacBryde escaped war duty, Colquhoun had disliked life in the Royal Army Medical Corps. Although tough, he found barracks life in Dalkeith in Scotland, followed by Harehills outside Leeds, just as psychologically difficult as Chopping had, even though MacBryde moved to each city to be near him. He had developed respiratory problems, and MacBryde had also struggled with illness as well as poverty.

Luck, though, was soon on their side. While staying in Edinburgh, MacBryde had met Peter Watson, a rich collector and publisher of Cyril Connolly's *Horizon*, which had been set up in 1940. Watson had invited him to come and stay at his flat whenever he came down to London. It was not long before he took up the offer with Colquhoun in tow. Colquhoun's unit was earmarked for service in the Far East, and MacBryde and their friend, the art critic John Tonge, had attempted to get him discharged on grounds of ill health. The ploy failed but just weeks later Colquhoun was discharged from the military, possibly following further medical problems but probably because of his homosexuality.

The Roberts arrived in London in February 1941 to stay with Peter Watson at his flat at Palace Gate, Kensington. Watson had amassed a collection of cubist and modernist works, and had an interest in neo-Romanticism. His generous patronage had not been curbed by the strictures of wartime London, and he became 'the gluepot of the Fitzrovian painters', as Andrew Sinclair put it.[25] Chopping and Wirth-Miller became part of the Watson set, and the collector would be a signatory of their visitors' book after the war.

John Craxton, who would become a significant figure in post-war British art, was another homosexual young artist who was taken under Watson's wing. Craxton met Watson in 1941 when he was just eighteen or nineteen:

> we talked until about four in the morning – about painting, style, architecture, poetry and music . . . Two major paintings by Graham Sutherland, *The Gorse in the Sea Wall* and *The Entrance to a Lane*, were hanging in his flat. Peter introduced me to Rimbaud and Kafka, and also to contemporary music. His library was full of French art publications like Cahiers d'Art, Minotaur, Verve, and one devoured them.[26]

Keith Vaughan, who like Colquhoun was forced to serve in the Royal Army Medical Corps when he tried to claim the status of conscientious objector, was also introduced to Peter Watson in 1941. Vaughan was a friend of Craxton and got to know Chopping and Wirth-Miller well as he would share premises with their friend John Minton after the war. When he met Colquhoun in Watson's flat in 1942, he surprisingly found the imposing Scot to be 'a fawn-like creature'.[27]

Vaughan, yet another untrained artist who would benefit from the democratic bohemia of the late 1930s and 1940s, was aided by Watson, even though he did not take to him to the same extent as Craxton, Minton or the Roberts. As reported by Philip Vann: 'he found him charming but rather sterile and with lizard-like eyes'.[28] Significantly, Watson introduced him to Graham Sutherland, who was very generous with his time in helping younger artists, including Bacon, Wirth-Miller and Minton. Vaughan regarded Sutherland as a wise mentor, visiting his family home in Kent and noting down his comments on painting.

The Roberts's own neo-Romantic work, with its heavy referencing of cubism, was a natural fit for Watson's modernist collection. Despite being an Old Etonian and the youngest son of a baronet, he appeared to see them as kindred spirits in need of assistance, and he was attracted to them. After he could no longer tolerate the drunkenness and chaos that accompanied their lives, Watson put them up at a different flat in St Alban's Grove, South Kensington. Eventually, they proved too much even for Watson's generosity and had to move on from there, too, but he still assisted them with handouts.

The Roberts were already on their way to being christened 'The Golden Boys of Bond Street'. Their work had been shown at the *Six Scottish Painters* exhibition at the Lefevre Gallery on New Bond Street in 1942, and the prestigious gallery was beginning to put its full weight behind them. In May of that year John Tonge wrote about them in *Horizon*, no doubt with Peter Watson's blessing.

The Roberts moved into a studio and flat at 77 Bedford Gardens, where, partly for the sake of financial security, they invited John Minton to join them after he suffered a nervous breakdown that saw him discharged from the army in 1943. In 1941–2, Minton and his close friend Michael Ayrton had designed costumes and scenery for John Gielgud's touring production of *Macbeth* and his career already seemed to be on an upward trajectory, but the production was not a critical success.

Minton took up a post at Camberwell College of Art in 1943 and proved to be a successful and well-liked teacher. He also benefited from his association with the Roberts, writing to his friend Edie Lamont: 'I have felt much better about painting since meeting the Scotsmen, and they have been a great help and encouragement to me.'[29] Their strong style and techniques started to bleed into his work.

Minton seemed to be on the mend from his breakdown until he became infatuated with the quiet, handsome Robert

Colquhoun, a passion that he was unable to hide when drunk. The often abrasive Roberts seemed untroubled for the first year, and MacBryde did not regard Minton as a threat. Minton's work was included in the Redfern Gallery's summer exhibition in 1943, and again in 1944 and 1945. The shows were in the less prestigious lower gallery, however, which the ever direct Roberts referred to as 'Min's bargain basement'.[30]

Shortly after they arrived at Bedford Gardens, Jankel Adler took a studio in the same building. An exiled Polish-Jewish painter, Adler, who was born in 1895, opened the eyes of Wirth-Miller, the Roberts and Minton to new artistic possibilities. They referred to him as 'the Master' and he became a touchstone for young modern artists in Britain. He was cosmopolitan, intellectual and self-assured, and had an unrivalled pedigree. Paul Klee, one of the most innovative figures in pre-war European art, had the studio next to him at the Düsseldorf Academy in the early 1930s, and they had become friends and exchanged ideas. His work, formerly monumental, now veered towards expressionism, and the paintings and prints of the Roberts became more expressionistic as they matured. Adler's works were included in major German museum collections until he was denounced as a 'degenerate' by the Nazis. He had fled from Berlin to Paris and on to Scotland, where he met Colquhoun and MacBryde. He soon started exhibiting in London, with a show at the Redfern in 1943.

The presence of Jankel Adler at Bedford Gardens was an additional lure for Wirth-Miller and Chopping. Wirth-Miller in particular took much from his artistic instruction – for a time, he stuck to Adler's command to paint from memory. Adler also taught them his technique for making monotypes, which he had learned directly from Klee.

Robert Colquhoun, Robert MacBryde, Denis Wirth-Miller,
Richard Chopping and Jankel Adler at the Storehouse in the mid-1940s.
(Author's personal collection)

The house at 77 Bedford Gardens became a chaotic
equivalent of a Paris salon, attended by many writers and artists
not still caught up in military service. Dylan and Caitlin
Thomas, the artist Michael Wishart, Cyril Connolly, the poets
W. S. Graham and Nessie Dunsmuir, and the writer Angus
Wilson all made frequent appearances at Bedford Gardens.
Francis Bacon, when he returned to London from Hampshire
later in 1943, was also a regular visitor, as was Lucian Freud (who
had briefly served in the merchant navy). Chopping and Wirth-
Miller became close to all of them (although it seems likely that
they tried to avoid Freud) and many of them would make
regular trips to Felix Hall and the couple's next house for parties.
Bedford Gardens was often full of artists working alongside each
other, while the conversations ranged from poetry to French
literature to philosophy to the advancements in contemporary

art. Graham and Thomas would give impromptu poetry readings. Ideas were swapped and alliances were formed but, more than anything, 77 Bedford Gardens was a place for wild parties and extreme drinking.

Despite the ongoing war, both Fitzrovia and Soho were reinvigorated by the return of many of the bohemian artists from civil or military service. Many of the group who regularly attended 77 Bedford Gardens could also be seen drinking in the Wheatsheaf, Fitzroy or Black Horse in Fitzrovia, and the Gargoyle Club or the York Minster pub on Dean Street.

The York Minster, now known as the French House, attracted Dylan Thomas, Augustus John and Wirth-Miller, and became a lifelong fixture of Francis Bacon's Soho routine. The pub is extremely small, to the point that its owner, Gaston Berlemont, refused to serve pints because there was no room for barrels. Bacon often made the York Minster his first port of call after he had finished painting in the morning. When Wirth-Miller was in London, he would often join Bacon at the counter, where they would have a couple of glasses of wine before lunch. The compactness of the pub added to its atmosphere, making it easy to strike up conversations with strangers and make new acquaintances, something Bacon particularly enjoyed.

Wirth-Miller now had the best of both worlds: a large workspace and immediate proximity to the natural environment at Felix Hall, and easy access to the rolling bohemian party in London. He also finally had his first artistic exposure of real note. In 1944, Wirth-Miller's work was included in the *British Landscape Painting* at the Lefevre, the same gallery that had recently shown the work of other promising young artists such as the Roberts and Keith Vaughan. There was no better commercial gallery in London at that time for his debut. The association gave him validity as an up-and-coming artist.

While it is not known what works were shown, the title of the exhibition confirms that he was starting to find his métier. *The Sphinx*, dating from 1945 and featuring a female sphinx with a distention of cheek and brow similar to *The Beekeeper*, shows that he was still pursuing figurative work at the same time, but from this point he would be increasingly defined as a landscape painter.

Despite this small success, he may have been riled that Freud's work was shown at the same gallery later that year: rather than taking part in a group exhibition, Freud was enjoying his first solo show. The exhibition featured the surrealist *Painter's Room*, in which a zebra's head sticks through a window into a room containing a shabby couch and a palm tree. John Piper reviewed the exhibition for the *Listener*, writing, 'he has a cultivated feeling for line, when he can be bothered with it, and a natural feeling for colour'.[31]

Wirth-Miller's success was also to be soon overshadowed by that of his increasingly close friend Francis Bacon in another exhibition at the Lefevre. After eight years away from the galleries, Bacon's re-emergence in April 1945 was sensational. It may have been a group exhibition, but it was completely dominated by Bacon's work, and by *Three Studies for Figures at the Base of a Crucifixion* in particular. The painting related both to Matthias Grünewald's *Mocking of Christ* (1503), which may have inspired the triptych form, and to Picasso, not least his *Guernica* (1937) in its expression of the horror of war. Whatever the influences, the rendering of three Furies, with distorted bird-like and animalistic bodies, extended necks and screaming mouths, was the work of an original and unclassifiable voice. Years later, in April 1974, Bacon would say to Dicky Chopping about the anguish of existence, 'Words have no meaning, sometimes a howl has more meaning . . . the only solution is your own dissolution.'

While *Three Figures* drew on Greek mythology and represented the vengeful pursuers of Orestes, it appeared to many to speak of the mental and physical impact of conflict as the end of the Second World War approached. The exhibition also included *Figure in a Landscape* (1945), with a featureless figure, seeming to express despair, trapped among metal and chaos.

The critic for *Apollo* wrote, 'I, I must confess, was so shocked and disturbed by the Surrealism of Francis Bacon that I was glad to escape this exhibition.'[32] Raymond Mortimer of the *New Statesman* attempted to look forward in hope: 'I have no doubt of Mr Bacon's uncommon gifts, but these pictures expressing his sense of the atrocious world into which we have survived seem to me symbols of outrage rather than works of art. If Peace redresses him, he may delight as he now dismays.'[33]

Wirth-Miller could count himself among a new movement – all young friends and acquaintances connected to the bohemian scene – that was rapidly emerging as a major force of change in modern British art. Nevertheless, it was already becoming clear that the likes of Johnny Minton, the Roberts and himself would be in the shadow of Bacon and Freud for the remainder of their lives.

At the same time as Denis Wirth-Miller was finding some level of success, Dicky Chopping was forging ahead in his career as an illustrator. Following the accomplishment of *Butterflies in Britain*, he had a very busy time in 1943–4. As well as the commission for the flower-book project, Chopping was given the go-ahead to write and illustrate four books that were published during the course of 1944: *A Book of Birds*, *The Old Woman and the Pedlar*, *The Tailor and the Mouse* and *Wild Flowers*. Noel Carrington was once again responsible for the commissions, publishing the books on behalf of the Bantam Picture Book imprint rather than his Puffin imprint. Chopping had now fully emerged from Morris's shadow. He was developing a graphic style of his own, incorporating increasingly more complex touches to bring particular details of the insects, animals, plants and characters to the reader's attention. He may have had to put his exhibiting career as a fine artist to one side, at least for the time being, but he was finding notable success as an originator of illustrated children's and natural history books.

It had been a very important year for both men. They were no longer just a handsome and charming couple who were good company and more than willing to join in the excesses of Bedford Gardens: they had become professional artists surefooted in their place among the group of ambitious friends.

That summer of 1944 the war hit home at a personal level. Chopping was summoned back to his mother's house in Colchester to hear news he had long feared. On the night of 25 August 1944, his elder brother Ralph, by then a squadron leader, disappeared with his Lancaster bomber after an air raid on the U-boat pens at Brest, Brittany. He was presumed dead.

Ralph's death seemed all the more useless to the pacifist Chopping as it followed the success of the D-Day landings in June. The war was already in its endgame; the Allied armies were pushing through France.

Nonetheless, Germany was not finished yet. V-1 flying bombs or 'doodlebugs' were terrifying Londoners. A few weeks after the first attack in June, Frances Partridge described the doodlebug as 'a robot plane about twenty-five feet long, projected from a concrete base in France; it flies low and with considerable noise and has a light in its tail. When the light goes out and the noise stops the doodle-bug is about to descend and everyone is advised to take cover instantly.'

In late July, Allen Lane cited the rocket attacks as the reason for cancelling a meeting with Chopping and Partridge. It was not only Londoners who had cause to fear the doodlebugs. A few days later, when Chopping and Partridge were sitting at the breakfast table at Ham Spray House, Julia Strachey told them she had heard an explosion in the night. She said it had shaken the house, and was convinced it had been a V-1. Chopping and Partridge laughed off the idea that a rocket would have fallen in the middle of nowhere.

'Pooh!' Chopping reported saying to Strachey. 'Probably a door banging or a carthorse stamping.'

Further investigation revealed that a doodlebug had landed less than a mile from where they were sitting.

Chapter 6

Prison and Wivenhoe

In late October 1944, Chopping and Wirth-Miller were sitting in the Windsor Castle pub in Kensington with John Minton, the Roberts and W. S. Graham. Known by his second name, Sydney, the Scottish neo-Romantic poet had just published *The Seven Journeys*, written while he was working in a torpedo factory. He would long be associated with fellow poets Dylan Thomas and George Barker, and like them was a heavy drinker.

The five young men had been drinking hard all day. Earlier that month the Roberts had shared a sell-out exhibition at the Lefevre. Colquhoun had shown twenty-five works, including seventeen oils, with MacBryde showing seventeen oils. Minton was included in the show too, although his work was in the ante-room and he suffered the indignity of his own friend Michael Ayrton writing in the *Spectator*, among some more complimentary comments, 'Of the three, John Minton is the weakest . . . His figure drawing remains very weak.' Nevertheless, his gouache *The Road to the Sea* was illustrated in that month's *Apollo* and purchased by John Lehmann, the managing director of Virginia and Leonard Woolf's Hogarth Press. He was an important admirer and would commission many illustrations from Minton.[34]

Chopping and Wirth-Miller also had cause to celebrate: to cap a successful year so far, the pair had just bought their first house, with financial assistance from Chopping's mother, Amy.

The Storehouse's facade (centre) prior to being painted black and the addition of a bow window. *(Author's personal collection)*

Located on the banks of the River Colne in Wivenhoe, Essex – just ten miles from Daffodil Cottage – the house had been built as a pub in the early 1800s. It was later converted into a grand townhouse for a wealthy merchant, but in more recent times it had become a sail storehouse for the fishermen who used the Colne. By 1944 the building was semi-derelict but it remained elegant. It offered views across the Colne and the marshes that ringed its estuary. In the distance, there was a white wooden mill that had once been owned by Chopping's father.

Wivenhoe was subject to wartime restrictions. Part of the riverside had been requisitioned by J. W. Cook & Co., who produced motor torpedo boats for the Royal Navy, which had a large base nearby. Consequently, Chopping and Wirth-Miller were informed that they would not be able to start making the house inhabitable until hostilities had ceased.

The group gathered in the Windsor Castle were still enjoying themselves when last orders were called, so Colquhoun and MacBryde suggested they bought off-sales to take back to Bedford Gardens. They wanted to drink throughout the night so, a couple of hours later when those supplies were drained, Colquhoun, Chopping and Wirth-Miller ventured back out into the blackout to find black-market alcohol.

By late 1944, few terraces around Bedford Gardens had been left intact and it was a rough area. The blackout provided cover for thieves and muggers but Colquhoun was capable with his fists, Wirth-Miller could fight if needed, and the young men were used to trawling the dark streets in search of entertainment. Somewhere among the streets of derelict housing, Colquhoun and Chopping lost Wirth-Miller, but they were unconcerned. He was familiar enough with the area around the Roberts's home to find his own way back. The next time they saw him, he would be under arrest.

Wirth-Miller had taken a detour down what he described as 'a bombed-out Blitz slum street'. He would later claim he had broken off to 'have a slash' but Minton had often spoke of the casual sexual encounters he had enjoyed around Bedford Gardens under cover of the blackout – Wirth-Miller may well have set out to test the claims for himself.

For the rest of his life, he maintained the story he gave in court: that, having relieved himself, he was collared by a police 'provocateur' as he did up his fly. He claimed entrapment, but he had little hope of being believed. As a bohemian artist, as a half-German conscientious objector who had never joined the war effort, as the brother of a convicted criminal, and as someone who lived with another 'single' man, his story did not elicit any sympathy in court.

Wirth-Miller was found guilty of gross indecency under Section 11 of the Criminal Law Amendment Act of 1885 and sentenced to nine weeks in prison. It could have been much worse. Even after the Second World War, homosexual men faced much longer terms for acts of 'indecency' and 'buggery'. In 1954, landowner Michael Pitt-Rivers, who would later marry Chopping's friend Sonia Brownell after the death of George Orwell, was sentenced to eighteen months under the 1533 Buggery Act. Alan Turing, the man who cracked the German 'Enigma' code, was prosecuted in 1952 and forced to undergo oestrogen treatment.

Wirth-Miller was sent to Wormwood Scrubs prison. Echoing Chopping's time in the army, he was stripped of his identity: he was now Prisoner No. 1071.

Letters coming in and out of Wormwood Scrubs were subject to rigorous controls and heavy censorship. The prisoners' writing paper was half-filled with official guidelines outlining what they could and could not write. They were not permitted to describe life inside the prison, but Wirth-Miller also had to abide by other unwritten restrictions. If he expressed his love too openly, it could be used as ('proof') of his homosexuality and also put Chopping at risk of arrest. Nevertheless, both his love for Chopping and his problems with the restrictions of prison life are evident in his letters, as are his powers of observation and continuing focus on artistic techniques and processes. Because of the long list of rules on the header, there was very little space in which to write so the few letters that reached Chopping were, according to Wirth-Miller, 'somewhat Joycian'.[35]

The first extant letter is dated 23 November 1944:

My dear Dick, I received your letter last Saturday, just before going out to exercise, after lunch. I was so afraid of what news it might contain that I kept it for an hour before I dared read it. I was afraid the paper would print the story, and I am sorry, not for myself but for the trouble and pain it will have caused other people. But I accept it all, philosophically. It is a great joy and pleasure to know of one's friends' loyalty. I ought never to have doubted it . . .

Here, time has an entirely different quality. It is the knowledge of the identical pattern of each day that creates it. It seems but a few moments since I left you and Robert, in that slum Street. I feel that, when I come out in January, if John [Minton], the Roberts and the Scots Bard [W. S. Graham] are not in the studio – just as they were – the world will be unintelligible to me. But I don't think it will last. I shall look back on November and December and see long vistas of mailbags & buttons, prison meals and prison clothes – which will all telescope themselves into a neat block to be neatly packed away like splints or crutches – but the simile isn't correct.

I do wonder how the lithography progresses – if the keys were possible from the pencil. I wonder if you tried extra oil or spirit on the tracing paper. I long to get back to my work. All the tasks here are such a waste of time. I come in contact with the most extraordinary people – but one never gets to know anyone. But perhaps it is too early to say that. Kretchsmer's physical types of delinquents are repeated over and over again – practically every prisoner has some sort of abnormality or physical exaggeration. I should think we could pick out the innocent, from the physically normal. I should like to make drawings – I try to in my head. The grey prison clothes accentuate colouring – sometimes during exercise periods – it looks like a Sisley or a Whistler nocturne. There have been some lovely hours of sunshine at midday. But it is in the morning at about ¼ to 8 when we go to the workshops, that it is beautiful. It has not been fully light these last few mornings and that half light is always kind to Victorian architecture . . .

I may have books sent in. But at the moment have a Life of Napoleon and a complete Shakespeare and there is only a certain amount of time in which to read, so unless you have bought anything wait until after you have visited me . . .

Have you been to the house on the river? It will be needing a fire to air it? Has your mother heard of my 'escapade'? Has the lean-to been repaired? Would you look at the B.hives and make sure no rain is getting in . . .

I had to put on my own clothes to have my photograph taken, on Monday. It was an odd sensation, because the only personal belongings I have are my glasses, toothbrush and comb. And seeing myself in a real suit was quite extraordinary. I can't tell you how I miss my grand piano, but at times I feel I have it with me in my cell. Especially at midday when I have my dinner . . .

I can truthfully say I get the best out of this experience. I am spared the burden of remorse and it is only in odd moments of weakness that I allow myself to dwell on the corrupt police and their methods . . .

Well Dick, this seems to be about all, give dear old Mog [Kathleen Hale] a special hug from me – where did you run into her? Robert C&M – I expect Graham is in Cornwall. Tell me the results of the RS exhibition. I can hear the footsteps of the warder and the click of the cell lights being turned off – so I must get into bed. It must be nine o'clock. We are woken at six, nine hours must be just right for prisoners – I mostly sleep all of it. This is a poor letter – but you know how it is.

On the few occasions that he was permitted to visit, Chopping felt that he could not risk showing emotion towards Wirth-Miller. They would be placed on either side of a wire grille, and given a few minutes to converse. Wirth-Miller described their goodbyes as 'the moment of separation obliterating the present'.

Before he left on one occasion, Chopping handed over the chocolate ration he had hoarded, and Wirth-Miller began to cry. As the other inmates started to jeer, Chopping wondered whether 'these new sweet flowers might have thorny stems'.

Wirth-Miller's cell was spartan but not, he thought, disagreeable. He had a corner washstand with a soap dish, bowl and white enamel jug. There was also a chair and a small writing table, which he scrubbed until its top was rendered 'quite white, like a work by Ben Nicholson'. The room itself measured around 14 x 8 ft. It had yellow walls up to a green, inch-thick border line, with white above. Wirth-Miller would lie back on his iron bed and stare into the depthless white of the ceiling, a 'surface which I never tire of'. The stuffed mattress was, he claimed, more comfortable than the one they had shared at Daffodil Cottage.

It was here that he would spend most of his day, projecting thoughts and ideas for paintings onto the blank canvas of the ceiling. Outside the four walls lay a prison that was 'full of tangible, melancholy silence, with the overwhelming stillness accentuated by a dense fog which muffles any distant external noises, making them sound like despairing sighs that gently tail off into the silence'. He was permitted no clock or watch, and his routines were timed to the clack of the warder's footsteps.

For the most part, prisoners were allowed to leave their cells only to go to the prison workshop for their afternoon duties. The inmates would spend hours sewing buttons onto uniforms or bar-stitching to strengthen button holes. On other days, they would haul mailbags around the prison; Wirth-Miller could never fathom the reason.

'Some men get 15 years,' he wrote, 'and I groan because of nine weeks.' He also remarked on the 'animal-like' sympathy extended to him by older prisoners. The closest thing he had to a friend was a frustrated Italian prisoner who had been interned when his native country had entered the war. At the merest mention of women, he would start to kiss his forefingers obsessively. Another prisoner, whose family lived in East Anglia, told Wirth-Miller that rockets shot down by the RAF were falling over the east of England. The thought of Chopping in danger worried him. 'I have no exceptional fear of death – but the thought of it for one who is so part of myself, alone, is torture,' he wrote incautiously.

As well as the complete works of Shakespeare and the Napoleon biography, he read *The Poet's Eye*, an anthology illustrated by his friend John Craxton, *The Saturday Book*, an annual miscellany that included contributions from leading writers and illustrators, and back issues of the *New Statesman*, *Picture Post* and John Lehmann's *New Writing*. He took to rationing himself to a reading quota in order not to run out before his time was up.

Despite the restrictions, in time he was given the tools with which to draw. He wrote to Chopping on 25 December: 'I have been able to make quite a lot more drawings – but I've no idea if they are good or bad. The padre says they are good, but he seems to like the Victorian paintings in the church here too.'

The same letter revealed his thoughts as Christmas approached. He was becoming worn down by his imprisonment:

I wish you with all my heart a happy Christmas but I know that it will [not] be for you. Perhaps wishes for the new year would sound more sensible and so I wish for the new year happiness, health & success with your work. I think I am sad because I am reminded that we planned to open the store [their new home] this Christmas . . . Perhaps I am sad because, surrounded as you will be by a happy family celebration, I know you will be sad. But think, by then, only fifteen more days of this stupid sentence will be left . . . oh how they pass. The more one tries to speed them the more ponderous they are. Do you know that now I've written this far I have lost my sadness & feel better. I know now why I am being a misery. I have not had your reply to my last letter. You see – one is only allowed a certain number of letters and those letters of sympathy from friends have cost me your letter. So please stop anyone else writing to me.

The worst thing about imprisonment is the great loneliness and writing to you seems to bridge the gulf . . . I wish I had the words and was able to say all I feel and all I want you to know . . . I find it so difficult to write easily – knowing that I must censor all I say . . . I wonder all the time how you are – what doing, where living. My whole mind is alive with thinking of the future. I plan – & look at everything from a thousand positions but always I come back to the same spot – prison & find I'm in the most hopeless mess & muddle mentally. My old optimism has deserted me – perhaps that's for the good. Perhaps I can turn myself into a realist instead of a sentimental romantic . . .

The whole point is there is nothing I can say – and now I've read this thro' I see I haven't expressed myself clearly at all. Where I say it makes me miserable – it's not self pity – it is thinking of you with the extra burden of thinking of me so that all your day on Christmas Day and every day – you have had anxiety and worry of me. Now I see this letter will make it worse – I think I won't write any more tonight but wait until tomorrow to finish it off. I think I will go to bed.

The 'happy family celebration' mentioned by Wirth-Miller was Christmas with Frances, Ralph and son Burgo Partridge in Wiltshire. Frances Partridge was 'touched to tears' by the situation, and did all she could to ensure that the sensitive Chopping was made to feel at home.

Other guests at Ham Spray House included the novelist Anthony West (the illegitimate son of H. G. Wells), the Russian artist Boris Anrep and the art critic Clive Bell, who was still married to Vanessa Bell but supported her relationship with Duncan Grant. Anrep, known for his mosaics at the National Gallery and in the octagonal room of the Tate, came to Britain before the First World War and fell in with the Bloomsbury Group. In 1912, Bell and Anrep both contributed essays for the catalogue of Roger Fry's *Second Post-Impressionist Exhibition*. Typical of the interplay of sexual relationships within the set, Anrep's wife, Helen Maitland, became Fry's long-term partner. Anrep, meanwhile, inspired several dozen poems by the great Russian writer, Anna Akhmatova.

Chopping's week-long Christmas stay at Ham Spray was a welcome diversion. The story of Wirth-Miller's conviction had not been kept out of the papers, with the *News of the World* quick to go into print. Wirth-Miller's mild success and the friends he kept made him a worthwhile target. Chopping began to sense animosity in the villages around Kelvedon and feared a homophobic beating. He sought to avoid places where he might be recognized.

After a few weeks of feeling isolated and vulnerable at Felix Hall, he decided that he had to leave but that meant abandoning his work. He sent two letters: the first was to Allen Lane to tell him he needed a break from the flower-book project to recover from a bad bout of flu; the second was a response to the Roberts after MacBryde had said, 'You've got to come here.' Chopping packed and left for London.

Chapter 7

The Storehouse

Denis Wirth-Miller passed through the gates of HMP Wormwood Scrubs shortly after 7.30 a.m. on Wednesday, 10 January 1945, and was embraced by Dicky Chopping and Kathleen 'Mog' Hale running towards him. His last written words to Chopping had been 'I think it promises to be the most wonderful day of my life.'

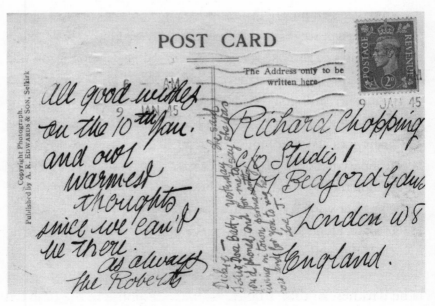

The Roberts and John Minton send Chopping wishes prior to
Wirth-Miller's release from prison in January 1945.
(The Estate of John Minton, Royal College of Art)

It is evident from his letters to Chopping that imprisonment affected him deeply and he became more vulnerable. Before being sentenced, Wirth-Miller felt that his life was coming together. His work had been displayed in a major gallery and he was beginning to find success as an artist. Moreover, his social circle had become wider and more vibrant, and he was enjoying wild revelries in London. He had kicked over the traces of being a fatherless, barely educated and impoverished boy. Nonetheless, in that final prison letter, sent on 5 January 1945, he revealed that he felt he had lost his way and he wished to recapture the days when he and Chopping had been alone at Daffodil Cottage:

I really have been making such a mess for the last two years. The future is like summer 1940 – from July onwards – I did my best work then & was wonderfully happy. In a way I have had smiles & glimpses of during the last two years – but not the sustained peace & completeness that I knew then . . . Where I say smiles & glimpses I may confuse you. To enlarge it is as [if] a great river that had been flowing peacefully & complete in 1940–41 during 1943 & 1944 was dammed up – so that only part of the former capacity of water flowed in its bed – the water was all there behind the dam – but it flowed over into strange country in streams & trickles – the water is still there behind the dam – which has now been fitted with floodgates. The river will soon be normal again and will with its flow & breadth, I hope, carry many great boats, birds and fish & sweep clean the banks of collected jetsam & flotsam.

The darkness of that 'strange country' would never be entirely erased from Wirth-Miller's psyche but he seemed certain that life in their newly bought house by the River Colne would allow him to focus on the two things that mattered most to him: his art and his love for Chopping.

The house in Wivenhoe, however, was still off-limits as the war dragged on. After his release, Wirth-Miller and Chopping stayed at Bedford Gardens as the guests of the Roberts and Minton. They worked in the mornings – Chopping on the flower-book project, and Wirth-Miller trying to rediscover the artistic confidence he had lost in Wormwood Scrubs – and drank with their hosts for the rest of the day.

Although glad of their friends' kindness, Wirth-Miller was unhappy. The couple wanted to be with each other in quiet privacy again, rather than drinking away the days at the Windsor Castle.

In prison, Wirth-Miller had recalled W. S. Graham describing the beauty of Cornwall, where he moved with his girlfriend, Nessie Dunsmuir, in 1944. He and Dunsmuir lived frugally in a caravan they had borrowed from friends, often unable to afford necessities. Wirth-Miller believed, however, that compared to 77 Bedford Gardens, with its parade of friends and artists looking for entertainment, the setting was more likely to offer the peace he craved.

Wirth-Miller had never travelled to Cornwall, but he had projected fantasies about it on to his cell's blank ceiling. The white blankness of table and ceiling also set in mind the works of Ben Nicholson, regarded as the leading abstract painter in the country, who had moved to St Ives in 1939.

With spring approaching, he persuaded Chopping that they should pool their money and buy train tickets to St Ives. It was the first holiday they had taken together in the eight years since they met. There was some artistic point to the destination: as well as Nicholson, the St Ives community included his wife, the leading contemporary sculptor Barbara Hepworth, and Naum

Gabo, the Russian constructivist who had joined them there during the war. Gabo lived with the leading critic and painter Adrian Stokes and the artist Margaret Mellis. Stokes had studied at the Euston Road School with William Coldstream and Victor Pasmore, whom Wirth-Miller and Chopping knew from their Fitzroy Street days.

From St Ives station, the couple walked along the seafront and met a fisherman who had just pulled his catch ashore. Chopping reported that they haggled with the fisherman for a large, still twitching cod and continued to a field of flowering violets, where they found Graham and Dunsmuir's caravan.

Their kitchen consisted of a portable stove in a cramped corner of the caravan, where Chopping cooked up a lunch of boiled cod with parsley sauce. They sat down and ate what by wartime standards was a luxuriant meal. 'It's delicious, Dicky – you're a smashing cook,' Graham said as he tasted his first mouthful. 'Now, where's the whisky?' The level of alcohol consumption would be no different than at Bedford Gardens.

Later on, their hosts took them back towards St Ives to visit the small cottage where the naive painter Alfred Wallis had lived until his death in 1942. The fisherman had taken up painting 'for company' after his wife's death in the 1920s. He had never had a painting lesson, and the child-like boldness and peculiarity of scale and perspective of his seascapes had appealed to Nicholson and his friend Christopher Wood when they visited St Ives in 1928. Nicholson's enthusiasm had led to the naive painter's works becoming prized. Graham was aware that it was still possible to buy some of the deceased fisherman's paintings cheaply at his cottage by the shore.

When Chopping and Wirth-Miller entered the cottage, they found that the floor was covered by Wallis's seascapes, which he had painted onto any available support from board and paper to cardboard boxes and empty cigarette packets. Wirth-Miller thought they would suit the new waterside house at Wivenhoe. He paid £14 for six paintings. It was a sum he could not afford, but it proved a wise investment. He would go on to sell them for £400 each in the 1980s, and their value accelerated in succeeding decades.

Wirth-Miller had a genuine and sustained interest in naive art. Decades later, in Wivenhoe, he lent his support to a similar artist, a local man named Ernie Turner (sometimes described as 'Wivenhoe's Alfred Wallis' although he never achieved the same level of fame). Turner began painting in 1964, having retired as a shipwright. Wirth-Miller gave him technical advice, encouraged him to experiment and helped his sales in London and overseas. Francis Bacon bought some of Turner's works, and there was a waiting list for his paintings.

On 8 May 1945, the war in Europe finally came to a close. A few weeks earlier, with the end inevitable, Denis Wirth-Miller and Dicky Chopping had been able to move into the Storehouse.

It was to be the most important place in their working and social lives, and the backdrop to the next sixty years of the ups-and-downs of their relationship. At first they referred to the house on Wivenhoe Quay as the 'Store' to reflect its immediate past as a sail store, or simply as 'the house on the river'. They could have drawn on the building's former names from when it was a public house – the Maidenhead and the Swan – but in the end they rechristened it the 'Storehouse'.

Since they had first found the Storehouse, it had been further battered by the winter storms that came from the North Sea. The roof was rotten and, if repairs were not made immediately, the damp would have made the house unsound. The restoration would take much time and money, neither of which they had, and building materials and labour were in short supply. Most of the able-bodied male workforce were still serving out the last six months of their military service; other skilled workers had headed to the major cities to join the rebuilding programme.

Help came from an unlikely source. Funeral directors and their employees were exempt from conscription, and coffin building gave them access to materials not available to other trades. Ernest Radford, a local undertaker, had capitalized on the labour shortage: he and his pallbearers supplemented their incomes with building work and were willing to patch up the Storehouse for the low fee Chopping and Wirth-Miller could afford. The house was soon ready for the next stage of renovation to begin once the two artists had the necessary funds.

For the time being, their quality of life was similar to that at Daffodil Cottage. Photographs reveal that both men, naturally slim, had become emaciated over their difficult winter, not helped by the cold conditions at Felix Hall, imprisonment and rationing, and by the need to put all their funds into the purchase of the house. They both fell ill frequently, taking turns to nurse each other back to health before the next bout struck. It was freezing inside the house, and there were holes in the floorboards and cracks in the plaster. All the walls and fixtures needed work before paint could be applied and paintings hung. Wivenhoe, if not hostile, was not immediately welcoming. There were many unconventional characters in the village, but the two artists, neither of whom were in military service, were treated with suspicion.

Chopping and Wirth-Miller were both tenacious, a quality that would see them through their first years at the Storehouse. Bearing in mind Wirth-Miller's final letter from prison, they were set on creating not only the house they wanted to live in, but the life they wanted to live together. There was a mutual determination and understanding between them that surprised even their closest friends.

Chopping and Wirth-Miller would buy fresh fish when money allowed, but prices for many foodstuffs remained beyond their reach. They would ask friends living elsewhere in East Anglia to bring them basic items including milk or butter. They would repay the favour with a trip to the oyster beds just downstream from their new house. When they could, they bought from the black market – Wivenhoe had a long history as a smugglers' village.

The house had a severe damp problem even after the roof had been fixed. The River Colne burst its banks several times a year, and the Storehouse was one of the properties most at risk from flooding. Following the floods, rats would sometimes invade the space below the ground-floor floorboards. Initially, Chopping and Wirth-Miller tried to exterminate them with poison, but it had little effect. Whenever one died, the stench of the rotting carcass would fill the ground floor, attracting bluebottles – flies were to become a regular feature of Chopping's work, both literary and artistic.

The men made do with provisional studio spaces inside their home for several years until they had the money to buy two small, conjoined cottages on Anchor Hill, adjacent to their house and accessible from their courtyard garden. The two little dwellings were knocked together to allow Wirth-Miller to paint upstairs in one and Chopping to draw, paint and write in the other. Chopping's studio overlooked Anchor Hill, the Colne and the marshland below nearby Fingringhoe. The interior of the studios was basic, lacking any luxury, but they installed a Baby Belling on which to heat drinks. In the late 1960s a small, primitive bathroom was added to the rear of the studios.

Despite the state of the house when they moved there in April 1945, guests started to arrive immediately. Even before they took up residence, Chopping and Wirth-Miller established a visitors' book as a jocular contrast to the informal atmosphere they hoped to create. The Storehouse would always be a convivial place of entertainment, with a regular stream of people making the trip up from London.

The final week of April 1945 started with a visit by the writer Patricia Cavendish, who had been introduced to Chopping when he stayed with Noel Carrington for a short time during Wirth-Miller's imprisonment. Cavendish was one of only two women with whom Chopping ever had a sexual relationship, the other being Olga the au pair when he was a teenager. The short affair occurred while Wirth-Miller was in prison, but he apparently knew about it and was forgiving, writing on 5 January 1945, 'No blame can be attached to either you or her.'

Just after her visit, the modern architect Ernö Goldfinger and his wife Ursula arrived. Goldfinger had built a modernist house for himself at 2 Willow Road, Hampstead, in 1939 and would remain a controversial architect for the rest of his life. It would amuse Chopping that he was later to design the cover for Ian Fleming's Bond novel *Goldfinger* (1959). The villain was named after Ernö because Fleming resented the removal of old cottages to make way for the Willow Road building. When Goldfinger considered legal action against Fleming, it was rumoured that the author threatened to change the name of the character to 'Goldprick'.

On the following day Ralph and Frances Partridge came with their son Burgo. Then, two days later, on 28 April, Robert Colquhoun and Robert MacBryde followed. During their stay, the four young artists rowed out into the middle of the lake at Wivenhoe Park, a country estate near the village, so that they

Pages from the Storehouse visitors' book; signatories include Bacon, Partridge, Colquhoun and MacBryde. *(Author's personal collection)*

could have a good view of a fireworks party taking place on the estate. The Roberts's biographer Roger Bristow reported:

> Spirits were running high and a kilt-wearing MacBryde, attempting to stand and raise a toast, unsettled the boat's balance and was unceremoniously toppled into the lake's murky water. Colquhoun and his two companions panicked, thinking that the weight of his sodden kilt would drag MacBryde under but instead, in the words of

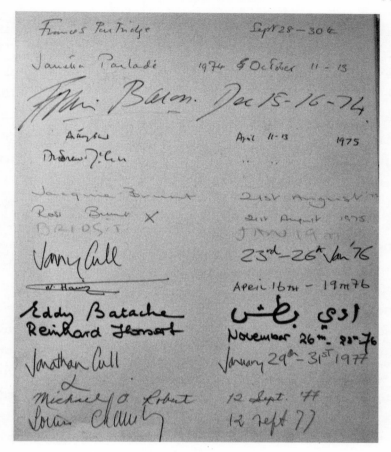

(Author's personal collection)

Wirth-Miller, 'he soon bobbed up, encircled and supported by the kilt floating on the water's surface'.[36]

A few weeks afterwards, they returned with John Minton,
but before long the Roberts and Minton would begin to loosen
their ties to each other. The Roberts's relationship with Minton
was collapsing into psychological warfare. Minton's obsession
with Colquhoun had continued. MacBryde's temper was savage
and he would lose control unpredictably, and the fragile Minton

was ill-equipped to counter his aggression. Frances Spalding wrote, 'According to Denis Wirth-Miller, it was "appalling" to see the intensity of Minton's feelings for Colquhoun.'[37] Minton attempted to bring a fourth man, Ronald Frame, another Scottish painter, into their delicate living and working arrangements but that did not work. While 77 Bedford Gardens still remained a destination for hedonistic artists and writers, there was an increasingly uncomfortable atmosphere.

In 1945, Minton graduated to having his own solo show at the Lefevre. Although he had learned much through his admiration of the eighteenth-century painter Samuel Palmer as well as Graham Sutherland, Colquhoun and MacBryde still denigrated him as a copyist of their own developments in neo-Romanticism. The tolerance that had to date kept things at least nominally civil disintegrated over the course of 1945–6. Increasingly often, Minton would be heard howling in despair in his room. MacBryde wrote to Minton after one episode, 'you would find some release by being parted from us . . . We couldn't be fonder of anyone than we are of you but I suppose you still meant it when you spoke of still loving Robert and sometimes feeling unhappy.'[38] In August 1946, when his friend Keith Vaughan invited him to share 37 Hamilton Terrace in St John's Wood, Minton accepted and would live there for the next six years.

The Roberts had always taken advantage of Minton's wealth and generosity. As they were now so successful as painters, and were also attracting illustration commissions and set-design work, the Roberts were unconcerned by his departure. Their progress was set to continue. By the summer of 1948, works by both artists had been bought for the collection of New York's Museum of Modern Art.

The Scottish artists wreaked havoc on the Storehouse when they came to stay. They frequently smashed glasses and drank to excess, and they would carry on even after vomiting. Their frequent visits inspired a drunken solution to one of the problems caused by the flooding. Whenever Colquhoun or MacBryde drank too much they would lift a ten-inch section of the floorboards above the flooded area and spew onto the rats below. The abyss became known as 'the sinkhole'.

The highly polished upper staircase at the Storehouse was perilous. As it was an original Georgian feature of the building, Chopping and Wirth-Miller never altered the staircase, despite the number of drunken artists and writers who fell down it. In the late 1980s Francis Bacon would show one of his biographers, Daniel Farson, the resultant bruises on his legs.[39]

After moving into the Storehouse, Dicky Chopping soon returned to the urgent work required on the flower-book project. Although both Chopping and Frances Partridge were knowledgeable about their subject in layman's terms, they needed someone with greater expertise. The series was meant to be accessible but it also needed to contain enough detail to interest informed readers. Lane consequently put the authors in touch with Noel Sandwich, a gentle, portly man who was a veteran botanist at Kew Gardens.

Although they made jokes to each other about his girth, Chopping and Partridge took to Sandwich immediately. He would often stay at Ham Spray House and the Storehouse, educating the co-authors about the finer points of botany and ensuring they read the 'fearful stuff', as Chopping called it, that he set them as homework.

Lane also visited Ham Spray in 1946 for a joint meeting with the authors and Sandwich. Chopping accepted a lift from London in Lane's Bentley. He described the journey as 'hair-raising' as Lane drove his enormous car fast, badly and arrogantly.

They tore along the 'dreadful middle passage' of the 'appalling Great West Road', and by the time the limousine drove up the narrow, hedge-lined roads leading to Ham Spray, Chopping's nerves were frayed. Partridge's view of Lane as a spiv was confirmed as the Bentley roared up her drive, smashing through overhanging branches.

Their dealings with Penguin's creative director Jan Tschichold and co-director Eunice Frost were more civilized. Chopping described Frost as 'a lady of very good and upright rectitude and character'. She had risen from the lowly position of secretary to become a major asset at Penguin. In 1941 she set up the company's New York office and was instrumental in bringing works by Evelyn Waugh, Dorothy L. Sayers and Graham Greene to the mass market.

The time-consuming hunt for specimens continued. It took the Partridges all over the country from the Lizard, where they looked for sea holly, to Cardigan Bay for yellow Welsh poppies, to the Quantocks in search of the bog pimpernel. Partridge's husband Ralph and son Burgo were often on hand to search with her. Burgo became so dedicated to the pastime that, on holiday in Switzerland one summer, Partridge noted him gasping at the sight of a field of gentians.

Noel Sandwich often assisted. Frances Partridge remembered setting out into the fields around Ham Spray with the botanist to look for a certain type of crocus verna. 'After much blundering, we found it at last,' she wrote to Chopping, 'and I must say it looked too sweet – lots and lots of little purple crocuses in a perfectly wild field.' At the moment of discovery, Sandwich launched into a florid condemnation of Proust's *Sodome et Gomorrhe*, forcing Partridge to hide her laughter.

Chopping's illustration work began to take up almost all of his time. He used extremely fine brushes for the intricate details and applied both watercolour and tempera for the coloration. Throughout his career he would prove to be too fastidious and too much of a perfectionist to be a fast worker, preferring to take extreme care with his illustrations. As deadlines approached, the Partridges took on more responsibility for the gathering of samples. Partridge would seal them in moistened biscuit tins and post them to Chopping in Wivenhoe. She would also affectionately berate him for his lack of progress.

The schedule became more punishing as the first publication date drew closer. Chopping was so pushed for time that he asked Wirth-Miller for help with the illustrations. Much to Partridge's annoyance, Chopping calculated that at the current rate it would take twelve years to finish the project.

Nonetheless, they continued to meet Eunice Frost's deadlines. Chopping's quota was for eight drawings every six weeks, the caliber of which Frost would then discuss with artists including Graham Sutherland, who would become a good friend to both Chopping and Wirth-Miller. The quota would have been more easily manageable if Chopping was not simultaneously pursuing other projects.

In 1945, he had followed up his illustrated children's books for Bantam with *Mr Postlethwaite's Reindeer and Other Stories*, published by Transatlantic Arts. The original title story led to interest from the BBC, which recorded a radio version broadcast at Christmas 1946. Chopping was eager to follow up its success and wrote many letters to the BBC suggesting other projects, but without success.

Around this time Chopping brought Wirth-Miller temporarily into the world of book illustration. The couple worked hand-in-hand on *Heads, Bodies and Legs*, which had the writing credit 'by Denis Wirth-Miller and Richard Chopping' in that order. It was published in 1946 by the Puffin imprint and was successful enough to be reprinted in 1951 and 1955. Each illustrated colour page was cut into three sections, made up of 'head', 'body' and 'legs', so a child could turn over different page-flaps and create a new character from the different sections. A haughty grand dame could end up with the body of a bird and the legs of another animal. The comical illustrations, probably executed by Wirth-Miller for the most part, were preceded by an explanatory children's story written by Chopping.

In autumn 1947, Chopping decided to discuss his workload with Eunice Frost. He had recently had dinner with her in London and felt it would not be too impudent to drop by her flat to broach the matter. Halfway down her street he changed his mind about arriving unannounced and decided to call her first. He saw a phone box nearby and shut himself inside what he described as its 'smelly confines'. As he dialled Frost's number, he registered the array of cards giving the numbers of local prostitutes, accompanied by lewd graffiti.

As the ringtone sounded, a piece of graffito caught his eye: 'If you want a good FUCK ring Eunice.' The number listed below the message was exactly the same as the one he had just dialled.

He was still bewildered when Frost answered the phone.

'Eunice, I am sorry to have to ask, but have you been bothered by indecent phone calls?'

She admitted that, in fact, she had been receiving two or three offensive calls every evening. He explained his line of questioning.

'My dear,' she said. 'Do me a favour and make it illegible.'

Chopping suspected that the graffito was the work of a disgruntled author. He scratched out the message and, after Frost invited him up to her flat, she rewarded him with a more lenient deadline.

★

Chopping was not too busy in 1947 to help Ralph Partridge. Frances was concerned about her husband's career. He was not receiving enough writing commissions and she felt that he had lost his ambition. She explained to Chopping that Ralph enjoyed writing reviews of crime novels when the opportunity arose and was interested in the psychology of the criminal mind. Chopping proposed a meeting with his cousin Dr J. Stanley Hopwood, who was the Superintendent at Broadmoor, the asylum for the criminally insane, at Crowthorne in Berkshire. Chopping suggested that there might be a possibility of Ralph writing a report on the institution under Hopwood's direction. Hopwood's liberal, progressive reforms were much criticized, and he welcomed the idea of an intellectual analysis of his methods.

In the spring, Ralph, Frances, Dicky and Denis undertook their first visit together to Broadmoor, where they stayed with Hopwood. The Superintendent, unaware of the nature of his cousin's relationship with Wirth–Miller, wrote prior to the visit apologizing that the pair would need to share a room 'but luckily not a bed'.

It was only two years since Wirth–Miller's release from Wormwood Scrubs, where he had discovered an interest in criminal psychology and physiognomy. His main concern, however, was to view the hospital's collection of paintings by the then under-appreciated Richard Dadd, the Victorian painter of fairies and supernatural subjects. Dadd, suffering from paranoid schizophrenia, had been a patient at the hospital after he stabbed his father to death in 1843.

After this initial visit Frances and Ralph wrote to Chopping thanking him:

We are truly most deeply grateful to you, and to your cousin, whom we both feel to be one of the most enlightened, absolutely admirable men we have come across, and courageous and independent-minded, and everything that one thinks valuable. He was so very kind to us, and he really is a charming little man and we liked everything about him – his soothing doctor's voice, his dry humour, and his attitude to his dog, cat and his old, fat mother up aloft.

Hopwood offered them unlimited access to the hospital. During the next year they visited regularly, usually on the weekend to attend plays or concerts staged by the patients, sports days and early-evening dances. The Partridges combined the trips with their work for the flower-book project, stopping off on the journey to look for varieties of flora.

After the first play that they attended, Frances Partridge recorded in her diary her speechless alarm as the stage curtain rose to reveal an imposing row of murderers dressed in hunting pink and singing the opening chorus: 'The young psychopathic tenor hero, I find rather gave me the creeps more than I realized at the time – I suppose it was all-consuming megalomania he seemed to suffer from.' At her first hospital dance she was asked to dance by a red-faced old man in a dinner jacket, who politely taught her the Boston two-step, gently resting his hand on her waist. Later she was to learn that 'his speciality was raping little girls'.

Chopping sometimes joined the Partridges on further visits and befriended a patient named Mrs Gordon, whose responsibilities included the costumes for the prisoners' shows. She had been imprisoned for murdering a member of her family. She had endured a difficult time at Holloway prison and thought of Broadmoor as a kind of sanctuary. At Broadmoor, she told

Chopping, she was at least allowed to fight the cold by curling up beneath her fur coat in her cell. She and Chopping corresponded for years, even after her release back to into the community in her home city of Sheffield.

Francis acknowledged in a letter to Chopping that the visits made her and Ralph feel humbled and ashamed never to have considered the difficulties endured by such patients and their families. Beforehand they had only ever thought of the suffering inflicted on their victims and the victims' loved ones.

Ralph Partridge's report led to his book, *Broadmoor: A History of Crime, Lunacy and its Problems*, published by Chatto in 1953. Dr Hopwood's liberal methods came under further public scrutiny at the same time; a Broadmoor patient called John Straffen, who was in the hospital having strangled two young girls, escaped in 1952 and strangled another. Chopping remained supportive of Hopwood's methods, and praised his approach to mental health in a national newspaper obituary following Hopwood's death in 1971.

Chapter 8

Bacon Arrives

The Storehouse's restoration would not reach the stage where guests could stay comfortably until the early 1950s, but the stream of visitors did not let up after the first burst in April 1945. In time the house would become a destination in itself, but before then the hosts and the waterside setting were the main attractions. Chopping and Wirth-Miller were charming, gregarious and intelligent, and were both good cooks. Their large cast of artistic friends arrived to socialize or work, or both. The drink would flow and the talk of art and literature would give way to the piano, singing and drunken entertainment. Wivenhoe became a mini-bohemia that appealed to their London friends' tastes. The direct rail service from Liverpool Street straight to the village made it easily accessible. Francis Bacon preferred to take a taxi.

Food was increasingly at the heart of the social life at the Storehouse. While rationing continued for many years after the war, guests would join Wirth-Miller in his small boat to collect gull's eggs to take back to London. Alternatively Chopping would take them in his 1928 Austin Tourer to a local farm to pick vegetables. He later had to sell the car to a local barge owner to raise money to pay the outstanding rates on the house. This amounted to £9.10s.

The kitchen was situated at the back of the house, with large windows that looked onto the courtyard garden. Wirth-Miller became interested in French cuisine after Janetta Woolley, with whom he became friends via Frances Partridge, introduced him to the country's gastronomy. A favourite meal for Wirth-Miller was an authentic peasant stew made of animal fat and little else. It was a dish, Chopping warned guests, that was only suited to committed carnivores.

Often, trips to the oyster sellers on the banks of the estuary would precede lunch. One visitor, Louise Cambon, wrote, 'I will always remember that day, in this nice oyster shop, the tall man, the nice wife, the bird and also the "hot" red wine.' Sonia Brownell commented that, 'it was sheer genius to have thought of the composition of the menu and to have laid down an oyster bed or two the very year when there are no oysters in France!'

The guests also took to Wivenhoe itself, which despite the beauty of its setting was a working village rather than quaint. The circle of highly social, urban friends would move from pub to pub in Wivenhoe much as they would from place to place in Fitzrovia and Soho. They would be introduced to the network of close friends that the couple made among the locals, before returning to the Storehouse for further drinking.

Chopping and Wirth-Miller kept up their friendship with Peter Watson that had first begun in the late 1930s or early 1940s, probably through Sonia Brownell or Colquhoun and MacBryde. He continued to publish *Horizon* until the end of the 1940s, and it would include the work of many of their friends and associates, among them Stephen Spender, Augustus John, Graham Sutherland, John Craxton, Robert Colquhoun, Lucian Freud. W. S. Graham, Julian MacLaren-Ross, Dylan Thomas, Denton Welch and Ian Fleming, who would contribute travel articles before he became a novelist.

Peter Watson's boyfriend Norman Fowler was a lesser known figure who stayed at the Storehouse. Watson's good faith and generosity, as the Roberts had proved, were easily manipulated, and he fell under the spell of Fowler, a former sailor he met in New York in 1946. He soon moved Fowler to England and funded his lifestyle, giving him a yacht. When Watson was found dead in his bath in 1956, fingers were pointed at his younger lover.

The most significant regular guest at the Storehouse was Francis Bacon, who over the decades would visit more than anyone. His exhibition of *Three Studies for Figures at the Base of a Crucifixion* at the Lefevre coincided exactly with the couple moving into the house in April 1945. With that single group exhibition, Bacon went from being a virtual unknown to one of the most talked about figures in British contemporary art. In retrospect, his cataclysmic triptych shifted the ground not just of art criticism. While many people did not know how to react to modern art, from cubism and surrealism to the neo-Romantic movement that drew on those genres, it was seemingly impossible not to react to Bacon's new work, even if that reaction was to turn away in horror.

Critics and gallery-goers appended to his work a narrative and meaning, perhaps led there by the storytelling nature of traditional religious triptychs and the suggestive title. Many saw *Three Studies* as a story and judgement of war, a comment on man's inhumanity to man. Bacon, however, did not mean his works to be narrative, judgemental or religious. The figures in *Three Studies* are Furies captured in a moment of anguish, not victims within a narrative of the extraordinary cruelty of the Second World War: the depicted moment gives the work power, not the backstory, not the 'why'. The strength of people's reactions would force them into conjecture to fill the void left by the absence of narrative, and this lack of narrative, combined with visceral power, gives his paintings continued resonance.

They speak to our own horror whatever the actuality of the situation, personal or global.

Michael Peppiatt wrote:

> For Bacon, the test of an image which 'worked', to use the artist's own term, was in part its resistance to any logical or coherent verbal explanation; everything that failed this stringent test fell into the despised category of 'illustration'. 'After all, if you could explain it,' he would insist with manic bonhomie, 'why would you go to the trouble of painting it?[40]

In his own small way, Wirth-Miller was experimenting with something similar. He was already developing non-narrative landscape at this time. The mood of the works may suggest a threat from nature, which would become more obvious in the darker, later paintings, but no story is explicit. The works are deliberately unpopulated and consciously full of movement: they are a moment and not a narrative in the manner of Constable's *The Haywain*. The only story-teller is the viewer.

Bacon was an impressive talker on art, as shown through his series of interviews with David Sylvester and his conversations with Peppiatt. During a long bout of drinking, he would announce a robust theory, often criticizing the work of other contemporaries but also in praise of Picasso or Giacometti, and return to it with further force throughout an evening. The deep friendship shared with Wirth-Miller was at least partly founded, beyond their outsider childhoods and capacity for drink, in a sympathetic intention in their art.

At this stage, Bacon was still nominally living and working at Cromwell Place with his nanny, Jessie Lightfoot. His lover, Eric Hall, was registered as resident there too by 1947, following the inevitable collapse of his marriage, but between 1946 and

1948 Bacon spent much of the time elsewhere. It was Hall who bought *Three Studies* at the Lefevre show, while Bacon's cousin, Diana Watson, bought *Figure in a Landscape*, but before long both works would be in the collection of the Tate. Bacon did not seem to be at all affected by his growing stature as an artist. He spent the money that came his way as fast as he earned it, and he continued frequenting the same locales, primarily the York Minster (the French) and the Gargoyle. There was only a handful of places that could drag him out of Soho and Kensington: Monte Carlo; Paris; Tangier; and Wivenhoe.

It was Monte Carlo where Bacon spent much of 1946 to 1948. Before he left he became close friends with Graham Sutherland, the living British painter he perhaps most admired at the time. Sutherland, born in 1903, had been influenced by William Blake and Samuel Palmer and was in turn influencing the young neo-Romantics such as Minton and the Roberts; Keith Vaughan and Minton, in particular, idolized him. Bacon never idolized any artist, but the two men got on very well despite having very different characters. Sutherland's work was a sympathetic precursor to that of Bacon. The work of both men carried a sense of ruination and the presence of the inexplicitly sinister both during and after the Second World War. Sutherland's *Horned Forms* (1944), painted at the same time as Bacon's *Three Studies* (which was not exhibited until 1945) has elements, including the bold, solid background and extended projections, that would come to be associated with Bacon's work.

Sutherland was attracted to the bohemian world and its recklessness and transgression while remaining conventional in his own domestic life. Bacon admired Sutherland's recent *Crucifixion*, writing to tell him that he found the work 'most awfully good'.[41] Later, the younger artist, as was his wont, would be cruel about Sutherland's work.

In 1946 Bacon sold *Painting 1946* – a disquieting work, full of threat, with hanging animal carcasses and symbolism reminiscent of Nazism – to his future dealer, Erica Brausen. She had been recommended to buy it by Sutherland. The more established painter had also taken Kenneth Clark, the director of the National Gallery, to Bacon's studio to see the work. Clark was offhand with Bacon and seemed outwardly unimpressed, but later told Sutherland, 'You and I may be in a minority of two, but we may still be right in thinking that Francis Bacon has genius.'[42] In 1948, Brausen sold *Painting 1946* to the Museum of Modern Art, New York, further enhancing Bacon's status. She was a German lesbian who had lived in Paris and was friends with Giacometti and Joan Miró, and was in the process of setting up the Hanover Gallery in London. It would become the single most important gallery for contemporary art in the capital in the 1950s. Her purchase of *Painting 1946* and continuing financial support of Bacon allowed the artist to escape from the dreariness of post-war London and head to Monte Carlo. There, he devoted more energy to gambling and his sybaritic tastes than to his art. His relish for a 'gilded gutter' life – mixing with both high-society figures and underworld criminals – endured from his teenage days, when he combined petty thievery with dining at the Ritz, through to his death.

The bond that Wirth-Miller and Bacon had struck back at Benton End was revived on Bacon's return from Monte Carlo in 1948. From that point onwards, Bacon would make his presence in Wivenhoe known by turning up at any hour of the day and banging on the door of the Storehouse. He would often arrive in a London taxi commandeered on the corner of Dean Street or Shaftesbury Avenue.

Chopping's diaries over the next few decades are peppered with references to Francis Bacon's frequent visits – 'FB down, late' is a common entry. Perhaps the most telling diary entries were those that featured entire days crossed out with a line and featuring the single word 'DRUNK'.

Chopping may have felt a twinge of jealousy when Bacon visited. For the best part of the previous decade, since the late 1930s, Chopping had fully captured Wirth-Miller's imagination. They had been co-conspirators on a shared adventure, sole confidants creating a new life on their own terms. Yet whenever Bacon walked through the door of the Storehouse, the privacy and quiet of their domestic construction was shattered. Bacon's force of character was so great that to some extent he monopolized Wirth-Miller's attention.

If Chopping had previously thought there were secrets that only he and Wirth-Miller could share, he now realized he was mistaken. Wirth-Miller hid very little from Bacon, and the candour was reciprocal. They were both often tender and compassionate, yet they were very direct in character, hated pretence and would say what they meant without reservation. Chopping should not have been surprised. In his final letter from prison on 5 January 1945, his partner had written, 'When I said yesterday I would never tell a lie again I meant that I would never conceal my opinions or my thoughts – because of fear of hurting someone – in the long run it causes much more hurt.' Bacon and Wirth-Miller were the successors to the Bloomsburian maxim that the transgression of excepted societal mores was irrelevant: expression and honesty were key.

Wirth-Miller felt liberated by his charismatic friend. Bacon's seriousness about his art very much reflected his own, and allowed him to discuss ideas and feelings that he felt may have been lost on Chopping, who was increasingly a professional illustrator rather than an artist attempting to express an interior, mental landscape. Wirth-Miller may have sought domestic bliss in the countryside, but his wildness was never far from the surface and his life had become too comfortable and risk-free for his liking.

On 12 April 1947, Wirth-Miller's work was included in the inaugural spring exhibition of the Colchester Art Society. The couple's notable older friends in the area, John Nash, Cedric Morris and Arthur Lett-Haines, had set up the organization (along with Henry Collins and Roderic Barrett) to promote the burgeoning art scene around the Essex and Suffolk border. One visitor to the exhibition, Tom Moody, recorded in his diary his pleasure at seeing works by John Nash (*Autumn Landscape, Wormingford*) and Cedric Miller (*Spoonbills*). He was less complimentary about more obviously modern works, but his full ire was saved for one work in particular:

> But we have on view a much more extreme specimen of sheer foolishness in the form of a lino-cut by Denis Wirth-Miller which would certainly attract astonished attention and excite controversy wherever it might be shown. This is a square foot of paper which appears to have been covered with boot blacking on which half-a-dozen thin white lines are irregularly traced, mostly straight but including a circle, in a style reminiscent of Paul Klee's 'Portrait of an Equilibrist'. The design – if it may be so dignified – is merely a scribble but Wirth-Miller has given it the title 'Fish-Face' and has marked its price as 'TWENTY GUINEAS!' [43]

Wirth-Miller had put Jankel Adler's tuition on monotype technique to good effect, if his desire was to stir up the anger of those who found modern art incomprehensible or in some way offensive. After the war, Adler had left 77 Bedford Gardens for a more sedate life in Aldbourne in Wiltshire. He died in 1949, the only one of ten siblings not to die in the Holocaust.

Wirth-Miller's relationship with the Lefevre Gallery was strengthening, and in January 1947 his work had been shown alongside that of the Roberts and Wyndham Lewis in *Gouaches and Drawings by British Artists*.

He often travelled to London to visit Bacon at his studio in Cromwell Place, from where the pair would head into Soho for nights of drinking and gambling. Bacon was in the course of completing his *Heads* series, having seemingly destroyed the works he produced while abroad. The mouths that first appeared in *Abstraction* (1937) and then the *Three Studies* (1944) were now human and screaming. The heads were caged and boxed in frames and the suggestion of extraordinary inner anguish was emphasized by the human figuration. Bacon had made the world smaller and stripped bare, with the figures more isolated and familiar, almost domestic – a man in a suit, the Pope – and the theatre was diminished. The anguish was now more recognizable to the viewer without the need of the drama of a crucifixion or vengeful Furies.

The author and critic Andrew Lambirth points to a similarity between a painting by Eileen Gray, who may well have influenced Bacon's furniture designs, and Bacon's *Heads*: 'Cage (*c.* 1940) contains a Francis Bacon-like space-frame, but it's unlikely that Gray would have known Bacon's work in 1940 – except perhaps as an interior designer. Bacon's own use of these skeletal boxes within a painting only really began in the mid-to-late 1940s.[44] The handling of the paint in *Cage* is very different from that of Bacon, but the form within the outlined cube and against a solid ground reveals that the two artists, perhaps unwittingly, shared an ability to transpose the tubularity of their furniture design into two-dimensional suggestions of imprisonment.

The last of the *Heads* series, *Head VI*, was the first of Bacon's works to be modelled on Diego Velázquez's *Portrait of Innocent X* (*c.* 1650). Bacon was said to be beginning to draw on his simultaneous sexual attraction to and dislike of his authoritarian father Edward, who had died during the war. To some, it was a further transgression to degrade the papal figure into a state of visceral, human anguish. The works were shown in Bacon's first solo exhibition, which took place in November 1949 at the Hanover Gallery – Erica Brausen finally had something to show for her faith and financial support of Bacon. Again, some critics recoiled, but the series confirmed that Bacon – this strange, make-up wearing outsider – could not be ignored as a force in contemporary painting. Wyndham Lewis responded to the series by calling Bacon 'one of the most powerful artists in Europe today and he is perfectly in tune with his time. Not like his namesake "the brightest, wisest of mankind", he is, on the other hand, one of the darkest and most possessed.'[45]

One afternoon in 1949, Wirth-Miller took Bacon to visit the Victoria and Albert Museum in order to show him the work of the Victorian photographer Eadweard Muybridge (1830–1904). Wirth-Miller had been fascinated by the photographic sequences of animals and human figures in motion since he had first arrived in London over a decade earlier. He understood his target audience, and how Bacon's interest in the triptych form could be related to Muybridge's series. As Peppiatt wrote of Bacon, 'his imagination was particularly stimulated by a sequence, with one form developing out of another'.[46]

Bacon was captivated. After that first exposure, he visited the Victoria and Albert Museum again before ordering a set of prints of his own. The images would have a significant effect on the work of both men over the next five years. After each of the artists' deaths, copies of Muybridge images were found littered on the ground of both their studios.

Following Dicky Chopping's death, the material in his own studio would reveal evidence of a little-known project that was occupying him at the time of Bacon's reintroduction into their lives. Chopping had persuaded Penguin to publish a quarterly magazine for children and it was vying for his attention with the immense flower-book project. He intended to fill the publication with work contributed by many of his friends. A manuscript of the proposed first issue contains a poem written by W. S. Graham, a story by Stephen Spender ('Pierino the Unicorn'), and illustrations produced by John Minton, Humphrey Spender (Stephen's brother) and Robert Colquhoun, as well as writing by Denton Welch ('The Burglar and the Packing Case').

Now little known, Welch, supported by Edith Sitwell and John Lehmann, found success in 1943 with his autobiographical work, *Maiden Voyage*. (Winston Churchill's secretary wrote, 'I have been told that it reeks of homosexuality. I think I must get it.'[47]) He had been a promising painter when he suffered a bad cycling accident in the mid-1930s. Despite his health problems, he associated with many members of the bohemian scene including John Minton, with whom he worked on vignettes for *Contemporary Cooking: Receipts from Vogue 1945–7*, and Chopping. He never fully recovered from his injuries and died in 1948 at the age of thirty-three, around the time that Chopping was attempting to publish the children's quarterly.

Weekend meetings concerning the progress of the magazine would take the contributors to the Storehouse or to Humphrey Spender's Wiltshire home in Sutton Veny. The magazine was never produced. The reasons remain unclear. Afterwards

Humphrey Spender wrote to Chopping, highlighting the problem with their esoteric occupations in the aftermath of war:

> It is only too easy to allow distractions to erode determination creating 'one more new botched beginning', to quote my brother Stephen. I think our predicament is to do with the validity of our occupation in a society which seems to shout that energies should be used to heal the wounds of the human race rather than to indulge our own creative urges. Certainly our society doesn't very clearly define roles for creative people.

The manuscript of the previously unknown Stephen Spender work, 'Pierino the Unicorn', found in the Storehouse archive, was corrected in Spender's hand and accompanied by Chopping's illustrations. Spender's son Matthew remembers that this story was written for him by his father, although he had never seen it. In the story, the children's enchanting, little white unicorn dies and the fools of the contemporary world are parodied. A character called 'The Word Master' challenges the brains of small children to reject conventional education and to think in an alternative manner. Spender and Chopping had attended the same school, Gresham's, but they had not known each other as Spender was eight years older. They later became friends, courtesy of Fitzrovia, Benton End and their overlapping social circles, and Spender was also much admired by Wirth-Miller. The couple attended Spender's events such as his seventieth birthday party at the Royal College of Art on 28 February 1979. In the summer of the same year they joined the Spenders, Lord and Lady Gladwyn and Lady Diana Cooper at the Aldeburgh Festival to honour the work of Benjamin Britten. The composer had died three years earlier in 1976. In the 1980s, Spender arranged for Chopping to attend the Hawthornden Castle writers' retreat.

As 1948 continued, Chopping and Frances Partridge were working exhaustively to hit their deadlines. The first volume of the flower-book series was due to go to press in December 1948.

As the publication date drew nearer, contact with Penguin became sparse. The authors found it difficult to get hold of Allen Lane, and instead of receiving any concrete information, they were palmed off with vague reassurances. Eventually, only days before the first volume was supposed to be printed, Penguin relayed some disquieting news: the date had to be shifted back by six months because the paper needed to print the book was 'still maturing'.

Partridge was outraged and, when Allen Lane tried to contact her, she 'left him simmering on the hob with no reply'. She told Chopping to 'issue a gnat's wail' to Eunice Frost in the hope that she might give them a realistic update. They were losing patience with their publisher and feeling despondent. 'One's libido in [Penguin's] direction is almost dead,' Partridge wrote to Chopping, 'but I do realise it is only dormant and could, were the signal to be given, start shooting sap along the veins, leaves, petioles and peduncles once more.'

When Chopping phoned Frost, she calmed his fears. She was adamant that Penguin was still fully behind the project, and that the delay genuinely was only a matter of logistics. He reported this back to Partridge, who said: 'You are too charitable by half about it. I think Eunice ought to be turned upside down and spanked. Oh I would like to spank that girl! I am sure that the old bird Lane was not to be caught so easily by showing his hand!' They cautiously continued their work, waiting for further word from Penguin. The publisher, however, fell silent again.

Chopping and Partridge were finally called to London for a meeting, without prior explanation, in the summer of 1949. Eunice Frost got straight to the point: if Penguin went any further with the project, it would bankrupt the company. The same accountants who had nodded so assuredly when they had backed the project in 1944 now repeated the gesture in confirmation of Frost's assertion.

Frost went on to explain that she had done everything in her power to keep the project alive. She had tried to get funding from the charitable Pilgrim Trust, but they had shown no interest. Chopping later described himself as sinking back into a red leather armchair, taking in the news. After the meeting, a Penguin employee told him that the furniture had been custom made for Heinrich Himmler's office in Berlin. Partridge thought it appropriately symbolic; Frost was Himmler to Lane's Little Hitler.

They spent much of the next year trying to persuade Penguin to relent, but Frost's verdict was final. The project was dead. Chopping and Partridge's five years of work had been for nothing.

Chopping had at least been on a retainer of £125 per quarter for the duration of his work on the books. Partridge was in a much worse position. Lane had promised her a fee upon completion so she would see no reward for her work. For some years afterwards, she claimed to be unable to look at a flower.

By the beginning of 1950, the Storehouse was starting to look like a home. Rather than turning his back on flowers Chopping helped Wirth–Miller in the long-neglected walled garden. They had learned the art of horticulture in the course of the odd jobs they had undertaken to earn their keep at Benton End, and had devoted much of their spare time at Felix Hall to cultivating its overgrown garden. On the rare weekends without guests at the Storehouse, they gradually created a three-tiered, stepped garden according to Wirth–Miller's design.

Wivenhoe had started to accept them. Everyone knew them, from the children working in shops at the weekend to the landlords who would have to push Chopping, Wirth-Miller, Bacon and visiting guests out of the Quayside pubs at closing time.

The Storehouse was once again a grand property, largely courtesy of Wirth-Miller. He sanded and waxed the wide oak floorboards of the upper two storeys, and plastered most of the house's walls in industrial brown wrapping paper. Together, they painted the ceilings a high-gloss off-white, and filled the house with books, *objets trouvés*, eclectic old furniture, and paintings and drawings they had bought or been given by friends.

Although Chopping's commitments meant that Wirth-Miller did most of the work on the house, the latter's career was also advancing. In 1948, his work was included in the *Colour-Prints* exhibition by the Society of London Painter-Printers at the Redfern Gallery, alongside Duncan Grant, Vanessa Bell, John Piper, Graham Sutherland and his close friends Colquhoun and MacBryde, John Minton and the recently deceased Jankel Adler. His painting, *The Bird-cage*, only commanded a price of four guineas and it was not illustrated in the catalogue, but it was significant for him to be listed among such high-profile names. In May of that year his friend Nina Hamnett was given a show of twenty-four watercolours, oils and drawings, mostly of Irish scenes, at the same gallery. (Also in the same year both Wirth-Miller and Chopping's work was included in *Contemporary Painting by East Anglian Artists*, an Arts Council exhibition at the Aldeburgh Festival – the beginning of a long association that the couple would have with Benjamin Britten's music and arts festival.)

The Londoners adored the improved Storehouse, trooping through the door and signing the visitors' book to formally announce that they had crossed into another world. It was not only the Soho crowd who were attracted there. Long after the end of her collaboration with Chopping, Frances Partridge and her circle of friends, including Janetta Woolley, would 'bust' the petrol ration to drive to Wivenhoe to spend time with Chopping and Wirth-Miller. Woolley, known in later life as Janetta Parladé after her marriage to the designer Jaime Parladé, would become a close friend to Bacon.

Partridge found Wivenhoe beautiful and particularly loved the Storehouse. She joked that their new interior could easily have been a page ripped from an imaginary magazine called 'House Comfortable, House Beautiful', saying the house was 'pure joy'. She liked its 'handsome black frontage standing proudly in the extraordinarily pure East Anglian light under a bright blue and white sky'. Together the three of them would lazily drift down the river in Wirth-Miller's boat to a remote creek off Rat Island. Here they would sunbathe, swim or read 'for days on end'.

In the winter, visitors could bolt themselves away with Chopping, Wirth-Miller and their stock of wine for company. On cold evenings when storms ripped across East Anglia, the couple would fill the house with the sound of Wagner's operas. Some guests loved it. Others were not so keen. Frances Partridge made it clear that she would refuse to have anything more to do with their dramatic Wagner evenings.

By this point, Chopping and Wirth-Miller had been together for over a decade. Their years of mutual experience had given them a sixth sense to pre-empt one another and they worked well together – as partners, hosts and sometimes in their professional endeavours – but they were as different as their closest friends: Frances and Francis. Their professional aims were sufficiently different to avoid jealousy or conflict of interest.

Chopping, mild, agreeable and easy to work with, had made a name for himself as an illustrator with a fluid, light style and attention to detail. Wirth-Miller was unpretentious but he was more the 'complicated artist', Nietzschean and internalized; he was beginning to focus on stark, brooding works.

Their differences in character would sometimes cause ructions. 'For years we have been tied together with the worst sort of strangling apron strings,' Chopping recorded in his diary. 'Denis feels things with painful acuteness and then starts to think, analyse, dissect and understand what he has felt . . . on the way he gets lost in a labyrinth and his original feeling is forgotten and replaced by another.'

When Wirth-Miller had been drinking, he was usually still entertaining, lucid and interesting, but sometimes he would lash out. Chopping called these unpredictable bursts 'the dark force'. Friends noticed the conflicts between them. Robert Gathorne-Hardy, whom they had met through the Nashes in Wormingford, wrote to them:

> I hope, passionately, that you will both follow my example in the matter of united bliss. Remember bliss does involve an absence of vexations and agonies. Kyrle [Leng] and I have known each other for twenty-nine years now, and in January will have lived together for twenty-five. Try and beat our record if it is remotely possible.

Despite the quarrels, they knew that they could. There was no one who could permanently come between them. Not even Francis Bacon.

Chapter 9
Colony of Artists

In the immediate post-war years, Fitzrovia thrived once more. Denis Wirth-Miller, Richard Chopping and their large circle of artists and writers continued to go to the Wheatsheaf and Fitzroy, and eat at the White Tower, a Greek restaurant that had replaced the Tour Eiffel. Fitzrovia would remain an important centre for working artists for some years to come. The notable *Weekend Exhibitions* featuring abstract work by Victor Pasmore, William Scott, Terry Frost and Roger Hilton took place at Adrian Heath's studio at 22 Fitzroy Street in 1952–3. Increasingly, however, those who wished to push boundaries and seek excess were drawn to Soho.

John Minton would often eat at Wheeler's, the fish restaurant in Old Compton Street. He was introduced to the restaurant, which opened in 1929, by the artist Rodrigo Moynihan, who was the professor of the painting school at the Royal College of Art, and his wife, Elinor Bellingham-Smith. The restaurant became a regular haunt of the bohemian crowd, including Chopping and Wirth-Miller, and was a staple of Francis Bacon's routine. He became a favoured customer because of his loyalty and generous tips, and his sometimes drunken behaviour became part of the restaurant's allure. Bacon, despite his alcohol intake, was careful about his diet and ate fish at Wheeler's on most days and forewent dessert.

Despite the fact that he was often rude to the fey and insecure Minton, they had similar taste. As well as Wheeler's, both men were also habitués of the Gargoyle. Minton became such a regular that the band leader would play one of his favourite tunes – 'I'm Going to Sit Right Down and Write Myself a Letter' or 'My Very Good Friend the Milkman' – when he came into the club. He was also commissioned to add a mural to Matisse and Lutyens's interior.

The Wivenhoe couple, the Roberts, the Moynihans, Lucian Freud, Philip Toynbee and the young artist Michael Wishart were all regulars at the Gargoyle, as were Angus Wilson and Cyril Connolly. Also included in the circle, courtesy of taking a studio alongside the Roberts at 77 Bedford Gardens, were Ronald Searle, creator of the St Trinian's stories, and his wife, Kaye Webb, a journalist who would become a major force at Puffin Books.

Minton was often the centre of attention at the Gargoyle because of his flamboyancy and generosity, as well as his unusual dancing. Ruthven Todd wrote:

In my pictorial memory, I have a coloured movie of his long, sad, clown's face, lashed by breakers of dark hair, as he danced a frenetic solo on the otherwise unoccupied dance-floor. His arms and legs were flying this way and that – the limbs of a loosely strung puppet, each of which was being worked by a strong conviction about what his limbs should do.[48]

Bacon's future biographer Daniel Farson encountered Minton and Wirth-Miller in the middle of a night of excess at the Gargoyle, alongside the aristocratic socialite, Lady Diana Cooper. Minton was fond of men in uniform and had brought a group of sailors to the club. While Minton did his strange dance, Wirth-Miller stood on his chair. He thrust a one-pound note into his mouth, followed by a five-pound note, and chewed, possibly drunkenly, to illustrate the meaningless of wealth. Minton managed to extract the five-pound note, and Wirth-Miller ran up the stairs to the lavatory. Farson suspected that he put a finger down his throat in order to retrieve the remaining note and wash it off.[49]

From 1948 onwards, there was a further reason to be in Soho rather than Fitzrovia. Muriel Belcher, who had formerly run a club called the Music Box in Leicester Square, opened the Colony Room club, often just called 'Muriel's', on 41 Dean Street. It was technically a members' club so it escaped the strict licensing laws that closed the pubs from 2.30 to 6.30 p.m. Bacon signed up on the first day it opened its doors. Belcher – Jewish, acerbic and lesbian – found him compelling and subsequently granted him free drinks, provided he could lure in a quota of friends and patrons. Wirth-Miller was one of the first Bacon brought in, and was quick to sign up himself. He thrived in the seedy club, but Chopping, whom he hauled in shortly afterwards, always described it as a 'hellhole'.

Belcher was archly camp and often used female pronouns for men. She called Bacon her 'daughter'. Christopher Hitchens recalled, 'Muriel, arguably the rudest person in England ("shut up cunty and order some more champagne"), almost never left her perch at the corner of the bar and was committed to that form of humour that insists on referring to all gentlemen as ladies.'[50] For Chopping the joke wore thin, but Bacon and Wirth-Miller persisted with that manner of speech for years to come, using it to make an arched point even though neither of them was very effeminate.

The Colony's décor was not as refined as the fading Gargoyle. The walls were painted an intense green, and the steps to its door smelt of rubbish and urine. It was anti-refinement, anti-pretention, anti-establishment and pro-hedonism. As well as Wirth-Miller and Bacon, it soon attracted what became a close-knit group of artists, actors, writers and misfits who disliked the ongoing conservatism of post-war Britain. Wirth-Miller's friends Nina Hamnett, John Minton and the Roberts were regulars, along with fellow artists Frank Auerbach, Patrick Caulfield and Michael Andrews. The clientele also included Lucian Freud, the actor Peter O'Toole, the musician George Melly and the photographer John Deakin. Its green walls became increasingly covered by artworks, some of which were executed by its members. During the 1950s, it may have sometimes seemed that all the major progressive players in the post-war British art world were crammed inside at the same time. And if Muriel Belcher was queen, Francis Bacon was king.

While Wirth-Miller became Bacon's most enduring friend, the more famous painter was also close to Wirth-Miller's enemy, Lucian Freud. The two men would often be seen at the club together until they fell out permanently in later life. The Colony gave Freud and Bacon plenty of opportunity to witness human interplay in a raw, raucous, unconstrained and sometimes obscene state. The Colony was a place of drunken arguments and excessive revelry, where the veneer of manners and respectability was often stripped away. As the author Douglas Sutherland wrote: 'You cannot really expect to have such diverse personalities packed in a small smoke-filled room, with the drinks rattling across the counter like bursts of machine gun fire, and maintain the calm of a tea party on the vicarage lawn.'[51] Among the arch campness and Polari, the base truth of character was exposed, and the observation of it seeped into both men's work.

When Freud married Caroline Blackwood in 1953, she was incorporated into their shambolic afternoons and evenings at

Wheeler's, the Colony and the Gargoyle. Freud and Bacon were so close that Blackwood would later say that she had dinner with Bacon every night for almost her entire five-year marriage to Freud.[52]

Many of the regulars in the Colony Room would become the subject of Bacon's paintings, particularly as he turned more towards portraiture in the 1960s. Colony Room regular Henrietta Moraes was painted many times by Bacon. She had a short marriage to a body-builder, Norman Bowler, who was also part of the Colony Room set. Johnny Minton, often drawn to the unobtainable, became obsessively interested in Bowler, and would monitor Moraes and Bowler's relationship in the Colony Room. One of Bowler and Moraes's children was later revealed to be the biological son of Colin Tennant, the nephew of the Gargoyle's owner, David Tennant.

One of Bacon's close friends and the subject of multiple paintings was the artist Isabel Rawsthorne, who was the sometime lover of Giacometti – one of the few living artists whom Bacon admired. Her world intersected with that of Chopping and Wirth-Miller. She was friends with Dylan Thomas, Peter Watson and Ian Fleming, and, once she married Alan Rawsthorne, settled at Thaxted in rural Essex, thirty-five miles from Wivenhoe. Originally concerned with expressionist renderings of dance and movement she, like Wirth-Miller, became inspired by the Essex countryside.

The Roberts and Nina Hamnett were eventually barred from the Colony Room so they would go to the Caves de France next door, as would Wirth-Miller, W. S. Graham when he was in London, the artist William Crozier, who was a close friend of the Roberts, and Bacon. It was a long bar with a subterranean atmosphere that was not as clique-ridden as the Colony, but the mood was similarly hedonistic. Another drinking establishment on Bacon and Wirth-Miller's radar was the Kismet, run by 'Maltese Mary' Douse, and frequented by both criminals and shady policemen. Fiona Green, a friend of Crozier, said that Douse, 'kept all Francis Bacon's cheques and said one day she would sell them for the signatures!'[53] Bacon would have been appalled.

While there were many planned parties and weekend stays at the Storehouse, it also became a more impromptu venue. In the late 1940s, Francis Bacon had befriended the younger artist Michael Wishart, who was born in 1928. They would spend long evenings talking about art and dining on the likes of spaghetti with walnuts and garlic at Bacon's studio in Cromwell Place – Bacon was an adventurous cook for the time. Wishart met the artist Anne Dunn not long after becoming friends with Bacon, and the two were soon engaged. An engagement party was held at Bacon's studio – for which the artist painted almost everything, including his chandeliers, red. The party continued for some days and every time the guests ran dry of champagne, Bacon would ask Ian Board, the barman at the Colony Room, to arrange further supplies. The party was finally starting to flag when Chopping and Wirth-Miller proposed a change of scene. The revellers headed to Wivenhoe in a fleet of taxis. The party would continue for two more days. David Tennant of the Gargoyle Club christened it as, 'The first great party since the war.'

Marathons like these were not uncommon. One Easter, Chopping and Wirth-Miller invited Francis Bacon, John Minton and Paul Danquah to lunch at the Storehouse. Danquah, who starred in *A Taste of Honey* in 1961, was the son of a Ghanaian statesman, J. B. Danquah, who is credited with giving the British Gold Coast the name of Ghana on its independence in 1957. Paul Danquah was a regular at the Colony and would later live at 5 Shaftesbury Villas, Allen Street, in the same building as

Minton. The latter also brought over his friend and occasional lover Ricky Stride, a body-building ex-sailor. Once everyone was drunk, Stride demanded the room's attention. He stood up, undid his flies, and shocked the room by revealing the double urinary slit of his penis.

Minton became the youngest teacher at the Royal College of Art in 1949, where he worked under Rodrigo Moynihan, following spells teaching at Camberwell School of Art and the Central School. He was inundated with illustration commissions and his gentle neo-Romanticism had seen him feted as one of the most promising young artists in the country. The Lefevre made him one of the principal artists in its stable and gave him a series of solo exhibitions, and he now seemed to be of more or less equal rank with the Roberts. In June 1950, the *Daily Express* summed him up as 'a brilliant exhibitioner in London and New York, and one of our most sought-after magazine illustrators'.[54] The neuroses that had become evident at Bedford Gardens were less obvious.

He often travelled up to Wivenhoe, where he and Wirth-Miller would spend afternoons sketching and painting landscapes and individual trees by the estuary. One Saturday, while they laid out their equipment next to the Colne, Minton told Wirth-Miller his method of warding off 'pesky, nosey busybodies' who interrupted his work when painting al fresco. He claimed that the best way to get rid of an intruder was to approach them with a straight face and daub a criss-cross of paint onto the front of their shirt.

'I have already used this method with Prussian blue on a white ground,' he continued. 'It really works wonders. By the time the recipient has cleaned off the mark or gone off to change you have ample time to finish in peace. With a child you would plant your brush strokes on the nose. A different psychology has to be applied to varying offenders. Well-meaning ones only need a mere wave of the brush to threaten.'

Their friendship was unlikely given that Minton was sensitive and took criticism badly, and Wirth-Miller was always honest and direct in his appraisal, but they were extremely close.

The hedonism of those years masked the effort Chopping and Wirth-Miller put into their work. By this time, they had set up their studios in the workers' cottages alongside the garden. Like Francis Bacon, Wirth-Miller worked with discipline, rising early whatever the effects of the night before, and he would paint through to the afternoon. His labours were paying off as he continued to hone the bleak marshland landscapes that would later bring him success.

At this stage, Wirth-Miller's domestic neatness led him to being ridiculed by some of his more artistically exuberant friends. John Minton said in a thank-you letter following one of his many trips to Wivenhoe: 'Your studio is far too tidy, personally I like a mess.' He admired Wirth-Miller's work, though, telling Chopping in a letter of 15 January 1949 that he 'liked his Redfern pictures'. In the same letter Minton apologized for some unknown action, saying 'Perhaps something more considered would have been better, but it's so difficult to organize and me never off the drink.'

Wirth-Miller was given further exposure in 1949–50. Francis Bacon and Graham Sutherland had rekindled their friendship following Bacon's time overseas. When they came to stay at the Storehouse together, they revealed that Alfred Hecht, the framer of choice for both artists, had a vacancy for a show in his shop's small exhibition space. Sutherland said he would lobby Hecht to hang some of Wirth-Miller's works. Following the visit, Bacon wrote to Wirth-Miller: 'Thank you and Dicky both so much for having me to stay. I enjoyed it so much in spite of my [illegible] – had a very good journey with Graham who is a great admirer of you both – thank you again.'

Bacon's letter to Wirth–Miller mentioning Graham Sutherland's admiration of both Wirth–Miller and Chopping. *(© The Estate of Francis Bacon. All rights reserved. DACS 2016)*

Sutherland may have only been a dozen years older than Wirth–Miller, but as part of a far more established generation of artists, his backing meant a great deal (as proven when Brausen bought *Painting 1946* on his recommendation). He was reaching the peak of his popularity and attracting major municipal commissions. As confirmation of his elevation, he had been appointed a trustee of the Tate Gallery in 1948. Hecht duly took Sutherland's advice and exhibited Wirth–Miller's works.

Sutherland became a supportive counsellor to Wirth–Miller. His artistic instruction and influence inspired the younger artist to develop his painting skills. Wirth–Miller later remembered Sutherland, who would return as a guest to the Storehouse, enjoying the lively gay banter of himself, Francis Bacon, Albert Hecht and the gallerist Arthur Jeffress. The straight, more conservative painter, sometimes dubbed 'an honorary homosexual', would happily join in.

While having a show at the framer's King's Road shop was not as prestigious as a solo exhibition at the Lefevre, it was another success for Wirth–Miller. As Hecht was the leading framer for contemporary art, many major artists and gallerists went through his doors. But if Wirth–Miller had hopes that Sutherland himself would attend the opening, he was to be disappointed. The older artist had become embroiled in a scandal at the Tate when he backed a campaign to oust the museum's director, John Rothenstein. Many in the art community and on the gallery's staff were opposed to Rothenstein, who appeared to dislike modern European art (and that of the Bloomsbury Group). In 1941, he chose not to purchase Matisse's *The Red Studio*, which had hung in the Gargoyle Club, from David Tennant for a few hundred pounds. The work consequently ended up in New York, at MoMA, in 1949 and many felt he had failed in his duty to keep such an important artwork for the nation. Donald Cooper, an art historian and collector of cubist works, led an open campaign against Rothenstein, which Sutherland supported. In 1950, the antagonism would come to a head when Rothenstein punched Cooper at an art reception. As a result of his involvement, Sutherland decided to lie low.

'I'm sorry I've been unable to get to your show,' Sutherland wrote to Wirth–Miller, 'and I'm grateful that you understand my reason for not being able to do so. I will try to see it.' He would, he said, encourage his patron Colin Anderson to pay a visit, although he could not promise anything. 'Owing to the Tate Affair,' he said, they were 'not much en-rapport'.

Francis Bacon's visits to the Storehouse were becoming more regular, and Chopping enjoyed his company. Although they would remain fond of each other for the remainder of their lives, Chopping was increasingly aware that Bacon was unwittingly driving a wedge between himself and Wirth-Miller. His partner would react by telling him that he was possessive and hypocritical, too. Chopping's own friendship with Frances Partridge was just as close and equally exclusive.

Their relationship was not helped by their continuing lack of money. The royalties from Chopping's illustrations and Wirth-Miller's few painting sales did not bring in enough revenue to instill any sense of security. Wirth-Miller was even struggling to pay for his artistic materials. He wrote to Bacon complaining that he had no way of competing with his peers if he could not afford the basic tools of his trade.

Nevertheless, the couple would carefully save enough funds so that they could occasionally travel abroad. Taking separate holidays, as they were advised to do by Partridge, became a solution to the bouts of cabin fever that would sweep through the Storehouse from time to time.

In May 1951, Chopping travelled to Spain alone for a few days. When he was having a drink alone at the bar of his hotel, an Englishman approached him and seemed very interested in getting to know more about him. At first, he was delighted to have the attention, but the stranger's line of questioning grew increasingly odd, verging on intrusive. Before long, other English-speaking men began to gather around him, asking him questions about a man called Guy Burgess. It became clear that the men were journalists who had been sent on a mission to track down Chopping, with a photographer in tow. He was forced to barricade himself in his room.

Chopping had heard of Burgess from Paul Danquah's new boyfriend, Peter Pollock, who had been a guest at the Storehouse. Burgess had been Pollock's lover until a few years earlier and he was also an acquaintance of one of Partridge's close friends, the novelist Rosamond Lehmann (brother of John Lehmann of the Hogarth Press), but Chopping had never met him. The little he knew about Burgess was that he was a high-level producer at the BBC, a homosexual, a chronic drunk and famously rude. Consequently, Chopping had no idea why, while he was on holiday, he was surrounded by journalists with a barrage of questions about him.

It emerged that, days earlier, Burgess had fled to the Soviet Union, leaving no explanation for his disappearance. The press soon found out that his travelling companion was Donald MacLean, a suspected spy. It transpired that Burgess was a committed Marxist who, prior to joining the BBC, had handled sensitive information for MI6 – which he had passed on to the Russians. The story hit the front pages, and journalists had started tracking down people connected to the pair. Chopping had become implicated.

When he finally got to the bottom of the mystery, he discovered the connection was tenuous. Rosamond Lehmann had written a letter to Stephen Spender that went some way to confirming Burgess's guilt. Spender, who like many left-wing intellectuals had turned against Stalin and Soviet communism after the Second World War, had leaked the document to the *Daily Express*. The papers started examining both Burgess's and Lehmann's circles, focusing on their homosexual friends. Paul Danquah and Peter Pollock fled the country shortly before the police ransacked their flat.

The *Express* obtained a photograph of Chopping, Wirth–Miller, Danquah and Pollock outside the Storehouse, leaning against Pollock's new Rolls-Royce. The paper erroneously stated that Danquah and Pollock shared the house together, and also claimed that Chopping had been a school friend of Donald MacLean at Gresham's. MacLean, who was five years older than Chopping, had left the school by the time he arrived there. The journalists imparted the false information with a homophobic undertone. Subsequently, Chopping had been tracked down to Spain, and the men haranguing him at the bar thought he was MacLean's friend and probably a 'queer' traitor.

Chopping returned to England and spent a few weeks living as a recluse in Wivenhoe until press interest died down. He was determined that the next time his name made the newspapers, the press would be reviewing his art rather than his sexual and political orientation.

In February 1952, George VI died, and a letter from Frances Partridge to Dicky Chopping, sent later that month, reveals how their worlds had continued to overlap since the demise of the flower-book project:

> I was up in London for 3 days over the King's Funeral time, partly to go to Quentin Bell's wedding party which was very gay with lots of champagne & dear old friends' faces. He has married a very nice, sweet girl, rather beautiful in a remote way, called Olivia Popham – who lived with painter Graham Bell shot down in the war. So she goes from Bell to Bell. We dined after the party with Angelica [daughter of Vanessa Ball and Duncan Grant] & Bunny Garnett [David Garnett, at whose Bloomsbury bookshop Partridge had worked in the 1920s] & Julia [Strachey] & Lawrence [Gowing] & I thought

all the old friends even with their grey heads were so gay & amusing & lively compared to the younger Gargoyle gin-drinkers whom I had spent the evening before with. That was a very odd evening starting with my taking Janetta out to the Ivy tête-à-tête. Later we met Derek Jackson [Janetta Woolley's fourth husband, a wealthy scientist and a 'rampant bisexual' according to Chopping] & Sonia Brownell at the Gargoyle – where we ran into Francis Bacon & his boyfriend & Lucian Freud & Francis Wyndham etc. etc. Bacon was most amusing & charming & stood everyone the Champagne in a reckless way. I thought him delightful – [he] was kissing Derek with great passion as they sat on the banquette – & then would turn & say 'we're talking about Homosexuality, if you know what I mean'. The boyfriend was as light as an owl & blinked unceasingly. I can hardly imagine that even when sober he could have been other than repulsive. Lucian Freud is a queer chap isn't he? – so deadly grave & self-conscious looking; no irony, no light touch & it seemed to me a great desire to be rude for the sheer love of the thing. I can't think how he gets so many rich girls to adore him – for he's no oil painting either. In the end we fetched up at Claridge's where all the Kings & Queens were staying & sat for a bit in Janetta & Derek's private sitting-room. It was hideous beyond your wildest dreams & the much vaunted log fire had gone out – I couldn't really see the point of paying such vast sums for nothing better than you get at the G.W. Hotel . . . I had an argument with Freud going home, who seemed to think it all wonderful.

Chopping had continued to draw and paint independently since the flower–book project had folded. In 1950 he fulfilled a commission to supply three butterfly and moth plates for *Nature Through the Seasons in Colour*, published by Odhams Press.

He then started adapting the skills he had learned from undertaking the vast number of botanical drawings into a new take on *trompe l'oeil*. The optical illusion of realistically depicting a three-dimensional object on a flat surface had a long history from ancient Classical murals onwards and reached a high point in Flemish and Dutch works in the sixteenth and seventeenth centuries. There was, however, no particular interest in the medium when Chopping started to lift his images of plants, animals and objects off the surface around the start of the 1950s.

In an interview with *La Revue Moderne* in 1952 he described his approach to *trompe l'oeil*: 'I try to see with the eye of a camera and I seek to paint what I see with the exactitude of a scientific observer allied to the sensibility of a painter.'

That interview followed sudden interest in his new style of work. He had been confident enough to put forward works for inclusion in the Royal Academy of Arts 1952 *Summer Exhibition* and they were accepted. Exhibit 849, *Apples*, and Exhibit 856, *Moss Rose*, were shown in the gallery's South Room. Exhibit 1030, *Stinking Hellebore*, was displayed in Gallery IV. Alfred Munnings, the former president of the Royal Academy and enemy of Morris and Lett-Haines, had made a drunken, scathing attack on modern art in 1949. Three years later, the gallery was still excluding work that leaned towards abstraction of the avant-garde. Wirth-Miller's work, and that of many of their friends, had been rejected, but the gallery's conservatism benefited Chopping.

The press praised his paintings, with one critic writing, 'Richard Wasey Chopping's "Apples" are witty but there is a tenderness about their wit. They glimmer beyond the picture. They are apples from a garden of the mind.' Another wrote, 'Richard Chopping's flowers are particularly fine'.[55] Chopping realized that his future could once again include an exhibiting career. He was now showing works alongside Stanley Spencer, John Nash, Edward Bawden and Munnings. Minton was included in the *Summer Exhibition*, and showed *The Death of Nelson* as well as his portrait of the wrestler Spencer Churchill. In the same show the unrelated Winston Churchill exhibited *Sunset over Jerusalem*.

Chopping hoped that a gallery might be interested in selling his works, including the illustrations for the aborted flower-book project. Having worked almost exclusively as an illustrator for the past decade, he was not confident in making an approach.

Francis Bacon stepped in to help, even though his private life was troubled. Eric Hall, the partner and father-figure who had helped support him since his early days as a painter, moved out of Cromwell Place in 1949–50. Perhaps not coincidentally, Bacon strengthened ties with his immediate family. He made the long trip to southern Africa to see his mother Winnie and sisters Ianthe and Winnie, in November 1950; his mother had remarried following the death of Edward Bacon and the family had relocated. Shortly after he returned, on 30 April 1951, Bacon lost one of the other key people in his life: his nanny, Jessie Lightfoot. In grief, he abandoned Cromwell Place and the studio in which he had productively worked since 1943. (Robert Buhler, Wirth-Miller and Chopping's old friend from their Fitzrovian days, took on the studio.)

Bacon introduced Chopping to Erica Brausen, and the head of the Hanover Gallery was taken by the *trompe l'oeil* paintings in his portfolio. She agreed with her financial backer, Arthur Jeffress, to include Chopping's work in a show, entitled *Contrast in Art*, later that year. It was a three-man show that would feature the work of Bacon on the ground floor and that of a French prince, Jean-Louis de Faucigny-Lucinge, in the upstairs gallery. The prince was a supporter and friend of Salvador Dalí. Chopping's work was hung in a small gallery at the back of the building, which he described as being 'like a kind of long lavatory'.

Brausen was forced to issue strongly worded letters to Chopping when he was panicking about completing enough works in time for the show. He wrote from London to Wirth-Miller saying how he longed to be able to match Bacon's swift productivity. In reply, his partner reminded him, 'Francis is a law unto himself and having invented his way of doing it can of course "slap the stuff down" . . . you don't need a watchmaker's lens to repair Big Ben – but both are time pieces. For you, your interest is not Big Ben.'

In the run-up to the show, Chopping stayed with John Minton, who had recently moved to 5 Shaftesbury Villas on Allen Street, Kensington. After six years, Minton and Keith Vaughan had given up the lease on the flat and studio they shared at Hamilton Terrace in St John's Wood. Like Minton, Vaughan, whom Chopping and Wirth-Miller knew well, was enjoying a very successful career with shows at the Lefevre, Redfern and Hanover. Although beset by his own issues, including about his sexuality, Vaughan may have been a stabilizing influence on Minton but their friendship had cooled.

Minton's flightiness may not have helped Chopping's anxiousness in the run-up to the exhibition. Chopping made an ill-considered complaint to the Hanover Gallery that revealed his insecurity:

> I have been extravagant over the framing, to a point which I can ill-afford, in order to live up to the Hanover Gallery, and I feel it is not unreasonable to ask for a really good card to announce me, rather than a flimsy piece of paper. I do feel there should be as little differentiation as possible between Francis, the Prince de F.L. and myself.

Robert Melville, the gallery's secretary who was also an esteemed critic, squashed the upstart:

> We are not amused by your remarks about our Invitation-Catalogues. Our clients like them, and since they receive them gratis the question of what you so unpleasantly call 'ill-advised economy' does not arise.
>
> The situation is this: the printers are setting up the material, and de Faucigny-Lucinge is having an invitation catalogue identical in format but with a different colour. Francis Bacon has an Invitation Card, but will have no catalogue at all.
>
> Artists who want special treatment contribute to the expense, and now it is too late to raise the issue.

Chopping's complaints immediately ceased.

His guest list for the Hanover show, which opened on 9 December 1952, was impressive. It included Quentin Bell, the Bloomsbury writer and artist, the writer Ruth Lowinsky and her surrealist painter husband Thomas, Ernest Thesinger, the actor from *The Bride of Frankenstein*, and Robert Kee, the journalist and author who was married to Janetta Woolley in 1948–50. Noel Carrington and the Partridges, who all attended the private view, were responsible for engineering some of those connections. Afterwards Carrington wrote to Chopping, 'I am very interested in the huge Francis Bacon paintings as they were not "tortured" or "hideous" or "obscene"! Evidently the wide open spaces suit him: but where can you hang such things? Only in liners or board-rooms.'

Coincidentally, Kathleen 'Mog' Hale, whose *Orlando the Marmalade Cat* series had by now made her a household name, promised to bring the art collector and shipping magnate Sir

Colin Anderson. The collector was looking for pictures for his new Orient Liner, *Oransay*, and had already purchased Graham Sutherland paintings for the vessel. Anderson bought several of Chopping's works. The artist gratefully thanked Mog, who replied, 'Well, we must never leave stones unturned', and in the same letter said she was arranging for a friend at *Vogue* to review the exhibition.

Two other friends that helped Chopping with his guest list were the artists Michael Wishart and Anne Dunn, the couple whose engagement party had been extended at the Storehouse. As many fellow artists did sooner or later, they had since fallen out with Francis Bacon. Dunn returned the invitation to the joint *Contrast in Art* show with the words: 'Mr Francis Bacon is my very least favourite artist and I won't be a patron.' Nevertheless, they compiled a list of invitees specifically for Chopping; Anne's family were well connected and the list included Christopher Fry, Alec Guinness and Michael Redgrave. Dunn, whose work was admired by the critic John Russell, would go on to have solo exhibitions in London and New York. After divorcing Wishart she married Rodrigo Moynihan, and co-edited an arts journal with Moynihan and another of Chopping and Wirth-Miller's friends, Sonia Orwell (née Brownell).

On 9 December, the weather was poor but the private view was packed. Fidelity, Countess Cranbrook, a philanthropist whom Chopping had met through Robert Gathorne-Hardy, commented that she was 'gloriously fiddle-fuddled' on the champagne. Joan 'Maudie' Warburton, the friend who had introduced Chopping and Wirth-Miller to Benton End, described the evening as 'an orgy of art, where I behaved very badly with all that lovely drink inside me'.

Nina Hamnett was also in attendance. She enthused about Chopping's work and gave him a pack of French playing cards that dated from 1816. The old bohemian had finally given him her vote of confidence; he painted the cards the following year and would keep them carefully stored in an envelope until he died.

Minton invited the guests to his flat for a post-show party, which was attended by Bacon, Rosamond Lehmann and Cecil Beaton. The photographer had planned to bring Peter Watson, but the philanthropist had been too ill.

Also absent was one of Chopping's former idols. His telegrams to John Gielgud had ceased after Wirth-Miller's false-teeth revelation, but he still took the opportunity to invite the actor to the private view. On 6 December 1952 Gielgud sent his apologies from Cowley Street, SW1, for being unable to attend the show 'and the after party at Mr Minton's'. Another person to reject an invitation was the Queen. Apparently she already had enough flower pictures.

The nature of the exhibition meant that Chopping's work was reviewed alongside that of Francis Bacon but, much to his surprise, he held his own. The *Daily Express*'s Bruce Blunt wrote on 17 December 1952:

Bacon makes no concession to anybody or anything. He offers no clue to his pictures. They have no titles. They are strangely terrifying and I think they are meant to be. The subjects are chiefly a single figure, animal or human, against a background of some phantasmal tropic scene. These creatures are charged with intensity of pity and terror. You feel they are burning to deliver a message. You are not quite sure what it is, but you have an uncomfortable feeling that it is far from being complimentary to the human race. The contrast is on the first floor, where there are small and exquisite watercolours of wild flowers and

the art of trompe l'oeil by Richard Chopping. This delicate
'deceive the eye' artistic joke has laughed quietly through
the centuries. The artist's aim is to paint a composite
picture with such skill that he tricks you into thinking that
a playing card, or a flower petal or a fly or a newspaper
cutting is the real thing and not painted. It is, in fact,
surrealism (which nails its kipper to the mast) in reverse.
And just because these pictures are amusing, it does not
prevent some of them also being beautiful.

Bruce Blunt may have been unaware that, a year earlier, his
paper had smeared Chopping's name and attempted to drag him
into the Burgess–MacLean affair.

The critic from the *Evening Standard* claimed to be able 'to
smell the scent of the flowers' in Chopping's art. Other articles
mentioned that a fly, a flower petal and a newspaper cutting were
fast becoming the motifs of Chopping's work – all would later
become components of his James Bond covers.

The commercial success of the show – a sell-out – helped
repair any rifts with the Hanover. It led to a sudden influx of
money for the artist, leading Brausen to begin one letter, 'Dear
Shopping Richard'.

Chopping and Wirth-Miller were taken aback at the speed
of his success. It soon opened the door to more fashionable
circles. They were now invited to mix with the rich, famous
and titled, and Chopping started receiving commissions,
including for portraits. He recalled attending a soirée at the
penthouse apartment of Helena Rubinstein, the multimillionaire
cosmetics mogul. The apartment, with a double-height atrium,
overlooked Hyde Park's South Carriage Drive. He described
Rubenstein as 'a wonderful gypsy-like creature with remarkable
dark hair tightly drawn-back across her skull'. His commissions

now included one from Princess Christina Margarethe of Hesse, who had purchased paintings from the Hanover show. He was also commissioned to produce a portrait for Viscount Waldorf Astor to be painted at his Cliveden home.

Just weeks before, Chopping and Wirth-Miller had been filling out their regular football pools coupon in an attempt to alleviate their constant lack of funds.

Chapter 10

The Party Line

The Hanover's *Contrasts in Art* closed in January 1953. Dicky Chopping packed up his things from John Minton's flat and went home. When he arrived, there was a letter waiting for him from Noel Carrington dated 21 January. 'I suppose you are basking in the success of the exhibition in the winter sunlight of the [Essex] Riviera,' it read, 'I continuously envy you living on the sea.'

On the evening of the 31 January, a storm hit Belgium, the Netherlands and Britain, destroying property and killing thousands. Essex and Suffolk suffered badly, and in Jaywick alone thirty-seven people lost their lives. Wivenhoe was spared the worst but, by the morning of 1 February, it was half-submerged. The properties by the Colne estuary bore the brunt.

Chopping and Wirth-Miller woke to find that the ground floor of the Storehouse was now underwater. The stench was intense because Wivenhoe's sewers had been overwhelmed. Over half a decade's work on their house had been ruined overnight.

One consolation was that Wirth-Miller's interior décor had already suffered due to the frequent, inebriated presence of Bacon, Colquhoun and MacBryde. The Roberts were at this point spending even more time at the Storehouse as they were often in the area. Between 1951 and 1954, they were somewhat improbably hired as nannies/housekeepers at Tilty Mill, the

Essex house that the Canadian poet Elizabeth Smart had sublet from Ruthven Todd, a friend of Dylan Thomas. More improbably still, they proved to be good babysitters. Smart had four children with the Roberts's friend, the poet George Barker, whom they had known since their early days in London. Smart had become a successful journalist and asked the artists to look after the children during the week while she was working in London. In return they could live at Tilty Mill rent-free and set up their studios there.

Babysitting may have been a forte, but housekeeping was not. The Roberts had not modified their behaviour since being feted by the art world. Like the Storehouse, Tilty Mill became another Essex offshoot of bohemia with visits from the Wivenhoe couple, W. S. Graham and John Deakin. They still drank heavily (by this time, according to their biographer Roger Bristow, they were 'classifiably alcoholic'[56]), were quick with their fists and promiscuous. On 25 February 1952, Keith Vaughan came home from dinner with John Minton, Christopher Isherwood and E. M. Forster to find his boyfriend Ramsay McClure in bed with Robert Colquhoun. He noted in his diary: 'Surprised to find myself just the least bit piqued.'[57]

Ruthven Todd returned to Tilty Mill in late 1953, having been with Dylan Thomas in the United States when the poet died, to find Graham and Nessie Dunsmuir also living there. Nearly all of the windows had been smashed and the furnishings damaged; he later wrote that 'all around, sluttishness and destruction had run riot'.[58]

Another consolation for Chopping and Wirth-Miller after the storm was that, thanks to Chopping's recent success, they had the money to decorate the house.

Once the flood had subsided, they began the process of surveying the damage while letters from worried friends arrived.

For decades to come, many of their friends would be concerned for the Storehouse whenever they heard of bad weather on the east coast. On 20 September 1968 Francis Bacon would write from Louis Trichardt in South Africa, where he was once again visiting his family: 'I do hope you have missed the floods which by the paper here seem to have been so bad.'

Wirth-Miller redesigned the interior to be simple and durable so it could survive both future storms and nights of hard drinking. Before the wood panelling was replaced, the couple marked where, when and what sexual antics had taken place against the walls. The aim was to shock any future inhabitant who removed the new panelling.

'They were notorious for their outrageous behaviour and seemed to know everybody from Frances Partridge to [man of letters] Brian Howard,' James Birch, the gallery owner, recalled from his childhood. He revealed that, like the Roberts, Wirth-Miller had a surprising softer side. 'They would come over or my family would visit them frequently, to the extent that Denis was known to me as "Nanny Worth-Millions", due to his nannying skills.'[59]

By the end of the year, the restoration of their home was almost complete and, on 4 December 1953, a telephone line was installed for the first time. The telephone came with a caveat: 'under the current statutory telephone regulations, telephone service provided by means of an exclusive line at the residence may at any time, if the Postmaster General so directs, be provided by means of a shared line'. It was no idle warning. Over the years, local party-line users would be shocked by the language and sexual details they heard when they inadvertently eavesdropped on their neighbours.

After the repair work on the Storehouse had been completed in 1954 it was photographed for *House and Garden*, where their friend David Hicks had influence. Hicks, a bohemian social climber, was responsible for some of the society connections that Wirth-Miller and Chopping made once they had established themselves, and he would also be pivotal in their future careers. They would often recall one of their first encounters with Hicks, whom they had met through Noel Carrington, and whom was also friendly with Arthur Jeffress and the socialite Bunny Roger. At his small house in Chelsea, they and several other guests were treated to supper, with the invisible staff raising the dishes into the dining room from the lower kitchen on a dumb waiter. At the end of the evening, as they all prepared to move on to a club, Hicks had called an imperious 'Goodnight and thank-you' down to the anonymous staff. The reply came back, 'Goodnight, David darling, have a lovely evening.' It was only at that point they realized that the staff consisted solely of his mother, who had cooked all the dishes but had not been invited to join them.

Despite his snobbish tendencies, Chopping and Wirth-Miller warmed to Hicks and found him amusing. At his suggestion, *House and Garden*'s art director Peter Coats came to photograph the Storehouse's newly refitted interior. A friendship developed with the art director and Coats later commissioned Chopping to create a rebus for his lover Sir Henry 'Chips' Channon, a Conservative Member of Parliament.

The ongoing restoration of the Storehouse during 1953 did not mean that the visitors' book was not in use. The Roberts, Minton and the wide assortment of friends that Chopping and Wirth-Miller had collected continued to walk through the front door in search of both entertainment and a release from city life. The Storehouse had new arrivals, too. Chopping's boxer Tosca had given birth to a litter of puppies.

Wivenhoe village had an annual regatta, and Chopping and Wirth-Miller would usually invite friends up for it. Sonia Orwell ('a voracious lioness on a constant social safari', as Francis Bacon described her) often made the journey up from London and described the Storehouse parties planned around the event as 'simply glorious'. She refused to take to the water, though. As a teenager she had been involved in a boating accident and had seen three of her friends drown. Wivenhoe planned a larger event to celebrate the coronation of Queen Elizabeth II on 2 June 1953.

There was no plan to have a party at the Storehouse that year due to the ongoing refurbishment. Chopping had been struck by tonsillitis and was recovering in hospital, having given Wirth-Miller instructions on how to look after the puppies. In his absence, the celebrations did not go to plan.

The painter Robert Buhler, whom the couple had known since frequenting his mother's café in Fitzrovia in the late 1930s, had remained a close friend and was now teaching at the Royal College of Art. As well as cityscapes and landscapes, he painted portraits of Spender, Minton and Bacon. Buhler had rented a cottage at Fingringhoe, on the opposite bank of the Colne, specifically for the public holiday. He and his girlfriend Mary found the small wooden boat that acted as a ferry service over to Wivenhoe and, on Coronation Day, they turned up early to drop in on Wirth-Miller. He persuaded them to join him at the Headgate pub in Colchester.

By the time they returned to Wivenhoe, they were drunk and the rudimentary ferry service had long since stopped operation. The thought crossed Robert and Mary's minds to swim over the estuary, but sense prevailed and they stayed at the Storehouse. They bade each other good night and the couple retired upstairs. Moments after they had headed upstairs, they heard the door slam: Wirth–Miller had gone out again. A few hours later, loud voices outside woke them up.

Buhler got out of bed to look out of the window. Wirth–Miller now had additional guests: six guardsmen, who appeared to be even more drunk than he was. Buhler quickly grabbed a chair to block the bedroom door; he did not want the squaddies to discover Mary in the state they were in.

Drunken noise and shouting continued downstairs for most of the rest of the night, with Buhler and his girlfriend sitting bolt upright in bed, ready to defend themselves if any of the soldiers tried to force an entry. They were left alone.

When Chopping returned from hospital a few days later, he realized that something had been going on in his absence. A pair of gold cufflinks was missing, as was a brand new leather jacket that Francis Bacon had given him. Suspicious about Wirth–Miller's unremarkable version of events relating to Coronation Day, he forced the truth out of Buhler. When Chopping confronted Wirth–Miller, the latter exploded in a show of protest and refused to apologize. Chopping was just relieved that the puppies were unharmed.

Following the success of the Hanover Gallery show, Dicky Chopping looked forward to solo exhibitions in the main space but there was trouble in Hanover Square. The relationship between Brausen and her backer and co-director Arthur Jeffress had turned sour, and the personal and financial dispute was damaging the gallery. Jeffress made plans to start his own gallery on Davies Street in Mayfair. He pulled his money out of the Hanover, and asked Dicky Chopping to join his new stable. The artist would have weighed up the options: Brausen was a risk taker dedicated to experimental contemporary art, and the future of her gallery could not be assured; Jeffress was flamboyant, more traditional in his tastes and rich. Chopping chose Jeffress.

As a director of the British-American Tobacco company, Jeffress's father had become extremely rich. When he died in 1926, Jeffress inherited a fortune and set about spending it in Paris and London. He became known as one of the 'Bright Young Things', the decadent aristocrats and socialites of the 1920s. In November 1931, at the height of the Great Depression, Jeffress threw a party, 'The Red and White Tea Party' in Regent's Park, which made him notorious. Members of the press infiltrated the event and saw Jeffress dressed up in 'Angel skin pyjamas, elbow-length white kid gloves, ruby and diamond bracelets'. He was vilified in the newspapers but he made no concession. He continued to dress extravagantly, and his mannerisms remained overtly camp, but he was now marked out to the authorities as 'disreputable'. In the following year, his home was ransacked by police and he was cross-examined following the murder of Michael Scott Stephen, a bisexual drug-dealer, even though Jeffress had almost no association with the case. He felt victimized.

His passion was art and the post-war art scene in London provided an arena in which he could flourish. His taste, however, was far from experimental or avant-garde. The tag-line for the new Arthur Jeffress Gallery was 'Sunday Painting, Trompe l'oeil and Magic Realism'.

This suited Chopping, who would be given greater exposure than at the more progressive galleries, where he would be considered an anachronism. Jeffress was also an extremely close friend of Graham Sutherland so Chopping would be able to strengthen that association. By this time, Sutherland was not just the most famous signatory of the Storehouse's visitors' book but also the most famous living painter in Britain. The liaison was socially convenient too as Jeffress shared many mutual friends and acquaintances with Chopping and Wirth-Miller. These included Bacon, Peter Pollock and Paul Danquah, Peter Coats and Chips Channon, and Alfred Hecht.

Jeffress was gossipy, gregarious and frivolous, and an over-consumer of food, alcohol and cigarettes. He was also generous. He suggested to Chopping that he should regularly dine at Claridge's and he would cover the bill. Chopping enjoyed the company of Jeffress but, more importantly, he proved to be a hard-working agent. His advice was invaluable to Chopping, as was his gentle prodding whenever a deadline approached. Jeffress had the versatile ability to play the camp fool one moment yet command respect and plausibility the next.

Shortly after he opened the new gallery, Jeffress went on holiday to Cyprus, possibly because of the military contingent stationed there. Jeffress, like Johnny Minton, was obsessed with men in uniform and would attend the colouring of the troop, the Royal Tournament (or the 'Royal Torment', as he referred to it) and military parades just to watch the soldiers and sailors. He would ask his friends and acquaintances to inform him if any ships were in port. Francis Bacon once wrote to Erica Brausen from the hills overlooking Monte Carlo: 'Do tell Arthur that I have not been able to track down the movements of the Fleet yet.'[60]

With the rise of sexual 'decadence' in London in the early 1950s, there was a police clampdown on homosexuality. Jeffress, after his previous experience of police harassment, was wary and sought pleasure abroad. He wrote to Chopping in 1953:

I would now no more go near a uniform in a pub than play football for Tottenham Hotspurs. A chummeroo of mine, rather a headstrong one of course, went into the Fitzroy last week and was quite soon asked to drink up and leave. In a dazed way, he asked why, and the reply was 'the manager saw you buying a drink for that sailor at the bar'! Talk about a police state! Anyway, go, he did, taking the sailor with him of course.

Jeffress continued working on behalf of his client despite the distractions in Nicosia. He sent a telegram to Wivenhoe that he had secured a commission for Chopping. The caveat was that the client was 'really rather on the dotty side': 'Lucian Freud can tell you about him as he is MAD about Lucian's pictures of youths . . . keeps making all sorts of strange offers. He hunts . . . what, I don't know . . . Fabergé and Freud. He is altogether a rum one.' Chopping's tightly controlled *trompe l'oeil* had little in common with Freud's direct and expressive nudes and free brushwork, but the commission was pursued, and it was only Chopping's need to focus on other projects that saw its incompletion.

Chopping's success continued under Jeffress's guidance. Proof that he was a leading figure in a renewed interest in *trompe l'oeil* came with his inclusion in *The Eye Deceived* mounted at the Graves Art Gallery. (The public gallery in Sheffield had opened in 1934 under the stewardship of John Rothenstein before he moved to the Tate.) The survey show of the *trompe l'oeil* form through the centuries featured works by Carlo Crivelli, Leonardo da Vinci, Grinling Gibbons, William Harnett, Edwin Lutyens and Stanley Spencer. Chopping's works were titled *Pansies and Snails*, *Pears* and *Still Life*, all of which were lent via Jeffress. The agent wrote from the opening, which Chopping did not attend: 'Your pictures looked a treat alongside such maîtres as [Evert] Collier and Harnett. Now I only need to be struck in public by Sir John Rothenstein to feel myself <u>really</u> in the news!'

Arthur Jeffress in his gondola, Venice, 1956. *(Author's personal collection)*

Chopping's works were seen on the walls of the Jeffress Gallery in a series of exhibitions, including *Trompe l'Oeil from the 18th Century to the Present Day* in 1955. A year later his paintings were hung alongside those of Freud, Sutherland, de Maistre and Spencer in *Unusual Juxtapositions*.

Chopping and Jeffress became very close within a few years. In September 1956 Chopping, who was always fond of the concept of a visitors' book, made Jeffress the gift of an illustration to fit into his visitors' book at his home in Venice. Jeffress had it bound into the book and reported back to Chopping that his work was much admired by the collector and socialite Peggy Guggenheim among others. Jeffress enrolled the help of Guggenheim and his guests to choose a suitable gift with which to thank Chopping. They settled on a pair of gondolier's espadrilles.

Arthur Jeffress was generous in sharing his contacts. One of Chopping's new acquaintances was Neil 'Bunny' Roger who, before the war, had made dresses for the actress Vivien Leigh. His standard attire was an Edwardian suit with the shoulders comically exaggerated and the waist pinned extremely tight, creating an avant-garde silhouette. When serving as an officer in the Western Desert and Italy, as legend had it, he would charge into battle clutching a copy of *Vogue* with a chiffon scarf around his neck. Another probably apocryphal story about his military service included giving his soldiers the advice, 'when in doubt, powder heavily', when they were faced by a bayonet charge. Nonetheless, he was known for his courage under fire.

He was always quick-witted, once saying, 'You can't call queer men "gay". Apart from anything else, they're all so miserable. The Greeks were more accurate when they called the Furies "the Kindly Ones".'

He invited Chopping and Wirth-Miller to a party to see in the New Year of 1954. They had been planning to go to the Chelsea Arts Ball, for which John Minton had designed the advertising and the set, at the Royal Albert Hall. To spare Minton's feelings, they decided to attend both parties.

Chopping and Wirth-Miller went as 'the Chocolate Soldier' and 'Russia' – but felt eclipsed by the costumes of the other guests at Roger's party. Jeffress, wearing a feathered mask, was also impressed. 'Really, how those girls get dressed up!' he remarked, referring to some of the young men.

The party continued until six in the morning but Chopping and Wirth-Miller left early to join their friends at the Chelsea Arts Ball, which had the theme of 'Fun'. Traditionally, the Chelsea Arts Ball climaxed with ornate tableaux parading through the Albert Hall before being torn apart by the revellers. The aim of the destruction was to rip apart old orthodoxies and welcome in a new year. The ball was famous for its nudity, open homosexuality and fighting, and would be abandoned in 1958.

At midnight, thousands of coloured balloons were released from the ceiling and the procession of tableaux began. The centrepiece was a Greek temple, on which rode partially clothed students dressed as satyrs and nymphs.

Footage of the ball, filmed by Pathé News, shows the frenzy and chaos that erupted. The central tableau was torn to the ground and the scantily clad students were forced to run. The ball became a brawl. Chopping dodged the fighting, but one of his friends was kicked in the eye and another's jaw was broken.

From what Chopping saw, it was not the partygoers who had started the fighting but the stewards. Nonetheless, the newspapers framed the Arts Ball as evidence of the moral bankruptcy of British youth, pointing the finger at the 'degenerate' artists and students.

It had been a memorable start to the year. It would be a significant one for Wirth-Miller.

Wirth-Miller's style as an artist and his career benefited from his close friendship with Bacon in the 1950s. They never permanently shared a studio but they collaborated on an unknown number of canvases in Wirth-Miller's studio, some of which are in the couple's archive. Bacon used the studio during his stays in Wivenhoe over the course of three decades, from approximately 1950 onwards.

After giving up his Cromwell Place studio in 1951, Bacon had a peripatetic existence for the next decade, which may partially explain his reliance on his hosts at the Storehouse and his frequent use of Wirth-Miller's studio. He was there so often, sometimes drunkenly working alongside Wirth-Miller, that

Chopping more or less abandoned his own studio in the adjoining cottage. He could not concentrate on his finely detailed *trompe l'oeil* works, illustrations and, later, writing while the other two artists behaved noisily next door.

One accredited collaboration between Wirth-Miller and Bacon is *House in Barbados* (1952), which they painted for Bacon's new lover, Peter Lacy. He met the former Royal Air Force pilot in the Colony Room and by 1952 they were in a relationship. Bacon would say:

> even though I was over forty when I met Peter I'd never really fallen in love with anyone until then. What Peter really liked was young boys . . . It was a kind of a mistake that he went with me at all. Of course, it was the most total disaster from the start.[61]

The relationship pushed Bacon's masochistic tendencies to the fore. He was a frequent visitor to Lacy's cottage in Hurst in Berkshire, where his new-found fame as a painter was irrelevant. Lacy was the dominant character, suggesting to Bacon that he should give up painting: 'you could live in a corner of my cottage of straw. You could sleep and shit there.'[62] The relationship was full of alcohol-fuelled rows, anger and violence.

A symbol of Bacon's infatuation was his agreement to Lacy's request for a painting of his house in Barbados, based on a photograph. The subject was a world away from the screaming popes that were Bacon's increasing obsession. Peppiatt reports that Bacon, who remained wary that his technique was largely self-taught and channelled only to render his own visions, 'asked a close friend, the painter Denis Wirth-Miller, whom he went to frequently for technical advice, to help him get the perspective right on this unusual commission'.[63]

Wirth-Miller's assistance went beyond technical advice. The doors in *House in Barbados* point to Bacon's brushwork, but many elements of the interior courtyard are suggestive of Wirth-Miller's similar but more detailed and disciplined style.

Seven years later in a letter dated 21 December 1959, Bacon seemingly forgot about Wirth-Miller's involvement. His main concern was that Lacy, his relationship with whom had disintegrated, was selling the work. Bacon was often generous, giving friends works for free, but he was appalled whenever he learned that one had been sold. This was partly due to the insult to his generosity, and partly because from 1958 onwards he had to pay commission to Marlborough Fine Art on sales he had made himself and works that were sold after he had given them away. The letter reveals his other frequent fears: he did not want a biography to be written in his lifetime, and he was having difficulty producing work when away from London (he was in St Ives). As usual, he spelled Denis's name incorrectly and used almost no punctuation.

My dear Dennis

   Thank you so much for your letter – I will write to Erica I do not in the least want any book to be done. I have really learnt my lesson this time never to move from a large town I can't wait to leave this dump – I doubt I shall ever get the pictures done for the show – Fischer [Heinrich Fischer of Marlborough Fine Art] could not come down thank god as he had to go to Germany but is coming now on 15th of January. I hope some miracle will happen that I can do the work. I am very upset to hear Peter hawked that awful picture I did for him of his home in Barbados all round London I made it look as awful as I could so that he would like it – he said he would never try to sell it but there you are I think this has been quite

the worst year of my life I just long to get back to London – I
know the show will be a disaster even if I do get it done.
Do write to me when you can I love to hear from you
    My fondest love and best wishes to you both –
Love
    Francis

    A second Francis Bacon work is recognized as involving some
level of cooperation. In 1964 Ronald Alley stated, when
discussing Bacon's *Landscape* (1952), a sparse, sketchy oil on
canvas: 'A few brush-strokes on the present work were added by
Denis Wirth-Miller.'[64] As the claim was made during Bacon's
lifetime in the *Francis Bacon* catalogue raisonné, the painter
presumably endorsed it. Bacon also admitted to James Birch that
he painted the tail in one of Wirth-Miller's dog paintings, and
Chopping's diaries reveal that Bacon worked on some of Wirth-
Miller's paintings in the 1970s. When Alley attempted to date
Bacon's works in sequence, Bacon instructed him to speak to
Wirth-Miller as no one knew the timeline better than the
Wivenhoe artist as they worked so closely together.
    Andrew Lambirth wrote in 2011 that, 'the spiky reds and
marsh grass that occasionally feature in [Bacon's] imagery would
seem to have an Essex provenance — more specifically deriving
from the paintings of his friend Wirth-Miller', and the critic
Louisa Buck makes a similar connection.[65] Meanwhile, it is
possible that striations in front or behind a subject, reminiscent
of a cage, were used by Wirth-Miller before Bacon.
    When in Wivenhoe, Bacon and Wirth-Miller would often
paint together late into the night. After their deaths, the detritus
of reference materials in Bacon's Reece Mews studio and
in Wirth-Miller's Storehouse studio was remarkably similar. In
Wirth-Miller's studio there were many Muybridge studies, news

clippings and newspaper photos depicting boxers, bullfights, Nazis and carcasses – all reminiscent of Bacon's subject-matter. The Francis Bacon MB Art Foundation in Monaco has investigated the crossover of material in the men's studios 'in order to deepen the understanding between Bacon and the artist Denis Wirth-Miller'. Its report, conducted by the Bacon scholar Katharina Günther, found that 'In the working environment provided by Wirth-Miller, Bacon had found an artistic home away from home.' She noted: 'Fragments of an early version of *Three Studies of Lucian Freud*, 1969 found in the studio after Wirth Miller's death and today held by the MB Art Collection bear testimony to Bacon's activities there.'[66]

Their styles may have rubbed off on each other and, in the case of some unattributed works discovered in Wirth-Miller's studio after his death, it is difficult to tell which painter is responsible. *Suited Man Walking through a Door* mixes Bacon's typical solid block of shadow, sense of structure and speed of application with more detailed sections on the trousers that are more obviously the work of Wirth-Miller. Similarly, a wrestler work, drawn from an Eadweard Muybridge photograph, was left in the studio; it gives the impression of Bacon's hand but scrutiny shows a level of detail that would be unusual for him.

There is unlikely to be a conclusive way of proving how much these works were a collaboration, or how much Wirth-Miller was toying with elements of Bacon's style in experimentation. While in the Wivenhoe studio, the two men would have used the same types of canvas and paints, so a distinction is unlikely to be made in terms of materials.

Whatever the truth, the works were left abandoned in the studio: they were the trials of ideas and often composed in a drunken state, and were never meant to be seen. Wirth-Miller sometimes nailed such works onto the floor of his studio in order to provide insulation as he worked on his own landscapes in winter.

The closeness of the two men meant that Wirth-Miller bore witness to the strange rituals Bacon would perform as he worked. Before starting out on a canvas at the Storehouse, he would write cryptic phrases onto small strips of paper or tape, which he then hung from the ceiling above his easel. One theory holds that scraps of paper such as this represented Bacon's idiosyncratic take on a voodoo doll. Once the painting was finished, he would rip them up and throw them away, but one strip from 1952 survived in a jam jar in Wirth-Miller's studio.

The inscription in block capitals reads 'ERYNX-SCHUNERANN-THEBES', followed by 'FRANCIS BACON'. He also signed and dated the other side. The inscription cannot be understood with any certainty, partly because Bacon's spelling was poor: ERYNX probably refers to Eryx, who challenged Heracles to a wrestling match; THEBES clearly relates to the Ancient Greek city-state; and SCHUNERANN, in the knowledge of Bacon's use of Nazi symbolism, may refer to Schuermann, the family of architects responsible for the velodrome at the Berlin Olympics in 1936. (That may suggest Greek wrestling in an arena, but the conjecture may be wildly off the mark.)

Wirth-Miller and Bacon's closeness in terms of working practice and influences is most apparent in their dog paintings. The works of both men are drawn from images of a white mastiff in Eadweard Muybridge's *Animals in Motion* (1899).

In 1952, Bacon interrupted his series of pope works to paint versions of *Dog*, in which a standing dog, small in proportion to the canvas, is isolated in the centre of the painting and confined by a red frame. These were followed by a similar image of the dog in *Man with Dog*, this time rendered more ectoplasmic and with more energy, near a street drain. The shadow of a man stretches ominously down from the dark top section of the canvas.

By 1953, Wirth-Miller was also working on a dog series, but these would be a more thoroughgoing examination of the Muybridge series of images. In form they are relatively remote from Bacon's 1952 works, considering they have a similar source, and have more in common with *Man with Dog* in terms of the palette of blacks and blues. While it is known that Wirth-Miller brought Muybridge's work to the attention of Bacon, it is not certain which of them introduced the palette that suggests a strong connection between Wirth-Miller's series and Bacon's *Man with Dog*.

Wirth-Miller's dog series gained the attention of one of the most important figures in British contemporary art at the time. Helen Lessore was born in London in 1907 and married the sculptor Frederick Lessore, twenty-eight years her senior, who had founded the Beaux Arts Gallery in the 1920s. She became secretary of the gallery in 1931. The gallery housed exhibitions by Christopher Wood and Barbara Hepworth, but its profile was raised when Lessore's husband died in 1951 and she took over. Lessore was a modernist artist herself and her passion was the radical contemporary art that was emerging in London following the Second World War. By 1953, John Berger had already identified that 'The Beaux Arts is quickly and deservedly gaining the reputation of being the one gallery where it is possible to see the serious work of young painters.'[67]

In that year, Helen Lessore presented a sell-out solo exhibition of Derrick Greaves's work, followed by an exhibition by John Bratby in 1954. She would become forever associated

with the Kitchen Sink school, a term unintentionally coined
by the critic David Sylvester that pointed to the realism of the
artworks. The term was used to cover a group of young artists
– Greaves, Bratby, Jack Smith and Edward Middleditch. They
presented stark images that portrayed working-class life and
everyday objects without any gloss or romance, perhaps drawing on the raw directness of Walter Sickert, followed by the
Euston Road School that had emerged in Fitzrovia when
Chopping and Wirth-Miller were living on Fitzroy Street.

John Minton had a hand in the artistic development of these
very young artists who studied under him at the Royal College
of Art. Greaves would say of his time at the RCA, 'one could
pick up a range of mannerisms from one's tutors including John
Minton's "way with Modernism", Rodrigo Moynihan's "suave
portraiture" and Ruskin Spear's "post-Sickertian dabbing and
splodging".' The gallerist and author James Hyman explains in
his Greaves monograph: 'Of all his teachers it was Minton who
was of most interest. Greaves respected him principally as a
draughtsman, a marvellous, fecund and fluent illustrator, and as
a convivial and witty performer, but as a teacher Minton was
almost monosyllabic.'[68] With Lessore's help, the 'Beaux-Art
Quartet', as they were also called, would become famous by their
mid-twenties and by 1956 were representing Britain at the
Venice Biennale. They soon dispersed from Lessore's patronage
and their careers as realist artists were almost immediately
subverted by the rise of abstract expressionism in the second half
of the decade.

Helen Lessore was an early collector of Bacon's paintings and
was able to gather enough works to mount a Bacon exhibition
in November 1953, much to Erica Brausen's chagrin.

Wirth-Miller could not have been in better hands when
Lessore showed an interest in hanging his dog series in a solo

exhibition in 1954. She became a close friend of Wirth-Miller and would join the list of visitors to the Storehouse, with some of her Beaux-Arts boys in tow.

The *Studies of a Dog in Movement* exhibition, which opened at the Beaux Arts on 21 October 1954, consisted of fourteen works exclusively from the dog series, with simple titles such as *Walking* and *Running*. It was Wirth-Miller's first solo exhibition, and he was described economically in the catalogue as 'Born 1917 at Folkestone, Kent. Self-taught'. Wirth-Miller was born in 1915; the incorrect date may have been a mistake or a deliberate deceit in order to present him as an up-and-coming young artist.

David Sylvester was off-hand in his review, claiming that 'an idea of Francis's Bacon's has been re-stated in a rather neon lit way'. Possibly as a direct result of his review, Wirth-Miller slapped the critic on the face in the presence of the Roberts and Keith Vaughan. Sylvester responded by breaking his nose.

Sylvester was not the only reviewer to make the comparison with Bacon. The *Times* critic, while calling Wirth-Miller an 'accomplished draughtsmen' and pointing to the benefits of 'blurring some part of the image with flickering lines', said Wirth-Miller 'used some of the more curious expedients to which Mr. Bacon has from time to time resorted'.[69] This made Wirth-Miller sound as if he was little more than a copyist and did not take into account the symbiotic nature of the two men's approach to the subject.

Whatever the route to canvas, Wirth-Miller's works combine an ethereality with a violence of force and motion that is not so coherent in Bacon's dog pictures. Andrew Wilson, the Curator of Modern and Contemporary Art at the Tate, described the energy of Wirth-Miller's *Running Dog* (1953):

The white spectral dog rushes forward out of the depthless blackness of the canvas. The body of the animal is made up of a web of lines that seem to dance on the painting's surface describing not just skin, flesh and muscle, but also the energy caught within the dog's taut body directing it forever forward.[70]

He went on to highlight further differences in execution:

Where Wirth-Miller's paintings isolate the dog on a black painted depthless field . . . Bacon's dogs are positioned on clearly defined stages. [Bacon's *Study for a Dog*, 1952] is broadly painted in a way that is quite different from the dancing web of lines in Wirth-Miller's paintings and gives a blurred impression of arrested movement.[71]

Works in the series, *Study of a Dog in Movement*, now in the collection of the Francis Bacon MB Art Foundation, and *Dog*, owned by New College, University of Oxford, have a regular succession of striations creating a sense of enclosure. While the striations might now be deemed reminiscent of Bacon, they draw directly from the original source: the cage in the background of Muybridge's images of the mastiff.

Arthur Jeffress wrote to Chopping after the show's private view: 'Please tell Denis once again how impressed I was by his exhibition.' An art-world friend of Jeffress had told him he wanted to buy one of the works, 'but that Mrs Lessore will not give him the usual trade discount. She must be an odd one and no mistake.'

Lessore, who was a forthright personality and suffered no fools, would continue to be helpful to Wirth-Miller and his career. In 1955, she fixed him up with a short stint teaching at Langford Grove girls' school near Lewes in Sussex. She had taught at the school herself, and would fix up positions there for her stable of young artists. Wirth-Miller was followed by Edward Middleditch and then Frank Auerbach. The headmistress, Miss Curtin, had some eccentric traits. Auerbach's biographer, Catherine Lampert, says that Curtin 'regularly invited him to share a lunch of scallops and gin, and at the end of the day threw down the stairs a cheque for three pounds'.[72]

Helen Lessore gave Wirth-Miller two further solo exhibitions at the Beaux Arts, in 1956 and 1958. These shows were both called *East Anglian Landscapes*: Wirth-Miller had finally settled down to his vocation and would rarely exhibit figurative work for the remainder of his career. Contemporary landscapes would never carry the kudos of the developments in figurative or abstract art, but Wirth-Miller found a distinct style free of the restrictions of neo-Romanticism. The paintings distilled a combination of his psyche and the local East Anglian topography, with its flatness and starkness. His works such as *Estuary Landscape I*, shown at the May 1956 exhibition, are confident and dark. They are full of motion, speed and violence emphasized by the horizontal stabs and strokes. The titles are simple – mostly numbered *Marsh Landscapes* and *Estuary Landscapes* – to underline that these works are the revelation of a moment rather than a narrative; the viewer's response to this disquieting natural world is not overtly directed. The technique and ominousness may be linked to Bacon, but Wirth-Miller was developing a unique language for landscape, born of modernity but equally primal.

One of the dog series and two of his works from 1956, a *Marsh Landscape* and a *Landscape*, would become his earliest works to enter public collections, with the influential Contemporary Art

Society responsible for purchasing *Landscape*. At the age of forty, Wirth-Miller had finally found his feet.

The new confidence led to sales. In 1957, Alfred Hecht wrote to Dicky Chopping after framing some of his new *trompe l'oeil* works, 'I hope you will get the increase now [in sale price]. In my view they will merit it. If not Denis will have to keep you. I'm glad Tommy Parr bought one of the landscapes, and I made Lord Beaverbrook buy the other.' Beaverbrook was the proprietor of the *Daily Express* and was at the time a great patron of Graham Sutherland, who may have pushed him towards Wirth-Miller's work. In later years, an argument with Sutherland resulted in Beaverbrook selling all his paintings by the artist at auction, which dented the prices of Sutherland's work.

While Wirth-Miller and Chopping underwent their transformations into successful landscape artist and *trompe l'oeil* artist respectively, Bacon pursued his variations based on Velázquez's *Portrait of Innocent X*, completed *Man in Blue I–VII* (1954) and turned to Muybridge again for his paintings of wrestlers (1953– 4). As had become commonplace, he was lauded by many critics, but others were unsettled by his works, particularly as the wrestling images were of male nudes.

Keith Vaughan, far from prurient and a progressive figurative artist himself, was not an admirer of Bacon, referring to his 'lack of permanent, formal, classical values, a sort of deliberate spiv-existentialist'.[73] His problem was partly political. Philip Vann explained:

> The disintegrative way Bacon depicted male figures – splayed out carcass-like on mattresses, wrestling erotically in couples under bare light bulbs or crouching on toilets in windowless interiors – was antithetical to Vaughan's

own desire to affirm the dignity of male out-of-doors figures who transcended their own petty quotidian personalities to discover fellowship with other men and unity with nature.[74]

Vaughan was not the only person to be unsettled by the works. Other complaints came from members of the public less bothered by the sensitivities of the political or cultural portrayal of homosexuality. They were disgusted, and called the police to report Bacon for obscenity when *Two Figures in the Grass* was shown at the Institute of Contemporary Arts, London, in 1955. The constable sent to assess the paintings was apparently bemused: 'But they're just wrestling in the grass.'

Bacon would have been immune to the thoughts of Vaughan or offended gallery-goers – in his view, he was his own best critic. Further, his success was becoming increasingly international in scope. He had been given his first one-man show in New York in 1953, at Durlacher Bros. Along with Lucian Freud and Ben Nicholson, he had represented Britain at the Venice Biennale in 1954, where the changing of the guard in terms of modern art was signified by Nicholson being relegated to a smaller room. Bacon was also about to be given his first solo exhibition in Paris.

Yet all was not well. One of Bacon's letters to Denis Wirth-Miller from Tangier, sent on 22 July 1956, revealed trouble in his relationship with Peter Lacy and in his work life, despite his apparent success. Paul Danquah and Peter Pollock allowed Bacon to share their Battersea address from 1955 onwards while he had no permanent London residence, but by 1956 Bacon was spending most of his time in Tangier as Lacy had gone to live there.

Hotel Cecil
Tangier
Morocco

July 22nd

Dearest Dennis

I have been meaning to write to you for ages I am staying
with Peter in a flat   everything is disastrous as you can
imagine – I have taken a cheap flat to work in unfurnished
– are you coming down to stay with Janetta at Malaga – I
may have to come back after a few weeks I am being sued
for dilapidations for about £1200 for the home I had in
Chelsea and assigned the lease to a house agent like a fool
I didn't go to a solicitor and I have been taken for a big ride
as he has been screwing the rents from the house for 11 years
and now refuses to pay the dilapidation and the landlords
have the right to come down on me – do let me know your
news and when and where you are going this summer. If I
can get the money would you like to come and work here
for a bit I have done nothing yet but am trying to start again
– do write when you have time I do hope you and Dickie
are flourishing
         all my love to you
         Francis

Bacon suffered from continual money and productivity
pressures during this period. In a letter to Wirth–Miller dated 7
September, and dated to 1956, he revealed his ongoing fears.

I must come back and work I have not been able to finish
anything here and feel I never will although from the work I
have done I shall be able to do the series I want to right away
but it is probably only wishful thinking – How are you I heard
you had gone to stay with Janetta in the Dordogne – I feel
I was very unfriendly to every one before I left London but I
think I was really a bit mental I hope you will forgive me I am
looking forward terribly to seeing you all but dreading
Battersea and the debts my only hope is if this series goes
I have got about 20 paintings I have worked out but this is as
you know only a shadow – the people here are superb looking
a great mixture but with predominately Berber strains and
terribly sympathetic it is necessary to speak Spanish here to
make much contact   I have learnt to swim a bit – but apart
from the wonderful looks of the people it is a dead town the
Europeans are terrible – Peter seems to like it and seems to
want to live here – but after a year I don't believe he could
stand it – I am longing to hear your news and to see your new
work I hear Norman Fowler warned you against me he tried
to warn Peter Watson I suppose it is part of his attractive
protestant-Buddhist New England puritanism to sound these
queenie warnings – I suppose she has retired to her island now
with the loot. All my love to you and Dickie
    love Francis

[P.S.] hope to get back about 24 or 25th I hope no one knows
as I want just to work and I am afraid they will all be down
on me with the awful debts

The series to which he referred rather than twenty paintings
would be just six works, inspired by Vincent van Gogh's *The
Painter on the Route to Tarascon* (1888), which would be shown at

the Hanover in 1957. Only one of those works dated from 1956, with the rest largely executed in a hurry to meet the deadline. As explained by the Estate of Francis Bacon:

> Necessity accelerated a process already in train; Bacon's application of paint became coarser, his impasto thick and ridged, and his colours far more strident in range and hue. Van Gogh was one stimulus, the Céret works of Chaim Soutine and the fierce light of Morocco were two others. It was a decisive break with the ghostly forms and sombre backgrounds of the first half of the 1950s, and a permanent one.[75]

Part of Bacon's financial problems lay in his over-generosity and compulsive gambling. He had to depend on the ever-loyal Erica Brausen to provide cash; she even subsidized some of his gambling losses. He was also disturbed that rivals in Soho were spreading rumours about him and sniping at his success.

Wirth-Miller was one of only a very few like minds he felt he could trust, and he poured out his grievances in a series of letters, sometimes prefaced by apologies for his latest bout of drunken antagonism. Increasingly, he would ask Wirth-Miller, and sometimes Chopping, to join him when he was abroad. He knew that Wirth-Miller could cope with the worst of his behaviour and would give as good as he got. Their friendship would remain stronger than their disagreements, of which there would be many.

Chapter 11

Escapades

Dicky Chopping's success brought much-needed cash flow to the Storehouse, but it came at a cost. Denis Wirth-Miller felt his work was as good as that of anyone, and he was now starting to be given solo exhibitions, but he was not afforded the same level of interest as Bacon, Freud, Minton, the Roberts or, as it now stood, Dicky Chopping.

To Wirth-Miller, who had concentrated almost solidly on painting since the late 1930s while his partner had been diverted towards illustration, Chopping seemed to have stumbled into success as if by accident. Within the space of a couple of years in the 1950s, Wirth-Miller had been rendered the lesser party in the relationship, and it showed in his outbursts. Chopping was considered the better looking and more charming, and it was he that was making the introductions in the more privileged circles – Wirth-Miller was there as 'Dicky's guest'. Wirth-Miller found solace in believing that his partner was an artistic lightweight – not a true artist, with the emotional complexity that involved. Bacon alone was worthy of his full attention.

Bacon himself was no stranger to relationship difficulties through his troubles with Lacy. The artist was under the spell of the former pilot; he would be the final long-term lover who could dominate him emotionally and psychologically.

Ralph and Frances Partridge with Richard Chopping
on the Quay, Wivenhoe. *(Author's personal collection)*

Bacon and Wirth-Miller's relationship troubles brought the
two men closer. They were of similar character; when they were
drunk, a stranger might meet them at a bar and find them
charming. Ten minutes later, either one of them might look the
same person in the eye and insult him with a cruel, almost
sadistic comment.

Chopping had always been the more level-headed in the
partnership, but this aspect of his character was now beginning
to stand out more starkly in contrast to Wirth-Miller's
increasingly mercurial temperament. Chopping's basic
decency seemed almost a weakness to some of his friends,
such as the Roberts, and out of keeping with the mood of
transgressing artistic and social boundaries in the 1950s. 'Does
Dicky want to be loved by *everybody*?' asked an exasperated
Francis Bacon on one occasion.

Chopping and Wirth-Miller were bound for collision. Chopping's own drinking prevented him from being able to put the brakes on any brewing conflict, and vicious arguments became a regular occurrence in the Storehouse kitchen. Frances Partridge had the misfortune to come between them during a fierce row, likening it to 'a nasty knot on a parcel which had all at once flown apart'.

Yet for all their rows, it never took long before rapprochement came. If one disturbed the other's work by answering the phone, they would leave a note, apologizing for the intrusion from 'the man from Porlock'. Even if one of them might initially find it a relief to be home alone when the other was away for a spell, they would soon be writing long letters – Wirth-Miller's written in punctuation-free block capitals, Chopping's in near-illegible cursive – clearly missing the other. They were mutually dependent; their love was too deeply ingrained for isolation, but their holidays away from each other were increasingly necessary.

Their ability to take these breaks was aided by Wirth-Miller. He set about changing their financial fortunes, despite the fact that he was less able to bring in money. The royalty deals that Chopping had made with Noel Carrington, Allen Lane and other publishers since the early 1940s were still bearing fruit – with *Butterflies in Britain* in particular, which he had re-illustrated for further editions, continuing to sell well. His exhibitions and commissions were now adding considerably to the flow of funds. Wirth-Miller persuaded Chopping to let him invest the royalties on the stock market.

This could have been a disastrous decision on Chopping's part. He placed their financial future in the hands of a gambler but his trust in Wirth-Miller paid off. His partner proved to be a capable player of the markets. Soon enough, he had netted them enough to qualify as comfortably off. His skill on the markets would later convince Bacon to let him invest some of the money earned from his paintings. In the meantime, Bacon was still spending much of the mid to late 1950s in Tangier, where his enjoyment of the city was tempered by problems with Peter Lacy.

Tangier was hot, exotic and colourful, and had become a bohemian destination. As Frances Partridge had remarked to Dicky Chopping on a holiday to Andalucía in 1953, Tangier had by accident of history become the unofficial capital of the homosexual world. It was this that had brought Peter Lacy to the city.

Morocco did not exist as a country until 1956. It was split between the Spanish and French empires, but Tangier, technically within the Spanish zone, was a colonial anomaly. In 1912, it was agreed that the city would remain a 'free port' jointly administered by Britain, France and Spain.

Tangier's extraterritorial status and relaxed laws made it a haven for outsiders. It became a hotbed of spies, exiles, criminals and persecuted homosexuals from across Europe and North America, many of them artists and writers. André Gide, Paul Bowles, Tennessee Williams, Gore Vidal and Truman Capote were among the American writers to spend time in Tangier in the 1950s, while the British contingent included Joe Orton, Kenneth Williams and Cecil Beaton. Chopping and Wirth-Miller's friends Peter Pollock and Paul Danquah would drive down in their Rolls-Royce, and the writer and broadcaster Dan Farson was often found in its bars. Tangier was a release from the homophobic persecution ongoing in the USA and Britain.

Bacon's admiration for the city extended beyond its liberalism. He wrote to Wirth-Miller of its horizons, skies and colour. His trips to Tangier became more frequent when Peter Lacy moved to the city permanently in 1956. Their relationship remained troubled and Bacon could only work in fits and starts. He wrote to Wirth-Miller later in 1956:

> Dearest Dennis
>
> Thank you so much for your card I am afraid the weather cannot have been very good it has also been bad and cold here – anyway it must have been lovely to have been together down there.
>
> I have been working a lot although I have only finished 4 paintings but I think and hope they are a lot better – Peter has been staying with me but he has now taken a flat on his own and is moving there soon – I am so pleased to feel I can work here now – either or both you and Dicky are welcome to come here when you like as there will be a spare room now – do write me your news and how the work is going when you have time my best love to you both

Bacon eventually persuaded his friend to come out and join him. Wirth-Miller had his reservations about Tangier, yet within hours of arriving he had changed his mind. The pastel-coloured houses, winding streets, souks and fabrics all appealed to the artist. He also admired the special quality of light and colour that had begun to infect Bacon's work. Wirth-Miller told Chopping that it was hard to believe that it was just a decade after the Holocaust and the atom bomb. Tangier seemed immune to the events that had caused deep desolation.

Wirth-Miller and Bacon's centre of gravity in Tangier was Dean's Bar, where Lacy was employed to play piano. The proprietor Joseph Dean had lent money to Lacy and forced him to play the piano all hours of the day and night to repay the debt. According to legend, Dean smuggled drugs out of Morocco by stuffing them up the anuses of carrier pigeons. Nobody was sure where he came from but he spoke with accent-less received pronunciation. His real name was possibly Donald Kimfull, who was involved in drugs and prostitution in London prior to 1919. Kimfull disappeared without trace after failing to attend court following the drugs-related death of an actress. Dean died in February 1963, having run the Tangier bar since 1937.

The bar was regarded as an ex-pats' 'Colony Room', and many of the people who frequented Muriel's also ended up in Dean's Bar while on holiday. It had a similar louche atmosphere, but the crowd included American writers, celebrities and Berber gigolos as well as the Soho contingent. Ian Fleming, who would soon become influential in Dicky Chopping's life, also visited the bar while in Tangier in the mid-1950s. He wrote to his wife, Ann, a friend to Bacon:

> My life has revolved round a place called Dean's Bar, a sort of mixture between Wiltons and the porter's lodge at White's. There's nothing but pansies, and I have been fresh meat for them . . . Francis Bacon is due next week to live with his pansy pianist friend.[76]

Tangier joined Soho and Wivenhoe as the satellites around which Wirth-Miller and Bacon's friendship revolved. The original aim was that Wirth-Miller would paint with Bacon on his trips to Tangier, but there is no evidence that he produced much work, and Bacon rarely kept paintings he attempted in the city. Inevitably most of their time was spent in their favourite bars.

When France and Spain granted Morocco its independence in 1956, Tangier's position as a form of free-port was taken away and the ex-pat community feared the repercussions. Bacon's friend, the painter Ahmad Yacoubi, was arrested and sentenced on a charge of paedophilia. Tangiers's protected status soon returned. As Bacon mentioned in a letter to Wirth-Miller in 1957, Morocco's sultan, Mohammed V, gave the city a special charter inspired by the foreign currency brought in by the American and British ex-pats and visitors.

Tangiers – Sept 20th

Dearest Dennis – thank you so much for your letter – I know one should never say anything about friends – I think in a letter to Paul [Danquah] I said I thought you were not writing this season I am sure we have both said much worse about one another so please don't let it worry you I am afraid I always say too much on the wrong thing – anyhow I was so glad to hear from you – I am living on my own now I have a very cheap flat which I like very much – I have not done any actual work but I feel on the edge of it now. I am going to Aix-en-Provence on the 5th of October. I am going to see how the casino works out for me and I expect I shall be in London about the middle of October or sooner if everything goes – I don't want to stay long in England if I can help it but I shall have to do a few paintings to get some money perhaps you would like to come back here for a bit in the winter and of course Dickie if he would like to – I am so pleased the painting has been going well and that you sold one at Helens – I could not understand about the picture for Beaverbrook your writing – I am so glad to be on my own please don't tell anyone I am coming back or have a flat here I am always saying this I know. The Sultan is here for a week to give the Charter to Tangier which means it will remain a free port & open money Market the town is crammed with people from the country and the South of Morocco I think they must be the most superb looking men in the world I am going to try and learn some Arabic. They are always so delighted and flattered if one can only speak a few words.

I long to go to Marrakech and further south the winter is the time to do it. I will telephone you when I get back. I do hope Paul passes this time.

All my fondest love to you both love Francis

Bacon remained so miserable about both the state of his finances and his relationship with Lacy that Wirth-Miller worried about his friend's mental health. He asked Joseph Dean to keep him abreast of Bacon's welfare.

Dean, a heavy drinker and cocaine user, was not the most reliable correspondent. He would sometimes reply to Wirth-Miller but his letters often concentrated on his own mounting problems rather than the health of Bacon. In one letter, he said he had recently had a 'go' of the heart, 'not bad enough as there is no thrombosis', but enough to confine him to bed. He added: 'I haven't had a word from Francis but am upset to hear he is going "off" again.' 'Off' implied that Bacon's relationship with Lacy had taken another turn for the worse.

Wirth-Miller could be direct and acerbic at times, but his caring nature would often reveal itself in his concern for friends and was extended to their children, as Frances Partridge discovered.

One of the main catalysts of Chopping and Wirth-Miller's expanding network, she was older, grander and altogether more sophisticated than them, even if they did find her slightly patronizing when she acted as a voice for the 'buggers', as she called them. Partridge had reservations about Wirth-Miller's temperament, but she nonetheless had a great deal of affection for him.

Burgo, her son, was a source of constant concern. When young, he suffered from pronounced anxiety problems and his parents could find no easy solution. When Wirth–Miller and Chopping joined the Partridges on holiday in the early 1950s, they noticed that the boy's problems were putting a strain on his relationship with Frances and Ralph. Ralph would lose his temper with him while Frances would fuss; both were aware that neither approach helped. Burgo's troubles deepened when he was sent to boarding school. Eventually, in the hope that a change of scene would benefit the teenager, Partridge wrote to Chopping to ask whether Burgo could stay at the Storehouse for a few days.

As James Birch's family were aware, the male couple, like the Roberts, were good with children. Burgo was delighted by his visit, as were his hosts and Frances Partridge, who wrote in February 1952, 'I meant to say how <u>very, very</u> kind of you it was to have Burgo down. He has just been down here this weekend & seemed to be fairly alright.' He soon made return visits to Wivenhoe, where the three of them took long walks into the countryside or drifted down the river in Wirth–Miller's boat, and stopped to sketch the scenery and picnic.

Wirth–Miller revealed his gentle side towards Burgo, who in turn looked up to him with respect. The artist encouraged him to embrace his imagination and conjure up surreal worlds filled with impossible animals and bizarre characters, and instructed him to write down his thoughts. After one stay at the Storehouse, Burgo returned home to show his parents some trees he had drawn 'for Mr Wirth–Miller's imaginary birds to sit on', and spoke of imaginary relatives who weaved smoking pipes from wool.

Chopping was concerned that Burgo was there often enough to notice his ongoing flare-ups with Wirth–Miller. 'Burgo noticed them all right,' Partridge wrote to him after her son had returned from one of his Wivenhoe trips, 'but did not say much on the subject and we did not really ask him.'

Burgo's headmaster acknowledged that his mood and work had improved, and suggested the boy might one day make a first-class writer for *Punch*. The careers advice did not go down well with Partridge, who simply remarked 'oh dear!' when she recounted the news to Chopping. The magazine was deemed old-fashioned and trivial. She need not have worried. Burgo did become a writer but his success came with the controversial *A History of Orgies* (1958).

Chopping and Wirth-Miller also became very close to Janetta Woolley, whom Partridge considered to be almost a daughter. Partridge had known her since she was a child, and had taken it on herself to look after her when her family were forced to flee their home in Spain when the Civil War broke out. Woolley had a series of short-lived marriages. Her fourth, to Derek Jackson, collapsed when Jackson eloped with her half-sister, Angela Culme-Seymour. Woolley was at the time heavily pregnant with Jackson's only son.

The divorce that followed made Woolley a rich woman and she bought a house in Montpelier Square in Knightsbridge. Chopping had known Woolley since the 1940s, when they would both stay at Ham Spray House, and she became a friend of Francis Bacon.

Chopping had been looking to rent a flat in London for some time but was still short of funds to pay for a second home. Janetta provided a solution by allowing Chopping and Wirth-Miller to use a flat below her Montpelier Square house for little money. Consequently, the couple had a Knightsbridge address.

The new London pied-à-terre was handy for both of them in terms of work. They could now court potential clients at leisure. Although Wivenhoe was still very much their home, the flat allowed for a more varied social life and, when necessary, gave them breathing space from each other.

Janetta noticed that when Chopping was staying alone downstairs, unfamiliar men would visit. This, she believed, was all perfectly normal and would have been fine had Chopping not boasted of his conquests to Wirth–Miller. Their relationship had been fairly open, but Chopping was sowing the seeds of further problems.

Wirth–Miller reacted in kind whenever he and Bacon hit the pubs and gambling dens of Soho together. The controversial Dutch writer Gerard van het Reve, a new friend who had lived with Minton at Shaftesbury Villas, wrote to Chopping expressing some concern about Wirth–Miller's nights on the town:

> I hope Denis is well and not hasting after prey that we are all far too old for. Tell him to get reconciled with old age, and to prepare for Death. And to kick all the pleasure boys with their tight trousers and sweating faces out of the house, and to lock himself up and paint – nothing else.

Dicky Chopping spent more time with Arthur Jeffress when the latter was not in Venice. Jeffress's appetites were taking their toll, and his increasing weight caused him discomfort. He would catalogue the problems 'Dame Time and Witch Gin' caused him but he ignored medical advice and was unwilling to change his lifestyle. He continued to overeat, chain-smoke cheroots and drink champagne and cocktails to excess.

Jeffress prefaced one letter from his palazzo with a caveat that it would be the 'dullest' he had ever written: it recounted a tea-time visit by Jean Cocteau and his patron Francine Weissweiller, who had immediately made a bid to buy Jeffress's Venice home.

In 1956, Jeffress invited Chopping to travel to Venice with him in his chauffeur-driven Rolls-Royce, stopping off en route at grand hotels.

Chopping returned from Venice full of energy and looked forward to telling Wirth-Miller the tales of what went on. Wirth-Miller was not so keen to hear them. In Chopping's absence he had spent six days drunk in London, having gone to the capital for a party thrown by Rodrigo Moynihan and attended by the old bohemian crowd. His behaviour had been spurred on by his loneliness.

Janetta Woolley was of the opinion that the couple's relationship would benefit if Wirth-Miller also went on holiday. He was stewing about Chopping's promiscuousness, spending too much time with his inner demons, and then acting rashly to try and banish them. Woolley rented a farmhouse near Assier in the Dordogne, with plans to buy it. Shortly before she left for France, she asked Wirth-Miller if he would join her.

Wirth-Miller's mood improved on French soil. He wrote daily to both Chopping and Bacon. The cattiness and the curt tone of some of his other letters were absent. Among Janetta's friends in France, he was accepted for whom he was – a charming, interesting and quite successful landscape painter – rather than either Dicky Chopping or Francis Bacon's friend.

The other guests belonged to a different generation and a higher stratum of society. They included Phyllis Nichols, a pacifist friend of the Partridges, who was by this time 'a muddled old thing'; Colin Davies, a landscape painter; and Robert Kee, the respected TV journalist who was one of Woolley's ex-husbands and had attended Chopping's Hanover opening. At first, Wirth-Miller's closest companion was Woolley and Kee's young daughter, Georgie. They got on well and, years later, she would credit Wirth-Miller for her love of champagne.

Woolley was aware that Wirth-Miller initially felt out of place, and attempted to get in touch with Francis Bacon in the hope that he could join them. Wirth-Miller, however, was fast becoming accustomed to the company. The letters he sent to Chopping reflected a growing social confidence. 'I have to dash off to see Julian Pitt-Rivers almost at once,' he wrote concerning the aristocratic anthropologist, who had a house nearby. 'He really is very nice. One could fall for him. He has that marvellous yet awful quality of making one seem the very special centre of his attention.'

Woolley had bumped into Pitt-Rivers, his wife and the writer and heiress Nancy Cunard 'on a road miles from anywhere'. Her party had then been invited up to Pitt-Rivers's house at Le Roc, where they swam in the pool and took 'simple' lunches. Wirth-Miller wrote enthusiastically about truffled *oeufs anglais*, cherries soaked in brandy, local cider and 'delicious, ice-cold' Château de Panisseau.

Beyond the refinement of Pitt-Rivers's hospitality, Wirth-Miller enjoyed the local peasant cuisine too – including the fatty stew he would later cook for guests at the Storehouse. The party would pack wicker baskets of local food for afternoon picnics by the River Lot. Reflecting on the walk to the picnic spot, Wirth-Miller wrote: 'On the bank in one place near a ford masses of small blue butterflies were sipping the juice of the cow's shit and also some huge swallowtails.' As an artist, he was always able to capture the beauty and horror of nature in the same frame.

The nights at Woolley's farmhouse were often warm enough for Wirth-Miller to sleep outside. He wrote to Chopping: 'This night is wonderful – deep navy blue – with a golden flush on the horizon and masses of glow worms. Janetta and Johnny [her new boyfriend] sleeping under the stars in the garden. I can hear giggles and springs creaking.'

Suited Man Walking Through Door, unstretched rolled canvas found in Wirth-Miller's Storehouse tudio. *Unattributed (Author's personal collection)*

Gust of Wind by Denis Wirth-Miller, 1970–71. *(Collection of James Birch)*

Garden Landscape by Denis Wirth-Miller, 1941. *(Collection of James Birch)*

Trees and Grass by Denis Wirth-Miller, 1972. *(Private Collection)*

Estuary Landscape by Denis Wirth-Miller, 1978. *(Private Collection)*

Bending Figure, found in Wirth–Miller's studio. *Unattributed (Author's personal collection)*

Landscape, found in Wirth–Miller's studio. *Unattributed (Author's personal collection)*

Trompe L'Oeil by Richard Chopping (1953), and the cover for his novel, *The Fly* (1965). *(Author's personal collection)*

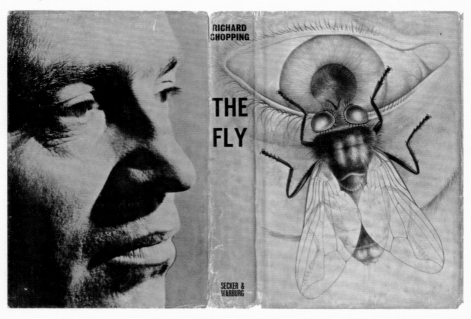

Facing page: Materials from the archive. *Clockwise from top left:* Wirth–Miller's studio; an Eadweard Muybridge dog; Bacon and Chopping; soldiers' buttons; Chopping when young; the studio's roulette wheel; the original *Goldfinger* skull; Bacon while on holiday in France with Chopping and Wirth–Miller; Chopping with a painting gifted by Bacon (©The Estate of Francis Bacon); a character from *Heads, Bodies and Legs*; Wirth–Miller's source photography for landscapes; Wirth–Miller and Zandra Rhodes; Chopping and Wirth–Miller in the late 1930s; a letter from Bacon (©The Estate of Francis Bacon). *(Author's personal collection)*

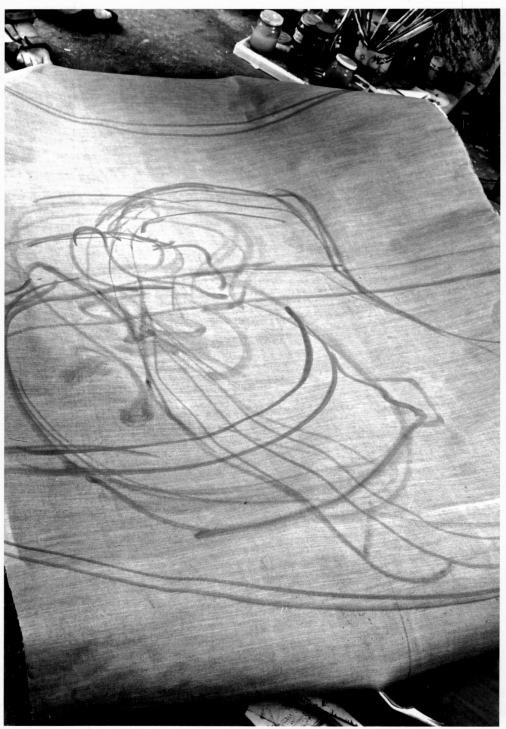

Large rolled painting by Francis Bacon.

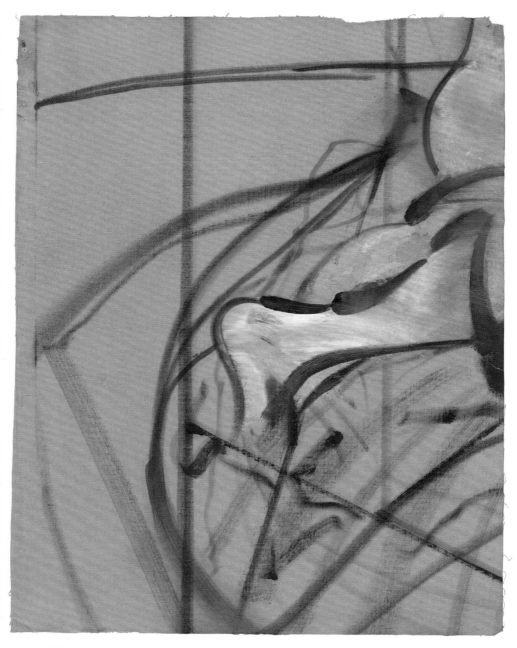

ERYNX SCHUNERANN — THEBES —   FRANCIS BACON

Top: Partial canvas painted by Francis Bacon found in Wirth–Miller's studio. (*©The Estate of Francis Bacon. All rights reserved. DACS 2016*)

Bottom: A strip hanging from the ceiling of Wirth–Miller's studio. (*Author's personal collection*)

Four dog paintings found in Wirth–Miller's studio. *Unattributed (Author's personal collection)*

The contested 'Freud' canvas owned by Chopping and Wirth–Miller. *Unattributed (Author's personal collection)*

The ground floor of the Storehouse. *(Author's personal collection)*

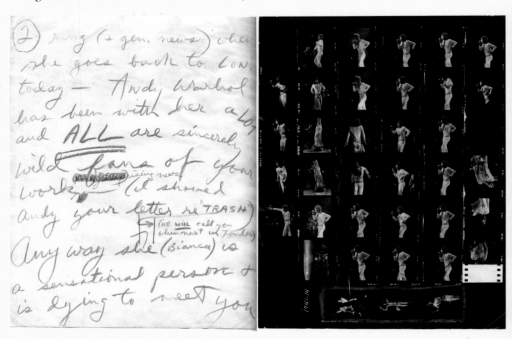

A letter from Peter Beard to Bacon on the reverse of a contact sheet of images of Mick Jagger. *(Peter Beard)*

Chopping and Wirth-Miller. *(Edward Morgan)*

An early painting of caged birds and boats. *Unattributed (Author's personal collection)*

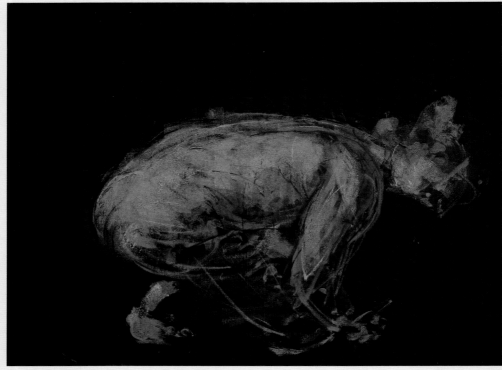

Crouching Beast. Unattributed (Author's personal collection)

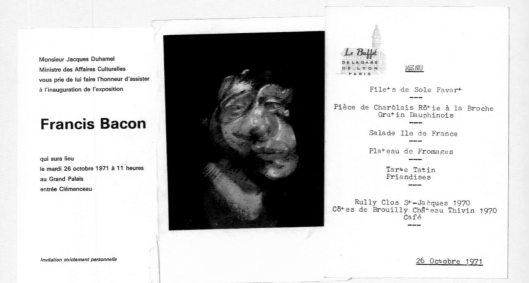

The invitation and dinner menu for Bacon's exhibition at the Grand Palais, Paris, 1971.

Materials, letters and photographs found in Wirth–Miller's studio. *(Author's personal collection)*

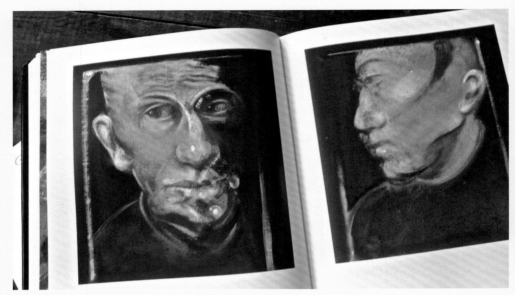

Francis Bacon's *Two Studies for a Portrait of Richard Chopping*, 1978.

Chopping and Wirth-Miller's ashes in a kitchen cupboard in the Storehouse.
(Author's personal collection)

He was full of remorse at the way he had treated Chopping, and wrote to him acknowledging it. Getting away from Britain had given him perspective, he wrote in one of his daily letters. He had been jealous and angry because he was lonely in Wivenhoe without him. He explained his own insecurities in reference to one of Chopping's trysts: 'I know I can never give to you what lies within Alex's power to provide – that alone is the sort of thought which makes me feel my inadequacy and therefore revert to childish behaviour with you when a concrete situation occurs – and I am reminded of my inadequacy.' In the mornings he waited for the post to arrive, hoping for news from Wivenhoe.

The correspondence had little effect on Chopping's desire for adventure, and he admitted as much in his replies. In one, he said he had felt the urge to have sex with a man he had met, pleading loneliness. Although Wirth-Miller found the letter upsetting, he remained realistic and conciliatory. If the act would help the relationship, he conceded, he should go ahead with it. 'About Wilbert,' he wrote, 'you are silly to deprive yourself of an experience – i.e. a black man – that you have always wished for.'

He wrote to Chopping asking him to come to France and offering to pay for his plane ticket. He was rebuffed even though the latter said being home alone was 'Miserable, miserable, miserable': 'there is no question whatever of me coming to France. I am afraid I shouldn't like it anyway. It all sounds too unreal for me and I suspect from the way you write that you are all in a permanent haze of alcohol.'

The holiday gave Wirth-Miller the distance he needed to consider his feelings, although his thoughtfulness went unreciprocated. Their relationship was strong, but when it came to important matters they had at least temporarily lost the ability to offer each other solace.

Chapter 12

From Dicky and Denis with Love

In April 1956, Dicky Chopping's work was included in a three-man show, *An Exhibition of Paintings and Drawings by Richard Chopping, Robert Ironside and Kenneth Rowell*, at the Arthur Jeffress Gallery. He was in good company. Ironside, a former assistant keeper at the Tate, was now enjoying a successful career as an artist. He had already exhibited at the Redfern and Hanover galleries, and had a joint exhibition with Keith Vaughan at Durlacher Bros. in New York, before joining the Jeffress stable. Rowell was a young Australian artist who would become well known for his theatre designs in his native country, and his lithographs would become part of the Tate collection.

The Times reviewer, under the title 'Present-day Romantics', praised Chopping's contemporary refashioning of *trompe l'oeil*:

> he is using the ambiguities of his technique to convey an allegory on the maturing of human wisdom in exactly the same spirit as the Dutch flower-painters when they allegorized the vanity of human wishes. The fly is the time-honoured symbol of the brevity of life and, in the Dutch tradition, bruises and patches of rot have begun to assail the mellow ripeness of Mr. Chopping's apples, cherries, and tomatoes.[77]

Chopping's paintings may have been a world away from those of Francis Bacon, but the latter thought that Chopping's work was interesting enough to bring it to the attention of his close friend Ann Fleming. Even though Bacon brought out the wild side in Wirth-Miller, he showed much loyalty to Chopping and consideration for his career. He insisted it would be worth Chopping's while giving Fleming a personal tour of the exhibition on the morning after the private view.

Chopping was nervous at the prospect of meeting Fleming. The former wife of the Viscount Rothermere, the proprietor of the *Daily Mail*, and a close friend of Noël Coward, she was known to not suffer fools.

While she was viewing his latest *trompe l'oeil* works, Fleming subjected Chopping to what he later described as her 'rapier tongue' in 'a fierce interrogation much as she might have interviewed a servant'. Afterwards, he had little sense that she liked his work.

Yet Bacon was correct: meeting Ann Fleming would prove to be worth his while. When Ann returned home she gave a positive report to her latest husband: the spy-thriller writer named Ian.

Chopping was summoned to an interview on the evening of 9 October 1956 at Ian Fleming's house in Victoria Square. Fleming was searching for an illustrator to work on his ongoing series of spy novels. The first four of these had sold well but he felt they deserved better packaging and decided to take matters into his own hands. He had just completed a new novel, and wanted a cover that would be effective on a billboard. The new book's title was *From Russia with Love*.

Ian Fleming's reputation was no less formidable than that of his wife. He was intelligent, self-centred, rakish and had a cruel wit. Born in 1908, during the war he had set up a unit of specialist intelligence troops called No. 30 Commando. They were covert agents trained in close combat, lock-picking and safe-cracking, with the mission of securing the enemy's secret documents. From running this network of agents, he was now looking after a network of correspondents for the *Sunday Times*. He took three months off every year to write the fictional adventures of James Bond, who was based on the secret intelligence agents with whom he worked during the war.

Dicky Chopping had not read any of the novels, but he knew of them. The first three novels, *Casino Royale* (1953), *Live and Let Die* (1954) and *Moonraker* (1955), had all sold well. The latest, *Diamonds Are Forever*, had sold out its first print run earlier in 1956. Sales were about to receive a further fillip when the Prime Minister, Anthony Eden, stayed at the Flemings' Goldeneye estate in Jamaica following the Suez Crisis.

Apart from the covers of his own books, Chopping's experience amounted to only two books. The first was an obscure work called *Alde Estuary: The Story of a Suffolk River* by W. G. Arnott, published locally in 1952. The second was the slightly more prestigious *The Saturday Book 15*, the 1955 edition of the annual book of miscellany published by Hutchinson, a previous edition of which Wirth-Miller had read while in prison. For the cover he had created a *trompe l'oeil* of a butterfly, a fly and an ivy leaf on a noticeboard. The board was also pinned with pieces of paper, one of which looked like it had been ripped from a calendar and featured the title. Chopping had craftily incorporated his own name on a strip of paper pinned to the noticeboard's frame. He had never produced a cover for a work of adult fiction.

Wirth-Miller and Bacon had been invited to join him at the Flemings's house. Chopping later wrote, 'Fleming himself

opened the door immediately ushering me upstairs to his study
. . . he said, as if I had appeared by chance: "You are just the man
I wanted to see!"[78] Chopping was surprised by his ebullience,
and reported that 'Fleming was very red-faced, with high blood
pressure from too much alcohol and too many cigars.' Meanwhile,
Wirth-Miller and Bacon joined Ann Fleming and were served
champagne and caviar.

Chopping described Fleming breathing cigar smoke out at
the same time as explaining the brief. He wanted to commission
Chopping to produce a picture to his specifications, which
would then be used for the cover of his new novel. By the time
he joined Bacon and Wirth-Miller, the commission had been
secured from Fleming. Regarding the fee, Chopping wrote,
'Ten guineas was the usual fee for a jacket, while my paintings
sold for around twenty (Francis Bacon's incidentally sold for one
hundred).' When Chopping had asked for £30 as his fee, 'he
replied "Oh no, my dear fellow, you must have more than that",
and wrote out a cheque for £40.'[79]

Chopping was pleased but had several reservations. He was
inexperienced with regard to book design, and it might prove
complicated to ensure that the painting would also work as a
front cover. Fleming did not want the painting to have gaps set
aside for the title: Chopping would need to incorporate the title
and author name himself. The author's list of requirements was
helpfully clear but very extensive: 'He wanted everything except
the kitchen sink to illustrate the overall straightforward message
of a murder done with a gun.'

The most problematic consideration for Chopping was that
the painting had to be completed quickly as the book was due
to be published in April 1957. Chopping was never a fast worker
and his *trompe l'oeil* works took a particularly long time.
Years later he learned that he had not been first choice for the

commission: Lucian Freud had turned it down. 'Perhaps just as well,' Chopping noted, 'for he was an even slower worker than I.'[80]

Fleming specified that he wanted a gun crossed with a red rose, and added that the rose was to include a stem, leaves and a tiny dewdrop on one of its petals. As for the gun, firearms expert Geoffrey Boothroyd had advised Fleming that a Smith & Wesson .38 Special MP with part of its trigger ring sawn off for faster firing was the only weapon that would realistically fit the narrative.

Chopping had no experience of typography. He said that he spent several days in his studio attempting to design an appropriate font. Wirth–Miller came to his assistance and offered a solution: he should use a basic, utilitarian font. In the James Bond novels, romance was secondary to the theme of intelligence, so an ornate, flowery typeface would be inappropriate. He suggested looking at typefaces used by the army, such as that stencilled onto ammunition boxes and vehicles. It was a masterstroke. Chopping discovered that the font was called 'Packing Case', which he applied in capitals. It became part of the Bond brand.[81]

For the *trompe l'oeil* image, Chopping began by drawing the objects individually to the required scale before incorporating them into the master image with carbon and tracing paper. The process was lengthy and he spent all of November 1956 confined to his studio. His experience of botanical drawing made the rose comparatively easy, but the gun posed problems.

As a pacifist, he had never previously been drawn to depicting weaponry, and the reproduction needed to be as exact as possible. Fleming consequently asked Geoffrey Boothroyd to lend Chopping the correct gun so he could paint it from life. The gun arrived by registered post.

He then combined the objects to find the correct balance for the overall work. The proofs show his method. He first laid down the bud of the rose and the grip of the gun, before filling in the details on the flower's stem and the metal body of the revolver. Last came the background for which he used a woodgrain pattern to suggest a table. The woodgrain would become another repeated feature of the Bond covers.

In his preliminary sketches for the gun, which he showed to Fleming, Chopping signed the work by painting 'CHOPPING' along the gun's frame between the grip and the trigger, in place of the manufacturer's trademark. Fleming ordered him to remove it.

'It has been the devil to complete, but fascinating', Chopping wrote to Fleming when he announced that the work was finished. Fleming summoned him to the *Sunday Times*'s offices on Gray's Inn Road.

Chopping took the painting with him on the train to London, wrapped in brown paper. Once again, he was nervous. Fleming had not seen anything beyond the preliminary sketches and had barely made comment. As far as Fleming was concerned, he would not expect Chopping to meddle with his writing, so neither would he tamper with Chopping's artistic style beyond the brief.

When Chopping reached the *Sunday Times*, he was shown up to Fleming's office. As he walked into the room, Fleming was in the process of finishing a telephone call and gestured for Chopping to be seated. Putting the receiver down Fleming laughed out loud and then explained that the call had been from a detective at Scotland Yard. He said that Chopping was now a wanted criminal and the police were about to come to arrest him. A gun identical to the one now sitting in Chopping's studio had recently been used in a very bloody triple murder. Fleming then flashed a warm smile and told Chopping not to worry, he had ironed out the technicalities with the police. The unnerving joke was typical of Fleming.

When Chopping unwrapped the package, Fleming was delighted. He gave him an additional £20.

He followed up the meeting with a letter: 'First of all a thousand congratulations on the jacket. It is quite in your topmost class and Annie loves it also. You and I are really a wonderful team.'

Their partnership would continue, almost uninterrupted, for the remainder of Fleming's life.

A few weeks later, on Sunday, 16 December 1956, the inhabitants of the Storehouse heard the news that Nina Hamnett was dead.

In 1953, not long after she had attended Chopping's breakthrough exhibition at the Hanover, she suffered a drunken fall. A botched operation left her with one leg shorter than the other, and she was incontinent, but she continued to go to the Fitzroy with the aid of a walking stick, with her trademark crooked hat perched on her head. Her circumstances worsened, forcing her to leave her beloved Fitzrovia. On 13 December 1956 she threw herself forty feet down from her bedroom window in Little Venice, impaling herself on the railings below. She survived the immediate impact and was reported to have said, 'Why won't they let me die?' Her wish was soon granted. She died in St Mary's Hospital, Paddington, three days afterwards. On receiving the news, Wirth–Miller remained silent, went out alone and returned very drunk.

The manner of her death was shocking, but her demise may have been anticipated due to her dipsomania and health problems. Her downward spiral had already begun by the time Wirth–Miller first met her twenty years earlier.

Wirth-Miller was simultaneously concerned about the health of other friends.

John, the 17-year-old son of Helen Lessore, became paralysed in May 1956 and faced a long period of hospital care. By this time Wirth-Miller was exhibiting at Lessore's Beaux Arts Gallery and he had become friendly with John, who recalls: 'During the first two months, Denis visited me in hospital at Neasden on every single day that I had no other visitor and then went back to central London to sit with my mother, who was distraught with my illness, so that she wouldn't be alone. He only stopped when I was off the danger list.'

Following his time in Neasden, in north-west London, John Lessore was transferred to the specialist hospital at Stoke Mandeville. Lessore described it as a 'sort of voluntary willy-nilly prison. If this is the top place in the country God knows what the others must be like. I think hospitals are the most dreadful places imaginable.' He reported on the limited view of the world from his hospital window in great detail. With his experiences of being in a prison cell, Wirth-Miller would have sympathized.

While some people were affronted by Wirth-Miller's occasional directness of opinion, children and young adults seemed to respond to his honesty and the seriousness with which he regarded them, as well as his personal support. John Lessore, who would go to the Slade and whose work is included in the collections of the Tate, Royal Academy and National Portrait Gallery, wrote to Wirth-Miller: 'I really owe you and mummy anything I do, since you two are the only ones who have ever taken any genuine interest in my painting.'

The young man also understood what both Wirth-Miller and Bacon were trying to achieve in some of their works:

I know you are an artist because when I look at your reeds I feel their reality, I can see them blowing in the wind, and when I look at Francis's people yelling I want to block some imaginary ears because the people are so real that there is a sort of void and I feel that since the man is screaming so violently there is something missing if I can't hear it.

John Lessore, who knew many of the leading artists of the day through his association with the Beaux Arts, was aware of the extent to which Wirth-Miller would go to help his other close friends, including Francis Bacon and John Minton: 'There were periods when Francis was suicidal and would ring Denis, who would drop everything, come down from Wivenhoe and sit and talk to him till the risk passed. He did the same for Johnny Minton, who was very depressive.'

It is not known how serious was Bacon's contemplation of suicide, and what in particular provoked these episodes. However, around the time of John Lessore's extended stay in hospital, it was becoming increasingly clear that John Minton, who had moved to Apollo Place in Chelsea in 1954, was in desperate need of emotional support.

Minton is often described as 'mercurial'. His mood swings were drastic and his self-belief – in everything from his appearance to his conversation to his art – was low despite his gregariousness. Throughout the time Wirth-Miller had known Minton, during their nights in Soho at the Gargoyle and the Colony Room, he would drink heavily and fall into self-pitying monologues.

His problems would also be evident during his frequent trips to see Wirth-Miller and Chopping in Wivenhoe. On a recent occasion, in April 1955, while the three men had been drinking at a pub in the village, Minton had been drawn towards a sailor who was friendly with Wirth-Miller in particular. The sailor rejected his advances and someone made the inference that, if Minton wanted sex, he would have to pay for it. Minton rushed out of the pub and left Wivenhoe without stopping to gather his things from the Storehouse. Wirth-Miller sent Minton a letter of apology. His friend responded:

> Thank you for returning my sponge-bag and for your letter. I do not see why you should apologise to me in any way, it is I who behaved like a little monster, I shall I daresay finally learn that he who wants to be loved by everyone and wants more than it is his right to have ends up with Nothing. I'm sorry, though, I ran away.[82]

For a decade, Minton had been one of the darlings of the art world and a highly successful illustrator. He had made a significant impact on decorative art and design, from contributing works for the Festival of Britain to illustrating Elizabeth David's Mediterranean cookery books. As a painter the success at his solo shows at the Lefevre allowed him to step out from the shadow of Colquhoun and MacBryde, although he still revered them. Furthermore, he was a respected teacher at the Royal College, and his instruction had played a part in helping the Kitchen Sink artists to break through.

His love life – beset by obsessions and complications involving several sailors, the former sailor and body-builder Ricky Stride, the wrestler Spencer Churchill and Norman Bowler – was made worse by his ingrained neediness. The success of his work provided a necessary anchor. As the 1950s progressed, that anchor was taken away.

The artist Patrick Heron was among notable voices decrying contemporary British art's need to illustrate and rely on draughtsmanship. It was parochial and constrained. The Kitchen Sink school, acclaimed so readily just a couple of years earlier, was quickly dismissed, as was the neo-Romanticism that fostered the rise of Graham Sutherland and then John Minton. Sutherland's reputation was receding and he witnessed Bacon assuming the albeit facile title of 'Britain's greatest living painter'. He was surprised when he was accused of borrowing from Bacon's work. His bitterness would increase when the man whom he regarded as a close friend started to make sarcastic comments about his work, including 'very nice . . . if you like the covers of *Time* magazine'.[83]

Sutherland, the master, was becoming outdated, and the Roberts were faring no better. The novelty of their kilts, abrasiveness, drinking, fighting and open homosexuality had worn thin. They were no longer young and dangerous: they were middle-aged alcoholics, unreliable, chaotic and difficult. Their softened, expressionist take on cubism was no longer fresh and, like other neo-Romantics, their slide towards obscurity was rapid. By the mid-1950s, there were new heroes to admire, and they came from across the Atlantic.

Abstract expressionism, which had taken hold in the United States through the works of Jackson Pollock, Barnett Newman, Mark Rothko and Willem de Kooning, was strong, daring and free of constraint. Contemporary British art seemed typified by intricate re-illustrations of Victorian fairy-tales in comparison to these bold, expressionist painters with their action painting, mark-making and colour fields. The point was underlined by the Tate's *Modern Art in the United States* exhibition in January 1956.

While the neo-Romantics fell from favour, Bacon and Freud, with their experimental and robust takes on the figurative, were immune. Curiously, while the damning of the work of many of his more successful friends was beginning, the career of Denis

Wirth-Miller was gaining momentum at the Beaux Arts. Like Bacon, but without anything like the acclaim, he was developing his own language; he would never be a household name, but neither was he a prisoner to stylistic trend.

Minton was. The students at the RCA were beginning to take note of the developments in abstract expressionism, and their teacher, still only in his late thirties, was becoming branded as an irrelevancy to the progress of contemporary art.

He was drinking too much and losing his way mentally. The quality of his work was suffering, and the reviewers of his February 1956 show at the Lefevre turned on him. Stephen Bone of the *Guardian* called the paintings 'a trifle dull'; John Berger wrote that the new works were 'only the framework for the paintings they could have been. [He] impatiently formalizes the scene into attractive toy blocks . . . seldom built up together to make a compulsive image of a street or a coastline'.[84]

Minton became deeply despondent and full of self-loathing. He drank himself senseless, attempting to keep pace with the likes of Wirth-Miller, Bacon and the Colony Room regulars such as John Deakin. He started to drink so much and so continually that it was no longer worthy of comment when he was found lying comatose under the tables at the Colony.

John Lehmann, who commissioned much of Minton's illustrative work, noted the change in him. In March 1956, after a dinner with Minton, Christopher Isherwood and the American portrait artist Don Bachardy, he noted: 'John M. dismayed us all by his frenzied, egocentric behaviour . . . in spite of his still spare, unbloated and youthful look, he has become a soak – with the nastily malicious undertone that soaks always betray. A tragedy.' Minton was aware he had a problem, saying to Carel Weight, who also taught at the RCA, 'I've always wondered what an alcoholic is like, and now I realize it's myself.'[85]

While his own reputation was faltering, he became obsessed with Francis Bacon's growing success. Bacon had tolerated Minton but he saw his brand of neo-Romanticism as a sentimental throwback and mere illustration. Most of the time, Bacon would be polite, and would join Minton for lunches with Buhler and Moynihan at the RCA, but occasionally their encounters would bring out his sadistic side: he openly despised weakness, and Minton's fragility annoyed him. At the Colony he once upended a glass of champagne over Minton's head and, as he rubbed the liquid into his hair, repeated his favourite adage: 'Champagne for real friends; real pain for sham friends.'

By April 1956, Minton was no longer capable of teaching due to his drinking and psychological issues. He took a year's leave of absence from the Royal College. 'Don't possess anything,' he used to counsel, 'or it will end up possessing you.' He gave away his drawings and paintings to friends, including Denis Wirth-Miller, and said he was turning his back on painting.

He tried to paint again in Spain that summer, but it was disastrous. He wrote to Jocelyn Herbert (also a friend of Chopping's since their time at the London Theatre Studio) to say that he had destroyed all the watercolours intended for an exhibition at the Leicester Galleries:

So now there are none. The Leicester Galleries will be Furious: I mean they gave me £250 to come to Spain, to paint. Paint, what's all that, I ask? What do they mean? I was of course mad, to try. After forty, one cannot be a promising Romantic artist . . . I daresay it's already done. I feel sadly out of date.[86]

In 1955, Minton had attempted to asphyxiate himself by wrapping a sweater around his head and putting a gas poker inside. In the latter part of 1956, he tried again and failed. He called Denis Wirth-Miller and asked him to stay with him at Apollo Place. Wirth-Miller, having returned from France, left immediately and stayed with Minton for the next ten days. Minton claimed that he was stopping drinking and went to his doctor every day to receive a shot of vitamin B. Nonetheless, whenever Wirth-Miller went out to meet Francis Bacon or to restock the groceries, he would return to find new bottles of gin hidden around the house.

Wirth-Miller took Minton to visit Paul Danquah in Battersea and remembered him shaking uncontrollably as they walked across the bridge. The Roberts, who still visited Minton despite the ructions that had occurred at 77 Bedford Gardens, once said they believed that their friend was taking drugs by this point of his life.

John Minton (left) as a guest at the Storehouse. *(Author's personal collection)*

Wirth-Miller tolerated Minton on the occasions when he descended into self-pity and drunkenness at the Colony Room, and his sympathy now extended to Minton's deeper depression. Unlike Bacon, he genuinely liked Minton and thought him talented.

Minton's final public act, on 3 December 1956, was to attack the new developments in contemporary art when he returned to the RCA to assess an exhibition of students' work. Two of the criticized students responded by publishing an open letter in the RCA's news-sheet, emphasizing that they were of a new generation, with new cultural reference points, producing art that Minton did not seem able to understand. Their riposte would have spoken to the fears he had already acknowledged to Jocelyn Herbert.

Minton had been working on a series of murals for the Reed Group and on the 19 January 1957, over a late-night coffee, he told the painter Stanley Ayres, 'I've decided I'm not a painter. I'm a decorator and muralist. I've no right to teach painting at the Royal College.'[87]

John Lessore recalls John Sykes, who lived at Apollo Place, telling him that Wirth-Miller phoned Minton on the following evening, but received no answer: 'he then rang the man in the flat below [Sykes], who went upstairs, looked in and said it was OK, Johnny was asleep'.

At about 10 p.m., Minton's friend Kevin Maybury noticed an empty bottle of sleeping tablets in the bathroom; he and Sykes realized that Minton was not sleeping, but in a comatose state. An ambulance was called but Minton was declared dead on arrival at St Stephen's hospital. He was thirty-nine. Chopping's diary entry for 21 January 1957 includes the stark note: 'Francis B telephoned to say Johnny had killed himself.'

The coroner declared that Minton had committed suicide. Despite the evidence, neither Wirth-Miller nor Chopping would

bring themselves to accept the official verdict. According to
Lessore, it seems that Minton may have thought that Wirth-
Miller was on his way to see him, and, as Frances Spalding
relates, Minton also expected Kevin Maybury to return to
Apollo Place earlier that evening. Wirth-Miller and Chopping
believed that his overdose was a cry for help or a tragic accident;
that if he had been found in time, he might have come back
from the brink, found a new way forward in his art, and returned
to sign the visitors' book once again.

Following Minton's suicide, Keith Vaughan, with whom he
had lived for six years, wrote in his journal:

> Much affected by the news of Johnny's death on Sunday
> night. Although long anticipated and felt to be inevitable
> the fact is profoundly shocking and hard to grasp. The one
> outstanding thing about him was that he was very much
> alive. He was never, as with some people, half in love with
> death. But he was in love with destruction . . . No one else
> could shine in his presence – his light was too strong – you
> were devoured and robbed of your identity – and he
> managed to persuade you that this did not really matter.[88]

Vaughan, for all his associations with the bohemia of Fitzrovia
and Soho, was a shy man, sensitive to being dominated by the
forceful characters in the art world. In his diary on 27 January
1955, he recorded at length the emasculation of Dennis
Williams, who idolized Bacon and lived in a small room
adjoining his temporary studio. He would do little things to
help Bacon but 'If I offered him a cup of tea he wouldn't drink
it. He just didn't see me.' Endlessly ignored, 'I felt absolutely
shattered, as though my personality had been wiped out.'[89]
Minton and Bacon may not have got on, but that was partly

because they both took centre stage, and others had to orbit around them. There was not enough space for both of them in a small room such as the Colony, or even in the wider art world, without there being friction.

Chapter 13

Golden Roses

Dicky Chopping and Denis Wirth-Miller had become friendly with the tenor Peter Pears when they were young men. They had been introduced to his partner, Benjamin Britten, when the composer returned to Britain from the United States in 1941, and a long-term friendship developed between the two couples.

Chopping harboured a schoolboy secret concerning Britten that he was loath to admit. In 1928, at the beginning of term, the headmaster of Gresham's asked Chopping's parents if their 11-year-old son could meet Benjamin Britten, a new-boy, at Ipswich station. Even though Britten was older − fifteen − Chopping was charged with making sure he made his way to the school without any problems. Chopping, who was travelling with a school friend, remembered:

> When we got to Ipswich we took into our carriage a shy, reserved, weedy-looking boy with the vulnerable appearance of a leveret. We didn't think much of him and virtually ignored him. Philistines that we were it did not interest us to know that he was a talented musician. We didn't care.

(Years later, Chopping's friend John Craxton would describe meeting the adult Britten as like talking to an oyster.)

When changing trains at Norwich Chopping and his friend set out to have 'a last-chance, blow-out tea' in the restaurant of the nearby cinema. 'He to our intense disgust went off by himself to the cathedral to play the organ. What a wet, we thought.' Then when they arrived at Holt station, they deserted the new boy: 'we gave our encumbrance a cruelly brief direction to Farfield [the house to which Britten had been assigned], a mile from the station'.

As adults, Britten, Piers, Chopping and Wirth-Miller were all involved in the arts scene in East Anglia. The friendship between the two couples strengthened and they met often, and the Wivenhoe couple would attend the opening of Britten's operas. On 7 June 1945, just a month after the end of the war in Europe, Britten's opera *Peter Grimes* was premiered at Sadler's Wells, with Chopping and Wirth-Miller in attendance with John Minton and Keith Vaughan, as well as Frances Partridge and Janetta Woolley. Four years later, in 1949, Graham Sutherland accompanied Chopping and Wirth-Miller to Britten's *Let's Make an Opera*, meeting beforehand at his home, The White House.

Later that year, on 12 December, Britten sent a postcard to the Storehouse from Illinois, asking about Wirth-Miller's small exhibition at the premises of the framer, Albert Hecht:

> We've nearly finished our dreary tour from college to college and ladies' music clubs to philharmonic forums. There have been lovely pictures to see but otherwise too much tension and too many nerves (and Martinis!) hope to see you when we get back? How's Albert H. going, Mister D? Love to you both from Ben and Peter.

Eventually, Chopping found the moment to apologize for his schoolboy behaviour. Chopping and Wirth-Miller exhibited their paintings at the first Aldeburgh Festival of Music and the Arts, founded by Britten and Pears in 1948, and did so again in 1954, when Wirth-Miller was in his more figurative phase. On seeing Wirth-Miller's work, Pears asked him to paint his portrait. A lunch was arranged in Wivenhoe, during which Chopping cut his hand badly while carving the lamb. After lunch, Wirth-Miller took Pears to his studio to begin the portrait. Meanwhile Britten and Chopping went for a walk down the River Colne towards Brightlingsea. While Chopping tried to hide the blood-sodden handkerchief wrapped around his right hand, he confessed to his childhood misdemeanour. On hearing the story, Britten, perhaps being kind, denied any knowledge of the event, saying that his parents drove him to school. But Chopping wrote:

> I know as clearly as I am writing these lines that it did happen . . . and I have always been ashamed that we were not nicer to him – not because he is now famous but considering how unhappy I was at the time, the least I could have done would have been to be nicer to him. My loss.

In June 1957 Chopping designed the artwork for the catalogue of Britten and Pears's festival. Arthur Jeffress described his work as 'an absolute dream'. He also confirmed that Chopping's *trompe l'oeil* works were still selling well in his Mayfair gallery as well as generating new commissions.

Britten and Pears's friends, brother and sister John and Rosamond Lehmann, were also part of Chopping and Wirth-Miller's circle. John Lehmann, as a leading literary figure and commissioner of modernist illustrations, was known to most of the artists in 1950s bohemia, although he was probably closest to Johnny Minton and Keith Vaughan. He was also friends with Stephen Spender and collaborated with Noel Carrington to produce *New Writing in Europe*. Rosamond, a novelist who had a nine-year affair with the Poet Laureate Cecil Day-Lewis, was a very close friend of the Partridges and it was this string of associations that had helped convince the press that Chopping was involved in the MacLean–Burgess spy scandal. In January 1956, Spender said of the Lehmanns (whose sister Beatrix was an actress), 'they think they're the Brontës when actually they are the Marx brothers'.[90]

Rosamond Lehmann had produced the English version of Jean Cocteau's 1929 novel *Les Enfants Terribles*, and for a while she and Chopping discussed the prospect of creating a new film version but the project fell by the wayside, partly due to Copping's other commitments.

Knowing of Rosamond Lehmann's fondness for Chopping and Wirth-Miller, Arthur Jeffress made sure he invited 'her chums' when, on 31 October 1957, he extended his first invitation to Lehmann to dine at his house. Lehmann unwittingly found herself playing referee to a waspish fight between Wirth-Miller and Chopping. Unperturbed, she took on a maternal role as the fixer of their rows. She would worry about the pair if she heard from Partridge that trouble was brewing and she would swiftly arrange to meet them.

Due to their workloads and the deaths and illnesses of their friends, the second half of the 1950s continued to be a troubled time for the Storehouse couple, despite their success as artists. Whatever peace of mind Wirth-Miller had found in France with Janetta Woolley continued to be usurped by Chopping's sexual liaisons.

Most of the time, Chopping and Wirth-Miller would turn a blind eye to each other's adventures but, as their friend David Queensberry put it, 'it is incredibly difficult to sustain a kind, loving relationship with endless, promiscuous fucking'.

The rows became worse and would sometimes end in brief periods of estrangement. Each reconciliation was passionate, and it was usually Wirth-Miller who made the first move towards it.

Both artists were tied down to pressing deadlines. Wirth-Miller was now on the treadmill of trying to produce enough quality work for solo exhibitions every two years. Simultaneously, Chopping was beginning to feel that he may have taken on too much work, and for clients too imposing to disappoint. Throughout the decade, Chopping was also involved with the Colchester School of Art, teaching 'Plant Drawing' part-time from 1951 onwards. He was well-liked at the college and was regarded as a natural teacher. Following his death, one of his former students, Mike Simkin, recalled in the *Guardian* his egoless approach during this busy time in the late 1950s: 'Nobody gave more encouragement with their work and spirit for life. He never spoke of his illustration work at the time, such as the covers for Ian Fleming's books, despite the fact that we were practising plant drawing and still life with fish, shells, flowers and grasses, the subjects of his own illustrations.'[91]

The couple's schedules were about to become even busier, against their better judgement.

Randolph Churchill, born in 1911, was not a universally popular man. The resoluteness, ambition and wit that had made Sir Winston an acclaimed wartime leader were reborn in his son as stubbornness, ruthlessness and rudeness. According to many who encountered him, he did not have the political skills or intelligence to make those character faults forgivable. Evelyn Waugh allegedly remarked when Randolph Churchill had a benign tumour removed: 'It was a typical triumph of modern science to find the one part of Randolph that was not malignant and to remove it.'[92] Waugh was one of his closest friends.

Churchill was, as David Queensberry identified, a control freak with self-destructive urges. He stood for Parliament in successive elections between the 1930s and the 1950s, but was successful only once: he won the seat of Preston in 1940 but lost it five years later. He committed himself to journalism and public speaking, relying on the attraction of his family name. On a lucrative lecture tour of the United States in the late 1940s, he was arrested and fined for reckless driving. He chose to conduct his own defence and failed.

His love life was less than harmonious. His first marriage, to the socialite Pamela Digby, became troubled partly due to his gambling debts. He married June Osborne in 1945 and had a daughter.

He retired to Stour House in East Bergholt in Suffolk, just to the north of the Essex border. Bobby and Natalie Bevan lived less than a mile away at Boxted House. Bobby was the son of the Camden Town Group painter Robert Polhill-Bevan, who had also been a member of the Cumberland Market Group alongside Chopping and Wirth-Miller's old friend John Nash. Bobby was an advertising executive with an extensive art collection, while Natalie was an artist. They would entertain a range of artists and writers, including Francis Bacon, Cedric Morris, Arthur Lett-Haines, Robert Gathorne-Hardy and the Wivenhoe couple, at Boxted House. Britten and Pears were also friends.

Natalie had been a fixture at Soho's Gargoyle club in the 1930s and associated with the artists Christopher Nevinson and Mark Gertler (who painted her twice). She had met Morris and Lett-Haines through her first husband, the writer and television producer Lance Sieveking, and became an integral player in the world of East Anglian bohemia.

Not long into her marriage to Bevan, Churchill fell in love with her, leading to an open relationship. Churchill believed he was the love of Natalie's life but, according to the artist

Glyn Morgan, who became a regular presence at Benton End, Churchill was just one of many men she saw in this period.

In 1958, Churchill sought Natalie Bevan's assistance when he was faced with finding a suitable present for the golden wedding anniversary of Sir Winston and Lady Clementine Churchill in October. As his father liked gardens, he had drawn up a plan to plant an avenue of varieties of golden rose at Chartwell, his parents' home. He contacted Cants Nursery in Essex, the oldest rose-growers in the country, but was informed that the roses would not flower in time for the celebration. Natalie Bevan provided a solution, which would be to commission a 'golden rose' certificate, gilt-framed and embellished with ornate calligraphy, which could be presented to the couple on the day of their anniversary as a foretaste of the avenue.

Consequently, she phoned Dicky Chopping. He was once again busy working for Ian Fleming. Furthermore, he had no experience of calligraphy and no interest in the commission so he turned her down. Churchill would not take no for an answer and, after much persuading, Natalie convinced Chopping and Wirth-Miller to come to Suffolk. Before the meeting, Chopping thought it would be prudent to ask David Queensberry for advice as Churchill was a friend of his mother.

Queensberry warned him that Churchill was 'not good news'. One night in the late 1940s, Queensberry had travelled to visit his mother at her house in Montpelier Square (the house Janetta Woolley bought, in which she set aside a flat for Chopping and Wirth-Miller's use). He walked in to find a drunken Churchill flirting with his mother. To put an end to the spectacle, Queensberry offered to drive Churchill home. The politician rudely turned him down, claiming that his personal chauffeur was outside. Queensbury was surprised but when he looked outside he acknowledged that there was a car at the kerb, but he didn't know that the term 'personal chauffeur' extended to a black-cab driver.

As Chopping reported, he and Wirth-Miller put on their best suits and travelled up to East Bergholt, prepared for the worst. They arrived to find a large Tudor house with an extensive garden overlooking the Stour Valley. They were shown inside and found Churchill pacing the floor of his drawing room, shakily clutching a tumbler of whisky, along with Natalie Bevan. Chopping's immediate impression was that he was an 'aggressive, weak bully'.

Chopping explained that he had neither the time nor the skill to fulfil the commission. 'No!' Churchill shouted, cutting him short. A tirade followed. When Churchill fell silent, Chopping recommended the services of a friend who might be more suitable. Churchill angrily dismissed the idea.

Wirth-Miller came up with the solution. While Churchill shouted over him, he suggested that, instead, the anniversary couple could be presented with a bound book of original paintings, each depicting a variety of golden rose that Churchill was going to plant in Chartwell's garden.

'But who is to paint them?' Churchill asked.

Neither Natalie nor their address books were short of artists' details, Wirth-Miller said. He was sure that many of their acquaintances would be eager to contribute.

It was 'as if a tactful breeze had blown across his brow', Chopping reported. Then Churchill shouted, 'Well, you two could both do a page!'

He appeared pleased with the names of possible contributors that Bevan, Wirth-Miller and Chopping began to list. He then issued two caveats: they would under no circumstances claim their idea as their own; and there was no question of being paid for their efforts.

Natalie Bevan later compiled a list of twenty-eight varieties of golden rose. Wirth–Miller chose 'Wheatcroft's Gold' and Chopping opted for 'Peace', a billowing rose that he knew from experience would take little time to paint. The work on the cover for *Goldfinger* was proving just as time-consuming as that for *From Russia with Love*, and Chopping was more interested in pleasing Fleming, a repeat client who paid well, than Randolph Churchill. *Dr No*, the Bond novel that immediately followed *From Russia with Love*, had not featured a Richard Chopping cover but Fleming had been keen to renew the relationship.

Prior to beginning the *Goldfinger* commission, Chopping had thought it might be a good idea to read the novel in order to ensure that the cover was appropriate, and also out of courtesy to his client. When he asked Fleming for the manuscript, the author laughed: 'Oh, you don't want to read any of *that* rubbish.' Chopping read it anyway.

The composition was macabre. At Fleming's behest, Chopping acquired a human skull from a local doctor. The author wanted the fatalistic romanticism of his plot to be symbolized by a rose clamped between the skull's teeth, with its thorny stem visible. A pair of coins were to be slotted into the eye sockets. Later, Fleming gave Chopping the coins as part-payment, and the artist kept the skull in his studio until his death.

Chopping's *trompe-l'oeil* process remained time-consuming and his attention to detail did not lessen for commercial commissions. He held Fleming in high regard. If he delivered, he knew he would be kept on board for future Bond titles, and the series was growing even more popular; Fleming's satisfaction would ensure him a decent living. He put all other projects on hold, including Randolph Churchill's birthday gift.

Wirth-Miller was also under pressure to produce work for his third solo show at the Beaux Arts. The exhibition was again called *East Anglian Landscapes*: the local landscape was now the sole focus of his work, and he was spending much of his time around the estuary and marshes. The works were still haunting and nearly always unpopulated. They were devoid of the romantic or sentimental, focusing instead on threat. In paintings such as *Landscape* (1957) and *Estuary in Flower – Ragweed* (*c.* 1960), a new aggressive luminosity and heightened colour were now bursting through the eeriness, suggesting that, like Bacon, his trips to Tangier had affected the way he understood and rendered colour.

These paintings, with their reedy vertical slashes, scratches, splashes and cross hatching, stand outside time through their dislocation from narrative and illustration. The splashes seem thrown onto the canvas with force and there is a new, stippled texture, suggesting that Wirth-Miller had incorporated something of the techniques of the abstract expressionists. In a 1958 *Landscape*, he experimented with electroplate and silver in the paint, with the paint dripped down the canvas to create regular striations. There is evidence from Wirth-Miller's studio that he was interested in a cut-up technique, slicing an image into vertical strips and then removing alternate strips. The result was partial obscuration while the form of the subject was still recognizable.

Several weeks after the initial meeting with Churchill, Chopping was summoned to East Bergholt for a progress report. He had yet to begin his rose painting. The list of twenty-eight artists who would contribute to the album, though, had taken shape. Drawing on Chopping, Wirth-Miller and Bevan's connections, it was impressive and included John Nash, Ivon Hitchens, Duncan Grant, Vanessa Bell, Cecil Beaton, Augustus

John, R. A. Butler and John Aldridge. Nash was to supply a rendering of the rose 'Lydia' while Augustus John had agreed to contribute a depiction of 'Golden Emblem'.[93]

Nonetheless, Churchill was in an unpleasant mood. Chopping explained that he had nothing to show: Ian Fleming needed his book jacket more than Winston Churchill needed a birthday present.

According to Chopping, Churchill exploded on hearing Fleming's name. 'Never mind *painting* for that Jewish . . . hack writer. *Get on with my father's painting!*'

Chopping found the anti-Semitic outburst bizarre. Fleming was a Scottish Protestant, and his father had been a drinking companion of Sir Winston.

Chopping weakened after a further onslaught from Churchill and agreed to prioritize the rose painting. His revenge, he decided, would be artistic. On top of one of the leaves of Randolph's rose, he painted a fat bluebottle. Later, Wirth-Miller would also take his revenge.

The golden rose album, which included an additional, twenty-ninth work by Matthew Smith, was presented on 12 September 1958. Initially it was supposed to be a surprise but a letter, dated a week earlier, from Winston's private secretary Sir Anthony Montague Browne reveals that Winston Churchill was forewarned of the plan and professed to be 'delighted'.

One Saturday morning shortly beforehand, Chopping and Wirth-Miller drove up to Suffolk for a friend's wedding. They had finished their rose pictures so they stopped off en route and handed their commissions over to Randolph Churchill. Chopping later wrote that he was 'full of illogical nervous relief and anticipation'. His 'Peace' was a finely detailed single, fully open rose and stem, plus bluebottle. He was surprised by Churchill's response when he showed the work: he liked it.

Wirth–Miller had completed two works for 'Wheatcroft's Gold', and he invited Churchill to choose between them. Churchill made his choice: a series of seven sketches on a single sheet, showing the rose in different states of opening.

'What are you going to do with the other one?' Churchill asked.

As described by Chopping, Wirth–Miller picked up the second picture, tore it into four pieces, and threw them into Churchill's lit fireplace.

'What the bloody hell did you do that for?' Churchill shouted. 'We could have sold it!'

The couple left, assuming that they would never have to see Churchill again.

They had not seen the last of the 'rebarbative, arrogant fellow', as Chopping called him. Just after Christmas, Churchill phoned the Storehouse and ordered them to come to his New Year's party. They had already accepted an invitation to Angus Wilson's party on the other side of Suffolk but Churchill insisted on their attendance. The couple found him pathetic but intimidating. They decided to arrive at Churchill's house early in the evening, stay a short while and race across the county to Wilson's party.

Chopping wrote that when they entered the house they found a lavish spread, with holly and mistletoe strewn across white tablecloths. Churchill and a young man, his secretary, stood in front of the fireplace into which Wirth–Miller had tossed his painting, holding glasses of champagne. There were no other guests.

Chapter 14

Chippy Chopping

Dicky Chopping delivered his cover for Ian Fleming's *Goldfinger* in March 1959 and reported that he was pleased with his handiwork. He felt it had the delicacy of his *From Russia with Love* cover, but it was more immediately eye-catching. The technical accomplishment of the composition was not lost on Fleming. He wrote to congratulate Chopping on the new jacket design. It was, he felt, 'quite as big a success as the first one', and enthused: 'no one in the history of thrillers has had such a totally brilliant artistic collaborator!'

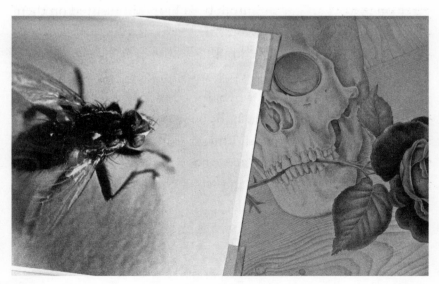

Some of Richard Chopping's preliminary images for Ian Fleming's *Goldfinger*.
(Author's personal collection)

The praise was not insincere: the author would go on to commission Chopping for every subsequent Bond cover until his death in 1964. It was apparent that Fleming regarded the dust jackets as part of the Bond image along with the dinner jacket and dry martini. Travelling on the London Underground, Chopping was delighted to see his work blown up to many times its original size on poster adverts.

In the knowledge that he was unlikely to be involved in any other enterprise that made so much money, Chopping asked whether he could keep the copyright to his covers. Fleming agreed. Chopping then asked if he could waive his fee in exchange for a small royalty: 'Whereupon, as rapidly as a shot from a Smith & Wesson, he said, "Oh no, my company wouldn't wear that."'[94] Nonetheless, the amount of money he received from Fleming dwarfed that received from other commissions, and it gave him the freedom to pick and choose other projects.

Denis Wirth-Miller, on the other hand, was not doing well. His latest show at the Beaux Arts had garnered sales, but circumstances had left him unable to keep up momentum. On one of his repeated trips to Morocco with Bacon, he had fallen seriously ill after an insect bite became infected. When he returned to England, doctors confirmed that the infection had damaged his left leg and right arm. He was in chronic pain whenever he stood up, and had severe difficulty walking. His weakened arm made it very difficult to paint.

Bacon, too, was going through a troubled time. In 1958, he had signed a contract with the Marlborough in London. The gallery represented some of the heavyweights of British modern art: Henry Moore, Ben Nicholson and Graham Sutherland. It was a major player in the art market, attracted collectors and had a relationship with the world's major public galleries. By this point Bacon had already had solo exhibitions abroad at Durlacher

Bros. in New York and Galerie Rive Droite in Paris, and a travelling exhibition in Italy. With the Marlborough's support, Bacon's exposure and reputation, and the price for his canvases, would be ratcheted up even further. Furthermore, the gallery had agreed to pay off Bacon's considerable gambling debts, amounting to over a thousand pounds. His contract, however, stipulated that he had to provide a certain number of pictures per year.

Erica Brausen was appalled by his abandonment of the Hanover Gallery after she had nurtured his early career and invested so much money in him. The split was acrimonious, but Bacon may have felt guilty. It is thought that he gave her £100,000 when, in old age, she could not cover her medical bills.

Bacon was still spending much of his time in Tangier, with Wirth-Miller sporadically in tow. He may have remained hopeful that the light and being away from the Colony Room and the York Minister would help his work. As it turned out, he kept only one work he completed there in the late 1950s: *Painting*, also known as *Pope with Owls*. In contrast to the screaming popes, the work is almost comic, with owls replacing the finials of Pope Innocent X's throne. The pope figure, rather than in obvious anguish or fury, seems reflective. The purple of the robes is bold and luminous.

His relationship with Peter Lacy was finally reaching breaking point. Lacy's alcoholism had become chronic – he was drinking several bottles of whisky a day. Bacon spent time with the American writers, Allen Ginsberg and William Burroughs, as well as the more refined bisexual couple, Paul and Jane Bowles. Bowles, who moved to Tangiers in 1947, remained there until he died fifty-two years later. Stimulants and hedonism played a part in all their lives.

Ginsberg elicited from Bacon a telling remark about his painting. On asking how he completed a work, Bacon told him he did it 'with a chance brushstroke that locked the magic in – a fortuitous thing that he couldn't predict or orchestrate'.[95] The overall image and structure of the work was not usually improvised and he often used photographic source material, but he explained to Dicky Chopping in 1974 that the creation of the image was a process of evolution: 'I don't see pictures at once. I let them seep into my consciousness.' He did not like to draw in preparation for a painting – saying to Chopping, 'I feel that if I did drawings I would only be illustrating my own ideas' – and few Bacon drawings exist. There was a spontaneity in the application of paint; the particular way the paint coalesced to form a feature involved accident or 'magic'.

Wirth-Miller, by the end of 1958, was making headway in his career despite his debilitating illness. Following his three solo exhibitions at the Beaux Arts, he now had the interest of the prestigious Lefevre Gallery. Bacon wrote three letters to him from Cannes, before and after Christmas, shortly after he had made one of his regular trips to the Storehouse. Bacon was in the south of France with Lacy, and their main focus was gambling.

Poste Restante
14th CANNES
France A.M.

Dearest Dennis,

Thank you both so much for the week-end. I do hope I didn't behave too badly getting so drunk.

I give you the address poste restante as I do not know how long I shall be here – I am afraid things are going just as badly as they ever have it is so depressing – I know now once and forever not to go on ever trying again to go on living together. I do hope your lunch with Willie Peploe [of the Lefevre Gallery] went off well I should like to hear I am sure it is far the best gallery in London. do write and let me know when you have a moment – in my rush I forgot all my brushes I had so carefully washed – I've been a bit lucky in the Casino – Fondest love to you both & all best wishes for Christmas love Francis

Dearest Dennis,

Thank you so much for your letter – I am so delighted with your news you have every reason to feel elated I am sure Lefevre are the best gallery – I cannot tell you how pleased I am – and about selling the other pictures – you told me about the commission but not who it was for I do hope it goes well – I hope to be back in London very early in March – I am working on a lot of paintings but will not be able to finish them all here – I am going to try and go to Tangier early in April if by any chance you feel like coming over for a bit or both of you – you could have a room to work in it is lovely there at that time of the year – my love to Dicky and fondest love

    Francis

Bacon and Lacy's problems were not alleviated by the break in Cannes. The relationship was in its very final phase:

Dearest Dennis

It is lovely down here but still terribly crowded – we had a lovely week but now the rows have started really because I have made a little money in the Casino – but this is just between us it is terrible I suppose to be frustrated as Peter is in so many directions. I wish he could get a break even in the

Casino. I had dinner at the next table to Giacometti the other evening I heard someone remark that the English became like rasberrys [*sic*] in the sun and turned around and saw it was him. I wish you were down here. I know you would love it. I so hope the suit[?] is going well. Peter packed his bag to leave last night but I don't know what is going to happen – there is lots of bag packing here it is a place made for rows in any case. I do hope the work is going well – all my love to you and Dickie

Love Francis

In 1959, the Marlborough became concerned by Bacon's lack of output. Even when he returned to London to paint, he still did not have a permanent studio of his own and was relying on the continuing kindness of Paul Danquah and Peter Pollock in Battersea. The Marlborough staff were professional in looking

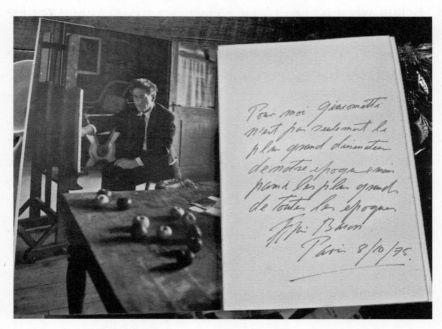

Francis Bacon's French dedication in *Alberto Giacometti: Dessins*, 1975.

after his interests but they were also professional in looking after their own. They persuaded Bacon that he should go to St Ives, renowned for the quality of light, in the hope that he would be able to work there in preparation for his first exhibition at the gallery in 1960.

Since Denis Wirth-Miller and Dicky Chopping had stayed in the town with the poet W. S. Graham, it had become the centre of abstraction in England. Local artist Peter Lanyon, who had his first solo show at the Lefevre in 1950, Patrick Heron, who had damned the illustrative motivation of much British modern art, Terry Frost and Bryan Wynter were all associated with St Ives and nearby Zennor. Despite the quality of the light, it was a strange destination for Bacon. He had little time for abstract art.

Bacon spent over three months in St Ives from September 1959 to January 1960. Now ostensibly free of his sado-masochistic relationship with Peter Lacy, he took Ron Belton with him. Belton was a previous conquest of the Colony Room regular Dan Farson, who described him as 'good looking in a dark, aggressive way'. Peppiatt and Farson's biographies of Bacon suggest that Belton was something of a London wide-boy; he had no interest in the art world; and he was willing to thrash Bacon. He was of a type that had a particular allure for the artist.

Bacon worked at 3 Porthmeor Studios, previously used by Ben Nicholson, Terry Frost and Patrick Heron, and he became friendly with the sculptor Barbara Hepworth. He also spent Christmas Day with the abstract artist Roger Hilton, who had just moved to the area and was set to become a great friend of W. S. Graham. Hilton was a former commando and a robust character with forthright views but in Bacon he met his match. Hilton told Bacon, 'I've always wanted to meet you because you are the only non-abstract painter worth consideration. Although of course you are not a painter – you don't know the first thing about painting.' Bacon replied: 'Good. I think my work is perfectly horrible. Now we can get together. You teach me how to paint, and I'll lend you my genius.'[96]

Michael Peppiatt reported that 'Bacon himself appears never to have talked about his stay in Cornwall', but his correspondence with Wirth-Miller provides some insight: he disliked it.[97] One letter reveals that Peter Lacy was still on his mind.

Segall House
The Wharf
St Ives
Cornwall

Monday 16th

Dearest Dennis

I often think of you and wonder how things are – it is terribly isolated here I have only finished 3 pictures so far but I hope they are a bit better but I could never live down here and am longing just to finish the work and leave. I often feel so lonely and unhappy. If Dennis dear you go to the Colony – would you try and find out from Leonard [a stockbroker who first introduced Bacon to Lacy] where Peter has gone if it is back to Mallorca or not and any news of him you can get – often I feel so distressed about him I do not know what to do. He wrote me such terribly unhappy letters and wanted to see me and then suddenly he wrote the letter I sent to Paul [probably Danquah] – I long to be free of Ron – I really wish he would get a job – I am in the most ghastly financial state I feel sure I shall never get straight – I do hope the work is going well. This is a stronghold of really dreary abstract stuff and they are all fanatical about it I cant tell you how bad it all is

– do let me know if Frank [Auerbach]'s show is good if you see it. If you ever felt like coming down you know I would love to see you both if you have a car it is the most wonderful country around this part. When you have time I would love to hear your news

Fondest love to you both

Francis

At some point during Bacon's trip, Wirth-Miller, seemingly without Chopping, went down to stay with Bacon in St Ives.

In another letter sent around this time, in which Bacon talks of Lacy selling *House in Barbados*, he calls St Ives 'a dump' and said he 'longs to get back to London'. His problems were not eased when, according to Peppiatt, Ron knocked out one of Bacon's teeth during a fight outside the harbour-side pub, the Sloop Inn.[98] When Bacon left, he abandoned his unfinished canvases, some of which were re-used by local artists.

When Bacon returned to London in January 1960, he went through a productive enough period to create new works for his first exhibition at the Marlborough, *Francis Bacon: Paintings 1959– 60*. The catalogue text was written by Robert Melville, whom he had known since his time at the Hanover Gallery. Some of the paintings from this period, such as those from the *Lying Figure* series, emphasize the positioning of the figure, rather than the expression of the face, to relay discomfort. These works were the preamble to a very productive decade, initiated by his move into a new permanent studio, 7 Reece Mews, very close to his former studio in Cromwell Place in South Kensington, in 1961.

When the Contemporary Art Society showed its recent acquisitions for the nation at the Arts Council Gallery in London in February 1959, three Francis Bacon works, including *Figure in a Landscape* (1956), were hung. The inclusion of works by Terry Frost, Roger Hilton, William Scott, Peter Lanyon and Patrick Heron revealed the strength of St Ives abstraction. There were also works by Wirth-Miller's friends Robert Colquhoun, Keith Vaughan and Michael Wishart, although Colquhoun's career was in its last throes. In 1958, he was given a retrospective at the Whitechapel Gallery in London; this was a blip in the downward spiral of the Roberts. Significantly Denis Wirth-Miller's *Landscape* (1956) was also included at the Arts Council Gallery show. His career was seemingly heading in the opposite direction. For the first time, his work was deemed worthy of being kept for the nation.

In April 1959, Chopping and Wirth-Miller, who always maintained their ties with the art community in Essex and Suffolk, were given a joint exhibition at The Minories, a new public gallery in Colchester. The building had been bought by the Victor Batte-Lay Foundation and, in a loose connection to Chopping and Wirth-Miller's early Fitzrovian days, the previous owner was Lucien Pissarro's sister-in-law, Dr Ruth Crawford.

Chopping exhibited sixty-three works, mostly of flowers and fruit, along with posters of his covers for *From Russia with Love* and *Goldfinger* and a drawing of the Smith & Wesson with the sawn-off trigger loop. The names of some of the lenders were notable, including his friends 'Mrs Ralph Partridge', Rosamond Lehmann and Peter Pears, as well as Paul Channon MP, the Earl and Countess of Cranbrook, Lord Medway and Lady Nichols. There was a rose drawing for the work commissioned for Sir Winston and Lady Churchill and a work-in-progress, 'Souvenir of Cliveden', commissioned by the Viscount Astor. It was obvious from the list of names that Richard Chopping had 'arrived' in social terms.

Denis Wirth-Miller showed twenty-eight paintings and eight drawings, principally from his three exhibitions at the

Beaux Arts Gallery. Most were marsh and estuary landscapes, but there were a couple of portraits as well as works from the dog series and *Wrestlers*, showing the influence of Muybridge on him in the early and mid-1950s. Again, some of the names of the lenders were socially prestigious, including the Cranbrooks and Prince and Princess Azamat Guirey.

There were only four works dating from 1959 as he was suffering from his infection, but Wirth-Miller's fortunes were about to improve. Two months later, on 12 June 1959, the Lefevre Gallery wrote to him, suggesting an exhibition date: 'I've been looking at the Exhibition programme, and from our point of view, the month of April next year would be best for an exhibition. I hope this is all right for you. We can go into the exact dates later on.' He was set to have his first solo show at the Lefevre. Dicky Chopping may have arrived as a painter of choice in society, but the news confirmed that Denis Wirth-Miller had 'arrived' as an artist.

Some of the collectors' names alongside his works at The Minories exhibition showed that he was attracting powerful patrons too. One of them was David Hicks, and the second half of the letter from the Lefevre indicates how important that name would become to Wirth-Miller: 'David Hicks came in this afternoon when I was out, and took one of your paintings on approval. If you are in touch with him before I see him myself, you might tell him that of course we will allow him ten percent on any business he introduces.'

David Hicks – who had amused Wirth-Miller and Chopping with his society pretensions – was now a leading interior designer for the rich. His support would be valuable to both men, but particularly Wirth-Miller. He would advise his clients to buy a Wirth-Miller landscape to complement his designs of their modern, but none too radical, high-spec interiors.

Chopping believed that Hicks was 'obviously gay', but that he wanted a high-class marriage to enhance his reputation. He proposed to Pamela Mountbatten – first cousin to Prince Philip and daughter of Louis Mountbatten, the last Viceroy of India. According to Hicks, they had met at a cocktail party, where she 'fell in love' with him instantly.

The couple came to stay at the Storehouse one weekend. Chopping and Wirth-Miller were usually relaxed hosts and had a very liberal stance when it came to the politics of sex, but the arrival of Pamela Mountbatten made them anxious about etiquette. They worried that it would not be 'proper' to offer them a double room straight away. They decided to give them separate bedrooms. Mountbatten took Chopping's room on the first floor, while Hicks was given the large, open-plan suite on the floor above.

Late at night, they heard Hicks furtively scramble down the stairs to Mountbatten's room, before creeping back up in the early hours of the morning. 'Poor girl – did she know what she was letting herself in for?' Chopping wondered years later.

The wedding was held on 13 January 1960 at Romsey Abbey close to Broadlands, the Mountbattens's Palladian-style seat in Hampshire. The Queen was invited to attend alongside entertainers such as Douglas Fairbanks and Noël Coward, as were Dicky Chopping and Denis Wirth-Miller.

On the day of the wedding the south of England was hit by blizzards, with several feet of snowfall. Chopping and Wirth-Miller had spent the previous night in London, and were given a lift down to Hampshire by the designer Tom Parr. He was Hicks's business partner and, as noted by Hecht in an aforementioned letter to Chopping, had bought a Wirth-Miller work in 1957. Progress in Parr's sports car through snowdrifts on country lanes was extremely slow and the passengers were 'frozen to the marrow', as Chopping put it. They were already dressed in tail-coats and had left their overcoats at home.

By the time they reached the abbey, the service had already begun. Chopping noted hundreds of disapproving glances as they tried quietly to take their seats. The church was as cold as the car.

At the end of the service, Chopping recorded, the royals paraded out of the abbey like 'bad-tempered dolls'. The remainder waited before being put aboard buses, which followed the royal convoy to the reception at Broadlands.

Chopping and Wirth–Miller were pleased to see that serving tables were laid out with champagne, lavish dishes and a wedding cake in the shape of Broadlands. While they were still queuing to shake hands with the wedding party, the lights cut out. Guests were knocked into by staff running to find candles, and Wirth–Miller claimed that the boy who accidentally hit him in the groin was the 11-year-old Prince Charles.

Once the staff had brought candles, the light was still dim but the handshaking ritual continued. As soon as that was concluded, Lord Mountbatten stood up and called for silence: the weather outside was becoming worse and any guest in need of transport back to London should leave immediately and take the buses to the station. There was no guarantee the rail lines would be operational if they waited any longer.

According to Chopping, there was a 'polite stampede' for the buses. Outside, he saw that Mountbatten had not been exaggerating. Parr, Chopping and Wirth–Miller decided to abandon the plan to drive back to London themselves and joined the crowd. The snow was falling so thickly that visibility was almost zero. The bus drivers were having difficulty getting the vehicles moving.

Chopping was standing directly behind the wheel of one of the buses that had started up; the driver was revving the engine in an attempt to move. Chopping quickly stepped to the side in case the wheels lost traction and the bus shot backwards. He then saw that Noël Coward and a friend were also behind the bus, chatting and oblivious. He shouted at them to step back. Immediately after Chopping's warning, the bus lost its purchase and hurtled backwards just as Coward and his friend jumped out of the way.

Coward approached Chopping and held him by the shoulders 'My dear, you have just, without a doubt, saved my life! What is your name?'

'Dicky Chopping.'

Coward misheard. 'Chippy Chopping?' he yelled. 'Chippy Chopping, I shall be seeing you on the train!'

On the bus journey, he heard Coward's voice again, coming from the backseat. 'There's Chippy Chopping! Chippy Chopping just saved my life . . . Chippy Chopping has *saved* my life!'

When they arrived at the station, the train had been held at the platform specially for their party. The train was old rolling stock, made up of Pullman cars – like 'little Edwardian drawing rooms', Chopping observed. There was not enough room for the party, which pressed through the carriage doors, taking the remaining seats and filling the corridors. Chopping lost contact with Wirth-Miller in the crush and was not sure he had made it onto the train.

Chopping managed to find a seat in a first-class carriage between a Rothschild heiress and a banker. Both were 'friendly enough, but a bit dull', so Chopping left his seat and tried to find Wirth-Miller.

He tracked him down and was glad to know that his partner was not still on the freezing platform. There were no seats anywhere near so Chopping forced his way back into the corridor. As he passed one carriage he heard, 'Chippy Chopping!'

Noël Coward poked his head out of a carriage and began repeating the story to the people packed into the corridor. When

Chopping moved off to return to his seat, Coward asked him where he was sitting. Ten minutes later, Coward put his head round the door of the first-class carriage, proffered a bottle of champagne, and squeezed in beside him.

To Chopping's surprise, during the long journey he got along very easily with the man he had strained to see at the 'Theatrical Garden Party' twenty years earlier. Coward was a friend of Ian Fleming and was impressed that Chopping was responsible for the Bond covers. When he found out that Chopping had met his rival, the playwright Terrence Rattigan, he launched into gossip. Coward then asked what Chopping and his partner were planning to do when the train reached London.

Chopping explained that they were due to meet the former Chanel jewellery designer Fulco di Verdura at Tom Parr's flat.

Coward threw his hands up in the air: 'Not darling Fulco? I must come with you. I haven't seen him for years!'

Di Verdura was reputedly one of Hicks's ex-lovers and consequently had not been invited to the wedding. He and Tom Parr were now a couple, and di Verdura was waiting for him to return from the wedding so that they could attend a dinner. A few months later, di Verdura would write to Chopping and Wirth-Miller from New York: 'I will *not* talk about the wedding . . . the only good thing is that it sends the Hickses to the oblivion where they belong.'

The train pulled into Victoria several hours late. Coward's white-gloved chauffeur was waiting at the kerb and ushered Coward, Chopping, Wirth-Miller and Tom Parr inside the vehicle. They were driven to Parr's flat, where champagne was awaiting them. The train was so delayed that di Verdura had already left for his dinner appointment and Tom Parr soon followed him.

Then, the 'imperturbable and patient chauffeur' drove the remaining party to Wheeler's on Old Compton Street. Chopping

found Coward to be one of the funniest men he had ever met. And
Coward liked him, too. They would remain friends, and Coward
would repeatedly invite Chopping and Wirth-Miller to his house
in Switzerland, although they never accepted the invitation.

David and Pamela Hicks, meanwhile, set off on honeymoon,
travelling to the West Indies on the *Queen Elizabeth*. They were
the only passengers on board.

In response to rumours that Hicks was homosexual,
Chopping wrote in his diary that Pamela 'did not appear to
deviate in her loyalty and love . . . Pammy wasn't a royal for
nothing; she had been trained to keep a stiff upper lip . . . it must
have cost her hard.' Whatever Chopping's concerns, the couple
had three children together and remained married until Hicks's
death in 1998.

Chopping and Wirth-Miller's work meant they were spending more time apart, but they wrote to each other daily wherever
they were, often signing off with 'dear old love'. When they
attended high-profile events together, there was a conspiratorial
air between them. Despite their delight at having made it to an
elevated social stratum, neither was entirely comfortable mixing
with the aristocracy.

Despite Chopping's public-school background, upper-class
acquaintances of the couple often took better to Wirth-Miller,
with his directness and raffish charm. Chopping's manners, good
nature and eagerness to please marked him out as 'bourgeois'.

Pamela Hicks appeared to dislike Chopping, but the Hickses
regularly invited the couple to their house in Chelsea and
Britwell House in Oxfordshire.

Chopping was starting to move away from the *trompe l'oeil*
paintings with which he had made his name. The Arthur Jeffress
Gallery was now selling his watercolour and tempera portraits

in which the central features of the face were close-up, detailed and sharply focused, and not framed by jawline or hair.

David Hicks admired the new works and commissioned Chopping to paint a small portrait of Pamela. It was one of his least successful works. Chopping described the setting of the painting as 'very 18th Century': she was portrayed lying in bed, having just given birth to her first daughter. Both found the process embarrassing.

'She hated it, shoved it in a drawer and never spoke to me again,' Chopping wrote. He also acknowledged his hubris: 'With [that portrait] died my shameful secret that the Pammie portrait might have led to painting the country's most revered lady, the Monarch. So much for secret ambition.'

Despite this, Hicks later commissioned Chopping to paint him for a companion portrait. In 1977, Chopping wrote to Hicks requesting the loan of both paintings for inclusion in that year's Aldeburgh Festival. Hicks agreed to send his own portrait, but would not send its companion: 'I am afraid Pammie would not want hers to be exhibited.'

The failure of the Mountbatten portrait more or less marked the end of Chopping's career as a professional portrait painter. He would continue to paint and to teach at art school, but from this point onwards his main passion would be writing.

Wirth-Miller, meanwhile, had his first exhibition at the Lefevre in April 1960. Some of the landscapes exhibited Wirth-Miller's recent changes in technique and use of luminescent colour. *The Times* reviewer acknowledged his skills while being disconcerted by his experimentalism:

The wide expanses of East Anglian marshland, its woody emptiness and monotony, have supplied the total subject of [Wirth-Miller's exhibition]. The pictorial limitations of the subject can be disguised if not indefinitely concealed by responsiveness to the change of light, weather and season that dominate such a landscape, and Mr. Wirth-Miller knows these intimately enough to convey their variety with rare economy when he chooses. But he is also a slave to his own rather clever prescription of stripes for reed-beds and serried blobs of paint for the shimmer of leaves and flowering grasses.[99]

Time and again in his career, Wirth-Miller would find that a radicalism in technique, admired in Bacon, Freud and the American abstract expressionists, would not be welcomed by the mainstream press in an English landscape painter.

Shortly after his first exhibition at the Marlborough in 1960, Bacon left on the SS *Kenya Castle*, presumably to visit Tangier, which was one of the stop-off points on the Union-Castle Line's 'Round Africa' service. Despite his apparent frustrations with Ron Belton while they were together in St Ives, the relationship was ongoing. Denis Wirth-Miller liked Ron, too, but must have made his desire too obvious.

Union-Castle-Line. S.S. "Kenya Castle"

I am so sorry I was annoyed with you at the station but I knew if you went to the other bar Ron would miss the train and have to take a taxi to the docks – you will be able to say I am an old governess but if I had made the same head on dash to seduce a friend of yours by trying to be outrageous you would not feel so good about it. But as you know it will make no difference as I shall always love you. It is very rough and Ron is in bed sick the crew are so handsome and charming and sweet on the boat they think we are a honeymoon couple isn't it camp, and are sweet to us – the boy who waits on us is so sweet and camp Ron has quite fallen for him. We drank your good luck and success with the bottle of champagne. At our table we have an old queer who has a physical training school in Nairobi and a charming young man and his wife going out to Uganda. The young man got drunk last night with me and confessed how he hated married life he said he hates homos, but gave me some luscious kisses in the cabin – will let you know how things go.

All my love to you both

Francis

In October 1960 he sent a further letter, this time from Monaco, where Wirth-Miller was due to meet him. Peter Lacy was evidently still on Bacon's mind, while the letter throws some light on the sado-masochistic relationship between Ron Belton and Bacon.

Dearest Dennis

Thank you so much for your sweet letter I did not show it to Ron so don't please mention anything about our exchange of letters when you come out. Do come with or without Tim Willoughby [a friend from the Colony Room] would you bring me £50 in £5 notes – I don't know long we shall last out here so come as soon as you can. I am terribly upset over Peter he looks so ill and is in such a state and can't speak to me. I cannot bear to see someone suffer because of me – do come out it would be wonderful to have you here. R sometimes is so violent I am afraid of him please don't mention to him I told you – I think Peter is going back to Mallorca I am afraid he will never forgive me and it is dreadful to see him looking

so ill   I feel desperate sometimes and feel I have done
something terrible. R is a really remarkable boy the more one
is with him he longs to see you. do come soon.

My fondest love to you and Dicky

love

Francis

After they met up in the south of France, both Bacon and
Wirth-Miller were initially knocked down by a bout of Asian flu.
After a few days of nursing each other back to health, they headed
to the beach, where they spent long days in the autumn sunshine.

Shortly before Wirth-Miller had left England, there had been
another bad argument at the Storehouse. Wirth-Miller, however,
was soon starting to pine for Chopping. 'I can't pretend I don't
miss you,' he wrote from Monte Carlo, 'and no matter what you
have been up to, I look forward to you and Wivenhoe.'

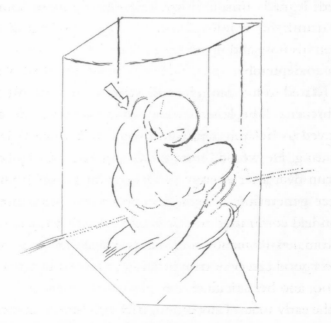

Chinagraph illustration found in Denis Wirth-Miller's studio.
(Author's personal collection)

Chapter 15

The Fire

The couple had now been together for twenty-five years, and were well into their forties. Chopping was going bald. He bought a hairpiece but Francis Bacon ridiculed it. He abandoned it after riding pillion on a suitor's motorbike: the wig had come off with his crash helmet.

By contrast, Wirth-Miller still had the hairstyle he had worn in 1937, but had taken to dyeing it black. He was aware that, as he aged, it made him look reminiscent of Hitler; sometimes when drunk he would clench a stamp-sized black rubber between his nose and upper lip.

On 20 September 1962, Robert Colquhoun died of a heart attack related to his alcoholism. By then he had rapidly slipped into obscurity. The other Robert, MacBryde, was devastated. He moved to Ireland shortly afterwards and more or less gave up painting. He would die just four years after Colquhoun, in 1966, run over after emerging drunk from a Dublin pub. The younger generation of neo-Romantics was no more. John Minton had committed suicide in 1957. Keith Vaughan moved away from neo-Romanticism towards abstraction, and continued to have a good career as an exhibiting artist, but by 1977 he was gone too, another suicide.

In the early 1960s, Chopping and Wirth-Miller suffered three personal losses in quick succession. Arthur Jeffress died on 21

September 1961. The by-now obese dealer's health had continued to suffer and he would not change his lifestyle. Also, following an argument with his gondoliers, they had allegedly denounced him as a homosexual to the illiberal Venetian authorities. He travelled to Paris, checked into an expensive hotel and committed suicide in his room.

In 1960, Frances Partridge's husband Ralph died from a heart attack, aged sixty-six. For the last few years, he had been ailing and was exhausted performing even simple tasks. The doctors warned Frances to keep him away from alcohol, but he was a gregarious host and continued to drink. By the end, Ralph was forbidden from entering the swimming pool at Ham Spray House: his doctor feared that the shock of cold water might kill him. 'Poor R. has gone nearly mad the last few days,' Frances Partridge wrote to Chopping on a hot summer's day, 'he sat on the edge and splashed himself rather pathetically. Then we took the water's temperature and found it over 70°! And the doctor (rung up) has said it will be all right.'

After Ralph's death, Frances Partridge sold Ham Spray House. She could not bear to be in the house she had shared with him for thirty years. On 7 September 1963, Burgo, her only child, collapsed from a heart attack while speaking to a friend on the phone, and died. He had recently married, and had become a father just three weeks earlier. He was twenty-eight.

In the midst of these events, Dicky Chopping furthered his career as an art-school teacher. In 1961 he had been introduced to David Queensberry, a Scottish aristocrat, potter and former soldier who had recently been appointed Professor of Ceramics at the Royal College of Art. Queensberry took an immediate liking to Chopping, and impressed by his work, invited him to join the college as a teacher of botanical drawing. It guaranteed a steady income, prestige and a reason to spend more time in London. In joining the staff of the RCA, he was following in the footsteps of his friends John Nash, John Minton, Robert Buhler and Rodrigo Moynihan.

Chopping proved to be a popular teacher at the RCA. Queensberry, who was liked by both Chopping and Wirth-Miller, showed faith in him when his first position was axed; he ensured that he was found a new role teaching drawing and applied arts. Finally, Chopping moved to the General Studies department to specialize in creative writing, a job he would keep until his retirement in 1983.

Wirth-Miller, meanwhile, was enjoying increased attention. Regaining his full strength and mobility since the infection he had caught in Tangiers, he was now able to capitalize on the success fostered by his shows at the Beaux Arts in 1954, 1956 and 1958 and the Lefevre in 1960. He was now an artist worthy of enough note for the *Burlington Magazine* to tell readers to look out for the exhibition of recent paintings by 'a talented artist Denis Wirth-Miller'.[100]

Works shown at the Lefevre exhibition in October 1962 revealed that his technique now included thick slicks of oil, applied with a palette knife, mimicking the heavy, glistening mud of the Essex marshland he studied. He was lifting the palette knife away from the canvas at an angle to create ridges that suggested the effect of the motion of water in *Wet Evening Landscape*. He was also sponging the oil to create texture in the mud in *The Estuary, Tide Rising*. One work from this period, *Water, White on White*, consisted solely of textured white paint. Not everyone was enamoured. One national newspaper critic wrote, 'He is an adroit painter and a sensitive admirer of what can, perhaps, be too easily regarded as conventional beauties of nature. But he continually gilds the lily with his heightened colour and a technique which is obtrusively clever.'[101]

Part of that technique included rigging up a device he had invented to throw paint at the canvas. It resembled a giant cake-icer that he would fill with oil paint and hang from the ceiling. He would swing it from side to side so that paint would spurt irregularly in thin arcs across the canvas, creating texture and a sense of motion in the marshland images.

The artistic breakthrough was rewarded with strong sales. Much of the interest in Wirth-Miller's art of this period came from the upper stratum of the British establishment. David Hicks was still including his paintings in the drawing rooms he was commissioned to decorate. In 1960, two of his oil paintings, a *Landscape* and an *Estuary Landscape*, had been purchased by the Royal Collection. 'I am so frightfully pleased that you are one of the first to be chosen for Royal patronage,' Dicky Chopping wrote by way of congratulation, 'wouldn't your poor mum be pleased?'

A combination of the Queen and David Hicks's seals of approval made high-society purchasers feel confident in paying large sums for his work. The Wirth-Miller name became briefly synonymous with a vein of tasteful luxury that was at odds with the experimental nature of the paintings themselves.

His name also became better known to the wider public, at least temporarily. In the autumn of 1963, the *Woman's Journal* made a major feature of its decision to reproduce two of the Queen's recent acquisitions in full colour: the magazine took out a quarter page in the *Daily Express*, advertising its scoop under the banner 'For the first time ever full colour reproduction of contemporary paintings from The Queen's private collection':

It is not possible to show them in this advertisement. Neither the space nor the limitation of black and white can do justice

to Wirth-Miller's 'Landscape' nor James Taylor's urban landscape 'Les Toits' . . . They are paintings chosen and bought
by The Queen for her own <u>private</u> pleasure; paintings
which, following the tradition of Royal Patronage, will
undoubtedly take their place in the history of twentieth
century art as works which have been honoured by Royal
acclaim.[102]

In fact, royal patronage did not prove enough to secure a place
in art history: both Taylor and Wirth-Miller fell into relative
obscurity during their lifetimes.

After the death of Ralph Partridge, Dicky Chopping proved to be
a supportive friend to Frances Partridge and they grew even closer.
At the same time, Denis Wirth-Miller became ever more dependent
on Francis Bacon for companionship. The neediness, though, was
mutual; by the late 1950s, they were already best friends.

Bacon was now financially secure due to the Marlborough's
management of his career and his rising reputation. Often, when
he became bored in Tangier, Monte Carlo or Soho, he would
try to persuade Wirth-Miller to join him.

Both men gambled hard, but while Bacon did so with
recklessness, Wirth-Miller was more prudent – he had less
money to squander. Although by the early 1960s Bacon was far
richer, Wirth-Miller would often have to subsidize him before
the end of the night. However drunk he became, Bacon would
post the money the next day along with a note: 'Here is the £100
I owe you'; 'Here is the cheque for £115'; 'A cheque of £150 for
the money you lent me at Charlie Chesters'. Even small amounts
were assiduously repaid: 'here is the £2 thank you so much'. It
is unclear whether the latter note was etched with sarcasm
following one of their rows.

Torn signature from a Francis Bacon cheque found in
Denis Wirth-Miller's studio. *(Author's personal collection)*

They had a shared sensibility in regard to art, gambling,
drinking and sex. It was perhaps inevitable that they would sleep
together at some point. When it did finally happen, Chopping
recorded that Bacon and Wirth-Miller 'tried it in turns' but it
was 'bread with bread' and 'no good for either of them'.
Chopping and Bacon also attempted to have sex; he noted in his
diary, 'attempted penetration with FB' over a bathroom sink,
'not successful – great trouble'. Their three-way relationship
remained platonic after those failed attempts.

Chopping and Bacon got on well, and Bacon in his letters to
Wirth-Miller almost unfailingly asked after Chopping's welfare
and sent his love, but their friendship was never as intense. They
had ongoing disagreements, particularly about Chopping's dog,
Tosca. Bacon, with his asthma, disliked dogs. His Muybridge-
inspired dog series was about form, motion and tension, and was
not born of any sentimental interest in the animals. 'Why don't
you just kill the fucking thing?' he once asked when Chopping
was giving his boxer some attention. He would moan that he
would become covered in dog hair whenever Chopping gave
him a lift in his car.

Chopping resigned himself to Bacon and Wirth-Miller's
noisy, hell-raising double act. If they were both at the Storehouse
at 6.30 p.m., regardless of the circumstances, they would head
to the pubs in Wivenhoe and stay there. Chopping found it a

tiresome routine, and would not always join them. He continued to dislike the Colony Room, so he often left them to their own devices in Soho. He would sometimes go on holiday with them but, more often than not, he sought his own entertainment.

Even when he was well into his forties that often meant sex. Chopping, always a neat artist, careful recorder of events and archivist, kept an extensive note of his conquests.

Spanking gardener in Stockwell – name escapes me

Dumpy man with rubber boots – by dustbins

Sailor – husband of textile secretary – not fulfilled

Egyptian watchman – Damp bed, tiny room

Rather plump middle-aged businessman – under bush

Man who borrowed brother's taxi – in taxi

Man in lift at British Museum – robbed me

Man with hair transplant – bus stop near Harrods

Man with poodle near Zandra's

Ex-policeman window cleaner – by-pass cottage then riverbank

Amsterdam. Male whore secretly when with FB & DW-M

Bed sitter-man near fish restaurant

Viennese night club performer

Black American Agromaniac – pox

Very bored ex of FB or DW-M – can't remember

Very camp motor mechanic

Ricky Stride, Paul Odo Cross (sock suspenders)

The list continues in Chopping's small handwriting for seven pages of A4; it is not complete.

Wirth-Miller never documented his promiscuity, but while he was less prolific, he was far from chaste. After Bacon had finished with Ron Belton, Wirth-Miller hoped he was finally free to have sex with him.

By 1961, Bacon was clear of his relationships with Ron Belton and Peter Lacy, and he moved into 7 Reece Mews. The dilapidated former coaching house on a cobbled street had only two rooms above a garage space he rarely used, but he lived and worked there for the rest of his life. It soon became a chaotic but productive studio: after only a few months he produced *Three Studies for a Crucifixion* (1962), a large-scale triptych and one of his best-known works.

In May 1962, Bacon's status was underlined with a retrospective at the Tate. With its triptych form and reference to the crucifixion, *Three Studies for a Crucifixion* effectively bookended the retrospective with *Three Studies for Figures at the Base of a Crucifixion*, the 1944 work that had announced him as a major artist, although some earlier works were also included. The palette is similar to the earlier work, but in place of the Furies the subject is now Bacon himself in the first panel, a mutilated body on a bed on the second, while in the third an upside-down, eviscerated carcass is screaming. The self-portrait makes it tempting to read the work as autobiographical, especially in consideration of Bacon's masochism, but the violence and anguish suggest a more universal relevance. The colours are now more solid and brighter. From this point on, Bacon would largely focus on the triptych form and portraiture, with many of the subjects drawn from his friends in the Colony Room.

There was great prestige in having a retrospective at the Tate in his own lifetime, but Bacon turned up in jeans to the private

view, with Janetta Woolley as his companion. As the focus of
the evening, he had not brought an invitation and, to his
amusement, was initially refused entry until someone recognized
him. The spatial proximity of his works over the last twenty
years underlined the power of Bacon's vision. In critical terms,
he had become untouchable.

On the day after the opening, Bacon received the news
that Peter Lacy had died as a result of alcohol abuse. He
responded by painting *Landscape Near Malabata, Tangier* (1963):
the forms are difficult to fathom, but the setting is the site of
Lacy's grave.

By 1963, Bacon was involved with George Dyer, a minor
gangland associate of the Kray twins described as 'hopelessly
weak' by Farson and 'a complete nutcase' by Queensberry.
Bacon was unable or unwilling to seek safety and security in a
relationship. His relationships with Belton and Dyer were linked
to his desire for transgression, the same disposition that helped
him to push at boundaries in his art.

Although described as charming when sober, Dyer was
aggressive and inarticulate when drunk, and he was drunk most
of the time. Bacon, though, was content in the early years and
took Dyer with him to Malta in spring 1964.

Dear Dennis

We are still in Malta – the weather had not been good. We
are going to Sicily tomorrow and trying to take a car to go
around Sicily and up to Naples. There are quite a lot of
American ships here. The bars are strange and it is strange
there is with the demand not a great pack of 'you know what's'
here. There is a strange and beautiful town called Mdima
[Mdina] built by the Crusaders. There is another in Rhodes I
believe but this is an impossible place to stay in for long. We

go most days to a fish restaurant about 15 miles from Valetta run by an Italian where there is lovely fresh fish and enormous crayfish as the fishing boats come in there otherwise the food is filthy. George seems to love it all and is looking marvellous. Do hope the work is going well. Will ring you as soon as I get back. Love to you both. This letter seems so stilted I can hardly read it myself.

Love
Francis

The relationship, perhaps inevitably, would go wrong. Bacon at times found Dyer so irritating that he would send him away for the evening or even to Tangier, with Wirth-Miller as a chaperone.

When a group of builders dismantled part of the roof of the Storehouse in order to convert an attic space into a new bedroom, they discovered the body of a blackened but otherwise preserved cat. One of the contractors recalled a story his grandfather had told him: when buildings were topped out in eighteenth-century Wivenhoe, a live cat would be released into the roof before it was sealed – it was believed that the trapped animal's spirit would ward off fire.

Wirth-Miller examined the mummified cat and said, 'It's rather beautiful – like a feline Modigliani.' Chopping reported that he was warier of its supposed supernatural powers.

In November 1963, Wirth-Miller, Bacon, Dyer and a young Canadian were involved in a typical afternoon of hard drinking in the Colony Room. Wirth-Miller invited them all to carry on drinking in Wivenhoe, so caught a taxi to take them into Essex. After drinks in the pub, they headed around the corner to the Storehouse, where they exhausted the wine stock.

George Dyer in the Storehouse garden. *(Author's personal collection)*

The four of them then took a taxi for a late-night dinner at the George Hotel in Colchester, where they drank more wine and bought additional supplies to see them through the night.

At some point after their return to the Storehouse, Bacon left them to use the lavatory and returned with a grave question:

'Denis – do you know your house is on fire?'

Wirth-Miller followed Bacon out of the room to find that the store room at the back of the house, which was used to house canvases, paperwork, old books and junk, was ablaze. The fire spread quickly and swept through the kitchen. The four men ran out onto the quay, and Wirth-Miller dialled the emergency services from a telephone box.

When two fire engines arrived at the scene of the fire, the sub-zero temperature froze the water in their hydrants. Fortunately, as the house was on the Quayside, they were able to pump salt water directly from the Colne and stopped the fire spreading beyond the store room and kitchen.

Chopping was in London. Having returned from the Royal College to the Montpelier Square basement they still rented from Janetta Woolley, he picked up the phone to hear his drunken lover greeting him with 'More glad tidings.' Wirth-Miller told him that the Storehouse was on fire and asked Chopping what he would like to save. Chopping's first thought was for his collection of Andrew Lang's Victorian fairy-tales.

'Oh, fuck your fairy books!' said Wirth-Miller.

The room had never been wired so the blaze could not have been caused by an electrical fault. The insurance company's report raised the unlikely possibility that the cause was 'a passing jackdaw with a glowing cigarette in its beak or even a rat with the same'. Both Wirth-Miller and Chopping were convinced that the culprit was George Dyer. They did not think that he had started it deliberately, but suspected that he had flicked a cigarette butt from a window, in the direction of the store room, while relieving himself in the first-floor toilet earlier that night.

Dyer did not admit to the possibility, but he was a career criminal used to denying the truth and covering his tracks. He even signed his name in the Storehouse's visitors' book as 'George Davies'. He often used a pseudonym, apparently on the advice of the Krays.

Like the flood in 1953, Wirth–Miller and Chopping eventually came to see the fire as a blessing. Terence Conran, then aged thirty-two, was an up-and-coming designer whom Chopping knew as he taught part-time at the Royal College of Art. Conran was in the process of setting up the first ever Habitat store, which would instigate a new interest in contemporary design within the average home. He agreed to design a chic new kitchen at the Storehouse in exchange for one of Wirth–Miller's landscapes and the opportunity to feature the finished design in promotional brochures.

The lost items listed in the insurance report included a 'flower piece' by Robert Colquhoun (£200) and original proofs of his illustrations for the anthology *Poems of Sleep and Dream* (£100). Their loss may have been particularly poignant as Colquhoun, who had spent so much time as a guest of the Storehouse, had died just a year earlier.

One object that did survive was the mummified cat, which would end up in a drawer in a guest bedroom. Wirth–Miller, who was fond of a practical joke, was amused by the idea of visitors discovering the artefact as they unpacked.

Chapter 16

Lust, Aberration and Death

As early as 1952, Chopping is on record in an interview as saying he considered himself a writer rather than an artist. He had already written some children's books, both fiction and non-fiction, and one of his stories was read on the BBC at Christmas 1945. Since the early 1950s, he had also been writing a novel with very adult themes.

Chopping may have published several books in the 1940s and been connected to the James Bond series, but he knew little about the world of fiction for adults. The natural person from whom to seek advice was Frances Partridge. Her connections made her an obvious contender to act as his mentor but he may not have wanted to threaten their friendship by putting it on a new footing, Additionally, the timing of the later, concentrated work on the novel coincided with the illness and death of her husband and then her son. Chopping sought to provide as much support as possible. He would visit Partridge at her Halkin Street flat when he was in London, and she in turn would stay at the Storehouse on weekends. Chopping would ensure that Francis Bacon was elsewhere. Like Wirth-Miller and Bacon, Chopping and Partridge spoke on the phone almost daily, and corresponded several times a week. Chopping owed her much; he found her proclamations on homosexuality and politics embarrassing, but she helped him and Wirth-Miller find a level of peace in their relationship, having advised them to holiday separately and, crucially, to listen to each other's concerns.

In the early days of the project, he turned to Partridge's close friend, Julia Strachey, to act as mentor. He had known her since his early visits to Ham Spray House during the Second World War. He had been in awe of Partridge's circle of established literary novelists and writers, composers and artists. Although these aristocratic proto-bohemians were mostly old and unfashionable by the 1940s, Chopping admired their achievements and confidence.

Julia Strachey was notable beyond her association with her Uncle Lytton. She had studied art at the Slade and gone on to be a model, photographer and author. In 1932, Hogarth Press, run by Virginia and Leonard Woolf, published her first novel, *Cheerful Weather for the Wedding*. A sharp black comedy, set during a single problematic day at a wedding, it became a cult classic, partly due to the insight it shed on the author's own life.

At the time she wrote it, Strachey was stuck in a love triangle between Dora Carrington and Stephen Tomlin, Julia's alcoholic husband, who was a sculptor. She left Tomlin not long after the book was published. She began a relationship with the artist Lawrence Gowing, who was seventeen years her junior, in 1939 and married him fifteen years later. Gowing was taught by William Coldstream at the Euston Road School in the late 1930s and later became the principal of the Slade. He also wrote a monograph on Lucian Freud.

Strachey continued to write, and after the Second World War became a reader for John Lehmann's new publishing company after he left Hogarth Press. When Partridge told her about Chopping's literary ambitions, Strachey offered her services.

They would meet regularly near her Mayfair office and go for lunch in a pub, where they would discuss his plans for the novel. Much as he appreciated her advice and criticism, Chopping found the process draining: Strachey was anxious and depressive. A typical letter she sent to the Storehouse read: 'This age is a particularly despairing one – we are all very near the brink of despair, are we not?'

Partridge had assured him that he could trust Strachey to give him a frank appraisal of his work. Despite his nervousness at her reaction, Chopping did not sanitize his writing, having taken his friend Gerard van het Reve's advice to dig deep into his psyche for inspiration.

For some time, Chopping had been interested in the notion that flies – a recurring motif in his art – were witness to all human life and its indignities, and signifiers of mortality. Much of the source material for *The Fly* was taken from Chopping's observations of fellow staff members in the Regent Street offices of *Decorations of the Modern Home* in the 1930s. He remembered the office workers as an unclean accountant, a terrifying secretary, a chirpy 13-year-old cockney office boy and a useless, impotent, middle-aged owner. The young Chopping had studied these characters, who would follow 'the discipline imposed by customary office routine whilst they frantically attempted to sexually ensnare one another'. In the novel, flies keep on appearing in their lives, which reach dark resolutions – one suicide, one heart attack and one incurable case of insanity.

He posted the first draft to Strachey with an explanatory note. There was a possibility, he wrote, that it might be a little too macabre for her tastes. She replied that she was 'too old, tough and hard to be materially affected by the horrors of whatever kind could be contained in any manuscript'.

She was nonetheless shocked when she read the work.

> I don't know how far you are yourself aware what a suicidal
> book it is Richard? What you hit a reader with is a hatred of
> life, you cast mud and shit and snot and vomit at it and never
> a good word does it get from you.

She implied that there was sadistic intent in his writing; his readers were being told that 'human beings are disgusting to look at, and full of rot and deterioration'. She asked how he could expect them to pay money to be told how 'purely filthy and repulsive' life is. He was 'only interested in the excreta of body and soul, to the exclusion of all else'.

Strachey wrote that she also feared that the book would not find a publisher due to its frank homosexual content as well as its dark tone. She refused to show the novel to John Lehmann for consideration.

Despite her reaction, she and Chopping remained friends. Strachey came to stay at the Storehouse several times over the next two decades.

Chopping persevered and wrote to V. S. Pritchett, who gave him positive enough feedback for him to carry on with the project. Chopping then sought out a new mentor. He had first met Angus Wilson in the early 1940s when Wilson and his partner of the time, Paul Odo Cross, would visit Cedric Morris at Benton End. Chopping was initially nervous in Cross's overtly flamboyant company. Cross, acknowledging this, wrote suggesting that Chopping should visit their Wiltshire home, where they could indulge in 'an orgy of being shy together, and get it all off discussing each other's ways of shyness'.

Wilson, born in 1913, was just a few years older than Chopping. After Oxford, he had worked briefly as a librarian at the British Museum before being assigned to Bletchley Park, where he cracked Italian naval codes.

Richard Chopping by Sir Cedric Morris, Benton End, 1941.
(© Estate of Cedric Morris)

After suffering a nervous breakdown, he returned to
Bletchley and spent the rest of the war there, continuing to write
on the side. In 1949, his short stories were published as *The Wrong
Set* and were reviewed in positive terms. He lived in Jamaica for
a while and would visit Ian and Ann Fleming at their Goldeneye
villa, from where Wilson wrote to Chopping, warning him that
his ears should have been burning. Wilson later settled in
Suffolk, not far from Chopping and Wirth-Miller.

Frances Partridge was also friendly with Wilson and would
renew her acquaintance while staying at the Storehouse. After
one particular dinner party in the early 1970s, she described
Wilson as having been 'in full flight with a gaggle of Essex

students'. Wilson and Malcolm Bradbury were at the time setting up the master's degree in Creative Writing, the first of its kind in the UK, at the University of East Anglia. The campus was at the top of Wivenhoe village and Chopping had been supportive. (The future Booker Prize-winning novelist Ian McEwan was one of the first students to complete the course.)

In the early sixties, Wilson agreed to help Chopping with his novel. Progress on the second draft was not rapid and Chopping noted that, whenever they met socially, Wilson would be pulling 'a sad little face and asking after the novel, as if he were worrying about the health of an ailing relation'. Over mussels at one Sunday dinner at the Storehouse, Wilson asked the question again, and Chopping was finally ready to hand it over. Wilson promised to read it and provide comments as soon as he could.

Several weeks later, Chopping travelled to Wilson's cottage for supper. After they had eaten, Wilson delivered a rapid commentary while flicking through the pages at high speed. Unlike Julia Strachey, Wilson remained completely neutral in tone, but he made it clear that he admired the 'bravery' of the putrid world Chopping had created. He said it was like nothing he had read before, but it needed 'choreography' and more recurring characters.

Chopping returned to Wivenhoe elated. Wirth-Miller was pleased for him and promised, despite the pressures of his ongoing exhibiting career, to take care of all household duties until the next draft was complete.

Chopping was busy working while also trying to write the novel. Between 1960 and 1964, he produced the covers for five Bond novels, as well as a jacket for *The Fourth of June*, David Benedictus's cult story of public-school rebellion. The *Sunday*

Times praised the Benedictus cover, which featured the close-up portrait of a boy, as 'striking'. Another reviewer said, 'Take a peek at the striking dust jacket . . . The artist is Richard Chopping, the expensive near-genius who provides Ian Fleming with cover-work for his James Bond chiller-dillers.' Innovatively, there was no author name or title on the front cover.

Chopping found his work as Fleming's illustrator progressively easier and more financially rewarding. Even so, each Bond commission presented new and unforeseen difficulties. For *Thunderball* (1961) he needed to track down a medical supplier who could lend the arm of a skeleton. Fleming asked him to depict a skeletal hand, with a knife thrust between the bones, picking up a pair of playing cards. Fleming, in his self-deprecating manner, told Chopping the novel was 'immensely long' and 'immensely dull'. 'Only your jacket can save it!' he added.

In July 1963 Chopping received a letter from a contact at Jonathan Cape, explaining in forensic detail exactly what the author required for the jacket of *You Only Live Twice* (1964): 'If you could manage a pink dragonfly sitting on one of the flowers, and perhaps just one epicanthic eye peering through them, [Fleming] thinks that will be just splendid.'

The principal image on the cover was to be a toad: 'an ordinary country toad will do perfectly well,' his contact at Jonathan Cape wrote, 'but make sure it really is a toad and not a common frog'. He continued: 'and try to get that deep red glow that one sees burning in their eyes at twilight. I think you would probably need to keep one to sit for you to ensure the right degree of inflation. Any dead ones I've ever seen looked awfully flat.'

Chopping set out with a jam jar and wellington boots to scour the banks of the Colne for a live toad. He was continually attacked by swarms of flies, whom he felt were taunting him for his lack of progress on his own book. He gave up and resorted to borrowing a toad from a neighbour's daughter. She taught natural history at a local school and kept her specimens at home during the holidays.

For *The Man with the Golden Gun* (1965), Chopping required another pistol – which he then put to effective use, extending its barrel across the spine and onto the back cover to emphasize the weapon's size. Chopping added his personal motif: two fat house flies, with one sitting on the pistol's grip.

Chopping thought that the attention to detail was worthwhile. Bond had become more than a literary franchise. In 1962, *Dr No*, the first novel in the film series, was released and became an unexpected blockbuster; it was named as the fifth-highest grossing film of the year in Britain even though it had only been released in October. The following year, shooting began on *From Russia with Love*. Towards the end of the shoot at Pinewood Studios, he received a letter from Jonathan Cape inviting him to a party at Pinewood Studios. The invitation was addressed to 'Mr & Mrs Chopping' so he asked Wirth-Miller to be his wife for the day. Francis Bacon came, too.

On board the specially arranged bus from central London to Pinewood, waiting staff hired by the studio walked up and down the aisle, repeatedly topping up the passengers' glasses with champagne, Bacon's drink of choice. 'We drank on the bus, we drank, we drank, we drank,' Chopping recorded. He remembered little from the party except for a brief chat with Fleming, who seemed surprised to see him. 'Oh you're here? They must have really scraped the bottom of the barrel.' As usual, he found Fleming's humour unsettling.

The films increased the sales of the books and the fame of Chopping's covers. After the *Thunderball* novel was released, Chopping travelled the full circuit of the Circle Line to see how many stations were displaying the full-length poster of his cover art: at least one poster was plastered onto the walls of every one of the line's twenty-seven stations. His jackets were attracting praise and leading to interviews. When he was interviewed about his design for *The Spy Who Loved Me* (1962), featuring a dagger and a carnation, he claimed that he had spent his fee on a new washing machine.

Ian Fleming died in 1964, but Chopping continued to be associated with the Bond brand. In 1966, the publishers Jonathan Cape released two novellas previously serialized in newspapers – *Octopussy* and *The Living Daylights* – as one book. Again they turned to Chopping for the cover art. He was asked to paint an elaborate conch and a spiny fish, and added his artistic signature of flies, now more numerous than ever before. He was paid the then-unheard of sum of £365. These were, as Chopping put it, 'dizzying heights'. According to the *New Yorker* magazine, he was now 'the world's highest-paid book jacket designer'.

He was also commissioned for the cover of Kingsley Amis's spin-off *The James Bond Dossier* (1965), which involved reusing recognizable motifs from previous covers. Following that, he was not asked to contribute to the franchise for a further fifteen years. Jonathan Cape abandoned *trompe l'oeil* and took the unusual decision to have a surrealist image for Kingsley Amis's next Bond title, while the films became so successful that they led the imagery on paperback reissues. Jonathan Cape went back to Chopping for the cover of *Licence Renewed* (1981), a new James Bond novel written by John Gardner. Familiar motifs returned in the forms of a gun, flowers, woodgrain and a fly.

Meanwhile, Chopping continued to enjoy teaching at the Royal College of Art. His students at the Royal College in the early 1960s included Zandra Rhodes and David Hockney. He encountered Rhodes in the textile department after he had moved from ceramics. The fashion designer, one of the innovators of the punk aesthetic before going on to design dresses for Diana, Princess of Wales, studied at the RCA in 1961–4. She described Chopping as her 'personal muse' and wrote that Chopping and Wirth-Miller 'introduced me to a totally new world and expanded my horizon'.[103] In one television interview together, Chopping, in a moment of self-deprecation, responded to her praise of his skills by saying, 'I just taught them about life. About wonderful, salacious life.'[104]

Towards the end of 1964, Chopping returned to Angus Wilson's cottage with the final draft of his novel. Wilson was pleased with the level of improvement, and offered to arrange an introduction to senior figures at the publisher Secker & Warburg.

Chopping worried that the publisher might fear that the novel's content would contravene the 1959 Obscene Publications Act. In 1960 Allen Lane and Penguin were taken to trial for obscenity for publishing an uncensored edition of *Lady Chatterley's Lover*. They were cleared, but there was still trepidation in the publishing industry.

Six weeks after his meeting with Wilson, he received a postcard from Egypt: Wilson had heard that Secker & Warburg were going to publish the novel.

Chopping travelled to London to meet Giles Gordon, who worked for Secker & Warburg. Gordon was just twenty-four but would become a leading figure in the publishing industry and a powerful agent.

The plan was to spend the weekend together at Gordon's home in order to edit *The Fly* into a concise 200-page novel. Chopping, however, bought a case of champagne with him to celebrate Gordon's recent wedding. According to Gordon's autobiography, his marriage never quite recovered from Chopping's stay. He also said that he found *The Fly* 'disgusting'.[105]

Pamela Warburg, the wife of the Secker & Warburg's co-founder Frederic, had a tradition of inviting new authors for a drink at her flat in St John's Wood. If she found them agreeable, she would invite them back to dinner. Chopping passed the test and was invited to dinner a few weeks later. He was intimidated by her, and remained on his best behaviour throughout the evening. Nonetheless, he discovered that she spread rumours that he had 'behaved outrageously': 'She said I held a metallic object to my crotch and made unsuitable sexual movements.' In reality, she would not stop 'bragging about her sexual conquests, both lesbian and heterosexual, as her simpering husband smiled indulgently'. She may have expected the openly homosexual writer of a disturbing and sexually scandalous novel to perform accordingly. When he failed to shock, she created her own fiction.

Chopping designed the cover of the book himself. It was a close-up, almost photo-realist image of a fly drinking at the rim of the staring eye of the dead female protagonist. While Chopping was working on the image, Wirth-Miller approached from the other side of the work-desk. He suggested that the image would look yet more sinister if shown inverted. Chopping took his advice. In the manner of the Benedictus design, he did not include any typography on the front cover, allowing the disturbing image alone to attract the reader. He was amused to hear that, 'the buyer for the bookstall at Heathrow had in 1965 ordered a substantial number of copies of my first novel *The Fly* because from the cover, which I had designed, he took it for a new Fleming James Bond'.[106]

Chopping wondered whether the novel would not receive much coverage due to its dark content. His anxiety proved groundless. Reviewers wrote about the novel with attention-grabbing turns of phrase. 'Lust, aberration and death are treated in the Grand Guignol manner. A shocker, only for those with cast-iron stomachs', the reviewer at the *Illustrated London News* wrote. It was 'just about the most unpleasant book of the year', according to the critic at the *Sunday Citizen*. 'But it held me like a fly in its spider's web of monstrous cruelty.'

A journalist at the *Sunday Times* wrote: 'There isn't a dull page in *The Fly* . . . highly startling. Rarely have the filthy, petty particulars of loneliness been given such a thorough going over. The book begins by being extremely cool and nasty, and ends in something like a dignified, sustained passion'.

The novel sold well in Britain, France and the United States. On 11 July 1967, the paperback edition reached number three in the *Evening Standard*'s bestseller list. Mrs Warburg presented Chopping with a copy of the hardback, which he described as 'revoltingly bound in tooled Moroccan leather, maybe fit for a *nouveau* country house library'. He was given a contract for a second novel. *The Fly* brought in several thousand pounds per year in royalties for some years to come.

The book was banned in Ireland and also, to Chopping's surprise, somewhere closer to home: Wivenhoe public library. 'Now it wouldn't raise so much as an eyebrow,' he commented twenty years later.

Chopping followed *The Fly* with a story published in the anthology, *Lie Ten Nights Awake*, subtitled *Ten Terrifying Tales of Horror and the Macabre* (1967). It was edited by Herbert van Thal, and also featured a contribution from Anthony Burgess, author of *A Clockwork Orange*. Chopping's tale, 'The Eagle', was a sinister story of taxidermy and cannibalism. The friends of Chopping and Wirth-Miller may have been surprised that such dark fiction was not the product of the more obviously tortured soul of the painter of barren and threatening landscapes, but the polite flower painter.

The success of *The Fly* inadvertently helped extend Chopping's teaching career at the RCA. The textile department was overhauled and, once again, Chopping was set to lose his job. With a bestselling novel to Chopping's name, David Queensberry was able to aid his move to the General Studies department as creative writing tutor. The move brought job security for the remainder of his career.

Chapter 17

Bad Behaviour

The Sexual Offences Act of 1967 effectively decriminalized homosexuality in England and Wales. On 27 July, Denis Wirth-Miller, Dicky Chopping and Frances Partridge listened to the parliamentary vote together on the radio in the Storehouse. Chopping saw the positive side of the legislation. Partridge, however, recorded in her diary: 'I wonder very much whether quite a few who get a kick from being outsiders and rebels won't feel a sense of disappointment and perhaps have to try some new eccentricity.'

Wirth-Miller, despite having been imprisoned effectively due to his homosexuality in 1944, saw the downside of the legislation. For thirty years, Chopping and Wirth-Miller had lived without orthodoxy or convention, defining their own moral parameters because they were outside both the law and social norms. Wirth-Miller was worried that his sexuality would suddenly become quantifiable and codified. The bohemia they had inhabited was born of a desire for a personal liberation, without boundaries, not a different type of codification. Right up to his death, he would continue to contend that he was right – the legislation meant another former of entrapment – even though he and Chopping registered as civil partners.

Wirth-Miller may have been arguing a philosophical point about sexual identity, but Partridge's diary note was echoed by

Bacon's reaction: that being gay was 'really so much more interesting when it was illegal'.[107] Bacon, Wirth-Miller and Chopping all enjoyed the trappings of the high life, but they were also attracted to dangerous liaisons in the underworld, the seedy bars, the back streets, the codes, signs and symbols that communicated carnal possibilities. They enjoyed the risk and the sense of transgression.

Earlier that day, Partridge, Wirth-Miller and Chopping had travelled down to Westminster in Frances's white Mini Cooper to watch the debate on the Sexual Offences Bill live prior to the vote. The Bill had been initiated by the Wolfenden Report, which concluded that 'homosexual behaviour between consenting adults in private should no longer be a criminal offence'. A preference for the same sex, the report committee decided, was not a 'disease', nor would its legalization lead to the moral collapse of society.

The Storehouse group found the debate in Parliament patronizing. According to Frances, even the liberally inclined Members of Parliament spoke about homosexuals as though they were 'creatures horribly deformed needing pity'. Chopping despaired as a Conservative, dressed in plus fours, declared that, 'there were three things you should never have on your ship – rats, buggery and thieves'.

The radical social changes of the 1960s and increasing liberal consensus were not matched by the views of many in Parliament, some of whom felt that the 1533 Buggery Act was still relevant to 1967. Even some of those who supported the decriminalization of homosexuality were disgusted by it.

When recess was called, Chopping was standing in a corridor when Lord Arran, a Conservative who had nevertheless sponsored the decriminalization Bill in the House of Lords, brushed past him. Chopping congratulated him.

Lord Arran turned round and said: 'So you think I did all right?' he asked.

Chopping nodded.

'I've loathed every minute of it,' the peer said and walked away. Later that day Arran would say, 'I ask those [homosexuals] to show their thanks by comporting themselves quietly and with dignity . . . any form of ostentatious behaviour now or in the future or any form of public flaunting would be utterly distasteful.'[108]

When, back in Wivenhoe, they listened to the voting and the Act was passed, it was, as Partridge wrote, a moment of 'modified jubilation'.

In 1967, Dicky Chopping turned fifty. Over the course of Chopping and Wirth-Miller's thirty-year relationship to date the bohemia that they had embraced in the 1930s had disappeared. Fitzrovia had become a tourist destination for those interested in Dylan Thomas. Although there were still a few artists' studios in the area, Fitzroy Street was no longer associated with new developments in British art; neo-Romanticism was dead and abstraction was no longer radical. Illicit sex in bombsites during the blackout was a distant memory. Soho was still a place for hard drinking and sexual antics, but the likes of the Colony Room were no longer attracting young artistic transgressors; it was the same old faces, increasingly alcoholic, their lives more chaotic. By now the poet Brian Patten's description of the Colony as 'a small urinal full of fractious old geezers bitching about each other' was already apt.[109] Bacon could still often be found at its counter, always democratic in that he was happy to talk to anyone who seemed interesting enough, but the place was moribund.

Chopping could see that his own culture – that of Fitzrovia, Soho jazz and Francophilia – was being superseded. Reading

Camus, ordering French food and playing Wagner loud were no longer signs of rebellion. Although he was interested in new cultural developments, he was several steps removed from what he now witnessed in the street or read about: tie-dye, Bridget Riley prints, conceptual art, 'mind-expanding' drugs and alienating pop music.

He and his friends were no longer among those spearheading the forward march of progress. To the students starting to protest in universities, they were now the old guard; they were part of the problem.

After the *succès de scandale* of *The Fly*, Chopping attempted to maintain momentum as a novelist. He wrote *The Ring*, which was published in 1967, hurriedly. It was the story of a homosexual man's relationships and had a central motif involving the protagonist's crotch. Angus Wilson helped out with the editing again, but this time with reluctance. Giles Gordon would recall: 'Chopping's second novel, and mercifully the last to be published, "The Ring", albeit embellished with a revoltingly clever cover, was a much more mundane affair than "The Fly" and sank with very little trace.'[110] That cover again showed his skill at jacket design, creating a thematic link to the previous novel through the close-up of an eye and the presence of flies, along with an intricately painted rose.

The Ring was ignored by the press. Chopping was not offered a contract for a third novel.

He published his final children's book in 1967. The set of seven tales, titled *The Last Dodo*, was credited to 'Richard Boyde': its publisher, Farrar, Straus & Giroux, did not want the book associated with the author of *The Fly*. The stories are linked by a pet shop and told from different species' points of view. The *Kirkus* magazine review implied that it was not ideal for children: 'Seven narratives for the days of the week, widely varied and highly original – but the underlying attitude is mature cynicism tinged with hope, informed by a mature sensibility . . . An intriguing lot with a lot of merit, little Juvenile appeal.'[111] No further Richard Boyde titles were released.

During 1967 Francis Bacon painted both *George Dyer Riding a Bicycle* and *Triptych – Inspired by T. S. Eliot's Poem 'Sweeney Agonistes'*. George Dyer would be the model for many of Bacon's works. He remained uninterested in art but was proud to be the subject of many paintings. According to Peppiatt he would delight in taking people around exhibitions to show Bacon's pictures of him, while claiming to be astonished that the works, which he thought were horrible, were worth so much money. *George Dyer Riding a Bicycle* captures Dyer's childish pride while also revealing his sullenness.

By 1967, Francis Bacon was making so much money he could afford a second property. He was worried about not having a long-term lease on 7 Reece Mews, which in any case was too small and, due to his working method, permanently squalid, with pieces of paper, photographs, newspaper cuttings, painting materials and tools all over the floor. The new studio was in a mansion block at Roland Gardens, on the other side of Old Brompton Road from Reece Mews. He had the large, grand property decorated to his taste, but he found he could not work there. It was too clean. He decided to stay at Reece Mews, where he could always work productively. He offered the unwanted studio to Chopping and Wirth-Miller for their temporary use while he figured out what to do with it.

Chopping and Wirth-Miller had ceased renting Janetta Woolley's basement flat in Montpelier Square and were grateful for a free London base. They stayed at Roland Gardens often and invited friends around to share in the drinking sessions that had been a regular feature of their lives together. Bacon would come across from Reece Mews for the company.

Younger tenants would often knock on the door in the small hours, asking them to keep the noise down. The couple and Bacon were particularly annoyed by three young men who lived below, who reported noise complaints to the police on several occasions. They were a hirsute, velvet-clad trio of Australians who, Wirth-Miller discovered from conversations with other neighbours, were 'pop stars'.

One night while Bacon was at the flat drinking heavily, he decided he would teach the pop stars downstairs a lesson. As he left with Chopping and Wirth-Miller to go to a gambling club, he paused, looked around, and then threw an empty bottle of Dom Pérignon through the Australians' front window, smashing the glass.

According to Chopping, the band was called 'something like the Gee Bees'. He added, 'They never got anywhere.'

Dicky Chopping's literary career was suffering but Denis Wirth-Miller was continuing to benefit, at least in terms of sales, from his association with David Hicks. He was no longer with the Lefevre but, from 1967, he was selling through the New Art Centre, a gallery on Sloane Street that attracted well-off Chelsea customers interested in contemporary art. Wirth-Miller's paintings were selling well but he was unhappy.

While the Tate retrospective in 1962 and a string of international exhibitions effectively crowned Bacon as the most important British painter of his generation, Wirth-Miller was aware that his own work was becoming an irrelevancy within more radical art circles. His association with David Hicks was double-edged; it guaranteed steady custom but it had cost him his artistic credibility. Success had allowed Bacon to pursue his art as he chose; albeit on a smaller scale, it had trapped

Wirth-Miller. While Bacon's work would be discussed in everything from academic articles to tabloid newspapers, his own was now relegated to interior design articles. A typical article discussed Hicks's design of an elegant but conservative bachelor pad, accompanied by a photograph of a large Wirth-Miller landscape given pride of place above the mantelpiece. Hicks's clientele of society figures had made Wirth-Miller's art a new form of 'Establishment' painting.

A letter, dated 1 January 1968, from the New Art Centre indicates the problem:

> I seem, already, to have made a dent in the number of landscapes we have, having sold two of the small ones (leaving me with only two), and also two large ones, one of these being the new landscape with the trees in the background, and the other a slightly older one, a rather blue marshy picture. When you can, I would like a few pictures to replace these ones. I'm afraid it would have to be the rather more conventional landscapes which people seem to be used to, and to want.

Wirth-Miller had passed fifty, but still wished to push the boundaries of his art. In c.1967, he produced *Landscape with Three Trees*, a radical painting in which the landscape was reduced to the simple form of thick black marks on an ochre ground. The three trees stand on the horizon line like urgently expressed Chinese calligraphy. By contrast, the New Art Centre wished to sell paintings such as the finicky *Essex Landscape – The End of Winter* and *Summer Landscape with Trees II*, which, while executed with skill and bravura, would suit a more conservative taste. Such paintings were traditional in form and the threat, which was characteristic of Wirth-Miller's complex personality as well as his marshlands, was absent.

Abstract expressionism had broadened possibilities in the 1940s and come to the fore in the 1950s. Now Pop Art, which had first emerged in the 1950s, had become a major force and further recategorized the framework of art through the work of Andy Warhol, Jasper Johns, Richard Hamilton and Peter Blake. A mixture of post-modern irony, reflection of the burgeoning consumer society and new techniques shifted the ground. As a genre, landscape was not readily associated with innovation or the zeitgeist, and when Wirth-Miller had attempted to bring more experimentation into his work at the Lefevre shows, he had been criticized.

He persisted in his relationships with both the New Art Centre and David Hicks. When a slot became available at the New Art Centre in July 1969, he accepted the gallery's offer to mount a solo exhibition. It was in the gallery's interests; a letter from February 1969 shows that it was continuing to sell numerous works from its stock, including one to the Ministry of Works, and people were interested in 'getting in early to your exhibition'. The work that had just joined the government art collection was the rather traditional *Summer Landscape with Trees II*.

The Ring's failure had shaken Chopping's confidence. Nevertheless, he wrote another novel. An interview in 1972 revealed that 'his third was not accepted by the eight publishers approached – "it wouldn't have made any money"'.[112] Bacon, however, gave Chopping encouragement. The latter wrote in his diary on 1 February 1974: 'He said he liked my new book. He does not agree with the others "after all where should I be if I took any notice of critics. One must do it the way one wants to and there it is."'

That interview in 1972 focused on the autobiography he had already been writing on and off for five years. His aptitude for writing fiction had quickly deserted him so he began mining his own life for inspiration. He had been filling up diaries for years and decided to put them to constructive use.

It was not a smooth or simple process. His archive of memoirs contains dozens of drafts on his meeting Wirth-Miller, and several more on his time at Benton End. Every time he believed he had made a breakthrough, he lost confidence, scrapped that version and started afresh, but soon he would become lost in trying to describe every moment in too much detail. While he attempted to write about his youth, he was frustrated by the ageing process; one draft reveals his unhappiness with his baldness, his expanding stomach and decreasing energy.

In November 1967, he wrote an extensive entry about the Queen's visit to the RCA. He had been scathing about the royal family seven years earlier at David Hicks's wedding, and his republican distaste was still evident. The evening was 'rather disappointing', he commented. He had started the day with a few sherries, before drinking too much white wine at the 'nasty lunch' that followed at the Albert Hall, prior to the royal event in the evening. They ate smoked trout, medallions of veal and 'pear *belle Hélène* – tinned pears with either Walls or Lyons ice cream'. He felt unsteady on his feet and became embroiled in an argument with one of the Albert Hall's officials who, for reasons unknown, called the police. Back in 1956, when his relationship with Wirth-Miller was at its lowest point, Chopping had written to his partner: 'I HATE drink and all the misery it causes, but only too conscious that it is necessary to some people. Alas you for one.' He was repeatedly critical of Wirth-Miller and Bacon's daily journey to oblivion. The truth was that he had also often drunk to excess when young, and was almost matching Wirth-Miller's intake in their middle age.

Undeterred by whatever had happened with the police, Chopping went back to the Royal College with the rest of the party. By 9.45 p.m. the royals still had not turned up, and Chopping was by his own account 'sloshed' on the college's champagne. When the guests of honour turned up, he was 'too drunk to take in anything other than a smiling face that belonged to the Queen' and a 'very ugly shade of pink' (the Queen Mother).

Following the day's events, there was an RCA inquiry into Chopping's behaviour. Ceramics teacher Peter O'Malley – the husband of his old friend Joan 'Maudie' Warburton from Benton End – fought his case. Chopping received an official caution rather than outright dismissal. He had been thrown off-kilter by the sudden failure of his writing career and had jeopardized his job. A drunk young bohemian with a promising art career might be indulged but a drunk ageing art teacher was unlikely to be tolerated for long.

In January 1970, while he was still trying to regain the confidence and sense of purpose he had lost, his mother Amy died. Their relationship had always been strong, and made closer by the early death of his father. She had steered him towards an artistic career, coped with his homosexuality despite the climate of the time, and helped him buy a house with his partner. His ability to pursue an unorthodox life had relied on the security and constancy of her affection. He was shattered by the news of her death.

On 27 January, Francis Bacon composed the simplest of condolence notes.

My dear Dicky

I am writing a letter which has nothing to say except that I do hope you are not too upset and distressed.

My love to you both.

Francis

★

Bacon had found a level of happiness with George Dyer, but he confessed to Chopping and Wirth-Miller that their sex life was suffering. After a few years together, Dyer had become self-conscious about sex. He was having episodes of impotency and Bacon said that on the rare occasions when Dyer managed to ejaculate, the result was 'unsatisfactory'. Dyer drank a great deal and may have had some level of dependency on drugs, but the impotency may also have been linked to his effective emasculation by Bacon, on whom he was increasingly financially and emotionally dependent. Dyer's role in the relationship was almost exclusively to be physically dominant – the father/bully that Bacon sought – but even that power was waning. Bacon told Wirth-Miller and Chopping that he had tried to boost Dyer's morale but there had been no improvement.

The couple made a bizarre drunken suggestion, which Bacon nonetheless agreed to try. Chopping spent several hours experimenting in the Storehouse kitchen, cooking batches of cornflour to try to match the consistency of sperm. The next time he spent the night with Dyer, Bacon was to put the cornflour enema up his anus so that it would pour out during sexual activity with Dyer. The results were not recorded.

Dyer's psychological issues remained. He became a needy victim and had lost his personality to the forcefulness of Bacon's character. As the relationship progressed, he sunk into self-loathing and hopelessness. From the outset of their relationship, he had demonstrated signs of weakness that brought out Bacon's more sadistic tendencies. A cycle of savagery began; the more pathetic Dyer became, the more Bacon despised and mentally bullied him. In time Dyer would become intent on self-destruction.

Long before their relationship ceased, Bacon wanted to be rid of Dyer but he was wary that the petty crook had become financially dependent on him and would no longer have the mental resolve to support himself. After they had been together for about five years, Bacon gave Dyer the flat in Roland Gardens, as well as £20,000, on condition that he would go his own way.

The plan did not work. One morning in the summer of 1969, Bacon rang Wirth-Miller in a panic. Dyer had broken into Reece Mews and destroyed his studio. He had ripped up several canvases and thrown the shreds into the bath before pouring bottles of wine over the remains.

Bacon was contractually obliged to provide the Marlborough with a certain number of paintings per year, and Dyer's actions had set him back by months. He knew that even if he changed the locks and returned to painting in the studio, there was a chance that Dyer would break in again.

Chopping was aware that the Royal College had studio space to spare and decided to speak to Robin Darwin, the college rector, to ask if Bacon might be able to use it temporarily. Darwin told Chopping that Bacon could have a studio on the Cromwell Road free of charge, on the agreement that he donated a painting to the college.

Bacon accepted Darwin's offer, and handed over one of the works from his *Bullfight* series, which Darwin agreed to lend back to the artist if it was needed for an exhibition. Darwin was replaced as rector by Lord Esher in 1971. On 6 August 1974, Chopping reported in his diary:

> FB rang up to tell us that someone at the RCA had refused to lend FB's painting of the bull-fight for the exhibition in America [at the Metropolitan Museum of Art, 1975]. Tried to call Lord Esher. I am determined to get permission for the loan since they would never have the painting had I not suggested to Francis that he might ask for a studio

there. Robin Darwin, FB said, always said he could borrow
it at any time that he wanted it. F sounded pissed.

He and Chopping conspired to work out how to wrest the
painting back from the RCA. Chopping claimed that, at one
point, he and Bacon considered stealing into the Senior Common
Room at the RCA and secretly replacing the bullfight painting
with a near-identical canvas from the series. On the following
day, Chopping sought to resolve the situation:

> If the picture is not lent I have said that I shall ask Esher
> to give his permission as a personal favour to me and if
> he doesn't that I shall resign. FB telephoned to say that it
> was Esher who had signed the letter of refusal. I spoke to
> him as arranged at lunchtime and he agreed that it would
> be a good idea if I spoke to Valerie Beston [of the
> Marlborough] which I did. I explained that Esher had not
> known that Darwin had promised that it could be lent.
> She said everything was most sympathetic with the RCA
> and FB had been over-wrought. She said the Marlborough
> could find them another Bacon to take its place . . . 'there
> are plenty about' which are not wanted for the show at
> the Metropolitan.

In the end, Esher agreed to allow Bacon to reclaim *Bullfight*,
and in 1975 accepted a permanent replacement work, *Study for
the Human Body: Man Turning on the Light* (1973). Chopping
reported on 24 May 1975 that Bacon 'hardly sounded pleased
and reiterated that he thought the bull-fight was the better
picture. However, he has now got rid of what had proved to
be an unsalable picture and has got one for which there have
been many requests.'

A few years later, Christopher Frayling wrote to Chopping declaring that it was 'by far the best rental agreement the College has ever made'. In 2007, the RCA sold the *Study for the Human Body* for £8,084,5000. As Bacon had indicated, despite that huge sum Esher may have done the RCA a disservice by not simply maintaining ownership of the bullfight work and allowing it to go out on loan. *Bullfight* would have probably reaped over twice that figure in 2007.

In pushing Dyer away, Bacon had given up the principal model for his 1960s works: Dyer's name crops up in countless titles, and his form is unmistakable in other works. In 1970, Bacon produced a triptych in which the central panel depicted two men wrestling or copulating, drawing on Muybridge's series. The other panels of *Triptych 1970* show a figure in a hammock, dressed in a suit in the left panel and naked in the other. The model did not appear to be Dyer, providing evidence that Bacon now felt free of his muse.

He was not free in reality. On 2 September 1970, Denis Wirth-Miller wrote: 'Francis arrested while I was talking to him on the telephone.'

In a further act of revenge, Dyer had tipped off the police that they would find drugs in the Reece Mews studio. The premises were searched and the police discovered a pipe stem and two grams of cannabis in silver foil.

Bacon stood trial in October 1970 despite the fact that he had no history of drug consumption. He would admit that he had tried to smoke cannabis fifteen years earlier but it brought on a bad asthma attack. Basil Wigoder, whom the Marlborough hired to defend the artist, questioned the detective in charge of the raid, and forced her to confess that it was Dyer who had tipped off the police. Dyer's record – involving borstal, thuggery and prison – and his alcoholism were enough to ensure that

Bacon was found not guilty. Despite the fact that a conviction would have ruined his ability to support his career abroad, particularly in the United States with its tight visa regulations, Bacon was magnanimous in victory, stating that he bore no animosity towards Dyer.

Denis Wirth-Miller followed up his 1970 solo exhibition at the New Art Centre, which had led to strong sales, with another in each of the next two years. It is clear that by then he had decided to ignore the New Art Centre's desire for 'rather more conventional' landscapes, and that he was no longer willing to pander to the taste of the more conservative members of David Hicks's client base. The works from 1970–72 were bold, unconstrained and original, with the paint streaked and swept across the canvas, sometimes with careful delineation, sometimes furiously, often against a visible white ground. Some had vertical lines and scratches for reeds and rough smears for trees, and some had a crazed cross-hatch of texture, while others had a more combed effect. In others such as *Granite, Upland and Road*, *Study of Landscape/Dartmoor* and *Road Descending and Mounting*, the topography was only delineated by the direction of the smears and subtle variation of the colour. The extreme motion found in these works was partly due to Wirth-Miller and Chopping combining to create a new type of source material. Chopping would drive at speed while Wirth-Miller clicked his camera, catching the topography rushing through the viewfinder.

As the New Art Centre gave Wirth-Miller exhibitions in such quick succession, his gamble of following his own instincts must have paid off. He was also asked to put together a solo show for Hintlesham Hall, courtesy of Robert Carrier, in 1972.

Carrier was a gregarious New Yorker who had originally trained as an actor before wartime service took him to Paris, where he learned about French cuisine. He moved to London in the early 1950s and, when British interest in food started to expand, established himself as a writer of cookery columns for *Harper's Bazaar* and *Vogue*. In 1959, he opened his first restaurant in Islington, and by the end of the 1960s he was a household name, mostly owing to his book *Great Dishes of the World*, which went on to sell more than 10 million copies.

In 1971, Carrier bought Hintlesham Hall, a decaying sixteenth-century manor house near Ipswich in Suffolk: according to Norman Scarfe, the East Anglian historian, 'Robert Carrier, the prestigious food and cookery writer, saw it, bought it, and undertook considerable rehabilitation of the fabric . . . In just ten years, he gave the house an international reputation, and after a very lively decade, he sold it.'[113] That reputation went beyond food. Hintlesham Hall became a country house hotel, with Michelin-starred food and arts events, including exhibitions, plays and concerts.

Carrier wanted to 'take the best parts of London into the country' but it was a high-risk strategy. The plan was that even if the restaurant lost money, the hotel would shore up the business. It would eventually fail because not enough people stayed in the hotel suites even though the restaurant did well. Carrier was cursed with 'too much enthusiasm, too little restraint', according to his friend Felicity Green, and 'in true Bob fashion, he just let all his friends stay free of charge.' Those friends included Wirth-Miller, Chopping and Bacon, who would stay whenever Carrier invited them, often with Sonia Orwell.

Maggi Hambling remembers one exhibition opening at Hintlesham Hall when Bacon was so drunk that he was unable to walk. Chopping stood to one side of him and Wirth-Miller the other. They slowly manoeuvred his slumped body around the exhibition as if carrying a ventriloquist's dummy.

Wirth–Miller's inaugural exhibition of eighteen paintings, all landscapes, sold well: 'a lot of country people are too frightened and afraid of appearing foolish if they buy [paintings] in London', Orwell wrote to them after one stay there. She disliked Carrier's choice of interior decoration, but conceded that, overall, she 'must give credit where it is, after all, very much due'. Wirth–Miller, true to form, was not the politest of guests. He once, while drunk, spat food back onto his plate and yelled an expletive, bringing the conversation in Carrier's restaurant to a halt. When Carrier threw his fiftieth birthday party at the hall in 1974, Wirth–Miller and Chopping were not invited.

The couple were ageing and their relationship was no longer illegal, but neither of them wanted to conform.

Chapter 18

The Death of Dyer

Francis Bacon had been a Francophile ever since he had stayed in Paris as a teenager. He had a great admiration for French culture, food and wine but he also prized the unstuffy French sensibility, passion and attitude to sex. It was in Paris in the late 1920s, while studying Picasso's drawings at the Galerie Paul Rosenberg, that he decided to become an artist. Bacon was not a man who required praise, but the French authorities' decision to grant him a full retrospective at the Grand Palais in October 1971 may have been the single endorsement that gave him the greatest pleasure. Pablo Picasso was the only living artist who had been given the same honour.

According to Terry Danziger–Miles, who installed the exhibition on behalf of the Marlborough, it had taken months of bureaucratic wrangling to put the exhibition together. Ann Fleming thought the show may have been under threat following a dinner at her Victoria Square residence: she described Francis Bacon, Sonia Orwell and another guest being 'very abusive to each other . . . French lady, unknown to me and imported by Francis; she is organizing a retrospective . . . tho' I should think the occasion is in some jeopardy now.'[114]

Despite that hiccup, the opening was scheduled for Tuesday 26 October 1971, with an additional reception hosted by President Pompidou's wife two nights beforehand.

Bacon had put together a British entourage for the occasion. It included a mix of characters – art-world fixers, friends and old Soho stagers – who all stayed with Bacon at the Hôtel des Saint-Pères in Paris's 6th arrondissement. Among its number were Dicky Chopping and Denis Wirth-Miller, Muriel Belcher and Ian Board of the Colony Room, Sonia Orwell, John Deakin (the Colony Room regular from whose photographs Bacon composed many portraits) and, from the Marlborough, his 'handler' Valerie 'Little V' Beston and Terry Danziger-Miles. Bacon's sister Ianthe was also there. Three years later, after Ianthe and Francis stayed together at the Storehouse, Chopping commented in his diary, 'the likeness of gesture and inflection of speech between them I found remarkable especially as in the past they have seen very little of [each other]. Their parents, we decided, must have both been monsters to have produced two so deviously complicated children.'

The Paris party was completed by George Dyer. Despite his misdemeanours, Bacon still pitied him and acquiesced to his plea to attend: 'There had been nothing between us for ages but since so many of the paintings were of him I could hardly say no.'[115]

Bacon, Wirth-Miller and Chopping had a long lunch in a brasserie and spent the afternoon going from bar to bar, before heading back to the hotel to prepare for Mme Pompidou's reception. Walking along the Right Bank of the Seine, they passed the Grand Palais, where they saw the honour guard drilling in preparation for the event and attendants unrolling a red carpet. Chopping reported that Bacon was taken aback at first, before swelling up with pride.

Back at the hotel, Chopping and Wirth-Miller were saying goodbye to Bacon outside his room while he opened the door. The air coming from the room stank and the three of them heard crashing noises coming from inside.

George Dyer was stumbling around the bed, knocking over everything within arm's reach. He tried to speak, but was so intoxicated that he was incomprehensible. A Moroccan rent boy stood in the corner with an unreadable expression.

Bacon later left for the reception without Dyer, whom he felt was in no fit state to control himself. Afterwards, Bacon and Wirth-Miller went gambling until the small hours of the morning. They returned to the hotel, drunk, and went their separate ways.

Bacon unlocked the door to his room and was hit by the stench again. He did not want to be in the foul-smelling room with the no-doubt still intoxicated Dyer. He remembered that Terry Danziger-Miles had a spare bed in his room so he banged on his door. Danziger-Miles let him in and he collapsed onto the bed.

In the morning, Bacon and Danziger-Miles left to go downstairs together for breakfast. As they were crossing the threshold into the corridor, Bacon asked Danziger-Miles to go up to his room to check on Dyer and handed him the key.

Danziger-Miles met Valerie Beston on the stairs, and she agreed to join him. They found Bacon's room in chaos but Dyer was nowhere to be seen. They were just about to leave and head downstairs when Danziger-Miles decided to check the bathroom. He opened the door and found Dyer 'all haemorrhaged' and slumped over the toilet. Blood was leaking from Dyer's mouth.

'George is in there,' Danziger-Miles said to Beston. 'He's not well. He's really not well.'

Beston pushed past him and went into the bathroom. She knelt down to take Dyer's pulse.

'George is dead,' she said.

Danziger-Miles ran down several flights of stairs to find Bacon.

When he saw the scene, the artist shouted: 'How am I going to have a big opening with this scandal? Oh, trust George to totally fuck it up!'

Valerie Beston took control of the situation. Described as 'a Miss Moneypenny to the M of Frank Lloyd, the gallery's less scrupulous founder', Beston was both capable and highly intelligent.[116] She had been at Bletchley Park before joining the Marlborough and working her way up from typist to director. She immediately went to speak to various officials to make arrangements so that Dyer's death would remain unreported for the time being. His demise, which was later found to be due to an overdose of barbiturates, would not be announced until the official opening of the Bacon exhibition on the following day.

The retrospective covered works from *Three Studies for Figures at the Base of a Crucifixion* in 1944 through to a series of five new triptychs painted since 1969 when the Paris retrospective had first been discussed. The impact that the work had on guests at the Grand Palais was just as forceful as it had been in London over twenty years earlier. The critic of *Le Monde* said he heard one phrase repeatedly uttered by the guests: 'It's like a punch in the face.'[117]

Unlike at the Tate retrospective, Bacon had dressed suitably for the occasion and behaved respectfully throughout the proceedings. As he walked among the paintings, talking to the guests, he would have seen image after image of George Dyer on the walls.

That night, Bacon, Chopping, Wirth-Miller and the rest of the British contingent went to the official dinner at the Train Bleu restaurant in the Gare de Lyon. News of Dyer's death spread as the evening progressed. Chopping and Wirth-Miller held onto a menu from the dinner. They ate sole fillets with glasses of Rully Clos Saint-Jacques, before moving on to a Brouilly and roasted Charolais beef, gratin dauphinoise and salad. They finished with tarte tatin. Photographs from the night show Wirth-Miller and Bacon laughing. Lacy had died the day after the Tate retrospective; Dyer had died just before the one in Paris; but Bacon reportedly remained emotionally composed for the whole evening.

Later during his stay in Paris, Bacon responded with mock tears, dabbing his eyes, when David Hockney offered his condolences. Peppiatt, however, discloses that Bacon was already feeling the weight of guilt that would accompany him for years: 'There it is. He's dead and nothing will make him come back. I've always known it would go wrong. If I'd stayed with him rather than going to see about the exhibition he would be here now. But I didn't and he's dead.'[118]

Rather than damaging the artist's reputation, the story only inflated the Francis Bacon legend. The lingering image of Dyer, and Bacon's feelings of grief and remorse, inhabited Bacon's work in a series known as the 'Black Triptychs'. He almost immediately painted *In Memory of George Dyer* (1971). Two years later he graphically portrayed the scene of Dyer's death in *Triptych, May–June 1973*, with Dyer in his final states of agony, slumped on and crouched over the hotel toilet bowl. Bacon had long pilloried 'painting as illustration', but in 1985 he said of *Triptych, May–June 1973*, 'it is in fact the nearest I've ever done to a story, because you know that is the triptych of how he was found'.[119] A few years later, he would say to Chopping that, in his painting, he was really only 'making records'.

When Bacon, Wirth-Miller and Chopping holidayed in France together in April 1972, travelling to Chartres, Cherbourg and Dinard, Chopping reported that Bacon, who was having trouble with double vision, was 'strangely quiet and low . . . FB had written two postcards and had posted them after which he seemed very quiet and moody. Who is to say why? Perhaps he was thinking of George or of Deakin?' John Deakin was ill and would die a month later.

Francis Bacon's success would come at a price. He had always been suspicious of sycophants, parasites and 'sham friends', but as his reputation grew they became unavoidable. He had been lonely since the end of his relationship with Dyer. On 15 January 1974, at the time that he was buying a new, rarely used studio at Narrow Street in east London, he stayed at the Storehouse with Sonia Orwell. Chopping noted in his diary that Bacon 'seemed drained and anxious looking'. (He added, 'She on the other hand was garrulous and fat, ate compulsively and hardly stopped talking.') On the following day, Chopping wrote:

> FB 'I don't mind being lonely, do you see, because I can think about my work. But she [Valerie Beston] sees nobody. She really is a very lonely little woman.' . . . F looks less haggard today. I hope it is because with us he has been able, even if only for a few hours, to relax in a 'queer' way.

Lucian Freud was among the lessening number of people he trusted and regarded as a true friend. That evening, Freud made a rare phone call to the Storehouse to talk to Bacon. Chopping reported:

> D [Denis] answered and [Freud] didn't even say who he was or attempt to be pleasant. He is worried about his show opening at The Tate on 24th Jan. D was very put out by being treated in such a cavalier fashion. Obviously it is not nice being disliked but he has said some pretty awful things about Lucian to a good many people in the past and some

of them must have got back . . . He behaved at the time
when Lucian rang as if somehow it was my fault that Lucian
doesn't like him.

Chopping went to Freud's retrospective at the Tate twice.
On the first occasion, on 20 February 1974, he wrote, 'For me
his paintings lack heart. Except for the head of a boy (no 70)
which seemed to me to suggest far more than just surface of a
painted face. The youthful informed look of a boy who would
be both tender and vicious.' He went again on the 26th,
following lunch with Bacon and Wirth-Miller at 'Le Français'
and still found the works 'cold and heartless'. In between, he
reported, 'Lucian in Muriel's – to me "it can't be true. You must
be wearing a mask" then later "I know what it is. It's a thick
layer of powder" . . . compliment or insult?' Freud also took to
referring to Wirth-Miller as 'Denis Worth-Nothing'. The adult
relationship of the former friends at Benton End would never
get beyond mutual antagonism.

A January 1975 entry in Chopping's diary mentions a
reflective conversation with Bacon that offers insight into some
of the divisions that emerged in the bohemian set in Soho: 'Long
conversation about Colquhoun + MacBryde's jealousy of
Francis, and Lucian's of Denis in relation to Francis.'

Soon afterwards Francis Bacon and Lucian Freud had a fall-
out, which was not unusual but this time it would be permanent.
They had been close friends since the war, and would often be
seen together in the Colony Room. They painted each other in
the early 1950s, with Freud capturing something of Bacon's inte-
riority in a tiny oil on metal work of 1952, while Freud was a
serial subject for Bacon. He had recently been painted alongside
Dyer and a self-portrait in one of the 'Black Triptychs'. Freud's
international profile did not match that of Bacon, but he was

widely acknowledged as one of the great post-war British painters. It is unlikely that artistic competitiveness was the key to the
impasse. Bacon and Freud were both strong characters with
forthright opinions, and the course of their lives was littered
with irreparably damaged friendships.

The row with Freud left Bacon without one of his closest
confidants. In 1974, however, Bacon struck up a friendship with
John Edwards, an apparently illiterate young East Ender he had
met one night in the Colony Room, whom he liked partly
because he did not lie to him. Their first meeting was illustrative.
Muriel Belcher had told Edwards to make sure that a pub he
helped his brothers to run, the Swan in Stratford East, had
champagne on ice as Bacon would be visiting with some friends.
Bacon never showed, leaving the pub with a quantity of
champagne that no regulars were ever likely to buy. When he
saw Bacon in the Colony, Edwards told him exactly what he
thought of the situation. Edwards and Bacon would be very close
throughout the 1980s, although the relationship was apparently
not sexual. Edwards would provide support to the artist through
illness and old age. One of the few other people that Bacon
trusted was Denis Wirth–Miller.

After the death of Dyer, Bacon became increasingly reliant
on Wirth–Miller, and vice versa; Bacon wrote in an undated
letter, 'you know you are one of the only people I can talk
to and I hold you in great esteem'. Their relationship went
beyond confidences and conversation: the two supported each
other's vices – drinking, gambling and rowing – without
repercussion.

As Peppiatt reported, 'True to his definition of friendship as
two people "pulling each other to pieces", Bacon developed a
no–holds–barred relationship with both of his Wivenhoe
friends'.[120] While Chopping and Bacon were close for four

decades, and their friendship would survive niggles and rows, it was Wirth-Miller who was his closest friend. Janetta Woolley, herself very close to Bacon, claimed that Bacon had one love of his life – Peter Lacy – and one lifelong friend – Denis Wirth-Miller.

Chopping's diaries of the mid-1970s reveal the depth of their friendship; the entries are littered with notes about Bacon's phone calls (often twice a day), his visits to the Storehouse, Wirth-Miller's stays with Bacon in London, holidays, and rows. On 10 February 1974, Chopping wrote, 'D said "all the people I have been attracted to are monsters. Janetta is a monster. Francis is a monster." What else does he infer in it but "and you are a monster"?'

After their nights in London, Bacon and Wirth-Miller would sometimes remember little of what had occurred. The likelihood, though, was that they had got into a vicious argument. Peppiatt knew the artist well enough to understand both the importance and nature of his relationship with Wirth-Miller:

> The quarrels, mainly between Bacon and Wirth-Miller (in many respects as close and long-suffering a friend as Bacon ever had), reached rare heights of camp invective, with the repartee turning so nasty (over subjects as sensitive as George Dyer's suicide) that it would have ended most relationships. In this particular case the friendship appeared to thrive on it.[121]

Bacon would send notes, such as one from November 1978, to the Storehouse apologizing for his suspected bad behaviour, even if he had been too incapacitated to know exactly what he had done.

Dear Dennis

I hope we did not have a terrible row in Mr Chows as I
meant to pay the bill and found I had the cheque the next
morning in my pocket. I must have been very drunk as I
cannot even remember leaving there please let me know what
I owe you for dinner – it is terrible with age what drink seems
to do

Yours

Francis

They would sometimes sulk with each other. The only
contact they made during these times would be a curt demand
to pay back whatever money one owed to the other. It was
usually Bacon who apologized, but he may have had more cause.
Even in the final years of Bacon's life, their emotional dependence
on each other was still matched by their fights. This apology
from Bacon was sent in the late 1980s:

I am so sorry I was so bad tempered when you telephoned
yesterday morning it was all quite illogical I don't expect you
will forgive me . . . I cannot sleep with disgust of myself and
I am at this early hour of the morning having some toast and
a glass of whiskey . . . I just felt I must write to apologise for
my illogical behaviour on the telephone yesterday

The two men could be possessive of each other, and spiteful
or complaining when they thought the other was not giving
them enough attention or answering their letters quickly
enough. They were addictive personalities, and their relationship
itself was one of their shared addictions. They continued to see
each other constantly even though they were aware of the
damage it caused.

On the evening of May Day 1974, Wirth-Miller and Bacon arranged to meet at Reece Mews for an aperitif and then head out for supper at La Meridiana, an Italian restaurant nearby. When Wirth-Miller arrived, he discovered that Bacon had also invited a new friend to join them. He was a student from America, and a teetotaller; Wirth-Miller resented the additional company.

They were turned away from La Meridiana and eventually settled for a table at La Popote, a restaurant on Walton Street. It was frequented by Rudolf Nureyev and Kingsley Amis, but Bacon and Wirth-Miller thought that the food was mediocre.

The tension mounted between Bacon and Wirth-Miller as they drank and the American looked on, apparently bemused by the animosity between the two older men.

They left together but, before they had reached the end of the street, Bacon spun round and started spitting insults at Wirth-Miller. This time Wirth-Miller was unsure of what he had done. He wrote to Chopping the next morning:

> As we were walking back Francis attacked me – verbally. I remember him saying something to the effect that he could understand your difficulties with me. I simply cannot face him and am writing this in case I go back to Wivenhoe – to ask if you would see him and him to tell you frankly whatever it was that I did or said.

Wirth-Miller's clarification that Bacon's attack had been verbal was necessary: they would have physical fights, sometimes in public. When Chopping invited both of them to a Royal College pantomime, they had inevitably both got drunk. Chopping winced as they tried to out-yell each other and attracted the attention of his colleagues. Chopping was already in a state of embarrassment when Bacon reeled around and slapped Wirth–Miller across the face.

Chopping disliked Bacon and Wirth–Miller's schoolboy in-jokes and their heightened use of the Queen's English but he fully understood how much Bacon's friendship meant to his partner. In 1974, Wirth–Miller was having a difficult time. Chopping wrote in his diary that Wirth–Miller 'says he would kill himself as soon as he could tidy up and dispose of our "joint estate" after my death. It is sometimes a heavy burden to be so needed.' Bacon helped Chopping to carry the burden of Wirth–Miller's depression and difficulties. He knew just how much Bacon wanted to help his partner. In that year, Wirth–Miller was struggling with his art, and Chopping's diary entry for 21 February revealed that Bacon was concerned:

> called on FB who was already painting in dressing gown with a split right across the bottom. Long conversation about how he felt he would be able to help D with his work if only he would let him. Tried to get to the root of why D was not able to work and was clearly unhappy. F very kind, understanding and seeming to want to be helpful.

Later, Bacon offered Wirth–Miller the use of the Narrow Street studio in the hope that a new environment would re-stimulate his painting, but his offer was not taken up.

Bacon himself was part of the problem. Foreshadowing the disastrous impact Bacon would have on Wirth–Miller's career in 1977, Chopping noted on 16 March 1974 that Wirth–Miller 'finds F very destructive about painting and everything and that he destroyed his confidence. "I can't talk about it." We have both therefore lost the confidence we usually have.'

The rows continued as 1974 progressed: 'F+D now screeching like parakeets as they get themselves dressed up to go out in the car to Ickworth. "65 year old piece of powder puff" screams Francis.' In May, Chopping wrote:

D told Francis that he only had sycophants for friends. FB replied 'I wonder Dicky doesn't cut your throat.' F said to me that he knows D hates his work because it has been repeated to him by other people, 'Why should he like it after all?' he said. I said I thought it was mischief making (I expect on the part of Lucian and David Sylvester). The fact of the matter is that they both (Denis and FB) want to dominate each other and neither will let the other do so.

Chopping did what he could to keep the peace, including playing go-between, and often helped smooth away the friction between the two friends. Bacon told Chopping that he and Wirth-Miller got on better when he was with them. Following a row between Bacon and Wirth-Miller, Chopping noted in his diary:

D said that FB felt 'depressed about Sunday night' so I went round to see him. He was in the bath and had to rise up like an ageing Venus. He couldn't look me in the eye. Said he wasn't depressed. We hardly alluded to Sunday but agreed that nobody could repeat what other people said accurately. He suggested Barbados. Went to travel agent for brochure.

The Storehouse couple and Bacon happily went on holiday to France again in the summer of 1974, and the three men spent Christmas at Narrow Street with Peter Beard, the American wildlife photographer, who was one of Bacon's close friends.

At this time Bacon was troubled by the health of another close friend. Muriel Belcher had a stroke and then broke her femur in the London Clinic. Chopping noted on 12 December 1974, 'FB has agreed to pay £100 a day to guarantee her stay in clinic. She wants him to be near at hand when she has the operation. FB, Denis says, is obviously very affected by the imminent possibility of her death.' Two days later he reported:

> Muriel did want to see us. She looked frail and frightened, her hands like elegant birds' feet, one plucking at the counterpane the other one thumbnail between her teeth like a child . . . Muriel and Carmel [her partner] touchingly tearful vulnerable – monoliths from the vituperative world of Soho club life. Over lunch in the restaurant at the Zoo Carmel told us of her suspicions that Ian [Broad] had been intentionally muddling Muriel up with pills, pot and drink so that her brain and physical condition was rapidly deteriorating.

Belcher recovered but remained weak and would survive only another five years. Just prior to the operation, Wirth-Miller had offered to put up Muriel and Carmel at the Storehouse, but they did not take up the offer. Chopping was relieved: 'If they came – God help us.'

In March 1975, Bacon was given a further accolade: a show at New York's Metropolitan Museum of Art. The exhibition concentrated on his recent work, including the 'Black Triptychs' that were painted in response to the death of George Dyer. Praise for Bacon was far from universal in the United States. Henry Geldzahler, the curator of the exhibition, was aware that it would divide opinion, writing in the catalogue, 'Bacon himself says his work is hated in America. This is both true and untrue. The audience that admires his work is large; the audience that dislikes it is smaller but more vociferous.'[122] The difference in critical opinion may have spurred interest: almost 200,000 people attended the exhibition.

Bacon wanted Dicky Chopping and Denis Wirth-Miller to once again be part of his British entourage, which again included Danziger-Miles and Beston of the Marlborough.

While grateful for the invitation, Wirth-Miller was concerned. Although it was thirty years since he had been imprisoned in Wormwood Scrubs, he feared that the strict immigration policy of the United States would prohibit him from entering the country. In the event, he neglected to mention his prison term on the tourist visa, but, for the entire ten-day visit, he was worried that he might be arrested for entering the country illegally. Two weeks before leaving for New York, Chopping, no doubt recalling the death of Dyer in Paris, wrote, 'I have a strange feeling of foreboding about America.'

Anne Dunn was also part of the Bacon group. She and her husband Michael Wishart had fallen out with Bacon in the early 1950s but the rift had long since healed. She had gone on to divorce Wishart and marry the artist Rodrigo Moynihan. Adding to Chopping's sense of foreboding, when Dunn was walking down Park Avenue from the Metropolitan she had to leap backwards to avoid a body falling from a seventeen-storey apartment block. It exploded onto the pavement in front of her. The result was reminiscent of an eviscerated carcass in a Bacon triptych. Dunn was undaunted: 'I suppose it's these things that make New York so charming.'

The group was scattered around midtown Manhattan – Chopping and Wirth-Miller were staying in Room 1635 on the sixteenth floor at the Hilton while Bacon was in the Carlyle

– but gathered regularly at bars and restaurants. Bacon left the telephone number of Anne Dunn's apartment for Wirth-Miller at the Hilton reception so that they could arrange to go to the private view together. Wirth-Miller rang but was unable to get a response to his call.

At 4 p.m. there was a knock on the door of Room 1635 while Wirth-Miller and Chopping were in bed. When Chopping opened the door, he was faced by two New York Police Department detectives. Chopping recalled them saying: "'Is there anyone here called Denis?" I woke him up and they both came in. In a very brusque way they shot questions at him about the telephone call he had made to Anne.'

The couple had no idea why they were being questioned. Wirth-Miller was certain that, whatever the cause, the police would discover that he had lied on his visa form and he would be arrested and imprisoned. Finally, one of the detectives explained that the apartment Wirth-Miller had rung had just become the scene of the homicide of three men. The police traced calls that had been made to the apartment and decided to investigate, leading them to the sixteenth floor of the Hilton.

The police questioned them and finally accepted their story that they had been trying to get in touch with Anne Dunn, but must have been given the incorrect telephone number. No further action was taken.

Wirth-Miller was angry and, although it was undoubtedly a coincidence, he suspected that Bacon had somehow set him up in the knowledge that he was already fearing imprisonment for the second time in his life. He walked up to Bacon while he was talking to guests at the private view, thumped him on the shoulder and said, 'You fucker!' After the confrontation, as was typical of their relationship, the two artists were soon hugging and laughing.

The British guests spent the private view drinking double whiskies courtesy of the museum. Dunn remembered next to nothing other than having been 'embraced passionately by a lady art critic and then someone pouring a glass of whiskey over my head'.

Even though Bacon and Wirth-Miller had made up, Valerie Beston, keen to keep a tight rein on events after the Paris tragedy, informed Wirth-Miller and Chopping that they were no longer invited to dinner. Nonetheless, they went to the opening at the Met on the next day, followed by a group dinner at Sardi's and drinks at the Algonquin. On the following day they met Bacon for lunch and the three men spent time with John Richardson, a British art historian who was working for the Knoedler gallery in New York. Chopping and, in particular, Wirth-Miller consumed a large amount of whiskey and experienced 'poppers up our noses'. Wirth-Miller was sixty years old at this time.

On Friday 21 March, Bacon arranged for them to visit Andy Warhol's Factory. Chopping described the visit:

Big scruffy building. Bullet proof door. Stuffed Great Dane in reception. Young man offered us champagne and magazines. Andy Warhol and Francis arrived. AW very frail, paint be-spattered. Back of his hair black with a white switch so that it looked like a badger. Red veined nose and strong glasses. Young swarthy man with cookies, girl photographer, sexy hairy man photographer . . . Strange atmosphere of dereliction. 'My pictures are so fresh they stick together' Warhol. Art deco desk of brass and black marble. Moose head given by John Richardson. Huge black kitchen under construction. Furniture arranged like movie lots so that the whole place had the appearance of being lived in by absent people. All rather sad and a 'has-been' feeling.

On his return to the United Kingdom, Chopping said, 'NY made our whole nervous system feel as if it had been in a food mixer.'

'What is there for me to do but get drunk?' Bacon said to Chopping shortly after his return from New York. Still lonely, Bacon called on the telephone so often that Wirth-Miller would sometimes ask Chopping to say that he was not home. In May 1975, Chopping wrote: 'Message from FB at the college. He claimed to have telephoned home yesterday and that someone answered and then rang off without speaking. I told him that the telephone had been off the hook all day but he didn't sound as if he believed me.'

Wirth-Miller was still struggling with his painting and his mental well-being. He asked Chopping if he thought he had suffered a nervous breakdown, and added, 'I want FB out of my life for a bit and shall be glad when he goes to Paris in July.'

Bacon was taking up residence in his new apartment on the rue Birague in Paris, and Chopping believed that this would be a turning point in Bacon's life: 'F really intends to make Paris his centre now. It should give D a chance to be independent of him, but at the same time he will be deprived of his stimulation.' Wirth-Miller was depressed when his friend departed, but the break did not last for long: the three men met up in Chartres just a few weeks later, and by August Bacon was back at the Storehouse.

In the meantime, Wirth-Miller finally had a breakthrough in his painting. Chopping happily reported on 17 June 1975:

D showed me the landscape he has been working on, after reading me an old review from the *Telegraph* which eulogised his Dartmoor pictures. This present landscape is beautiful. The application of the paint seems different.

I was afraid to say much for fear of saying the wrong thing.
But he should feel pleased that he has finished a landscape
which he says is better than the last one sold at the New
Art Centre.

During this period, Wirth-Miller admitted 'that he drinks
because he gets so wrought up over his work'. It had been a
difficult time in their relationship. Chopping was also looking
for purpose in his life and considered taking on volunteer work
as a hospital porter in Colchester when he was not teaching at
the RCA. When he talked to Bacon about it, the artist, perhaps
remembering his time as an ARP warden in the Second World
War, replied, 'Funnily enough I've often thought about doing
something like that'. Instead, Chopping, all too aware of the
suicidal tendency in Wirth-Miller's family, joined the Samaritans
following encouragement from their old friend Joan 'Maudie'
Warburton. He then persuaded friends, including Frances
Partridge, to donate to the charity.

Bacon was still visiting the Storehouse with great frequency.
Despite the fact that he was so metropolitan in nature, and had
disliked living in Hampshire and staying in St Ives, he was
drawn to Wivenhoe. In August 1975, he decided to buy a house
near Wirth-Miller and Chopping:

F and D went off to see Cameron's cottage. F and D
returned, F having made the decision to buy the place.
I have very mixed feelings but at least I have done nothing
to prevent either doing what they want. Hintlesham. Bottle
of champagne at bar. Then drank far too much at lunch.
Then pub. D and Francis spending lavishly. All staggered
home when pub shut. I went on duty at Samaritans. F and
D sat up till 2 a.m.

The house was a fairly ordinary Victorian red-brick terraced cottage at 68 Queen's Road. Bacon enjoyed luxury, and as the local newspaper commented when it reported on the purchase, Bacon's paintings were now selling for up to £100,000 (Wirth-Miller's were £1,000 each) so he had plenty of funds, but grandeur seemed to have little appeal when it came to purchasing property.

Bacon, as he had done at Roland Gardens, spent money on refurbishing the house. He had the ground-floor front-room ceiling removed in order to create a double-height, well-lit studio, and the walls were painted in sage. Once the house was completed, however, he used it almost as little as Roland Gardens, preferring to share Wirth-Miller's studio at the Storehouse. Even though they had both passed the age of sixty, the two artists would still usually begin the day early, working in the Storehouse studio. They would stop at lunchtime and head to the nearby Rose & Crown or the Black Buoy, depending on which landlord was tolerating them at the time. Bacon would rarely take the short uphill walk to his own house, which involved crossing a railway track, and he would return to the Storehouse, often sleeping there.

Wirth-Miller's bedroom had effectively become Francis Bacon's room, while Wirth-Miller stayed in the converted attic. The walls were lined from floor to ceiling with Michelin road maps of France, which appealed to his Francophile tastes (the rest of the house was lined with thick brown wrapping paper, one of Wirth-Miller's idiosyncratic interior-design ideas). As it had three exterior walls, the room was often freezing and Bacon called it 'the little igloo'. Despite his asthma, Bacon had a strong constitution and was willing to suffer the cold rather than walk back up the hill after several bottles of wine. A local person remembered meeting Bacon and Wirth-Miller as they were

A work by Francis Bacon in Denis Wirth–Miller's studio.

drunkenly attempting to walk up the hill. Bacon had tripped up and fallen backwards onto the canvas he had been painting, and the imprint of the oils was visible on his raincoat.

In September 1975, Bacon was once again involving himself directly in Wirth–Miller's painting. Chopping wrote: 'After lunch Francis said he could help D with his painting and to my amazement he let him, adding quite a lot of thick paint. F lay down to rest. D and I went up to my studio . . . I got them to bed with sleeping pills and I left at 10 p.m.' By this point, all three men were regularly taking sleeping pills.

Bacon stayed at the Storehouse for Christmas 1975. As part of Wirth–Miller's attempt to reinvigorate his painting practice, he had returned to figurative subjects. On Christmas Day, Wirth–Miller remained out drinking while Bacon and Chopping sat in the kitchen. Bacon confessed that he had seen Wirth–Miller's nudes but had been unable to conceal the fact that he did not like them. When Wirth-Miller finally returned, Bacon put him to bed with a sleeping pill.

The drawback of Wivenhoe was that there was no opportunity to gamble. The small roulette wheel they kept in the studio offered none of the thrill of the casino. Often, when it was late and Bacon and Wirth-Miller were already inebriated, they would pursue their mutual craving and head back to London, usually by taxi. Chopping rarely joined them as he had little interest in gambling, reporting in 1974, 'I had a conversation with FB about relating gambling to painting, saying I wished I was more of a gambler as it might enable me to loosen up my style of painting. He maintained that it had never done that for Lucian.'

They would head to Charlie Chester's casino, named after the comedian who had been popular in the 1960s. It was not one of the exclusive Mayfair casinos. Former croupier Chris Moore, who worked there in the mid-1970s, recalled that 'The operation was targeted squarely at the bottom of the market', with the focus on blackjack, roulette and craps.[123] It would stay open until 3 a.m., affording Wirth-Miller and Bacon more drinking time, and the downmarket nature of the casino meant they were more likely to be allowed to misbehave.

Moore said, 'There was a slightly dangerous side to working [there] in those days. The casino attracted thousands of passers -by, many much the worse for drink.' It was also a destination for football fans: 'On the nights when England played Scotland at Wembley it seemed that the drunkest and most violent of the supporters found their way to the door of Charlie Chester's.' The remnants of the Kray gang were connected to the establishment (including a doorman known as 'Mick the Hammer'), which was an additional attraction for Bacon and Wirth-Miller.

Bacon would wake up at Reece Mews, unsure what had happened to the thick bundles of notes he often carried with him. Often he would have lost it all at the tables or given it to the taxi driver who took him home. Wirth-Miller, the less impetuous of the two when it came to stakes, was a good gambler. When he had won, he would often not wake Chopping up with the news, but rather leave a scrawled note on the kitchen table, 'won you a little present . . . £200 or more . . . much more'.

According to the artist Michael Leventis, who was a close friend of the artist, Bacon would foist cash onto John Edwards when he had a big win, instructing that it was under no circumstances to be returned. He would then lose badly and demand that Edwards return every penny. Edwards always obliged.

Charlie Chester's was convenient, but Wirth-Miller and Bacon would also travel to Monte Carlo for serious gambling. On one trip to the south of France in July 1976, Dicky Chopping went with them, somewhat reassured that Wirth-Miller and Francis Bacon were trying to control their alcohol intake. Rather than heading for the gambling hotspots of Monaco and Nice, the plan was to drive to Marseille for the opening of Bacon's exhibition of recent works at the Musée Cantini. Chopping wrote, 'D brought up the subject of us going to Marseille for FB's exhibition. He has been so nice since he has been off the drink that I can hardly refuse to drive them although I am not without misgivings. FB seems very pleased at the suggestion and immediately fell in with it.' He also reported, 'F very snarky until he suddenly said he had decided not to say anything bitchy until Christmas.'

First, they stayed at Bacon's cramped, messy apartment at 14 rue de Birague in Paris. Gaston Defferre, the mayor of Marseille and a former Socialist presidential candidate, had been instrumental in arranging the Bacon exhibition. He was in Paris with his wife, Marie-Antoinette, and went to Bacon's flat for dinner. Chopping cooked for them, and Marie-Antoinette, or 'Paly' as she was known, later asked for his recipe for a gratin. Unfortunately, she had not been able to recreate it: 'I tried to get the right potatoes,' she wrote to him, 'maybe we should let them grow in Francis's cupboard again.'

James Birch, a mutual friend of the Wivenhoe couple and Bacon, was studying history of art in Aix-en-Provence. On their way to Marseille, the three men dropped by and demanded that he join them for the rest of the journey.

Compared to the retrospectives and the New York show, it was a modest exhibition of only sixteen works. The four British men enjoyed themselves, but Wirth-Miller made them rise early in search of more alcohol and bouillabaisse.

While Wirth-Miller and Bacon were going from bar to bar in Wivenhoe or Soho, Chopping would often stay elsewhere. The Royal College allowed him to rent a room at minimal cost in a student residential building at Evelyn Gardens, near the Fulham Road. He would sit in his room, writing long, reflective diary entries, and sometimes attempting to make progress with the memoir he had now been writing for almost a decade. He was so focused on his memoir that in 1976 he turned down an approach to design the cover for a Kingsley Amis novel and the chance to write and illustrate a children's book. He would often walk up to Belgravia to see Frances Partridge, who was now in her mid-seventies, or take the Underground into town and go to the 'Elephant's Graveyard', the nickname of the Quebec, near Marble Arch, so-called because of its older, gay clientele.

Chopping continued to be a popular tutor at the Royal College after he took up his creative writing role. Mike Simkin at the Colchester School of Art remembered 'Richard's love of fun and sartorial elegance, which was captivating for us as students, particularly when he dressed up for our Christmas parties in military uniform and regalia or striped blazer and boater – not unlike the illustrations depicted on the covers of Denis and Richard's book [*Head, Bodies and Legs*].'[124] He continued his passion for dressing up by regularly playing the 'leading lady' at the RCA's annual pantomime.

Chopping had an informal approach to teaching. Halfway through a tutorial, he might decide to take a student to his friend Peter Langan's new brasserie next to Green Park station, and on at least one occasion 'to a saucy club' in Soho. He was having coffee in St James's with a student one morning when he heard Langan shout his name across the street. The restaurateur came towards them, drunkenly swinging a large lobster. He delivered a wet kiss on Chopping's face and careered off, leaving the live lobster on the table.

Chopping would sometimes invite celebrities to talk to his RCA students about their creative lives. On 4 December 1975 it was the turn of Quentin Crisp:

Quentin Crisp arrived. Very demure, slightly sad grand-dame with involved pile-up mauve and grey hair. Clothes pathetically old but the manner very, very gracious, but on the surface totally passive. Not so underneath I guess. Lunch in SCR [Senior Common Room] with a bottle of wine mostly drunk by me . . . Q talked for 2 hours. Very opinionated but interesting. Offering no solution but self analysis and 'doing one's own thing' with obsession.

In 1976, with the help of Chopping's introductions, Crisp made his acting debut as Polonius in the RCA's low-budget film of *Hamlet*, which also featured Helen Mirren. Between 1976 and

1983, Adam Ant, Diana Dors, Frankie Howerd, Ronnie Barker, Anthony Newley, Dick Francis, Robert Carrier and Elizabeth David all gave talks to Chopping's students.

One of the friends Chopping made at the RCA was Iris Murdoch. The Booker Prize–winning author was a frequent lunchtime companion in the Senior Common Room. For a while, she had been a fellow tutor in the General Studies department, having joined the RCA in 1963. She would also occasionally join Bacon, Chopping and Wirth-Miller at Sonia Orwell's soirées in her Gloucester Road home. Their friend Stephen Spender described these gatherings as the closest he had seen to an English salon.

Chopping introduced Partridge, who had long admired the writer, to Murdoch and her husband John Bayley. In 1975, Murdoch helped Partridge decide what to do with her large archive, which is now held alongside Rosamond Lehmann's archive at King's College, Cambridge.

Chopping liked Murdoch but found her intellect and talent imposing. Following her death in 1999, he wrote in a letter to an ex-student:

> I was, to a certain extent, in awe of her but she always seemed to me austere, unapproachable, too intellectual for the likes of me. I felt I was her inferior. I find her weird really. I realise how very unusual it is that such a woman, with her appearance and intellect, could write so brilliantly about sex, not completely directly, but potently, even the attraction of a middle-aged refugee for the naked body of a fifteen year old boy lying face down on the beach. Quite extraordinary. She writes in an odd sensual way as if she's turning it all over in her mind, as if she wanted to experience the scenes about which she is writing. Inventing, because she can't have been a middle-aged man. But must have had a very strong sexual urge.

In 1995 Partridge reported back to Chopping that she had seen the Bayleys in Oxfordshire, and again at Charleston, where she was astounded to have found Iris Murdoch drunk. It emerged that Murdoch had Alzheimer's disease. She died in 1999.

By the late 1970s, Chopping was contemplating his retirement from the RCA. In April 1977, he threw a grand sixtieth birthday party. David Hicks, still practising the art of self-advancement, was unable to attend: 'I shall be gleaning the last rays of Carribbean [sic] sun on the porch of my Egyptian-inspired house on Eleuthera,' he wrote. 'I am madly busy . . . my new book, *The David Hicks Book of Flower-Arranging*, is doing well . . .'

'Why is David Hicks such a little shit?' Chopping noted.

Chapter 19

In a Muddle

In 1977, while Francis Bacon was set to have exhibitions in Paris and Mexico, Denis Wirth-Miller was invited to exhibit at the Wivenhoe Arts Club. It hardly offered the same status, but Wirth-Miller had long been a supporter of local arts. The club had been set up by the couple's near-neighbour George Gale, a former editor of the *Spectator* magazine. Further solo exhibitions at the New Art Centre and Hintlesham Hall were already scheduled to take place over the course of the next year. He had emerged from his artistic crisis of 1975–6 and, at the age of sixty-two, Wirth-Miller was again enjoying respectable attention as a career artist.

Meanwhile, Dicky Chopping had also returned as an exhibiting artist through Wirth-Miller's association with the New Art Centre. In May 1977, he had a solo show of recent work in the Lower Gallery, while Eileen Agar was shown in the more prestigious Upper Gallery. He was now creating highly detailed realist watercolours, rather than *trompe l'oeil* works, and the gallery produced a postcard of his *Cream Cake* (1978). It also produced a postcard of one of Wirth-Miller's recent works, *Landscape* (1977).

The techniques that had inhabited Wirth-Miller's work in the early 1970s were still evident, with slashes, splashes, smears and woven marks, but the impression now was of a calmer artist. Some of the works leaned back towards a more traditional, formal landscape structure but they were distinctive and confident;

despite his traumas, the works from the mid-1970s onwards suggested an artist who was in full control of a wide range of
innovative techniques.

Just as he was setting to work on new paintings in preparation
for the series of exhibitions, Wirth-Miller slipped while cutting
a canvas and sliced off the top of a finger. The finger quickly
became badly infected, and he could not paint at all. A doctor
warned him that the finger might have to be amputated.

Chopping tried to help Wirth-Miller through this troubling
period but the dark side of Wirth-Miller's personality took over.
Chopping found the level of anger, insults and complaints
directed at him increasingly unbearable. The finger was no
longer in danger of amputation so, when Chopping received a
letter inviting him on holiday to Tuscany at short notice, he left.

Wirth-Miller, still in need of care and company, phoned
Francis Bacon, who immediately headed to Wivenhoe. The
unlikely care worker looked after Wirth-Miller and helped him
ease his way back into painting.

Wirth-Miller regretted his treatment of Chopping and did
not blame him for absconding. A few days after Bacon arrived,
he wrote to him in Italy: '[Bacon] was terribly kind and slept in
your bed in case I needed anything. Much as I feared he tried
to cheer me up with champagne but I was able to keep in check.'
Robert Carrier arrived a few days later and offered to cook.
When he started cooking eggs with butter, Bacon, according to
Wirth-Miller, started 'bleating' for him to use Flora instead –
Bacon, despite his self-destructive habits, always feared high
cholesterol and tried to avoid desserts and egg yolks.

Wirth-Miller recovered in time to produce enough work for
his forthcoming exhibition at the Wivenhoe Arts Club. He was
nervous as he had not exhibited for five years, but he had won
the battle against his lack of self-confidence. He invited everyone

he knew of any consequence, including leading figures from the arts scene in Essex and Suffolk. The star guest was Francis Bacon.

Wirth-Miller met Bacon outside the gallery at the opening, and shepherded him inside. His friend was already drunk and unsteady on his feet. When he started to take in Wirth-Miller's new paintings, he began to rock back and forth. The guests waited respectfully to hear his opinion.

Bacon stopped rocking on his heels and started laughing. For the next ten minutes, he went around the exhibition, stopping to laugh, gesticulate and insult various works – even though he was acutely familiar with the psychological crisis his friend had endured in relation to his work. Wirth-Miller's friends and neighbours looked on in shock.

Wirth-Miller had listened to Bacon pillory the work of many leading contemporary artists, including some who had been close friends, not least Graham Sutherland, but Bacon had always been respectful of his work, even though he had disliked his attempted move back to the figurative. Now, the criticism was unremitting and belittling, and directed at his landscapes.

That night, Wirth-Miller vowed to give up painting for good. He fulfilled his obligations to the New Art Centre and Hintlesham Hall and continued to work occasionally in private, but from that moment on he was finished as a public artist. He claimed to David Hicks and the New Art Centre that his eyesight was failing. It is possible that he had mild synchysis scintillans by that early stage, with crystals of cholesterol forming in his right eye, but, in truth, he was humiliated.

James Birch reported, 'Denis always said that Francis Bacon was his muse', and he told Louisa Buck that Wirth-Miller's 'response was to destroy the entire show'.[125]

As Wirth-Miller told Terence Conran, he gave up painting as a profession 'because I will never be as good as Francis'.

The confidence that had carried him from a difficult child-hood in Folkestone and Northumbria to the heart of bohemia and on to become an acclaimed artist had irretrievably buckled.

Wirth-Miller held true to his vow for the remaining thirty-three years of his life. From that point on he devoted himself to garden-ing, foreign travel and drinking. Despite all their arguments, Bacon and Wirth-Miller always had a similar sensibility towards art. Now, he simply accepted that Bacon was right about his own art, too.

There were no long-term repercussions for Bacon and Wirth-Miller's friendship. Their strange relationship, in which tenderness and squabbling were balanced in equal measure, remained largely unchanged.

Although Bacon painted many of his friends and associates, he never completed a portrait of Wirth-Miller (although he destroyed so much work that it is impossible to know whether he attempted one). He completed a double portrait of Dicky Chopping in the year after the Arts Club debacle. Chopping always claimed that Bacon made him look as hideous as possible, but the work captures his personality and the rendering in profile is an unmistakable likeness. For a Bacon portrait, it is peculiarly muted, sympathetic and respectful, and devoid of grotesquery.

That summer of 1978, Chopping and Wirth-Miller were lent Terence Conran's holiday home on the Dordogne; the designer had remained a friend since his days at the RCA when he designed the Storehouse kitchen. He had gone on to become the most famous furniture and design retailer in Britain; coincidentally, when he acquired other retail companies in the 1980s he named the parent company Storehouse plc. Staying at Conran's cottage in Suffolk once, after a drunken lunch, Chopping and Wirth-Miller had ventured out into the countryside to collect puffball mushrooms. That evening, they walked back into the sitting room with triumphant looks on their faces. Wirth–Miller had a pair of huge mushrooms stuffed into his underwear, while Chopping had a pair stuffed up his jumper. 'We are off to the pub. Who will bet on which of us will have the most luck with the local menfolk? Will it be big balls or big tits?' Conran could not remember the outcome, but he did remember having the mushrooms fried for breakfast the next day: 'quite delicious they were'.

Before the trip to France, it was clear to Chopping that Wirth–Miller was having trouble adjusting to the idea that he was no longer a 'painter', the single word that had defined him for the past forty years. His alcohol intake increased to fill the void and, typically, he turned on the person closest to him. For a few hours in the morning Chopping would find him in a reasonable mood, but he would later become antagonistic, shouting insults.

Chopping wrote to Wirth–Miller, 'I don't know how I can endure those days when I see you tired, drifting towards dark humour and on the horizon looms an attack on me for what I have inflicted on you.'

The Conrans' house near Souillac was surrounded by tobacco fields and overshadowed by a chateau. The dry-stone walls, gorges and medieval towns that peppered the area reminded Wirth–Miller of becoming besotted with France for the first time more than twenty years before. Unlike Chopping, he was not a man given to sentimentality or nostalgia, but he had fond memories of long walks with Janetta Woolley and her friends, exploring the riverbanks and ruined castles.

While on holiday, Wirth–Miller and Chopping were at peace. They only needed a change of environment to reawaken the compatibility and affection that had seen them through forty years together. During this calm period, Wirth–Miller worked out how he could give himself some sense of purpose and self-worth now he was no longer a painter.

Almost as soon as they were back in Essex, Wirth-Miller returned to France, this time with Bacon. While Bacon would often have what Cyril Connolly described as 'bad attacks of the Parlay-Voos' (in reference to Sonia Orwell), smattering his conversation with French, Wirth-Miller wanted to use his unexpected free time to learn French properly.

He enrolled on a four-month language course in Villefranche-sur-Mer, a town on the Riviera placed between the gambling destinations of Nice and Monaco. The town had been in the headlines a few years earlier when the Rolling Stones decamped there for tax reasons. Wirth-Miller intended to finish the course speaking better French than Bacon. The older artist persuaded him that, prior to starting his studies, they should spend Christmas together in Monte Carlo playing roulette.

The trip started badly, according to Wirth-Miller, when he turned up at Reece Mews the night before heading to the airport. Bacon was in a foul mood. He wanted to head out for dinner and the inevitable drinking and gambling that would follow. Wirth-Miller protested that he was feeling unwell, and wanted to go to bed with some Complan he had brought with him. Bacon was furious but offered Wirth-Miller his own bed for the night.

Wirth-Miller began writing to Chopping about the trip in great detail very soon after he arrived in France. He and Bacon had lunch at Nice airport ('a fortunate dish of the day – filet de loup with vegetables cooked in aluminium foil – cuisine minceur influence I think – but very good for me'), and headed to the Hôtel Westminster on the Promenade des Anglais, where Bacon had booked rooms.

At nightfall, they repeated their argument of the previous evening. Bacon wanted to go out gambling; Wirth-Miller felt too weak to do anything more strenuous than lie on his bed with some Complan and read *Dr Faustus*. He refused outright to leave the hotel. Once again, Bacon conceded defeat and appeared to be glad that Wirth-Miller had refused to bend to his will.

Wirth-Miller's resolve had ebbed away by the following evening. They returned to their familiar routine, eating and drinking heavily and gambling at the roulette table. The grand casinos reminded Wirth-Miller of the sets for the James Bond films, and therefore Chopping. He missed the simplicity of the weeks he had spent with Chopping in Dordogne.

On 21 December 1978, three days into the trip, they left Nice for Monaco and were joined by Bacon's cousin, Diana Crawford. They had a run of luck at the casino initially and both won £100 on the first day. On Christmas Eve, Bacon had a large win, but Wirth-Miller seemed tired of the activity, reporting an 'appalling ghastly day of intense gambling', followed by an evening drinking champagne.

Bacon was soon losing money: 'I don't know how much Francis lost but I lent him 2500 francs.' Wirth-Miller, too, had a 'terrible loss' but quickly won it back 'and more'. At midnight, they went outside with Diana Crawford to watch the Christmas fireworks exploding over the Royal Palace.

The next morning began with a bloody Mary at the bar of the Hôtel de Paris and they went into the restaurant for lunch. They began with vodka and caviar, followed by spit-roast turkey, caramelized cocktail onions and chestnuts, accompanied by champagne. Wirth-Miller decided to pay and was astonished by the bill: 'Thank god I have won the price of a hundred meals.'

The heavy gambling continued with wins for Wirth-Miller and losses for Bacon: 'I tried to deter him but he eventually got 24,000 francs off me – the same old song – "when I think of what I've done for you" and so on. Parted virtually no speak.'

For the next few days, Bacon abstained from the casino, brooding over his losses. They spent their last night in Monte Carlo with Muriel Spark, the author of *The Prime of Miss Jean Brodie*, who was by then living with her female partner in Tuscany. Diana Crawford left for England and New Year passed with further nights of gambling, which ended in a net gain for both men.

At the language school, Wirth–Miller installed himself in the communal student accommodation, where he was to spend the next four months with a group of classmates whose ages ranged from eighteen to seventy.

Bacon decided to stay nearby and often interrupted Wirth–Miller's studies. Wirth–Miller began to find this irritating: he genuinely wanted to study rather than be at Bacon's beck and call. He also liked the frugal living arrangements and the sobriety of most of the other students. This was a relief after the excesses of Nice and Monte Carlo. The persistent undercurrent of Wirth–Miller's letters to Chopping is that he needed to re-determine whom he was, to give himself a new point of focus, and he wanted to be free of Bacon's dominating and sometimes needy presence to achieve that.

Eventually, Wirth–Miller spoke to Bacon frankly and told him that he had to leave him to his studies. Bacon seemed genuinely sad. He said that although he could not face returning to Reece Mews yet, he would be lonely if he stayed in the south of France without Wirth–Miller. He decided to go to Paris, and would return to pick up Wirth–Miller when the course finished. As a concession, Wirth–Miller agreed to join Bacon for a final night of gambling.

'I got to school at 8 a.m. on the 3rd having gone to bed at 3:30 . . . silly fool!' he wrote to Chopping the following evening. 'But I was having one of those runs of luck and Francis was feeling upset because he was leaving. He returns to Paris on the 10th as he feels he will feel so lonely.'

★

In the absence of his friend, Wirth-Miller found himself able to focus and found a new resolve in living a monastic life: 'Undoubtedly living in this more temperate climate is a great help not drinking since Francis left.' He took the monastic theme further, forgoing meat and living off bread, fruit and vegetables. He concentrated on his homework, which was initially more difficult than he had anticipated.

He was writing to Chopping in an honest, conciliatory tone. 'I feel in a bit of a muddle,' he admitted, 'you may think it strange but I keep on thinking of those last days in Wormwood Scrubs.' His experiences back in 1945 had damaged him deeply, even though he rarely discussed them. They came to the fore because Robert Carrier had written to him with a proposal that grabbed his interest but also made him anxious.

Carrier had bought a restaurant on New York's 63rd Street and, as at Hintlesham Hall, he planned to mount exhibitions of British contemporary art. He wrote to Wirth-Miller offering him a solo exhibition in September 1979. Wirth-Miller was tempted but remained apprehensive of the American authorities, and his fears had been made worse by the police incident in New York. He could not risk failing to inform the authorities, for a second time, of his conviction. Yet if he did inform them, he might not be allowed into the country in any case.

More than that, he had lost all confidence following the Wivenhoe Arts Club show eighteen months previously. He doubted that he was strong enough to subject his work to possibly cruel scrutiny ever again. He was beginning to miss Chopping terribly, admitting, 'It all makes me feel terribly in need of your practical and calming presence.'

He was nervous what Bacon would say, but eventually seemed to make up his mind: 'Subject to ringing Robert again and seeing photographs of the restaurant I am going to accept his invitation whatever Francis says (I know in my bones he will be against it).' He was going to return to being a professional artist once more, saying he would be 'stupid to miss such a chance'.

But miss it he did. He either prevaricated too long or let Bacon dissuade him after all. Wirth–Miller gave up the opportunity to get a foothold in the American market. The works he was creating at the time of the Wivenhoe debacle combined technical adventurism with a commercially friendly sense of composure; they may well have attracted both critical interest and good sales – Robert Carrier had thought so. Wirth–Miller had lost faith. To some extent Bacon had made his friend, like his lovers, psychologically reliant on him and then dealt a hammer blow.

In his letters to Chopping, it is clear that Wirth–Miller realized how difficult he had been since he had given up painting, and the language course seemed to have given him a sense of perspective and contrition. 'I came here as I felt I had to discipline myself,' he wrote, 'also I know that I have got into a mess with my life and in some way this was the only way I could find of regaining something that I have lost.' As often happened when they were apart, Wirth–Miller's pride gave way to honesty about his true feelings towards Chopping.

Without any distractions, he excelled at the language school and was awarded a merit. It was the sort of education that had been denied to him in his youth, and he derived pleasure and some renewed confidence from it. Despite his success as an artist, the bullying he endured at school and his lack of formal qualifications had rooted an insecurity that manifested itself in obnoxious behaviour. As he explained to Chopping in a letter he wrote on results day: 'I so *hated* my school. I have never experienced a day like this in which I am not just a persecuted half German.'

Bacon was due to arrive on the day that the course finished, driving down from Paris with the artist Eddy Batache and the art historian Reinhard Hassert, both of whom he painted. The two men became a regular feature of Bacon's life, and therefore of Wirth-Miller's trips to France. Wirth-Miller was worried about his friend's impending return. He had found a peace of sorts in the school's ascetic lifestyle, and that was likely to be shattered as soon as he returned to his normal routines.

'I just don't know,' he wrote to Chopping, 'I just know that the round of restaurant eating holds little attraction for me as now I expect a meal out to be the exception not the daily form. I just get bored.' The simplicity of the school had been 'so much more enjoyable' than the 'arid restaurant meals' he had with Bacon in Monaco and Nice.

Tellingly, he was still concerned about Bacon's opinion, even on trivial matters. 'My hair has got so long I'm going to have to cut it today,' he wrote on the eve of his friend's arrival, 'or I'll look like too much of a hippy for Madame Bacon.'

Bacon began mocking him within minutes of arriving at the school. He ridiculed his student lifestyle and taunted him for being taken in by it, while also pointing out Wirth-Miller's diminished frame.

Bacon had immediately reasserted his dominance. 'What Francis said is TRUE. I have got terribly thin – I thought that the breakfast and lunch at the school was enough,' he wrote that evening. 'I was so anxious during those first days. I used to leave my food – all nerves.'

Wirth-Miller, Bacon and his two friends booked into a hotel. 'I fear "reprisals" from Francis if I stick to no drink at all – but I think I will have to – I feel like "Sid Rotten" or whatever the punk rocker was called as I have just lost my tolerance for alcohol.' He added: 'You know, there are times when he is bitchy almost out of some need.'

As they wound their way north through the French provinces, Wirth-Miller was soon drinking again, but in Paris he attempted to keep it under control. While there he again underlined that Chopping was always in his thoughts: 'That friend of Dalí was in the casino but not as beautiful as you . . . his teeth seemed all wrong and yours do not.'

Dicky Chopping's bond with Frances Partridge was similarly close to that of Wirth-Miller and Bacon, but they shared discussions and tea rather than arguments and alcohol. For the first time since they had worked on the flower-book project together, however, they found themselves at odds.

Partridge was now well-known outside the last remnants of the Bloomsbury set. In 1978, the Hogarth Press published her wartime diaries under the title *A Pacifist's War*. Extracts were serialized in Sunday newspapers, and Partridge herself received a good deal of publicity as a result. According to her biographer Anne Chisholm, she was greatly surprised that anyone was interested, and even more so by the fact that she rather enjoyed the attention. For the first time since the death of Ralph and then Burgo over fifteen years before, she was drawing some satisfaction from life.

The interest in Partridge's diaries was symptomatic of a wider shift in British culture. The 1950s and 1960s had been decades in which to look forward, with the advent of greater consumer spending power, new household technologies and the space age. In the 1970s, there was a growing nostalgia for the past. Britain entered a new era of globalization in which it became clear it was no longer a major power. The oil crisis, the diminishing coal industry, economic uncertainty, high inflation, the three-day week and strikes led to greater political polarization.

Chopping had always been uncomfortable with Partridge's upper-class socialism. As a liberal young man, he had respected her views, but he often found her political evangelizing to be patronizing. As the 1979 general election approached, Chopping believed that Britain should free itself of the constriction of the trade unions. He found himself leaning towards the Conservatives and Margaret Thatcher. He was not alone: on 3 May 1979, the Conservatives were returned to power with a majority of forty-four seats.

Partridge found it difficult to countenance the support of Chopping – a pacifist artist – for the Conservatives when Britain went to war over the Falkland Islands in 1982. She wrote to him, chastising him for his political shift and expressing her horror at the jingoism surrounding the conflict:

> I must confess I have been quite staggered by the violent wave of 'Patriotism', flag-waving, open excitement quite intelligent people are indulging in. Everyone is enjoying the F.I. so rapturously. I feel I've been dropped by parachute in a country where only Czechoslovak is spoken. I loathe it all. UGH!! And Mrs T – the great horror of horrors – (have you noticed her resemblance, physical and otherwise to Arthur Scargill?) . . . In the Observer I said 'I should love to strangle Mrs Thatcher' . . . I have daydreams that she might go off her head, or otherwise explode, but what then?

Politics were not Chopping's most pressing concern at the time. After he had finished his final Bond cover in April 1981 – for *Licence Renewed* written by John Gardner – he went on holiday to France with Bacon and Wirth–Miller, whose attempts at abstinence had collapsed following his return from the French course in 1979. Bacon later heard rumours that Wirth–Miller had been sniping about his lack of generosity during the latest holiday and was furious. Their fallouts usually lasted no more than a couple of days, but their relationship was very much weakened by Wirth–Miller's alleged accusations. Although Bacon remained an occasional presence in their lives, the bitterness continued. In December 1981, not long after the death of his close friend Ann Fleming, Bacon said to Chopping about Wirth–Miller, 'It's no good. We can't get on. There it is.' Chopping reported a week later, 'everything seems to have gone wrong since the break with FB', and the Wivenhoe couple had a dreadful Christmas without Bacon.

By then, Bacon was spending more time with John Edwards. (Chopping described in his diary arriving early at Bacon's studio on 6 March 1981: 'John was sleeping having been in a fight. F had avoided the police but John hadn't; broken tooth, bad ear, black eye.') The support Edwards and his family gave to Bacon allowed him to resist mending his relationship with Wirth–Miller.

Wirth–Miller's life was hollowed out by the absence of his closest friend. With few pastimes other than gardening on which to focus his attention, he started to drink before lunchtime. The Storehouse couple's fights worsened and were becoming more physical, with objects regularly thrown at each other across the kitchen.

The impasse continued for two years. On 2 May 1983:

Afternoon: D drunk telephoned FB. I spoke to him. D went out. Francis told me he realized that we had nothing in common and there was no use our having any relationship. Talked half an hour. I felt very sad. D back then he went to the pub. Back around 11 p.m., abuse until around 12.45. Violence. We both hit each other. He tried to kick me in the balls.

Zandra Rhodes, a former RCA student with whom Chopping had remained close, drove up from London for lunch at the Storehouse one Sunday in the early 1980s. When she pulled up outside, it struck her as strange that the front door had been left ajar. As she approached, she heard muffled yells coming from inside. She followed the noise until she reached the kitchen at the back of the house. Chopping and Wirth-Miller were facing each other from across the room, and each was holding a knife. Screaming at them, she prised them apart before being able to negotiate a truce.

Both men were frustrated with their inability to communicate with each other properly in person. 'It is as if I am trying to tear myself out of a natal sac made of tough plastic which cannot be penetrated by human fingernails,' Wirth-Miller wrote to Chopping after one fight, which had ended with Chopping leaving for London. '[It is] turning my brain into a tangled mass resembling the plastic pan scraper by the kitchen sink.' Neither wanted the antagonism, but they could not break the cycle. The critic Louisa Buck, a friend to both of them, believed their relationship needed the conflict: 'Their presence animated many a staid Essex gathering, sometimes overly so when too many drinks resulted in one of their legendary rows which seemed to fuel rather than deplete their relationship.'[126]

In term time, Chopping was able to escape the ongoing traumas at the Storehouse several days a week to fulfil his teaching duties at the RCA, and even at the age of sixty-five he would sometimes spend those evenings in London seeking out casual sex. Yet he knew that this excuse to get away would soon be denied him.

In 1983, at the end of the academic year, he retired for good and once again began thinking about the past.

Chapter 20

A Monstrous Companion

'I hope you are still alive,' Frances Partridge wrote to Dicky Chopping in the 1990s; by then she was in her nineties and most of her friends were deceased. On her death, she would be known as the 'last of the Bloomsbury Group'. Her 'young friend' was well into his seventies, and many of the people whose names were written in the first pages of the Storehouse's visitors' book were now dead.

By the time Chopping retired from the Royal College in 1982, the Fitzrovia and Soho of the bohemians was long gone. There were a few survivors, and the Colony Room was still going, but Muriel Belcher had died in 1979. Earlier that year, Wirth-Miller wrote to Chopping:

Muriel has had a fall and knocked out two of her front teeth. Francis is terribly saddened by her obvious breaking up. Robert [Carrier] had been at the club one evening when she fell on the floor and he was the only person who attempted to pick her up.

By 1983, the deceased Nina Hammett, Robert Colquhoun, Robert MacBryde, John Minton and Jankel Adler were almost forgotten by the art world. Sonia Orwell, Graham Sutherland and Keith Vaughan had died in recent years. Robert Buhler and

W. S. Graham would not survive for much longer. Chopping's most famous friends and associates – Britten, Fleming and Coward – were all gone too.

Cedric Morris and Arthur Lett-Haines had died within a few years of each other, but Maudie Warburton, who had arrived on her bicycle in 1941 to tell the Daffodil Cottage boys about Benton End, was alive and still visiting the Storehouse.

Although many of the names had changed, the visitors' book was in frequent use. Friends and students from the Royal College, including Zandra Rhodes and David Queensbury, would visit, as would James Birch and other members of the arts world who were associated with Essex and Suffolk. Francis Bacon was again sometimes sleeping in the 'igloo'.

During his retirement, Chopping's main reoccupation was his writing – even though his most recent published book dated from 1967. He had assumed that he would finally be able to complete his memoir. As his retirement progressed, however, the prospect of its publication, or even of it being completed, receded. The memoir increasingly became a process rather than a project with a deadline. Sieving through the ephemera, remembering details, and fashioning and refashioning his memories on paper became an act through which he was trying to hold onto the facts of his life for himself, rather than for public consumption. Similar to his process for flower illustrations, he was slowly and painstakingly trying to represent the exact details for his own satisfaction, and would not be hurried.

He still had a great deal of free time to fill. Despite a few uncomfortable, years since Wirth–Miller had started to play the stock market and make savvy investments in the 1950s, they had slowly become better off and bought two rental properties in Wivenhoe. Bacon wanted to sell his Wivenhoe house. Shortly after Chopping retired in 1983, the Storehouse couple agreed to purchase the property with a view to letting it out.

> 7 Reece Mews
> London SW7
> 24/9/83
>
> Dear Dennis
>   Thank you for the £500 towards the £5,000 we verbally agreed on, and also for the B.P applications form which I have not got the money to take up at the moment – I have found the key of Queens Rd and will send it to you
>   with best wishes
>   Francis
>
> P.S. I cannot make out from your letter if you want Frank Auerbach to look at the house or not if you want him to will you please let me know also if I give him the key or send it to you next week-end as it is too late for this one

In late 1983, Bacon's coldness towards Wirth-Miller thawed. They had been in France together earlier in the year, but it had not been a success. It is apparent from Chopping's diary entries that Wirth-Miller was uncomfortable in the presence of John Edwards and resented the increasingly important role he played in Bacon's life. In November, Wirth-Miller and Bacon spent time in Paris, and the holiday was more enjoyable, with Chopping reporting that Denis 'seems to have had a very nice unquarrelsome time and seen quite a lot of Eddie and Rheinhardt'. The relationship would be somewhat restored for the remainder of Bacon's life, although the quarrels returned as a constant feature.

When Chopping and Wirth-Miller set about preparing the house for rental (nothing came of the Auerbach lead), they found it in a dirty and chaotic state. Bacon's green army blankets lay strewn across the floor and there was ingrained dirt on the surfaces. Every light switch in the building was covered in 'dark grey jam'.

In 1985 Bacon was given a second retrospective at the Tate. Wirth-Miller and Chopping attended the private view on 20 May; they returned to the gallery with Bacon on the following day and were photographed together on the steps of the gallery. The photograph is telling. Bacon, of course, is the central figure; the Storehouse couple are his satellites.

The retrospective was large, featuring 125 works. A calmness that had entered some of his portraiture, including the double portrait of Chopping, in the late 1970s was increasingly evident in new works such as the triptych *Three Studies for a Portrait of John Edwards* (1984). They stood in marked contrast to the anguish and viscera of earlier works. They were the paintings of an older and, perhaps due to the influence of John Edwards, more content man. Bacon's personality remained forceful, but he was occasionally checking his hedonistic excesses.

Chopping and Wirth-Miller decided to deal with their restlessness and lack of occupation by going on holiday as often as possible. Wirth-Miller and Bacon were frequently in Paris or on the French Riviera, and Chopping joined them in France twice in the second half of 1985. Bacon's art may have been calmer, but Bacon and Wirth-Miller had fallen into the same cycle of rows that preceded the hiatus in the friendship in 1981–3. In between trips to France in 1985, on 22 September the three men had dinner at Langan's. Chopping wrote in his diary, 'Francis hit Denis who then stormed in and out. I managed to persuade [Denis] to go home. Then I went back and said "you shouldn't have hit him".'

On 19 October, Wirth-Miller wrote to Chopping from Cannes that he had been able to swim daily while Francis remained in the shadows of the casino. Wirth-Miller was again sporadically trying to control his drinking.

Incredibly F & I have kept each other off drink. We have had fantastic meals – here and one in Marseilles at the cheap place. Francis bought 2 tickets on a boat to Casablanca on Oct 27th. It is two days on the boat and will be more rest. We are still up. Tonight I refuse to play as I want to stay up. I wonder what he is doing now. It seems we will go to Tangier and when I get the address of the hotel from Francis I will send it to you so you can send a line. If Francis wins he says he will take me to Marrakesh – what a very tantalizing thing. Tomorrow we are going to Nîmes. Francis has not been at all well but I think today he feels a bit better – I don't think you would believe without seeing it the way we prevent drinking, so far only one Pernod and only wine – no spirits at all. Never been drunk – only very over-excited by winning. Because we are not drinking we plan our meals with great care, and so far have not, except on the train, had anything less than good and much superb. The sky is now the colour of a Frances W-E [Frances Wynne Eyton, a neighbour] picture only vibrating and glowing.

Wirth-Miller may have turned his back on painting, but he saw the natural landscape with the eye of an artist, observing the colours and the smallest details. He wrote to Chopping:

The narcissus are breaking into bloom like little star rocket bursts just above the ground. Mimosa have come out. The prettiest scraps of feather and gristle kept shooting out of the mimosa. The light in the sky is golden, peach on the horizon shading up thru green into blue. The rain has darkened the leaves of the tangerine trees and made them shine. When it's grey it's a nacreous and pearly greyness – if I had paints I think I would like to try and paint it. Everything – green trees – olives specially are tinged with a mauve-ish pink and the sea below Cap Ferrat is the strangest combination of cobalt green with quite deep purplish streaks and reflections – some bouffante-light, cumulus clouds have come up behind Cap Ferrat – more like white smoke than clouds.

The letter returned to the business in hand: 'I have had some good runs of luck and have won the equivalent of £2,000 but a lot can go wrong tomorrow.'

Chopping took holidays of his own, including a trip to Greece with the *Evening Standard*'s food critic Fay Maschler and her sister, Beth Coventry, who ran Green's restaurant in London. The people of Greece fascinated him: 'There is, apparently, one of those old black and brown dressed peasant ladies who has a tame duck which swims with her in the sea. I long to see her.' The housekeeper, he reported, was stealing the sisters' underwear.

Against Frances Partridge's advice when their relationship reached its lowest period in the 1950s, the Storehouse couple planned to take holidays together again. Often, however, Wirth-Miller would invite Bacon to join them. The trio went to Amsterdam and made several trips to the south of France by car. Bacon and Wirth-Miller preferred not to drive, leaving Chopping as the permanent designated driver, which suited their drinking habits. While Chopping drove Wirth-Miller would navigate; Bacon would sit in the back of the car with a handkerchief tied round his head, frequently complaining.

On one holiday, as they were travelling along a dual carriageway past Sête, Chopping could take no more of Bacon's complaints and antagonism. He drove towards the railway

Francis Bacon's postcard to Denis Wirth-Miller from Sête, France.

station, stopped the car and made Bacon get out. He left him standing at the side of the road.

Chopping and Wirth-Miller did not hear from him again until he sent a postcard when they were back in England. It featured an image of two empty deckchairs on a beach at Sête. Bacon wrote on the reverse: 'Where is the 3rd chair, tweetie pie?'

Wirth-Miller's comment in his letter of 19 October 1985, 'Francis has not been at all well', was among the first of many indications that Bacon was ailing. He was soon in and out of Harley Street clinics. Despite a greater concern for his health, he still often went to the Colony Room, the French House (as the York Minster became after a fire in 1984) and the Golden Lion.

It was around this time that the tables turned in his friendship with Wirth-Miller; he had again started to become more reliant on him. He had known Wirth-Miller since the Second World War: their shared history and artistic sensibility gave a broader frame of reference than a conversation with younger men, including John Edwards. Bacon was six years older, but they had kept in step on the same self-destructive road for the greater part of their lives. The tempestuous of their relationship never lessened, though, even as they advanced towards old age.

Maggi Hambling, who was a student at Benton End twenty years after Chopping and Wirth-Miller, remembers being told about a party held to celebrate the opening of an antiques shop in Suffolk. The shop was owned by their mutual friends Angus McBean and David Ball, who were long-term partners. As a young man, McBean, a highly acclaimed photographer, designed some of the scenery and a pair of shoes for the production of *Richard of Bordeaux* that led to Chopping becoming obsessed with John Gielgud. Like Wirth-Miller, he was arrested during the war for homosexual-related activity, and served over two years.

McBean was around eighty when he opened the antiques shop with Ball. The genteel party was disturbed when Chopping and Wirth-Miller arrived with Bacon in tow. The latter pair were drunk and stood outside the shop, arguing furiously. Bacon then marched into the shop, pointed at a plate and said he wanted to buy it. He handed over £40 in cash, walked back towards Wirth-Miller, and smashed it over his head.

'Now will you fucking shut up?' he yelled.

In their seventies, Chopping and Wirth-Miller still went to London independently a few times per week – Wirth-Miller to spend time with Bacon, Chopping to stay with Zandra Rhodes in Bayswater. They would also go into town together for supper at Langan's Brasserie or Green's. They made a point of visiting the galleries; even if they felt alienated by the work of some of the rising American artists – Jeff Koons, Jean-Michel Basquiat and Julian Schnabel – both remained interested and open to new ideas.

They also continued to host lunches at the Storehouse. They each invited their own friends, which led to unusual pairings. Zandra Rhodes, dressed in chic clothes and high-heeled ankle boots, did not drink alcohol, but might find herself opposite Bacon, slightly dishevelled, who would drink several bottles worth of wine.

On one occasion, they were both hesitant about heading out on a post-lunch walk proposed by their hosts. Wirth-Miller led the way through Wivenhoe's winding streets and into the marshland. He then took a shortcut home across muddy fields, at which point Rhodes's stiletto heel became stuck in a cow pat. She failed to shake it free and called out for help. Bacon was the first to react, jogging back to sink onto his knees and carefully prise the shoe out of the manure.

Still ignoring Frances Partridge's advice, Chopping and Wirth-Miller continued to take holidays together – to Madeira, Gambia, Malta and, regularly, to the Conran family's house in Dordogne. Wirth-Miller increasingly resisted inviting Bacon. Despite their ongoing fractiousness at Wivenhoe, the couple enjoyed each other's company, especially when left to their own devices, but Wirth-Miller's argumentativeness would sometimes take hold.

One of their breaks was to Bacon country, Cannes, but they still travelled without him, despite his request:

Dear Dennis
    If you and Dicky decide to go to the South of France I would love to come as far as Monte Carlo do hope you have enjoyed Malta.
    love
    Francis

On the day of their arrival they went to a bar and drank several *suzes* before heading to a restaurant. They ordered the most expensive menu, beginning with glasses of champagne and twelve large oysters. Next came a *salade gourmande*, studded with duck livers, slices of breast and a roasted quail leg. This was followed by a whole grilled lobster each and then puff-pastry tarts.

Shortly afterwards, both were hit by chronic indigestion – 'feeling sick and up till 2AM feeling as if I had swallowed a crown of thorns,' Chopping recorded.

Chopping wanted to go to bed but Wirth-Miller was keen to continue drinking and a row ensued. Wirth-Miller phoned Bacon, whom he felt would take his side. They spoke briefly, but Wirth-Miller soon forgot and dialled him again. When Bacon did not pick up, he pulled out his address book and began calling Chopping's friends. His partner urged him to come to bed, but Wirth-Miller spent an hour dialling numbers, receiving little by way of response. Chopping again told him to stop, and Wirth-Miller inevitably started shouting. He threatened to abandon the holiday and get on a plane home immediately. Chopping suggested that, in that case, he should call a taxi. Wirth-Miller ignored him and started emptying the minibar. When there was nothing left to drink, he took two sleeping pills and passed out. Only then could Chopping get to sleep.

Their rows were getting worse and, increasingly often, they were erupting in public. Joan Warburton wrote to Chopping warning that if they did not keep their problems to themselves, people would cut them off. She wrote, 'I heard third hand of a young couple having a meal in a local restaurant in Nayland who said there were two extraordinary old men quarrelling and I'm afraid it was you two. Can't you resolve your quarrels at home? People won't invite you and are afraid to mention it.'

It was Wirth-Miller whom friends chose to cut off.

Alcohol remained an over-bearing issue for Wirth-Miller. Even in old age, the self-defence mechanisms he had developed as a boy came to the surface when he had been drinking, and he was quick to argue. Over the years since he had stopped being an artist, he had lost direction and self-control. He had always had a dangerous side, coupled with an unnervingly direct way of speaking, but he was also interesting, charming, loyal and kind. Those facets were being eroded by alcohol and bitterness. When drunk, he was a loose cannon and he was now upsetting people too often for them to be able to pass off the episodes as isolated incidents.

Zandra Rhodes remembers being greeted by Wirth-Miller when she arrived for lunch at the Storehouse one day. He leaned in as if angling to give her a peck on the cheek, then suddenly grabbed her and stuck his tongue down her throat. He also said to another lunch guest's horror: 'My, my – I had forgotten just how big your nose is!'

'Dicky, you will probably have heard from your friend of his performance last night,' read one complaint. '[Denis] was insufferably offensive. Words live, and cannot be un-said, and have put "paid" to our relationship. That's the end of the road as far as he and I are concerned. He has a genius for destruction: for laying waste.'

The actress Joan Hickson, the star of the BBC's *Miss Marple*, lived a few streets away from the Storehouse and often invited her neighbours to her house for drinks. Shortly after his eightieth birthday, Wirth-Miller turned up alone, already drunk. He behaved appallingly, and Hickson cut off all communication with the couple.

'I see my memories as a patchwork,' Chopping wrote in one of the many introductions to his attempted autobiography. 'I see them as episodes, stills flashed for minutes together as a magic lantern slide thrown onto a screen in focus one minute, then, click! It goes and is replaced by another. Sometimes in full colour, sometimes in sharp focus.'

He revealed that he was getting lost in his own archive material: 'I have been trying in the process of regurgitation and cud-chewing to assess it all . . . this squirrel hoard of material which has cluttered up my writing room the past 40 years. Like Patricia Highsmith . . . I never throw anything I've written away.' As well as his own writing, diaries and letters from friends, the hoard included newspaper cuttings, train timetables, restaurant menus, account books, receipts, invitations and porn magazines. It was an obsessive undertaking. 'The depressing realisation that has come to me is that owing to the dotty way I put together a piece of writing (or even a picture, really, done like a pointilliste) by re-writing overlaying pieces here and there like a species of patchwork, by putting it all away for weeks, even years and then having another scratch at it – is never going to get finished.'

He felt that in order to be a proper writer again he needed clarity, which he believed could only be achieved away from the archive and away from Denis Wirth-Miller. In 1987, he applied to become a writer-in-residence at Hawthornden Castle in Midlothian, backed by a letter of recommendation from his old friend Stephen Spender. The castle had been built in the seventeenth century, and Dr Johnson had visited it on his tour of Scotland in 1773. Drue Heinz, heiress to Heinz food empire, bought the castle in the early 1980s, refurbished it and turned it into a writers' retreat. In 1982, she launched the Hawthornden Castle Fellowship, a residency open to published authors.

Chopping had not published any new work for twenty years but his application for the fellowship was successful. When he began the six-week residency, he decided to put his memoir to one side and concentrate on producing something at speed, training his writing muscles to work again. He aimed to produce a contemporary re-write of *The Fly*.

Rather than writing fiction, he spent much of the time exchanging letters with Wirth-Miller. As ever when they were apart, they were each other's closest confidants. Chopping enjoyed the setting of the castle – he wrote to Wirth-Miller of a sunset's 'burnished copper shield of sky' – but he took against the local former mining village: 'Rosewell is one of the last places God made and He forgot to finish it. The village butcher looks like the Scots cousin of Sweeney Todd and this is the most dismal and depressing pub I have ever seen.'

He did not take to Drue Heinz either. 'The staff speak of her as if she is a dragon,' he noted, before adding: 'Don't breathe a word to FB.' Bacon knew of Heinz and had told Wirth-Miller, 'I believe she is very sympathetic.' 'Mrs Beans', as Chopping called her, had an apartment at the Albany, an exclusive apartment complex in London that had been the address of a long line of writers and actors including Byron and Aldous Huxley. 'I expect F. has met her [there] with Stephen Spender.'

In his letters, Chopping assassinated the characters of his fellow writers and described 'a strange young man with a face like a boiled potato'. He was surprised how interested they were in his own life story, and particularly his friendship with W. S. Graham. The poet, who had recently died, had a growing cult following. 'The two single beds in my room remind me of his shitting the bed story,' Chopping wrote, 'but these are not the kind one could tell that to.'

'It all sounds a bit like being in prison without a crime,' Wirth-Miller wrote to him, 'how fortunate it is all so much to your taste.'

'I feel like a cranky old hermit in a romper suit,' he wrote back. Later, he admitted his fears about death. 'I hope I don't die in my sleep up here in Hawthornden, choking to death with the hind leg of tonight's haggis, it would be such a nuisance for you to get all my stuff back.'

Writing with candour, Wirth–Miller expressed the same sentiment:

> I'm afraid 'old age' is a monstrous companion. It has taken a great shine to me and is always around with little and big attentions, more I think to remind – like Oscar Wilde's remark about falling in love with yourself – it's a life-long affair. Oh dear! Such a gentle smooth-tongued creature always ready to excuse exertion or effort and if I'm not careful I will begin to confuse his identity and think him a friend.

While still in his seventies, Wirth–Miller began to exhibit worrying traits. He was drinking more than ever, picking up a large weekly stock of wine from the local supplier and sometimes having to replenish before the week was out. He had turned the basement of his old studio in the garden into a makeshift cellar, and would find excuses to fetch more bottles. He was also becoming more insular. He wanted to stay at home, alone with his memories. Sometimes, Bacon had trouble getting hold of him. 'I was supposed to confirm a lunch date with Francis for today but I felt I didn't want to go, so buried the telephone under the cushions,' he wrote to Chopping when the latter was staying in London.

Without explanation, he now frequently pulled the telephone cord out of its socket. Chopping would replace it, but the next time he came to make a call he would find it disconnected again.

Wirth-Miller's temper, increasingly erratic behaviour and the offence he was now regularly causing were not down to alcohol alone. He was suffering from the onset of senility.

That year, 1987, the stock market crashed, and a large part of Chopping and Wirth-Miller's retirement fund disappeared. They were also concerned what would happen if one of them died. As a gay couple, they were not entitled to tax breaks when it came to death duties. If Chopping, the legal owner of the Storehouse, was to die first, Wirth-Miller would receive a bill he would be unable to pay and would have to sell the Storehouse. They decided to dispose of their assets in the hope of keeping their bequests beneath the tax threshold. This meant selling part of the art collection they had built up over the decades.

Firstly, they sold three Richard Hamilton collotypes that Bacon had given them in 1974, followed by most of the Alfred Wallis canvases Wirth-Miller had bought in Cornwall in 1945. They then sold the most valuable item in their collection: a portrait of a head smoking a cigarette that Bacon had given them. It sold for £20,000 – but the sale angered Bacon greatly. The Marlborough still took a 20 per cent commission on any works sold, regardless of whether he stood to profit.

Chopping had already annoyed Bacon when he revealed that he had written a stage play called *Intimate Enemies: A Day in the Life of Tom, Dick and Harry*, based on their three-way relationship. The play emerged out of a conversation the men had in 1974. Chopping noted in his diary that Bacon said, '"what fun it would be if we could live this whole thing out on the stage." I suggested that with all his money he took a theatre and we did it . . . cooked dinner, ate it, lived our lives, talking, arguing, going to bed and so on.' Bacon initially urged him to write the play.

The resulting draft was a failure as a writing exercise, but it throws some light on the fraught relationship of the three men. Tom (Wirth-Miller) and Harry (Bacon) spend much of the first act talking about dyeing their hair, which both artists did. Meanwhile, Dick (Chopping) sits by the telephone, anxiously waiting for them to leave the stage. As soon as they exit, he shouts 'NOW!' into the receiver and is immediately swept into the arms of a muscular black lover.

Harry returns almost immediately. Dick's reaction is telling:

DICK: *Why don't you bugger off you old scarecrow and wreck someone else's life? We don't need you. You have done enough damage.*

In the next act, Harry and Tom speak to each other on the phone, discussing Harry's new boyfriend. He is half Greek, half Arab and leaves Harry satisfied five times a night. He is 'very well proportioned where it matters', Harry boasts.

TOM: *Does he know how to use it?*
HARRY: *Very definitely.*
PAUSE
HARRY: *I'm afraid he may want a picture.*
TOM: *Well give him one, and enjoy the rest while it lasts – really! At your age.*

When Wirth-Miller told Bacon about the play, his initial enthusiasm had long since vanished and he forbade any use of his likeness. He was disturbed that someone whom he had trusted would dare to think of profiting from their association and would reveal salacious details about his private life.

Following the 1985 Tate retrospective, his private life had taken on a new dimension. He became close to a much younger Spaniard named José Capelo, who had sent him letters of appreciation after seeing the exhibition. Unlike the paternalistic relationship with John Edwards, Bacon would claim that this was a physical affair, which appeared to energize the painter. Capelo would later deny the 'veracity or correctness' of the allegations made about him and Bacon.

In 1988, the art dealer James Birch, who had known Denis Wirth-Miller and Richard Chopping since he was a child and remained a close friend, mounted a ground-breaking Francis Bacon retrospective in Moscow. Held at the New Tretyakov Central House of Artists, it marked the first time that a major living artist from any Western country had been given an exhibition in the Soviet Union. Some of the works originally slated to appear in the show were rejected on the grounds of being too sexually explicit. Nonetheless, mounting the exhibition of work by a controversial British artist was illustrative of the new era of *glasnost* and *perestroika* initiated by Mikhail Gorbachev.

Bacon was interested in seeing Russia, and in the catalogue wrote, 'I feel I was very much helped towards painting after I saw Eisenstein's film *Strike* and *The Battleship Potemkin* by their remarkable visual imagery.' A still of the screaming nurse in *Battleship Potemkin* had been a major reference point for his own screaming figures. In the end, he did not attend the opening due to growing concerns about his health. He did not feel up to facing the rigmarole of events around the opening and feared the effect a long flight would have on his asthma. He wrote to James Birch, saying that 'bad goes of the asthma' would preclude his attendance.[127] John Edwards went as his ambassador.

Nevertheless, Bacon was still inhabiting his old haunts in Soho and, if José Capelo was in London, he would show off the handsome and erudite Spaniard to his friends. He was also still enjoying adventures with Chopping and Wirth-Miller. In autumn 1988 the Storehouse couple travelled to London to stay at Hazlitt's Hotel in Soho for a few nights. They met Bacon for lunch accompanied by wine, and all three returned to the hotel for a few bottles of champagne.

They settled on the White Tower for supper. It was a nostalgic return to Fitzrovia and the days when Wirth-Miller and Chopping had lived on Fitzroy Street. Sonia Orwell had lived above the premises and, while it was still Le Tour Eiffel, it had been a regular haunt for Wyndham Lewis and the Vorticists. The restaurant was tolerant enough of Bacon and Wirth-Miller's behaviour to have made it a frequent port-of-call throughout their friendship.

I had known Chopping, Wirth-Miller and Bacon since I first became a student at the RCA in 1981, and had often visited the Wivenhoe couple at the Storehouse. On their way towards Fitzrovia, they stopped at the office of Fitch & Co., the design consultancy where I was employed. I agreed to join them for dinner, despite the fact that they were already legless.

When I had first met Bacon, his attitude was that, as one of Chopping's students, I was to be tolerated with a smile of disinterest. I had made the mistake of showing sentimentality about some matter and, as he loathed sentimentalism, he had written me off. Once, while the three artists were drunkenly arranging a holiday for all four of us to the Conran house in France, he started yelling 'she's not coming' while stabbing a finger continuously in my face. Over the course of many more meetings in the 1980s, he thawed towards me.

As we handed over our coats at the White Tower, Bacon

passed a wad of notes to an attendant, who seemed startled to receive money from a customer before they had left. Bacon ordered several bottles of wine with dinner, followed by several more. He was slurring, and when he tried to get up on his feet to make a point, he could not keep his balance. When the wine waiter passed him, oblivious to his incomprehensible request, Bacon grabbed an empty bottle and lobbed it at another waiter. The waiter returned with a new bottle and Bacon stuffed a £50 note into his pocket. The three old friends laughed and were clearly enjoying each other's company.

When Bacon needed to go to the lavatory, he inched himself up from the banquette seat and lurched sideways. Before anyone could catch him, he fell headlong into the wooden trellis that separated our table from the couple next to us. Bacon took out more £50 notes and pushed them into their hands.

After he had settled the bill, Bacon forgot about it almost immediately and shouted at a waiter to bring it again. After he had been corrected on his mistake, he foisted more £50 notes on both the maître d' and the coatroom attendant. I helped him into a taxi.

Bacon could be charming and amusing and would be helpful when discussing my future, while always conveying the complexity and slight edge of danger that underscored his personality. On that occasion, though, it was as if he had become a caricature of himself – an ageing man diminished into following the tropes of behaviour he had established over the decades.

The next morning, Bacon rang Wirth-Miller at Hazlitt's and accused me of robbing him: he swore that he still had £1,600 when he got in the cab, none of which remained. Wirth-Miller laughed at him, telling him that he had handed around most of the money at the restaurant and had probably thrown whatever remained at the taxi driver.

Bacon found security in having large amounts of cash at his disposal: enough to help cover his whims, generosity and failings. Terence Conran remembers visiting the Reece Mews studio once and seeing a pile of dusty bricks dividing the mess of Bacon's work area from the mess of his living room. He eventually realized that the bricks were blocks of £50 notes.

In 1989, Francis Bacon had a cancerous kidney removed. He became weaker and thinner but, in the spring of 1990, he invited Wirth-Miller, Chopping and myself to lunch at Reece Mews to celebrate Dicky's seventy-third birthday. His house was always in a state of chaos, but we were struck by the terrible conditions in which he was living. Weakened by his illnesses and his operation, he was now unable to properly look after himself. The rope on the stairs, which had been in place for years in lieu of a proper banister, was thick with grease. A trail of diarrhoea marked Bacon's progress from his bed to the lavatory. The door of the oven hung on a single hinge, and the bath in which George Dyer had destroyed Bacon's paintings in 1969 appeared to be stained with excrement. Bacon was breathing heavily and unsteady on his feet.

He had cleared the table so that there was space to eat and retreated. Believing that Bacon was at the cooker, I went to the lavatory. When I opened the door, I found him standing there, his hand against the wall in an attempt to keep himself steady as he urinated. He was missing the bowl and urinating down the wall.

During his final years, Bacon spoke to Wirth-Miller on the phone almost every day when they were not together. He was still seeing José Capelo whenever he could, and, Bacon told me that lunchtime, the two men's relationship continued to be sexual, despite his health. Capelo has seemingly denied this. He is believed to be the subject of one of Bacon's final works, *Triptych 1991*. As he confessed to Wirth-Miller, Bacon felt that his young companion, a successful man with his own life in Spain, would sometimes find an excuse to be 'away'. Bacon had become accustomed to being in control of his relationships, but controlling Capelo was beyond his power. A letter he wrote to Wirth-Miller on 21 August 1990, when the Storehouse couple were again staying at Terence Conran's house, reveals Bacon's frustration, but also that he was still looking to the future. He had given up his flat in the rue Birague sometime before, instead staying in hotels when in Paris:

> Dear Dennis,
>
> Thank you so much for your card I went several times to the Petit St. Benoit [a restaurant in Paris] I do hope you are enjoying your time near Souillac – I really love being in France I think I may rent the old flat in Paris from Michael [Leiris] as he has bought another place
>
> Trying to work – I think in october Jose is going to take one of the cheap tickets to go around the world – I don't see much of him as he is nearly always traveling – do hope I shall see you when you get back – all my love to you and Dickie
>
> Fondest love
>
> Francis

Wirth-Miller and Bacon continued to come to blows, as they always had. When the art critic Richard Cork interviewed Bacon in August 1991, there had evidently been something of a fall-out: he described Wirth-Miller as 'somebody who used to be a friend of mine'. The two men were no doubt amid another row when the interview took place. Nevertheless, Bacon still credited Wirth-Miller with introducing him to Muybridge's images at the Victoria and Albert Museum in the late 1940s.

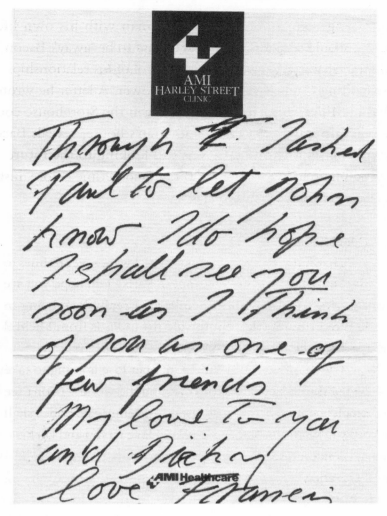

A letter sent by Bacon while he was recovering in a Harley Street clinic.

In December 1991, Bacon had another operation at the AMI Harley Street Clinic. He had entered the clinic in trepidation, fearing that he would die, but he did not want the press, hangers-on or even John Edwards to know the situation. Prior to the letter, during a call on 2 December, it seems that Wirth-Miller, who always strictly guarded Bacon's privacy, was insulted that Bacon felt he had to ask for his discretion:

Dear Dennis

When I telephoned yesterday evening the very last thing I wanted was to be rude to you – all I asked was not to mention that I was in hospital as I do not want my sister [Ianthe] coming over to see me – when I came in for the operation I only mentioned it to Valerie [Beston] and Jose it was only after the operation which I did not expect to come through I asked Paul [Danquah] to let John know I do hope I shall see you soon as I think of you as one of few friends

My love to you and Dicky

love

Francis

Within days, Wirth-Miller received a more specific letter, in which Bacon made the confession for which his friend had perhaps always longed: 'I consider you my only true friend.'

Worried that he would die soon, Bacon made plans to visit Capelo in Madrid in April 1992. By then he was so ill that he was usually confined to Reece Mews and his doctor advised him not to fly. The night before he was meant to depart, his friends Michael and Geraldine Leventis spent hours trying to talk him out of the trip. He went anyway – it was his final transgression.

He was so weak that he required assistance to leave the plane. He became critically ill and was having difficulty breathing. After four days in Madrid, he was taken by ambulance and placed in intensive care at a medical centre, the Clínica Ruber, which was run by nuns and specialized in respiratory problems. On 28 April 1992, he had a heart attack and died at the age of eighty-two. He was cremated in Spain two days later. In accordance with his wishes, none of his friends was invited to attend. There was no ceremony.

Chapter 21

Absence

'I'm afraid it will be a shattering blow to Denis,' Frances Partridge wrote to Dicky Chopping a few days after the news went public. Wirth–Miller was distraught at the loss of his closest friend. With his mind already weakening, his life threatened to unravel.

In the absence of any funeral ceremony, his feeling of rootlessness was worsened when Bacon did not leave him anything in his will. Wirth–Miller did not expect to receive any part of Bacon's by now vast estate, but he had hoped to be left a memento mori, perhaps a painting, that acknowledged the importance of their friendship over the course of half a century. None of Bacon's other close friends such as Paul Danquah received anything either, but Wirth–Miller was still left feeling bereft that he had nothing tangible on which to focus his grief. Bacon's entire fortune was left to John Edwards, although tapes of a conversation he had with a friend and neighbour, Barry Joule, appear to reveal that he had already given \$4 million to his sister and the same amount to José Capelo.[128]

As was to be expected, journalists and biographers sought out Bacon's friends. Dicky Chopping and Denis Wirth–Miller did not comment. Bacon had vetoed biographies during his lifetime and did not want his life discussed in the press. When Daniel Farson approached them for his long-planned biography, Chopping and Wirth–Miller refused to talk to him.

When Farson's book, *The Gilded Gutter Life of Francis Bacon*, was published, Wirth-Miller angrily went through it with a red marker pen, noting scores of perceived inaccuracies. Wirth-Miller and Chopping were barely mentioned in the book, although Farson acknowledged Wirth-Miller to be one of Bacon's closest friends. His description of the incident in which Bacon showed him bruises after failing downstairs hurt them as it implied that they wanted to be given Bacon's house in Wivenhoe for free:

> Francis was at his most expansive, dropping his trousers to reveal some bruises sustained when falling down the stairs of the house he had bought in Wivenhoe in Essex on one of his visits to Dennis [*sic*] Wirth-Miller and Dickie [*sic*] Chopping. He surprised the hustlers in the Lion with his explanation for the bruises: 'I think they polished the stairs on purpose in order to kill me before I changed my mind. You see, I've promised to leave them the place.'[129]

Farson claimed he had met Bacon that day to discuss writing his obituary with David Lewis-Jones, the *Daily Telegraph*'s deputy obituaries editor. Lewis-Jones took up his *Telegraph* post in 1986, three years after Wirth-Miller and Chopping had already bought Bacon's Wivenhoe house, rendering the story inaccurate. Farson may have accidentally conflated comments made by Bacon, but Wirth-Miller and Chopping thought he was being deliberately sensationalist in misrepresenting them. The Wivenhoe couple were offended that they were made to seem like they were 'sham friends'. Wirth-Miller further resolved not to talk to people approaching him for information about his friend.

★

In place of a memento mori, Wirth-Miller, still inconsolable several years later, spent much of his time re-reading and annotating the large pile of letters he had received from Francis Bacon since the Second World War. They were the only connection he still had with his old friend and, in his eighties, he was retreating into his memories. In his increasingly frustrated and senile state, he projected his anger onto the letters themselves. He ripped up and burned many of them; those that remain were discreetly taken away by Chopping or had been left hidden between the pages of books.

While Wirth-Miller started to retreat from the world and became more introverted, Chopping was still full of enthusiasm for human contact. He went to London often, staying with Zandra Rhodes, his former student Su Thomas or myself, and often visited Frances Partridge, who was in her nineties. He dreaded returning home.

When Chopping arrived back in Wivenhoe, Wirth-Miller would usually be drunk, and often accompanied by strangers he had met in the pub. Chopping thought it was as though Wirth-Miller was trying to send out a message that the Storehouse was his house, and his house alone.

Wirth-Miller talked about the Storehouse as if he had built it from scratch. He had been responsible for much of the decorating, but Chopping had bought the house and had played a large part in its upkeep. Whenever he attempted to counter Wirth-Miller's drunken grandstanding, he received a barrage of abuse, both physical and mental.

The violence was escalating and Chopping was increasingly worried: 'I suppose the final straw was Denis shrieking at me as I went upstairs to get away from his attack,' Chopping wrote of one afternoon in 1999. He barricaded himself into a bedroom, and then Wirth-Miller refused to let him out: 'after we had come to blows, he was in danger of falling down the stairs but he still refused to let me leave the room. I threw up the window and called for help. Needless to say, no one answered.'

If an escape to London was too daunting or could not be arranged, Chopping went to Colchester, where he would book into his favourite hotel room. As he recorded, it had a 'TV and 2 beds – £60 for 2 nights'.

After more than half a century, the Storehouse was no longer a place for social gatherings and pleasure. It was now a place ruled by a bitter, confused old man. Chopping started to be absent for longer periods. He would arrive at friends' houses and install himself, sometimes for weeks. He often claimed that he was never going back to the Storehouse, but every time Wirth-Miller wrote him a letter pleading loneliness, he would return to Wivenhoe.

Sometimes Wirth-Miller would be at peace and the two of them would take long walks together in the countryside, just as they had done when they lived at Daffodil Cottage during the war. They shared their hatred of the ageing process and deep concerns. Wirth-Miller wrote:

> I do seem very old . . . as if all my veins and arteries are nearly clogged up and the blood is just managing to squeeze through . . . I meant to write a list of things to prepare and complete for 'old age' and now I'm in it and not very well prepared.

He also confessed to his mental state. 'Watching a documentary about a man mourning his dead friend of thirty years made me cry,' he wrote. He was 'overwhelmed with grief'.

The Storehouse was starting to fall into decay. There were cobwebs on the walls and mould grew in the corners. Chopping's hoarding had led to damp piles of material – from correspondence to magazines to bills – that he could not let go without admitting defeat in his attempts to complete his memoir.

The house was reverting to the state in which they had found it half a century before. Once again, there was a problem with rats. The bay window they had installed in the 1960s was leaking and threatened to fall out of its frame. Neither Chopping nor Wirth-Miller had the strength to resist the decline.

Their bodies were similarly on a path to decrepitude. 'I have a long mirror in my bedroom and I am appalled, every time I pass it, at the image of a ghastly old bald man, hunched and tottering,' Chopping recorded, 'it can't be me.' He was now in and out of Colchester hospital with ailment after ailment; his spine was crumbling; he was suffering from a rare blood condition; he had a throat-cancer scare. 'Never get old,' he would warn his younger friends.

He remained terrified by Wirth-Miller's drinking. 'He doesn't understand how on edge I get as I see the level of wine lowering,' Chopping wrote to a friend. 'I used to have to take calming pills while I waited for the Minotaur to be released.' Wirth-Miller had usually drunk two bottles of wine by the early afternoon, and was trying to cover up the scale of his consumption. Chopping suggested that they should both restrict themselves to half a bottle each at lunchtime, but Wirth-Miller could not comply.

One night, Wirth-Miller slipped on the polished Georgian staircase. Grasping for something to hold onto, he brought a large bell-jar down after him. It smashed over his head. The accident seemed to accelerate his senility.

His accusations were becoming confused and he was drawing fire from across the decades. He claimed that they had never met at the Theatrical Garden Party, that Chopping had 'manipulated' Allen Lane into commissioning the flower-book project, and that he had behaved immorally during the war. When visitors came round, he sometimes claimed not to recognize them. Chopping initially thought it was a ruse, concocted to belittle his guests and embarrass him. He slowly realized that that there was a deeper problem, which had started long before the fall. He suspected that his partner had Alzheimer's.

'All I want to do is live in peace with him,' Chopping wrote, 'having each his own independence, when necessary, for the few years, months, weeks, days, or possibly hours we have left to us.'

Wirth-Miller, when he was calm and lucid, wished for much the same. He wrote after Chopping had once again left for London:

> Being up in your studio has given me a great punch in the solar plexus, leaving me burdened with feelings of regret and guilt, and shame too. As all partings foreshadow the great final one – so empty rooms bereft of a familiar presence mournfully whisper what your room or mine must one day be. I miss you very much. Hopefully I will be more appreciative of you when you come back. All my love to his dreadfully missed friend. D.

Around the turn of the millennium, Chopping walked out yet again. This time he refused to return unless Wirth-Miller began to keep a chart of his alcohol consumption. Wirth-Miller agreed and stuck to it with honesty. Within a few months, he was so appalled by his dependence that he gave up drinking entirely.

Now sober, he renewed some of his past enthusiasms; he re-read his favourite writers – Nietzsche, Georges Bataille and Nicolas Boileau-Despréaux – listened to music and watched the news. He was still brooding, though, and his mind continued to deteriorate. When friends came for dinner, Wirth–Miller would often sit in silence, speaking only to say: 'When one has known a genius. . .' Having known Francis Bacon, he deemed few people worthy of his attention.

Friends of their own generation, with whom they could reminisce about the vanished world they had inhabited, were now few. Nevertheless, they had maintained contact with Janetta Woolley and stayed with her and her husband Jaime Palardé in Spain in 2001. (Chopping noted in his diary, 'She let out that José Capelo has stayed here, more than once I think.') Chopping had made friends with a younger set of people, but he was sentimental about the past, about the excitement of being part of a bohemia that seemed capable of rearranging the universe, and about the old friends from that time, now deceased. Wirth–Miller, meanwhile, retreated further into his troubled memories: his treatment as a child; his imprisonment; and his final failure as an artist. He was sieving the past to see where his life had gone wrong. Referring to the David Sylvester incident that took place decades earlier, he now admitted, 'it served me right, for instance, that he broke my nose because I slapped his face in the presence of the Roberts and Keith Vaughan'.

Frances Partridge was now talking or writing to Chopping almost every day. He noted in his diary on 22 July 2001 that he had tried to ring her but 'No reply. Dead on the floor or gallivanting? I hope the latter.' He asked her in a letter if she, too, worried about the uncertainty that now defined their lives. She replied:

Death – oh yes, I think of it most days. But if one could only guarantee to drop off in sleep I wouldn't fear it at all. Like Burgo I can't imagine what it's like and am frightened of it. I know I don't want any paraphernalia and had none for Ralph or Burgo. I don't feel people one loves are in any sense themselves once they are dead, and celebration of the fact in dying flowers and hymns is a mockery. But people do seem to find satisfaction in it, so good luck to them.

In 2002, Partridge went into hospital. She was 102 and Chopping feared the worst. He asked to speak to her doctor but was told only family members were permitted to do so. This upset him as she had few close relatives left and he had been a close friend for over fifty years.

When he spoke to Frances, he was able to offer her little solace: 'She kept bleating, "I'm in prison, I'm in prison."'

He was in pain from his hip, which he had damaged in a drunken fall in the garden, returning from a village wedding at 2 a.m. He had lain out in the rain for three hours before he was found.

'I have it in mind when I get the name of her apparently young surgeon that if he can operate on a patient of 102 and not kill her, perhaps he would do the same for an 85 year-old and, I suppose I should add, "not kill him",' Chopping wrote to Robert Kee, Janetta Woolley's ex-husband, 'although frankly I am getting sick of it all, lucky as I am to be as well as I am.'

Frances Partridge died on 5 February 2004 at the age of 103. Within a few weeks, Chopping was in hospital himself for an operation to remove a retina. The procedure was a failure and it left him with poor sight in that eye, and soon afterwards, the retina of his other eye detached. He could not read without a magnifying glass. His sense of isolation increased but the death of one of his final links with the past spurred him to return to work on his memoir again. His handwriting was even more unruly than his usual scrawl, but with the help of thickly lined paper he was writing more in terms of volume than at any point since the 1960s.

While Chopping sought to bring his memories onto the page, Wirth-Miller was still destroying traces of his own life. Chopping hid more of the letters and ephemera of their lives to save them from destruction. He knew that his own autobiography would never see the light of day, and he wanted to safeguard their story for posterity.

Both of the old men were still inundated by interview requests. Had they been the subject of interest they may have responded, but the approaches mostly concerned either Francis Bacon or Ian Fleming. They resented existing only in the light of those two men and spurned most approaches, thereby largely writing themselves out of their histories.

Nonetheless, there were clearly things Wirth-Miller wished to say about Bacon, given the right circumstances. In 2004, letters from Adam Low, a television producer, indicate that Wirth-Miller considered contributing to a BBC *Arena* documentary on Francis Bacon. True to the lack of decisiveness and self-worth that had plagued him since he had given up painting, he could not think the matter through clearly and took to his bed for two days.

Chopping put an end to the matter: 'It has obviously stirred up in your memory some unresolved problems, incidents, attitudes, I don't know what to call them, which are making you suffer,' he wrote in a note that he left on Wirth-Miller's bedside table. 'If you do the film interview I predict that it will become worse for you (and of course for me) but it is you I am thinking about. I think [Adam Low] should be put out of his misery at once.' For his part, Chopping had a clear line on his involvement with Fleming's legacy. 'Quite honestly I'm sick of it,' he responded when pestered for another commemorative article.

Wirth-Miller suffered greater humiliation. He discovered that amateur collectors were buying his work at auction for low prices, but not out of interest in his landscapes. They were futilely scraping off the surface layer of paint in the hope of discovering a lost work by Bacon.

Chopping and Wirth-Miller's happiness in Wivenhoe had always been fostered by their love of the surrounding landscape of marshes and wild flatlands. Their ramblings became increasingly infrequent and shorter, to the point where they no longer had the energy to leave the village. Soon they were having difficulty doing basic tasks and looking after themselves. Chopping could barely walk; Wirth-Miller's mind was continuing to degenerate. He stopped dying his hair black and rarely shaved. He lost so much weight that his skin sagged. The hollows of his eyes became deeper, making his stare seem perpetually menacing. He was drifting towards agoraphobia, hardly venturing out of the house. The two men became increasingly dependent on outside help.

Neither wanted to have to trust a carer they did not know, although health workers became necessary at certain times. Dan Chapman, a long-time family friend from the area, selflessly looked after them most of the time, with young friends in London also making the journey to help when time – or Wirth-Miller – permitted.

In 2004, the government passed the Civil Partnership Act, allowing gay couples almost the same legal rights as their heterosexual peers. Chopping and Wirth-Miller had been together for almost seventy years, since a time when a homosexual act was a prison offence; they had witnessed the birth of legislation decriminalizing homosexuality in 1967; and, in December 2005, they became one of the first gay couples in the country to be legally bound. Richard Chopping was eighty-eight; Denis Wirth-Miller was ninety.

★

Chopping suffered a stroke shortly afterwards. It was relatively
minor, but it left him even more fragile. When he became ill,
he was immediately transferred to a retirement home. He was
allowed to return to the Storehouse for a while, but took a turn
for the worse and was once again taken into care.

He pleaded to return to the Storehouse but he was initially
not allowed. The by-now senile Wirth–Miller did not want him
to return, and health visitors could see the squalor into which
the Storehouse had descended. Dan Chapman kindly volunteered
to move Chopping into his own house, but the elderly man was
intent on returning to his home of sixty years.

Eventually, the local services conceded in the knowledge that
he probably did not have long to live. Wirth–Miller, now a
hermit with a continually fogged mind, watched in silence as
Dan Chapman installed a hospital bed on the ground floor of the
Storehouse. The bed was visible from the Quayside through the
bay window, so next came a screen that would allow Chopping
a degree of privacy whenever a carer arrived to wash him.

Chopping then came home, reliant on either a Zimmer frame
or a crutch to walk. As soon as the carers and Chapman had left,
Wirth–Miller, despite being over ninety years old, tore down
the screen, wrenched the Zimmer frame from Chopping's grip
and hurled them both through the front door onto the Quayside.

Chopping spent most of his time lying in bed, and could only
move into an orthopaedic chair with help from his carers. He was
always desperate for visitors to come and help him onto his feet.

When I was at the Storehouse one day, I supported Chopping
to a chair next to the passage to the kitchen. He poked at the
floor with his white stick and revealed a secret: beneath the floorboards lay a Francis Bacon painting. A drunken, late-night session
had ended in a terrible argument. Bacon had walked out and

Wirth-Miller, furious, had slashed the canvas he was working on. The couple buried the evidence under the floorboards, and when Bacon returned he seemed to have completely forgotten about the painting. Rats and flood waters then destroyed them.

April 2008.

The church bell rings again and Dicky opens his eyes.

He is beyond cold. He can no longer feel the difference between his body and the cold, hard floor. He should not have tried to reach the kitchen tap.

Denis has now been and gone three times. He may come again in a few more hours but Dicky knows the outcome will be no different. He will step over Dicky as if he is just rubbish on the floor.

Seventy years. Through obscurity, decadence, success and back to obscurity, hand in hand with Denis. Walks along the Stour from Daffodil Cottage. Johnny Minton dancing in the Gargoyle and the Roberts being sick. Frances Partridge affectionately berating him. Caviar at Ian Fleming's house with a cheque for £40 in his pocket. 'Chippy Chopping saved my life!' The shadow of Bacon still there even a decade and a half after he had died. Arguments, terrible arguments. But all worth it.

Dicky closes his eyes again. All worth it.

Retrospective

Dan Chapman found Dicky Chopping on the floor of the Storehouse kitchen late that afternoon. He called an ambulance and Chopping was rushed to Colchester hospital.

He had pneumonia and hypothermia, and was flickering in and out of consciousness as friends came to his bedside. I was lucky to find him awake. He told me, in terrible detail, what had happened over the twenty-two hours he had been on the floor and how he had waited for death.

His moments of lucidity became fewer and farther between over the course of the next week, in which he had his ninety-first birthday. His pneumonia worsened and he writhed in his bed, pleading for water.

At first Denis Wirth-Miller refused to visit him. He was questioned about the fall and the smashed phone, but he would only say: 'He deserved it because he was irritating.'

Dan Chapman eventually coaxed him out of the Storehouse and took him up to the hospital. As soon as he saw Chopping lying in the bed, Wirth-Miller's anger disappeared. Chapman left them alone, and when he returned a few hours later, he found that Wirth-Miller was still in the room. He was sitting there, holding his partner's hand, looking down at him and crying.

Dicky Chopping died at 6.30 p.m. on the following evening, 17 April 2008, after ten days in hospital. Wirth-Miller requested to see his corpse. He had invited a friend with a camera, whom he asked to take pictures of his partner's dead body. That night, he positioned the photographs around his pillow, and went to sleep surrounded by them.

Wirth-Miller was ninety-two. Although he may have been liable for manslaughter the authorities decided that there was no point in holding him to account. He had already been subjected to many psychiatric tests, which had not offered a clear diagnosis. It was obvious there was something amiss with him, but it was impossible to distinguish whether his answers were concocted for his own amusement or were the result of genuine dementia.

Wirth-Miller insisted on a private memorial service – to which he did not turn up. Then, as unpredictable as ever, he relented and agreed to a small church service. He did not wish to attend but Dan Chapman eventually changed his mind and walked him up to St Mary's church. He sat stony-faced throughout.

Both Wirth-Miller's appearance and his mind deteriorated further. He was not capable of living alone so Dan Chapman – the only person to whom he would still speak – moved him into an old people's home nearby. He was completely passive. The first room available was small and without much natural light. It may have reminded him of his cell in Wormwood Scrubs but he seemed content. When a fellow patient died, Wirth-Miller was moved to a room with a view over the garden but he kept the curtains closed all day and rarely left the room.

He ate well and was relatively strong but in 2010 he suffered a stroke. Shortly afterwards, he had a fall and broke his arm in two places. He was taken to Colchester hospital, but it was clear he had no intention of leaving. In a room just yards from the one in which he had sat with his partner, he refused food and drips, effectively inviting death.

Denis Wirth-Miller died on 27 October 2010, a week before his ninety-fifth birthday. He left his body to medical research, but age had shrivelled it to the point where it was scientifically useless. His brain, the only organ of interest, was taken to Addenbrooke's Hospital in Cambridge by motorcycle courier.

As an atheist, Wirth-Miller shared Francis Bacon's disdain for posthumous commemoration. Religious sentimentality, as he saw it, was an aberration. There was no funeral.

Three months after Wirth-Miller's death, a retrospective of his work opened at The Minories Galleries in Colchester, where the Wivenhoe couple had been given a joint exhibition in 1959. James Birch, who had mounted the Francis Bacon exhibition in Moscow in 1998, sourced many paintings that had not been seen in public for decades.

The couple's old friend Louisa Buck put together the catalogue, in which Zandra Rhodes called Wirth-Miller 'a very colourful and tortured character'.[130] Buck praised the 'relentless, unpeopled emptiness' of his work and described him as 'volatile and cuttingly intolerant of any perceived pretension'.[131]

Birch had tracked down works that dated as far back as 1941 right up to the Wivenhoe Arts Club exhibition and Wirth-Miller's sudden retirement in the late 1970s. Wivenhoe itself had changed since he and Chopping had first arrived in the 1940s but Wirth-Miller's eerie, often violent landscapes were instantly evocative of the region. When Andrew Lambirth reviewed the exhibition for the *Spectator*, he wrote of Wirth-Miller's 'slashing diagonals of rain' and trees 'like spinning tops, almost Futurist in their suggested motion'. As he noted, the 'knotted and ribbed and combed' textures of these paintings made them stand out.[132]

Lambirth believed that Wirth-Miller's last works, 'swirling forcefields of raised, almost woven paint', were his best. For all that The Minories exhibition revealed his originality and dexterity, his ability to push at boundaries and still capture a sense of place, it underscored that Wirth-Miller's sudden retirement was a waste of talent. The shadow of Bacon overhung the works. In some ways he had made Wirth-Miller and had allowed his transgressive personality to bloom, but he had destroyed him too.

Endnotes

1 Jane Rye, *Adrian Heath* (Farnham: Lund Humphries, 2012), p.53.

2 See Colin Hayes, *Robert Buhler* (London: Weidenfeld and Nicolson, 1986) for more on Buhler's career.

3 Denise Hooker, *Nina Hamnett: Queen of Bohemia* (London: Constable, 1986), p.212.

4 James Norton, 'Bacon's Beginnings', *Burlington Magazine*, vol. 158 (January 2016), pp. 19–25. Mark Stevens and Annalyn Swan, for whom Norton worked as a researcher, intend to clarify the details of Bacon's early life in a biography to be published in autumn 2017.

5 Michael Peppiatt, *Francis Bacon: Anatomy of an Enigma* (London: Constable, 2008), p.27.

6 Francis Bacon discussed his early criminal adventures with Richard Chopping, who reports in his diary entry for 4 April 1972: 'Francis told us about his abortive career as a pickpocket.'

7 Peppiatt, *Francis Bacon*, p.33.

8 ——, *Francis Bacon*, p.46.

9 Norton, 'Bacon's Beginnings'.

10 ——, 'Bacon's Beginnings'.

11 'The 1930 Look in British Decoration', *The Studio* (August 1930), no. 100, pp. 140–1.

12 Norton, 'Bacon's Beginnings'.

13 'Death After Son's Sentence', *Gloucestershire Echo*, 18 November 1938.

14 'Father of Gaoled Playboy is Gassed', *Daily Mail*, 19 November 1938.

15 Frances Partridge, *A Pacifist's War* (London: Hogarth Press, 1978). Many quotes by Partridge recounted here are sourced from her letters in the Richard Chopping/Denis Wirth-Miller Archive. Quotes from Partridge's diaries are taken from *A Pacifist's War*, plus the books covering later years: *Everything to Lose* (London: Gollancz, 1985); *Hanging On* (London: Collins, 1990); *Other People* (London: HarperCollins, 1993); *Good Company* (London: HarperCollins, 1994); *Life Regained* (London: Weidenfeld & Nicolson, 1998); *Ups and Downs* (London: Weidenfeld & Nicolson, 2001); with additional information from Anne Chisholm, *Frances Partridge: The*

Biography (London: Weidenfeld & Nicolson, 2009).

16 Elizabeth Knowles, *Looking West: Paintings Inspired by Cornwall, 1880s to Present Day*, exhibition catalogue (Newlyn: Newlyn Orion, 1987).

17 David Herbert, 'Little Known Painters . . . Lucy Harwood', *It Started with a Jug . . .*, itstartedwithajug.blogspot.co.uk (undated).

18 David Buckman, 'Denis Wirth-Miller: Bohemian Artist Who Enjoyed a Close Association with Francis Bacon', *Independent* (19 January 2011).

19 David Buckman, 'Richard Chopping: Versatile Illustrator Best Known for His Bond Jackets', *Independent* (22 April 2008).

20 Kathleen Hale, *A Slender Reputation: An Autobiography* (London: Warne, 1998).

21 Fiona MacCarthy, 'Obituary: Kathleen Hale', *Guardian* (28 January 2000).

22 James Lee-Milne, 'Obituary: Geoffrey Houghton Brown', *Independent* (10 February 1993).

23 Quentin Crisp, *The Naked Civil Servant* (London: Jonathan Cape, 1968).

24 Peppiatt, *Francis Bacon*, p. 97.

25 Andrew Sinclair, *War Like a Wasp: The Lost Decade of the Forties* (London: Faber & Faber, 2011).

26 Philip Vann, 'The Intimate Figurative Impulse', in Philip Vann and Gerard Hastings, *Keith Vaughan* (Farnham: Lund Humphries/Osborne Samuel, 2012), p. 55.

27 Vann, 'The Intimate Figurative Impulse', p. 55.

28 Vann, 'The Intimate Figurative Impulse', p. 55.

29 Frances Spalding, *John Minton: Dance till the Stars Come Down* (Aldershot: Lund Humphries, 2005), p. 64.

30 Spalding, *John Minton*, p. 66.

31 William Feaver, 'Lucian Freud: Life into Art', *Lucian Freud*, exhibition catalogue (London: Tate, 2002), p. 22.

32 *Apollo* (May 1945), p. 108.

33 Raymond Mortimer, *New Statesman and Nation* (14 April 1945), p. 239.

34 Spalding, *John Minton*, p. 71.

35 The extracts from the letters have been lightly edited for the sake of spelling and punctuation.

36 Bristow, *The Last Bohemians*, p. 178.

37 Spalding, *John Minton*, p. 77.

38 Spalding, *John Minton*, p. 84.

39 Daniel Farson, *The Gilded Gutter Life of Francis Bacon* (London: Vintage, 1993), ch. 12. Farson thought Bacon was talking about the stairs at his own house in Wivenhoe, but he was referring to the Storehouse.

40 Peppiatt, *Francis Bacon*, p. 117.

41 Roger Berthoud, *Graham Sutherland: A Biography* (London:

Faber & Faber, 1982), p. 131.

42 Berthoud, *Graham Sutherland*, pp. 110–11.

43 With thanks to James Birch, who curated the Denis Wirth-Miller exhibition at The Minories, Colchester, 2011.

44 Andrew Lambirth, 'A Lifelong Business', in Peter Adam and Andrew Lambirth, *Eileen Gray: The Private Painter* (London: Lund Humphries/Osborne Samuel, 2015) p. 14.

45 Wyndham Lewis, 'Round the London Art Galleries', *The Listener*, 17 November 1949, p. 860.

46 Peppiatt, *Francis Bacon*, p. 105.

47 Denton Welch, *Maiden Voyage* (Norwich: Gallery Beggar Classics, 2014), Preface.

48 Ruthven Todd, *Fitzrovia and the Road to the York Minster or Down Dean Street* (London: Michael Parkin Fine Art, 1973).

49 Farson, *The Gilded Gutter Life*, ch. 6.

50 Christopher Hitchens, *Hitch-22*, (London: Atlantic, 2011), p. 152.

51 Douglas Sutherland, *Portrait of a Decade: London Life 1945–55* (London: Harrap, 1988).

52 Nancy Schoenberg, *Dangerous Muse: A Life of Caroline Blackwood* (London: Nan A. Talese, 2001), p. 97.

53 Fiona Green, 'William Crozier: Artist', *Soho Memories* (6 August 2011), http://www.sohomemories.org.uk/page_id__72_path__0p3p.aspx.

54 Spalding, *John Minton*, p. 152.

55 Publications unknown; clippings from the Storehouse archive.

56 Bristow, *The Last Bohemians*, p. 248.

57 Vann, 'The Intimate Figurative Impulse', p. 71.

58 Bristow, *The Last Bohemians*, p. 256.

59 James Birch, 'Preface', in *Denis Wirth-Miller*, exhibition catalogue (Colchester: The Minories Galleries, 2011), p. 7.

60 Peppiatt, *Francis Bacon*, pp. 147.

61 Peppiatt, *Francis Bacon*, pp. 176–7.

62 Peppiatt, *Francis Bacon*, p. 178.

63 Peppiatt, *Francis Bacon*, p. 177.

64 Ronald Alley, *Francis Bacon*, Introduction by John Rothenstein (London: Thames & Hudson, 1964), p. 60.

65 Andrew Lambirth, 'East Anglian Friends', *Spectator* (26 March 2011).

66 Katherina Günther, 'The Wivenhoe Chapter – Francis Bacon and Denis Wirth Miller', MB Art Foundation, http://www.mbartfoundation.com/news/item/304 (28 July 2015).

67 John Berger, 'The Young Generation', *New Statesman* (15 July 1953), p. 101.

68 Quotes, including the Derrick Greaves quote, from James Hyman, *Derrick Greaves: From Kitchen-Sink to Shangri-La* (Aldershot: Lund Humphries, 2007), p. 21.

69 David Sylvester, 'Round the London Galleries', *Listener* (17 May 1956), p. 648; 'Beaux Arts Gallery: Studies of Movement by

Mr. Wirth-Miller', *The Times* (4 November 1954).

70 Andrew Wilson, 'Always the Viewer', in *Denis Wirth-Miller*, exhibition catalogue (Colchester: The Minories Galleries, 2011), p. 19.

71 Wilson, 'Always the Viewer', p. 20.

72 Catherine Lampert, *Frank Auerbach: Speaking and Painting* (London: Thames & Hudson, 2015), p, 72.

73 Michael Yorke, *Keith Vaughan, His Life and Work* (London: Constable, 1990), p.162.

74 Vann, 'The Intimate Figurative Impulse', p. 114.

75 'Biography – 1950s', The Estate of Francis Bacon, http:// francis-bacon.com/life/ biography/1950s (accessed 5 January 2015).

76 Mark Armory (ed.), *The Letters of Ann Fleming* (London: Collins Harvill, 1985), p. 197.

77 'By Ways of English Painting: Present-day Romantics', *The Times* (14 May 1956).

78 Richard Chopping, 'Writers Remembered: Ian Fleming', *The Author* (Winter 1995), p. 134.

79 Chopping, 'Writers Remembered'.

80 Chopping, 'Writers Remembered'.

81 In contrast to his version of the design process relayed here, Chopping also stated in an article in 1995 that Fleming 'chose the Packing Case lettering' (Chopping, 'Writers Remembered'). By then he was seventy-eight and his recall was becoming erratic.

82 Spalding, *John Minton*, p. 204.

83 Farson, *The Gilded Gutter Life*, p. 197.

84 Stephen Bone, *Guardian* (24 February 1956); John Berger, *New Statesman & Nation* (17 March 1956).

85 Spalding, *John Minton*, p. 212; p. 215.

86 Spalding, *John Minton*, p. 226.

87 Spalding, *John Minton*, p. 236.

88 Vann, 'The Intimate Figurative Impulse', p. 72.

89 Vann, 'The Intimate Figurative Impulse', p. 99.

90 David Leeming, *Stephen Spender: A Life in Modernism* (London: Henry Holt, 1999).

91 Mike Simkin, 'Letter: Richard Chopping', *Guardian* (19 June 2008).

92 Michael Davie (ed.), *The Diaries of Evelyn Waugh* (Harmondsworth: Penguin, 1982).

93 Information from the Churchill Archive, file CHUR 1/57.

94 Chopping, 'Writers Remembered'.

95 Ted Morgan, *Literary Outlaw: The Life and Times of William S. Burroughs* (London: Pimlico, 1991).

96 Ben Tuffnell, *Francis Bacon in St Ives*, exhibition catalogue (St Ives: Tate, 2007), p. 30.

97 Peppiatt, *Francis Bacon*, p. 221.

98 Peppiatt, *Francis Bacon*, p. 222.

99 'Mr. Denis Wirth-Miller',

The Times (13 April 1960).

100 Keith Roberts, *Burlington Magazine*, vol. 104, no. 716 (November 1962), pp. 504–10.

101 Publication unknown; clipping from the Storehouse archive.

102 *Daily Express* (25 October 1963).

103 Zandra Rhodes, 'Foreword', in *Denis Wirth-Miller*, exhibition catalogue (Colchester: The Minories Galleries, 2011), p. 9.

104 *School Days*, BBC TV, date unknown [1990s].

105 Giles Gordon, *Aren't We Due a Royalty Statement?* (London: Chatto & Windus, 1993).

106 Chopping, 'Writers Remembered'.

107 Peppiatt, *Francis Bacon*, p. 216.

108 *The Times*, 28 July 1967.

109 Quoted in Sophie Parkin, *The Colony Room Club 1948–2008: A History of Bohemian Soho* (London: Palmtree, 2013).

110 Gordon, *Aren't We Due a Royalty Statement?*.

111 *Kirkus* (undated [1967]).

112 Clipping from the Storehouse archive; publication unknown.

113 Norman Scarfe, *Hintlesham Hall: The House and Its Associations* (Hintlesham: Hintlesham Hall, 1988).

114 Armory, *The Letters of Ann Fleming*, p. 400.

115 Peppiatt, *Francis Bacon*, pp. 293–4.

116 Charles Darwent, 'Valerie Beston: Francis Bacon's Loyal "Miss B"', *Independent* (2005).

117 Michel Conil Lacoste, *Le Monde* (3 November 1971), quoted in Peppiatt, *Francis Bacon*, p. 290.

118 Peppiatt, *Francis Bacon*, p. 296.

119 'Francis Bacon', *South Bank Show*, ITV (9 June 1985).

120 Peppiatt, *Francis Bacon*, p. 312.

121 Peppiatt, *Francis Bacon*, pp. 312–13.

122 Henry Geldzahler, 'Introduction', *Francis Bacon: Recent Paintings 1968–1974*, exhibition catalogue (New York: Metropolitan Museum of Art, 1975).

123 Chris Moore, 'Recollections – Charlie Chester's London, 1973', *Casino Life* (3 March 2013), http://www.casinolifemagazine. com/article/ recollections-charlie-chesters-london-1973.

124 Simkin, 'Letter: Richard Chopping'.

125 Birch, 'Preface', p. 8; Louisa Buck, 'Denis Wirth-Miller: A Partial Memory', in *Denis Wirth-Miller* exhibition catalogue (Colchester: The Minories Galleries, 2011), p. 17.

126 Buck, 'Denis Wirth-Miller: A Partial Memory', p. 11.

127 Letter to James Birch, 23 August 1988, quoted in Peppiatt, *Francis Bacon*, p. 388.

128 Dalya Alberge, 'Francis Bacon Gave Secret $4m to Beloved Banker', *Sunday Times* (2 February 2014).

129 Farson, *The Gilded Gutter Life*, ch. 12.

130 Rhodes, 'Foreword', p. 9.

131 Buck, 'Denis Wirth-Miller: A Partial Memory', p. 11.

132 Lambirth, 'East Anglian Friends'.

Acknowledgements

With much gratitude to Howard Watson, Digby Warde-Aldam, Michael Anderson, Clare Conville, Andreas Campomar and Claire Chesser, without whom this book would not have been realized.

And with many thanks to:

The Estate of Francis Bacon; Nejma and Peter Beard; Madeleine Bessborough; James Birch; Erica Brealey; Louisa Buck; Vicky Butler; Rachel Campbell Johnston; Dan Chapman; Adrian Clark; Reverend Richard Coles; Paul Conran; Sir Terence Conran; Jonathan E. Cull; Thomas J. Cull; Robert Davey; Terry Danziger-Miles; Sir Christopher Frayling; The Lucian Freud Archive; Greg Gorman; Felicity Green; Liz and Peter Griffiths; Maggi Hambling CBE; Martin and Amanda Harrison; Rachel Jardine; Kim Jones; John Lessore; Michael and Geraldine Leventis; Catherine Mayer; The Estate of John Minton (Royal College of Art); The Estate of Cedric Morris; Milo O'Sullivan; The Estate of Frances Partridge; David, Marquis of Queensberry; Dame Zandra Rhodes; Annie Rice; Linda Silverman; Jack Smyth; Frances Spalding; Mark Stevens; Su Thomas; Helen Upton; Dr Andrew Wilson; Sophie Wogden; Sir Peregrine Worsthorne.

And to the many other friends of Richard Chopping and Denis Wirth-Miller whose records helped the completion of this book.

Bibliography

Much of the information in this book is sourced from the archive of Richard Chopping and Denis Wirth-Miller owned by the author, and from personal interviews and correspondence. Information relating to many exhibitions is partially drawn from the collections of catalogues at the National Art Library Archive (Victoria and Albert Museum), not all of which are listed here.

All words and images attributed to Francis Bacon ©The Estate of Francis Bacon. All rights reserved. DACS 2016.

All words attributed to Frances Partridge reproduced with the permission of the Estate of Frances Partridge.

All words attributed to John Minton reproduced with the permission of the Estate of John Minton (Royal College of Art).

Ades, Dawn and Andrew Forge, *Francis Bacon*, exhibition catalogue (London: Tate, 1985).

Alberge, Dalya, 'Francis Bacon Gave Secret $4m to Beloved Banker', *Sunday Times* (2 February 2014).

Alley, Ronald, *Francis Bacon*, exhibition catalogue (London: Tate Gallery, 1962).

——, *Francis Bacon*, Introduction by John Rothenstein (London: Thames & Hudson, 1964).

Armory, Mark (ed.), *The Letters of Ann Fleming* (London: Collins Harvill, 1985).

Arnott, W. G., *Alde Estuary: The Story of a Suffolk River* (Ipswich: Norman Adlard, 1952).

Arya, Rina, *Francis Bacon: Painting in a Godless World* (Farnham: Lund Humphries, 2012).

'Beaux Arts Gallery: Studies of Movement by Mr. Wirth-Miller', *The Times* (4 November 1954).

Benedictus, David, *The Fourth of July* (London: Anthony Blond, 1962).

Berger, John, 'The Young Generation', *New Statesman* (15 July 1953), p. 101.

Berthoud, Roger, *Graham Sutherland: A Biography* (London: Faber & Faber, 1982).

Birch, James, 'Preface', in *Denis Wirth-Miller*, exhibition catalogue (Colchester: The Minories Galleries, 2011).

Boyde, Richard, *The Last Dodo* (London: Farrar, Straus & Giroux, 1967).

Brighton, Andrew, *Francis Bacon* (London, 2001).

Bristow, Roger, *The Last Bohemians: The Two Roberts – Colquhoun and MacBryde* (Bristol: Sansom, 2009).

Buck, Louisa, 'Denis Wirth-Miller: A Partial Memory', in *Denis Wirth-Miller*, exhibition catalogue (Colchester: The Minories Galleries, 2011).

Buckman, David, 'Denis Wirth-Miller: Bohemian Artist Who Enjoyed a Close Association with Francis Bacon', *Independent* (19 January 2011).

——, 'Richard Chopping: Versatile Illustrator Best Known for His Bond Jackets', *Independent* (22 April 2008).

'By Ways of English Painting: Present-day Romantics', *The Times* (14 May 1956).

Calvocoressi, Richard and Martin Hammer, *Francis Bacon: Portraits and Heads*, exhibition catalogue (Edinburgh: National Galleries of Scotland, 2005).

Chisholm, Anne, *Frances Partridge: The Biography* (London: Weidenfeld & Nicolson, 2009).

Chopping, Richard, *Butterflies in Britain* (London: Puffin, 1943).

——, *The Old Woman and the Pedlar* (London: Bantam Picture Book, 1944)

——, *The Tailor and the Mouse* (London: Bantam Picture Book, 1944).

——, *Wild Flowers* (London: Bantam Picture Book, 1944).

——, *A Book of Birds* (London: Bantam Picture Book, 1944).

——, *The Fly* (London: Secker & Warburg, 1965).

——, *Mr Postlethwaite's Reindeer and Other Stories* (London: Transatlantic Arts, 1945).

——, *The Ring* (London: Secker & Warburg, 1965).

——, 'Writers Remembered: Ian Fleming', *The Author* (Winter 1995).

Conil Lacoste, Michel, *Le Monde* (3 November 1971).

Crisp, Quentin, *The Naked Civil Servant* (London: Jonathan Cape, 1968).

Darwent, Charles, 'Valerie Beston: Francis Bacon's Loyal "Miss B"', *Independent* (2005).

Davie, Michael (ed.), *The Diaries of Evelyn Waugh* (Harmondsworth: Penguin, 1982).

Davies, Hugh and Sally Yard, *Francis Bacon* (New York: Abbeville Press, 1992).

Dawson, Barbara and Martin Harrison (eds.), *Francis Bacon: A Terrible Beauty*, exhibition catalogue (Dublin: The Hugh Lane Gallery, 2010).

Denis Wirth-Miller, exhibition catalogue (Colchester: The Minories Galleries, 2011).

Farson, Daniel, *The Gilded Gutter Life of Francis Bacon* (London: Vintage, 1993).

Feaver, William, 'Lucian Freud: Life into Art', *Lucian Freud*, exhibition catalogue (London: Tate, 2002).

'Francis Bacon', *South Bank Show*, ITV (9 June 1985).

Fryer, Jonathan, *Soho in the Fifties and Sixties* (London: Thistle, 2013).

Gale, Matthew and Chris Stephens (eds.), *Francis Bacon*, exhibition catalogue (London: Tate, 2008).

Geldzahler, Henry, 'Introduction', *Francis Bacon: Recent Paintings 1968–1974*, exhibition catalogue (New York: Metropolitan Museum of Art, 1975).

Gordon, Giles, *Aren't We Due a Royalty Statement?* (London: Chatto & Windus, 1993).

Green, Fiona, 'William Crozier: Artist', *Soho Memories* (6 August 2011), http://www.sohomemories.org.uk/page_id__72_path__op3p.aspx.

Günther, Katherina, 'The Wivenhoe Chapter – Francis Bacon and Denis Wirth Miller', *MB Art Foundation*, http://www.mbartfoundation.com/news/item/304 (28 July 2015).

Hadfield, John (ed.), *The Saturday Book 15* (London: Hutchinson, 1955).

Hale, Kathleen, *A Slender Reputation: An Autobiography* (London: Warne, 1998).

Hammer, Martin, *Bacon and Sutherland* (New Haven and London: Yale University Press, 2005).

——, *Francis Bacon* (London: Phaidon, 2013).

Harrison, Martin (ed.), *In Camera – Francis Bacon, Photography, Film and the Practice of Painting* (London: Thames & Hudson, 2005).

——, *Francis Bacon: Catalogue Raisonné* (London: The Estate of Francis Bacon, 2016).

Hayes, Colin, *Robert Buhler* (London: Weidenfeld and Nicolson, 1986).

Herbert, David, 'Little Known Painters . . . Lucy Harwood', *It Started with a Jug . . .*, itstartedwithajug.blogspot.co.uk (undated).

Hitchens, Christopher, *Hitch-22,* (London: Atlantic, 2011).

Hooker, Denise, *Nina Hamnett: Queen of Bohemia* (London: Constable, 1986).

Howgate, Sarah, with Michael Auping and John Richardson, *Lucian Freud: Portraits* (London: National Portrait Gallery, 2012).

Hyman, James, *Derrick Greaves: From Kitchen-Sink to Shangri-La* (Aldershot: Lund Humphries, 2007).

Kirkus (undated [1967]).

Knowles, Elizabeth, *Looking West: Paintings Inspired by Cornwall, 1880s to Present Day*, exhibition catalogue (Newlyn: Newlyn Orion, 1987).

Lambirth, Andrew, 'East Anglian Friends', *Spectator* (26 March 2011).

——, 'A Lifelong Business', in Peter Adam and Andrew Lambirth, *Eileen Gray: The Private Painter* (London: Lund Humphries/Osborne Samuel, 2015).

Lampert, Catherine, *Frank Auerbach: Speaking and Painting* (London: Thames & Hudson, 2015).

Lee-Milne, James, 'Obituary: Geoffrey Houghton-Browne', *Independent* (10 February 1993).

Leeming, David, *Stephen Spender: A Life in Modernism* (London: Henry Holt, 1999).

Leiris, Michel, *Francis Bacon: Full Face and In Profile* (London, 1983).

Lewis, Wyndham, 'Round the London Art Galleries', *The Listener* 17 November 1949, p. 860.

MacCarthy, Fiona, 'Obituary: Kathleen Hale', *Guardian* (28 January 2000).

Moore, Chris, 'Recollections – Charlie Chester's London, 1973', *Casino Life* (3 March 2013), http://www.casinolifemagazine.com/article/recollections-charlie-chesters-london-1973.

Morgan, Ted, *Literary Outlaw: The Life and Times of William S. Burroughs* (London: Pimlico, 1991).

Mortimer, Raymond, *New Statesman and Nation* (14 April 1945).

'Mr. Denis Wirth-Miller', *The Times* (13 April 1960).

Naylor, Gillian (ed.), *Bloomsbury* (London: Pyramid, 1990).

Nicholson, Virginia, *Among the Bohemians: Experiments in Living 1900–1939* (London: Penguin, 2003).

Norton, James, 'Bacon's Beginnings', *Burlington Magazine* (January 2016).

Parkin, Sophie, *The Colony Room Club 1948–2008: A History of Bohemian Soho* (London: Palmtree, 2013).

Partridge, Frances, *A Pacifist's War* (London: Hogarth Press, 1978).

——, *Everything to Lose* (London: Gollancz, 1985).

——, *Hanging On* (London: Collins, 1990).

——, *Other People* (London: HarperCollins, 1993).

——, *Good Company* (London: HarperCollins, 1994).

——, *Life Regained* (London: Weidenfeld & Nicolson, 1998)

——, *Ups and Downs* (London: Weidenfeld & Nicolson, 2001).

Peppiatt, Michael, *Francis Bacon: Anatomy of an Enigma* (London: Constable, 2008).

——, *Francis Bacon in Your Blood: A Memoir* (London: Bloomsbury, 2015).

——, *Studies for a Portrait* (New Haven and London: Yale University Press, 2008).

Powers, Alan, *Eric Ravilious: Artist and Designer* (Farnham: Lund Humphries, 2013).

Rhodes, Zandra, 'Foreword', in *Denis Wirth-Miller*, exhibition catalogue (Colchester: The Minories Galleries, 2011).

Roberts, Keith, *Burlington Magazine*, vol. 104, no. 716 (November 1962), pp. 504–10.

Russell, John, *Francis Bacon* (London: Thames & Hudson, 1993).

Rye, Jane, *Adrian Heath* (Farnham: Lund Humphries, 2012).

Scarfe, Norman, *Hintlesham Hall: The House and Its Associations* (Hintlesham: Hintlesham Hall, 1988).

Schoenberg, Nancy, *Dangerous Muse: A Life of Caroline Blackwood* (London: Nan A. Talese, 2001).

Simkin, Mike, 'Letter: Richard Chopping', *Guardian* (19 June 2008).

Sinclair, Andrew, *War Like a Wasp: The Lost Decade of the Forties* (London: Faber & Faber, 2011).

Spalding, Frances, *John Minton: Dance Till the Stars Come Down* (Aldershot: Lund Humphries, 2005).

Stevens, Mark and Annalyn Swan, *Francis Bacon* (London: HarperCollins, forthcoming).

Sutherland, Douglas, *Portrait of a Decade: London Life 1945–55* (London: Harrap, 1988).

Sylvester, David, 'Round the London Galleries', *Listener* (17 May 1956), p. 648

——, *Interviews with Francis Bacon* (London, 1993).

——, *Looking Back at Francis Bacon* (London, 2000).

Todd, Ruthven, *Fitzrovia and the Road to the York Minster or Down Dean Street* (London: Michael Parkin Fine Art, 1973).

Tuffnell, Ben, *Francis Bacon in St Ives*, exhibition catalogue (St Ives: Tate, 2007).

Vann, Philip and Gerard Hastings, *Keith Vaughan* (Farnham: Lund Humphries/Osborne Samuel, 2012).

Welch, Denton, *Maiden Voyage* (Norwich: Gallery Beggar Classics, 2014).

Wilson, Andrew, 'Always the Viewer', in *Denis Wirth-Miller*, exhibition catalogue (Colchester: The Minories Galleries, 2011), p. 19.

Wirth-Miller, Denis and Richard Chopping, *Heads, Bodies and Legs* (London: Puffin, 1946).

Yorke, Michael, *Keith Vaughan, His Life and Work* (London: Constable, 1990).

Index

Abstraction (by FB) 41, 53, 130
Adler, Jankel 87, 129–30, 136, 336
Air Raid Protection (ARP) 45, 53, 312
Aldeburgh Festival of Music and the Arts 133, 136, 221
Allden, Eric 39, 41
An Exhibition of Paintings and Drawings (1956) 202–3
Anderson, Colin 157
Anrep, Boris 103
Arran, Lord 278–9
Art & Industry magazine 62
Arthur Jeffress Gallery 166–8, 169–70, 202, 221, 246–7
The Ash-grounds (by RC) 42
Astor, Viscount Waldorf 160, 240
Ayrton, Michael 36, 86, 94

Bacon, Edward 38, 131
Bacon, Francis 4, 31, 33, 53, 72–3, 88, 108, 168, 214, 217–18, 292, 300–1, 367, 368
   art and career 39–41, 72, 90–1, 124–5, 127, 130–2, 157, 158, 173–8, 180–1, 183–7, 232–4, 236–40, 258–9, 281, 282–3, 288–9, 294–5, 297, 298, 307–8, 339, 352, 355
   Cromwell Place 81, 125, 144, 154
   early life 38–9
   Eric Hall 40, 41, 81, 125–6, 154
   family 38, 131, 154, 295, 359
   friendship with DWM 41–2, 66, 125, 127–8, 130–1, 141, 146, 149, 172–7, 184–6, 187, 189, 191–3, 194–5, 210, 234–6, 238–9, 248–50, 255–7, 259–60, 301–6, 311, 313–16, 322, 323–4, 326–8, 330–2, 333–4, 338, 339–40, 341–3, 355, 356–7
   friendship with RC 41–2, 90, 149, 154, 203, 256–7, 284, 286, 288–9, 301–2, 306, 314–15, 341–2, 350–1
   gambling 127, 187, 233, 255, 315–16, 327–8
   George Dyer 259–60, 281, 287–8, 290–1, 295–7, 298
   Grand Palais retrospective (1971) 294–5, 297
   health and death of 355, 357–9
   Jessie Lightfoot 39, 81, 125, 154
   John Edwards 301, 316, 334, 352, 359
   José Capelo 352, 353, 355–6, 358, 359
   London social life 37, 41, 89, 139–40, 141–4, 152, 279, 315–16, 353–4
   New York exhibition (1975) 307–11
   Monte Carlo, Monaco 126, 127, 316
   Moscow retrospective (1988) 352
   New York exhibition (1975) 307–11
   painting donated to Royal College of Art 288–90
   Paintings 1959–60 exhibition (1960) 239
   Peter Lacy 173–5, 184–5, 188, 191–2, 233, 235–6, 249–50, 259, 298, 302
   Reece Mews studio 239, 258, 281, 288, 355
   Ron Belton 237, 239, 248–9
   Tangier, Morocco 184, 191–5, 233
   Tate Gallery retrospective (1962) 258–9
   Tate Gallery retrospective (1985) 339
   Wivenhoe property 312–13, 337–8, 339, 360
Bacon, Ianthe 295, 359
BBC (British Broadcasting Company) 117, 150, 367
Beaux Arts Gallery 178–81, 182, 213, 228, 232, 234
Beaverbrook, Lord 183
Bedford Gardens, London 83, 86, 87–9, 103, 106, 114
The Beekeeper (by DWM) 62
Belcher, Muriel 141–2, 301, 307, 336
Bell, Vanessa 5, 19, 26, 40, 64, 78, 103, 136
Belton, Ron 237, 239, 248–9
Benton End art school 58–70
Berger, John 213
Beston, Valerie 289, 295, 296–7, 308, 310
Bevan, Natalie and Bobby 224–5, 226, 227
Birch, James 62, 163, 196, 317, 323, 337, 352, 373
The Bird-cage (by DWM) 136
Blackmore, Peter 6, 22
Bloomsbury Group 5, 25, 26, 30, 78–9, 103
Blunt, Bruce 158–9

Blythe, Ronald 60
Bone, Stephen 213
Bowler, Norman 143
Brausen, Erica 127, 131, 147, 154, 155, 159,
    166–7, 187, 233
Bristowe, William Syer 77
British Landscape Painting exhibition (1944) 89–90
Britten, Benjamin 133, 136, 219–21, 337
Broadmoor hospital 119–21
Brownell (later Orwell), Sonia 30–1, 97, 123
Buck, Louisa 175, 373
Buckle, Richard 30
Buhler, Robert 30, 154, 165–6, 336–7
Bullfight (by FB) 288–90
Burgess, Guy 149–51
Burlington Magazine 253
Butterflies in Britain (by RC) 75, 76, 190

Café Royal, Piccadilly 17–19, 27, 34
Capelo, José 352, 353, 355–6, 358, 359
Carrier, Robert 291–3, 322, 329–30
Carrington, Dora 78–9, 265
Carrington, Noel 65, 70, 75–6, 78, 80, 156,
    161, 164
Cavendish, Patricia 111
Caves de France club 143
Chapman, Dan 368, 369, 371, 372
Charlie Chester's casino 315
Chelsea Arts Ball 171–2
children's magazine project, RC's 132–3
Chopping, Amy (RC's mother) 8, 13, 44, 95, 286
Chopping, Ezekiel (RC's father) 8–9
Chopping, Ralph (RC's brother) 8, 92
Chopping, Richard 'Dicky'
    accident in the Storehouse kitchen 2–4,
        370, 371
    Aldeburgh Festival of Music and the Arts 221
    An Exhibition of Paintings and Drawings (1956)
        202–3
    Andy Warhol's Factory 310
    apprenticeship to Barry Hart 13, 14–15
    Arthur Jeffress Gallery 166–8, 169–70, 202,
        221, 246–7
    Benton End 58–70
    book illustrations 65, 72, 75–8, 81, 91–2,
        138, 152–3, 269–70, 274, 280 (*see
        also* flower-book project; James Bond
        books)
    character 33, 138, 189, 246
    children's magazine project 132–3
    commission for the Churchills 225–7,
        228–30
    conflicts with DWM 138, 166, 190, 198, 199,
        201, 222–3, 250, 322, 325, 334, 344–5,
        361–2, 364
    Contrast in Art exhibition 154–60, 161

Daffodil Cottage 45–6, 48, 55, 60
    deaths in family 92, 286
    early art and career 28, 42, 48, 49, 61–2
    early employment 11–13
    early relationship with DWM 18–19, 20–1,
        22, 27, 28–9, 42, 43–4
    exhibition at The Minories 240–1
    Eye Deceived exhibition 169
    family background 8–9
    Felix Hall 73–4, 88, 103
    flower-book project 77–8, 81–2, 103, 115–
        17, 118, 134–5
    The Fly 12, 266–7, 269, 273, 274–6
    friendship with FB 41–2, 90, 149, 154, 203,
        256–7, 284, 286, 288–9, 301–2, 306,
        314–15, 341–2, 350–1
    Guy Burgess scandal 149–51
    Hawthornden Castle Fellowship 347–9
    health and death 109, 363, 366, 368, 369,
        371–2
    James Bond books 111, 159, 203–8, 227,
        231–2, 240, 269–72, 367
    London Theatre Studio 15–16
    Mountbatten and Hicks wedding day 242–6
    National Service 51–3
    New Art Centre exhibition (1977) 321
    portraits of 63, 324, 339
    Samaritans work 312
    school trip to Nazi Germany 9–11
    sexuality 5, 6, 12, 21, 22, 28–9, 111, 257–8
    Summer Exhibition (1952) 153–4
    Royal College of Art 252–3, 272–3, 276,
        285–6, 288–90, 317–19, 335
    trompe l'oeil work 153, 154, 169, 202, 205,
        206, 221, 227
    writing 75, 76, 117–18, 190, 264–7, 269,
        273, 274–6, 280–1, 284–5, 337, 346–9,
        350–1, 366–7
    see also Partridge, Frances; Roberts;
        Storehouse; Wirth-Miller, Denis
Churchill, Randolph 223–7, 228–30
Clark, Kenneth 30, 54, 127
Coats, Peter 164
Colchester Art Society 129
Colchester School of Art 223
Coldstream, William 30–1, 107, 265
Colony Room (Muriel's) 141–3, 213, 279, 336
Colour Prints exhibition (1948) 136
Colquhoun, Robert 34–5, 54, 66, 83, 84, 85–7,
    94, 96, 111–14, 132, 136, 161–2, 240, 251,
    263, 336
    see also Roberts
Conran, Terence 263, 324–5, 355
Contemporary Art Society 182–3, 239–40
Contemporary Painting by East Anglian Artists
    (1948) 136

Contrasts in Art exhibition 154–60, 161
Cooper, Donald 148
Coward, Noël 5, 6, 244–6, 337
Cranbrook, Countess 49, 157, 240
Craxton, John 84–5
Crisp, Quentin 74–5, 318
Cross, Paul Odo 267

Dadd, Richard 119
Daffodil Cottage, Essex15, 45–6, 48, 60
Daily Express 150, 151, 158–9, 254
Daily Mail 41, 43
Danquah, Paul 144–5, 150, 184, 236
Danziger-Miles, Terry 294, 296
Darwin, Robin 288–9
de Maistre, Roy 40, 72, 170
Deakin, John 142, 162, 213, 295, 299
Dean, Joseph 192–3, 195
Dean's Bar, Tangier 192–3
Decorations of the Modern Home magazine 11–13, 266
di Verdura, Fulco 245
Dog series (by FB) 177–8
Dordogne, France 199–200, 324, 344
Douse, 'Maltese Mary' 144
Dunn, Anne 144, 157, 308, 309, 310
Dunsmuir, Nessie 106, 107, 162
Durlacher Bros., New York 184, 202
Dyer, George 259, 262–3, 281, 287–8, 290–1, 295–7, 298

'The Eagle' (by RC) 275
East Anglian Landscapes exhibitions 182, 228
East Anglian School of Painting and Drawing 57–70
Edwards, John 301, 316, 334, 338, 352, 359
Elizabeth II, Queen 158, 165, 242, 254–5, 285, 286
Esher, Lord 288–9
Estuary in Flower – Ragweed (by DWM) 228
Estuary Landscape I (by DWM) 182
Euston Road School 19, 107, 265
Evening Standard 159, 275
Eye Deceived exhibition 169

Farson, Daniel 140–1, 237, 259, 359–60
Felix Hall, Essex 73–4, 88, 103
Figure in a Landscape (by FB) 91, 126
First World War 23, 47, 79
Fish-Face (by DWM) 129
Fitzrovia 5, 19, 25–7, 29–35, 36–7, 45, 50, 53–4, 74, 89, 139, 279, 353
Fleming, Ann 193, 203, 294
Fleming, Ian 111, 193, 203–8, 227, 229, 231–2, 245, 270, 271, 272, 337, 367
Flowers with Hands (by RC) 42

The Fly (by RC) 12, 266–7, 269, 273, 274–6
Fowler, Norman 123–4, 186
Francis Bacon MB Art Foundation 176, 181
Francis Bacon: Paintings 1959–60 exhibition (1960) 239
Frayling, Christopher 290
Freud, Lucian 11, 31, 57, 62, 63, 64, 67, 68–9, 70–1, 88, 90, 142–3, 152, 169, 206, 265, 299–301
From Russia with Love (I. Fleming) 203, 240
Frost, Eunice 116, 117, 118, 134–5
Garden Landscape (by DWM) 62
Gargoyle Club 36–7, 41, 89, 126, 140–1, 148, 152
Gathorne-Hardy, Robert 49, 138, 157
Geldzahler, Henry 307–8
Germany, RC's school trip to 9–11
Giacometti, Alberto 125, 127, 143, 236
Gielgud, John 12, 13–14, 15–17, 28–9, 158
Ginsberg, Allen 233–4
Goldfinger (I. Fleming) 111, 227, 231, 240
Goldfinger, Ernö 31, 111
Gordon, Giles 273, 280
Gouaches and Drawings by British Artists (1947) 130
Goupil Gallery Salon 42, 47
Gowing, Lawrence 19, 265
Graham, W. S. 88, 89, 94, 106, 107, 132, 143, 162, 237, 336–7, 348
Grant, Duncan 5, 19, 26, 40, 64, 78, 103, 136
Graves Art Gallery 169
Greaves, Derrick 178, 179
Green, John 49–50
Gresham's School 9–11, 133, 219–20
Guggenheim, Peggy 170

Hale, Kathleen 'Mog' 64–6, 69, 75, 104, 156–7
Hall, Eric 40, 41, 81, 125–6, 154
Ham Spray House, Wiltshire 78, 79, 93, 103, 252
Hambling, Maggi 58, 292, 343
Hamnett, Nina 20–1, 31–3, 43–4, 45, 66, 136, 142, 143, 157–8, 208, 336
Hanover Gallery 127, 131, 154–7, 166–7, 187, 202, 233
Hart, Barry 13, 14
Hawthornden Castle Fellowship 347–9
Head VI (by FB) 131
Heads, Bodies and Legs (by DWM and RC) 117
Heath, Adrian 19, 139
Hecht, Alfred 146, 147, 148, 183
Heinz, Drue 347, 348
Herbert, Jocelyn 28, 214
Heron, Patrick 211–12, 237, 240
Hicks, David 164, 241–3, 245, 246, 247, 254, 282, 284, 291, 320
Hickson, Joan 346

Hilton, Roger 237–8, 240
Hintlesham Hall, Suffolk 291–2, 293, 321
Hitler Youth 9–10
homosexuality, laws against 96–7, 168–9, 277–9, 368
Hopwood, Stanley 119, 120, 121
Horizon magazine 67, 84, 86, 123
Houghton Brown, Geoffrey 72–3
House and Garden magazine 163–4
House in Barbados (by FB and DWM) 173–5
Hyman, James 179

Illustrated London News 275
Intimate Enemies (by RC) 350–1
Ironside, Robert 202

James Bond book covers 111, 203–8, 227, 231–2, 240, 245, 269–72
Jameson, John 68
Jeffress, Arthur 154, 164, 166–71, 181, 198–9, 221, 251–2
John, Augustus 19, 26, 31, 36, 54, 64, 89, 228–9
Jonathan Cape publishing 270–1, 272

Kirkus magazine 280–1
Kismet club 144
Kitchen Sink art 179, 211, 212
Klee, Paul 87

La Revue Moderne magazine 153
Lacy, Peter 173–5, 184–5, 188, 191–2, 233, 235–6, 249–50, 259, 298, 302
Lambirth, Andrew 130, 175, 373–4
Landscape – 1956 (by DWM) 240
Landscape – 1957 (by DWM) 228
Landscape – 1952 (by FB and DWM) 175
Landscape with Three Trees (by DWM) 283
Lane, Allen 75–6, 77–8, 80, 81–2, 93, 103, 115–16, 134, 273
Langford Grove girls' school 182
The Last Dodo (by RC) 280–1
Le Monde newspaper 297
Le Tour Eiffel restaurant, Fitzrovia 26, 31, 353
Lefevre Gallery 86, 89–90, 94, 114, 130, 145, 155, 213, 234, 241, 253–4
Lehmann, John 94, 150, 213, 221–2, 265, 267
Lehmann, Rosamund 150, 221–2, 319
Lessore, Helen 178–80, 181–2
Lessore, John 209–10, 216, 217
Lett-Haines, Arthur 55–8, 59–61, 64, 65, 67, 69, 129, 337
Leventis, Michael 316
Lewis, Wyndham 19, 42, 130, 131, 353
Lie Ten Nights Awake (ed. H. van Thal) 275
Lightfoot, Jessie 39, 81, 125, 154
Listener magazine 90

London Group 42, 47
London Theatre Studio 15–16, 28

MacBryde, Robert 34–5, 54, 66, 83, 84, 85–7, 94, 96, 103, 111–14, 136, 161–2, 251, 336
see also Roberts
Marlborough Fine Art 174, 232–3, 236–7, 239, 288, 294, 350
Matisse, Henri 37, 148
McBean, Angus 343
Melville, Robert 156
Metropolitan Museum of Art 307–8
Miller, William John (DWM's brother) 42–3
The Minories Gallery, Colchester 240, 373–4
Minton, John 35–6, 37, 54, 66, 85, 86–7, 94, 96, 106, 113–14, 126, 132, 136, 139–41, 142, 143, 145–6, 154, 155, 158, 168, 171, 179, 210–12, 213–18, 251, 336
Modern Art in the United States exhibition (1956) 212
Monte Carlo, Monaco 126, 127, 316
Moody, Tom 129
Moore, Chris 315
Moraes, Henrietta 143
Morgan, Glyn 68
Morris, Cedric 55–8, 59–62, 63–4, 65, 67, 69, 75, 129, 337
Mortimer, Raymond 91
Moscow retrospective (1988), FB's exhibition 352
Mountbatten (later Hicks), Pamela 242–3, 246, 247
Moynihan, Rodrigo 19, 139, 145, 157, 179, 199, 214, 308
Mr Postlethwaite's Reindeer (by RC) 117
Munnings, Alfred 56, 57–8, 153
Murdoch, Iris 319–20
Museum of Modern Art, New York 114, 127, 148
Muybridge, Eadweard 131–2, 175, 177, 178, 183

Nash, Christine 47, 48, 54
Nash, John 47, 48–9, 54, 81, 129, 228, 229
Nash, Paul 36, 47
National Gallery 30, 35, 103
National Service 51–3
Nature Through the Seasons in Colour 152
neo-Romanticism 35, 85–6, 114, 145, 212, 251
New Art Centre 282, 283, 284, 321
New Burlington Galleries 42
New Statesman magazine 91
New Yorker magazine 272
Nicholson, Ben 106, 184

Orwell (née Brownell), Sonia 157, 165, 292, 293, 299, 336, 353

Painting – 'Pope with Owls' (by FB) 233
Painting 1946 (by FB) 127, 147
Paris retrospective (1971), FB's 294–5, 297–8
Parr, Tom 242–3, 245
Partridge, Burgo 79, 103, 111, 116, 196–7, 252
Partridge, Frances 45, 50–1, 55, 78, 79–83, 92,
    93, 103, 111, 115, 116–17, 119–20, 121,
    134–5, 137, 149, 151–2, 156, 190, 195–7,
    252, 255, 264–5, 266, 268–9, 277, 319,
    332–3, 336, 361, 365–6
Partridge, Ralph 78–9, 111, 116, 119–20, 121,
    196, 252
Pasmore, Victor 19, 31, 107
Pears, Peter 219, 221
Penguin publishers 75–7, 82, 116, 132, 134–5,
    273
Peppiatt, Michael 38, 75, 125, 131, 173, 237,
    281, 302
Picasso, Pablo 32, 39, 90, 294
Pinewood Studios, party at 271
Piper, John 35, 41, 54, 90, 136
Pissarro, Lucian 31, 42
Pitt-Rivers, Julian 200
Pitt-Rivers, Michael 97
Pollock, Peter 150, 184, 236
Pop Art 31, 284
Prichett, V. S. 267
Puffin Books 75, 76, 117–18

Queensberry, David 17, 23, 222, 224, 225–6,
    252–3, 259, 276, 337

Ravilious, Eric 54
Rawsthorne, Isabel 143
Read, Herbert 40, 41
Redfern Gallery 87, 136, 155, 202
Reve, Gerard van het 198, 266
Rhodes, Zandra 272–3, 335, 337, 343, 344, 346,
    361, 373
The Ring (by RC) 280, 284
the Roberts 34–5, 54, 83–4, 85–8, 94, 106,
    111–15, 130, 142, 143, 161–2, 212, 251
Rogers, Neil 'Bunny' 164, 171
Rothenstein, John 148
Rowell, Kenneth 202
Royal Academy of Arts 153
Royal Collection 254–5
Royal College of Art 30, 47, 145, 179, 213, 214,
    216, 252–3, 272–3, 276, 285–6, 288–90,
    317–19, 335
Royal Opera House programmes 30
Rubinstein, Helena 159–60
Running Dog (by DWM) 180–1
Russell-Smith, Mollie 62

Saint-Denis, Michel 16

the Samaritans 312
Sandwich, Noel 115, 116
Second World War 45, 51–4, 55, 74–5, 79, 84,
    92–3, 108
Sickert, Walter 17, 20, 29, 31, 42
Six Scottish Painters exhibition (1942) 86
Skeaping, John 56–7
Slade School of Fine Art 31, 209, 265
Smart, Elizabeth 162
Smithells, Philip 9
Society of London Painter-Printers 136
Soho 36–7, 54, 89, 139–44, 279
    see also Colony Room; Gargoyle Club
Spectator magazine 94, 373
Spender, Humphrey 132–3
Spender, Stephen 66, 68, 132, 133, 150, 222, 319
The Sphinx (by DWM) 90
St Ives, Cornwall 106–8, 237–9, 240
Stokes, Adrian 107
the Storehouse 1
    cooking and dining 122–3
    decay of 362–3, 369
    flood 161, 162–3
    gardening 135
    House and Garden feature 163–4
    house fire 260, 262–3
    moving in 108–11
    purchase of 94–5
    restoration of 109, 136–7, 162–4
Strachey, Julia 78, 93, 265–7
Strachey, Lytton 5, 78–9
Studies of a Dog in Movement (1954) 180–1
Summer Exhibition (1952) 153–4
Sunday Citizen 275
Sunday Times 270, 275
Sutherland, Donald 142
Sutherland, Graham 35, 36, 41, 54, 85, 117, 126–7,
    136, 146–9, 157, 167–8, 183, 212, 336
Sylvester, David 180, 365

Tangier, Morocco 184, 191–5, 233
Tate Gallery 35, 63, 103, 126, 147, 148, 202,
    258–9, 339
Tennant, David 37, 144, 148
The Times 40–1, 180, 202, 247–8
Theatrical Garden Party, Regent's Park 6–8
Thomas, Caitlin 26, 88
Thomas, Dylan 26, 34, 66, 88, 89
Three Studies for a Crucifixion (by FB) 258
*Three Studies for Figures at the Base of a
    Crucifixion* (FB's – painting and
    exhibition) 72, 90–1, 124–5, 126, 130,
    258, 297
Tilty Mill, Essex 161–2
Todd, Ruthven 140, 162
Tonge, John 84, 86

Tootal Broadhurst Lee 24–5, 28, 45
Tosca (pet boxer dog) 164, 256
Toynbee, Philip 37, 140
Transition Gallery 40
Trompe l'Oeil from the 18th C. to the Present Day (1955) 170
Turner, Ernie 108
Turner, Jon Lys (author) 353–4, 361

Unusual Juxtapositions exhibition (1956) 170
U.S. servicemen in London 74–5

Vann, Philip 183–4
Vaughan, Keith 35, 85, 114, 126, 155, 162, 183–4, 202, 217, 240, 251, 336
Venice Biennale exhibitions 179, 184
Victoria and Albert Museum 131–2

Wallis, Alfred 107–8
Warburg, Pamela 274, 275
Warburton, Joan 58–9, 157, 312, 337
Warhol, Andy 284, 310
Warthmiller, Johann (DWM's father) 23, 43
Watson, Peter 84–6, 123–4, 186
Waugh, Evelyn 223
Weekend Exhibitions, Fitzrovia 139
Welch, Denton 123, 132
Wheatsheaf, Fitzrovia 26, 34, 89
Wheeler's restaurant, Soho 139–40, 245–6
White Tower restaurant, Fitzrovia 139, 353–4
Wickham, Anna 34
Wilde, Oscar 17
Williams, Dennis 217
Wilson, Andrew 180–1
Wilson, Angus 88, 140, 230, 267–9, 273, 280
Wirth-Miller, Denis
    Albert Hecht's shop exhibits 146–9
    alcohol problem 346, 349, 363, 364
    art and career 24, 30, 31, 47, 48, 62, 73–4, 83, 87, 89–90, 91, 117–18, 125, 128–31, 136, 138, 146–8, 173–8, 180–3, 188, 212–13, 223, 228, 232, 234, 240, 253–4, 282–4, 291, 305, 311–12, 314–15, 321–4, 329–30, 368, 373–4
    Benton End 58–70
    British Landscape Painting (1944) 89–90
    character 23, 67–8, 105, 138, 163, 189, 195, 246
    Colchester Art Society 129
    collaborations with FB 173–7
    Colour Prints exhibition (1948 136
    conflicts with RC 138, 166, 188, 190, 198, 199, 201, 222–3, 250, 322, 325, 334, 344–5, 361–2, 364
    Contemporary Painting by East Anglian Artists (1948) 136
    Daffodil Cottage 45–6, 48, 55, 60
    death of 373
    death of FB 359–61
    death of RC 371–2
    Dog series 178, 179–81
    early employment 24–5, 28, 45
    early relationship with RC 18–19, 20–1, 22, 27, 28–9, 42, 43–4
    East Anglian Landscapes exhibitions 182, 228
    exhibitions at The Minories 240–1, 373–4
    family background 22–4
    Felix Hall, Essex 73–4, 88
    friendship with FB 41–2, 66, 89, 125, 127–8, 130, 131, 141, 146, 149, 172–7, 184–6, 187, 189, 191–3, 194–5, 210, 234–6, 238–9, 248–50, 255–7, 259–60, 301–5, 311, 313–16, 322, 323–4, 326–8, 330–2, 333–4, 338, 339–40, 341–3, 355, 356–7, 367
    Gouaches and Drawings by British Artists (1947) 130
    health and dementia 2–4, 109, 232, 241, 322, 323, 349, 350, 361, 363–5, 368, 369, 372
    Hintlesham Hall exhibition (1972) 291, 293
    House in Barbados (by FB and DWM) 173–5
    imprisonment 96–102, 104–5, 308, 309, 329
    Landscape 1952 (by FB and DWM) 175
    language school in France 326, 328, 329, 330
    paintings purchased for Royal Collection 254–5
    RC's accident in the Storehouse kitchen 2–4, 370, 371
    commission for the Churchills 226–7, 229–30
    Royal Opera House programmes 30
    sexuality 24, 80–1, 277
    solo exhibition Lefevre Gallery (1960) 241, 247–8, 253–4
    solo New Art Centre exhibition (1969) 284, 291
    Studies of a Dog in Movement (1954) 180–1
    Wivenhoe Arts Club exhibition 321, 322–3
    see also Bacon, Francis; Chopping, Richard 'Dicky'
Wirthmiller, Eleanor (DWM's mother) 23, 24
Wirthmiller, Eleanor (DWM's sister) 23, 24
Wishart, Michael 88, 140, 144, 157, 240, 308
Wivenhoe Arts Club 321, 322–3
Wivenhoe regatta 165
Woman's Journal 254–5
Woolley, Janetta 80, 123, 137, 197–8, 199, 200, 259, 302, 365
Wormwood Scrubs prison 97–102

Yacoubi, Ahamad 193–4
York Minster pub, Soho 89, 126, 342
Young British Painters exhibition (1937) 41